The Special-Needs Collection

Second Edition

CHILDREN with AUTISM

A Parents' Guide

Edited by Michael D. Powers, Psy.D.

Foreword by Temple Grandin

Woodbine House ❖ 2000

Cover Illustration: Charlotte Fremaux

The following publishers have given permission to use extended quotations from copyrighted works: From *A Difference in the Family: Life with a Disabled Child*, by Helen Featherstone. Copyright (c) 1980 Basic Books, Inc. Reprinted by permission of Basic Books, Inc., Publishers. From *The Siege: The First Eight Years of an Autistic Child*, by Clara Claiborne Park. Copyright (c) 1967, 1972, 1982 by Clara Claiborne Park. By permission of Little, Brown and Company.

Diagnostic Criteria For Pervasive Development Disorders reprinted in Appendix A with permission of the American Psychiatric Association.

Library of Congress Cataloging-in-Publication Data

Children with autism: a parents' guide/edited by Michael D. Powers; foreword by Temple Grandin—2nd ed.
    p. cm
    Includes bibliographical references and index
    ISBN 1-890627-04-6 (pbk.)
    1. Autistic children—Popular works. 2. Autism—Popular works. I. Powers, Michael D.

RJ506.A9 C45 2000   00-035165
618.92'8982-dc21

TABLE

OF

CONTENTS

106260

DEDICATION

This book could never have been written without the participation of the thousands of families of children and adults with autism whom we—as contributors—have known professionally and personally over the years. They have allowed us into their lives to share their hopes, fears, tough times, and triumphs, enriching our lives and our work. It is to them that we dedicate this book.

ACKNOWLEDGEMENTS

There has been tremendous change in the field of autism and developmental disabilities in the 11 years since the first edition of *Children with Autism: A Parents' Guide* was published. From how autism is diagnosed, to how children with autism are educated, to the "Individuals with Disabilities Education Act," to improvements in medications, and to the tremendous impact of technology on the field, the second edition of *Children with Autism* represents a substantial updating and expansion of the information the book provides. This extensive revision and updating could not have been possible without the hard work of each author, and I want to thank them first and foremost. Their commitment to helping children with autism and their families is matched only by the expertise they bring to their work.

To Temple Grandin, Beverly Sills Greenough and Peter Greenough, Lillian and Joe Tommasone, and Bernard Rimland I owe a special thanks: Their willingness to share their stories gives hope to every parent who reads this book.

I have learned much from the feedback from hundreds of parents who have read *Children with Autism* over the past 11 years. Their expert observations, praise and criticism, and recommendations have been a source of encouragement and reflection for me. If I have done justice to those suggestions, I have them to thank. Omissions, however, are my responsibility solely.

Temple Grandin, Jerry Newport, Mark Romoser, and Joseph Stobierski, Jr. are successful adult women and men with autism and Asperger's Disorder whose courage, diligence, intellect, and humor have given me a privileged glimpse of their world and experience. I could never repay them for this.

My colleagues at the Yale Child Study Center, particularly Fred Volkmar, M.D., Ami Klin, Ph.D., and Sara Sparrow, Ph.D., have provided an intellectually stimulating and supportive environment to share information and learn. It is a privilege to be associated with a group of individuals for whom "in the best interest of the child" is not merely a phrase, but a code of conduct.

For nearly 20 years Nancy Richardson, past Executive Director of COSAC in New Jersey, has provided me and countless parents and professionals with her special vision of empowerment and support for families of children with autism. She has been a marvelous teacher and a good friend. Thanks also to COSAC for permission to reprint their Program Checklist.

Liz Noble and Dawn Kelleher provided invaluable support and assistance in the preparation of the second edition of *Children with Autism*. Their good nature and careful attention to detail made the entire process run much more smoothly, as they do every day in the management and staffing of our Center. Thank you Liz and Dawn.

For many years I have been most fortunate to work with a creative and talented group of professionals at the *Center for Children with Special Needs* in Tolland, Connecticut. Felicia Morgan, Ph.D., James Loomis, Ph.D., and Lisa Nystrom-Mule, MA, S/LP, CCC provide people with autism and their families a sensitive blend of clinical expertise and knowledge of schools and communities that bridges the gap between hope and possibility and effective practice. I am indebted to them for their willingness to share their skill, and for their friendship.

Few authors or editors would argue about the importance of working with a publisher who shares the author's vision about his or her work. More than just sharing my vision about children with special needs the staff at Woodbine House has helped shape my vision through their development of the "Special Needs Collection" over the past 15 years. With an unwavering eye and uncanny perceptiveness, Susan Stokes, Fran Marinacio, Sarah Strickler, Beth Binns, Gena Daggett, Brenda Ruby, Cathryn Smith, and Sarah Glenner have shepherded the second edition of *Children with Autism* through many revisions, countless e-mails, and numerous deadlines to a finished product. It is a pleasure, indeed, to work with such a group of committed professionals.

Sandra L. Harris, Ph.D. has been the mentor, teacher, colleague, and friend that too few of us ever are fortunate enough to know. From my early days at the Douglass Developmental Disabilities Center, through my graduate studies at GSAPP at Rutgers, to joint professional endeavors too numerous to name, she has been the model of the clinical standard to which I aspire, but doubt will ever attain. With a clear empirical eye and a compassionate soul, she has provided guidance, nurturance, and critique to my work for nearly 25 years. Continuing her legacy of service would be the best thanks I could give her.

It is to my sons Seth and Evan that I owe my deepest gratitude. Both have literally grown up through the tenure of the first edition of *Children with Autism*. During that time they have taught me more about the power of being a compassionate and thoughtful classmate and friend to students with autism and other disabilities than any textbook or research study. More than keeping the sense of wonder in my life, they are among my finest teachers about life. It is a privilege to be their father.

FOREWORD TO THE SECOND EDITION

Temple Grandin

I have autism....
I was lucky to begin early educational intervention when I was two and a half years old. Back in 1949 most children with autism were sent away to institutions. At age two and a half I had all the full blown symptoms of autism: no language, no eye contact, and lots of tantrums. Mother fought with many professionals who wanted to put me in an institution, but she was also lucky to find professionals who were willing to help. The first was a neurologist at the Boston Children's Hospital named Dr. Bronson Cruthers. She told my mother that I was an "odd little girl" and to give me "normal therapy." Dr. Cruthers referred my mother to a speech therapist who worked with speech handicapped children in her house. Miss Reynolds, the speech therapist, was one of those excellent teachers who had just the right instincts for working with children. She knew just how much to intrude into my world. If she pushed me too hard I had a tantrum and if she did not push at all there was no progress. She helped my brain to hear hard consonant sounds by stretching out those sounds. I used to say "bah" for ball because I did not hear speech sounds correctly. If adults spoke slowly I understood, but if they spoke fast it sounded like gibberish. I thought that adults had a special "grownup" language.

When I was three my mother hired a governess who had experience with working with autistic children. She spent hours playing structured children's games with me and my sister. I remember that there was a lot of emphasis on turn taking. I would slide on the sled and then it was my sister's turn. Because of our governess, from age three to six my day was highly structured. I even had one and a half hours per day of "Miss Manners" meals. In the 1950s children were expected to sit at the table and behave. When we had Sunday dinner at Granny's I had to have good table manners. Today I appreciate my strict upbringing. Being autistic is no excuse for being a slob.

At age six I was enrolled in a typical first grade. The school was small and the class had only 12 kids. It was an old fashioned, very structured classroom. Looking back, I know that a chaotic, unstructured classroom full of 30 kids doing lots of different things would not have worked for me. At home my mother worked with me to develop my art talents. Painting with watercolors and doing art was strongly encouraged. Overall my educational program really lasted all day. This is important. If I had been allowed to spend hours each day doing meaningless things, or staying disconnected from the world, my brain would not have developed in the same way.

My sensory problems were the one part of my early education program that was handled badly. I had to wear horrid scratchy petticoats to church. They felt like sandpaper, and I hated them. In the early 1950s nobody understood sensory sensitivities. Sounds bothered me a lot. Even our governess, who did a lot of good things with me, did not understand sound sensitivity. When we went on the ferryboat she made me sit under the foghorn. When it blew I screamed in pain because it hurt my ears. Accommodations for sensory problems are really important for people with autism. One can find comfortable clothes that do not itch or scratch. A piece of tape applied to a school bell will make it quieter and easier to tolerate. Lots of exercise and lots of sensory activities with deep pressure and swinging can help calm the nervous system and make it easier to tolerate these things.

As I got older, the people who helped me the most were the more unconventional, creative individuals. In high school I had a science teacher who encouraged my interest in science. Looking back, I cannot emphasize enough the importance of mentors both in high school and in the business world. These people can help develop talents, and also skills for life. One mentor I had at my first job had his secretaries work with me so I would learn to pay more attention to how I looked and acted. He realized that this would affect how people viewed my work. At the time I was angry with him. Today I thank him.

I often wonder how my education would have been handled differently today. Some things would have been much easier because so much more is known about autism. It is likely that my mother would have found a good speech therapist, teachers, and doctors to work with me. But the lack of structure and clear rules in today's world would be a major problem for me. I was brought up in a world where what was right and wrong were very clear. The structured environment of the 1950s was good for me. Children with autism need clear rules.

Another problem would have been mainstreaming me into a noisy chaotic unstructured class with 30 kids doing 6 different things. That would not have worked. Much of the structure I had in my education was just part of the structure of the 1950s, but the orderliness and clear rules were very important to me.

Looking back on my education things were handled extremely well except for the lack of understanding about sensory problems. The lack of support groups and doctors blaming parents for making a child autistic were things that made it hard for my mother. It is very good that so much has changed.

Parents of children with autism today have more information and support available to them than when I was young. *Children with Autism: A Parents' Guide* is a big part of that support system. Parents will find it full of up-to-date information that will help them understand their child with autism, and help get that child off to the right start.

Foreword to the
First Edition
Beverly Sills Greenough

"I know just how you feel...."

Over the years (some 36 now), I wish I could tell you how many times I have heard these words from well-meaning people attempting to empathize with me over the problems of my son who has autism.

They don't know. Really, they have no idea of what we go through. I say this not in any way as a sob sister. It's just fact. No one knows except those who have undergone the same thing.

However, just as my husband, Pete, and I learned early on, parents of children with autism quickly start saying "Why them?" instead of "Why us?" They also are greatly benefitted by the growing depth of understanding and general knowledge about autism, as is abundantly demonstrated in this guide.

But let me go back 32 years to when I first met this puzzling condition head-on. These recollections are largely drawn from an autobiography of mine.

Bucky was two months old when we summoned a photographer to take pictures of our adorable, perfect, beautiful son (are there any other kinds?).

The photographer startled me when he observed: "There's

something wrong with your kid, Mrs. Greenough. He won't follow the birdie" (the fake canary attached to his camera).

We began watching Bucky very closely. He seemed to have spasms and peculiar movements when his eyes crossed badly and when he lost control of his hands. I began worrying that Bucky might have some sort of nerve affliction. But then he'd calm down. Bucky was a cheerful and extraordinarily handsome boy (he still is), but it was impossible to make eye contact with him.

So we took him to Children's Hospital in Boston. A woman doctor there (not exactly tactful, but blunt) told us: "There are so many things wrong with this boy that if I listed what they are today, they would be only half of what you're going to be facing."

The first thing she cited was *"retardation."*

What did she know about autism? Zilch. Very few doctors in the sixties had any notion about it.

That doctor also stated flatly that Bucky would never talk or be toilet-trained. And that he'd have to be fed for life. She did not know that he was, or would later become, deaf. Or that he was capable of learning sign language.

Nor did she know that in our household was a wonderful young Irish girl named Ona McCarthy. Purely by instinct and intelligence, Ona just knew how to work with a kid with autism. Through repetition and reward—boy, did we buy a lot of fruit Lifesavers—she not only trained Bucky but she also taught him how to use table utensils. Soon he could feed himself.

We managed, not easily, to keep Bucky at home until 1969. He was able to play outdoors a lot, within the confines of a very large, protected backyard. We also had a trained sheepherding dog—a Welsh corgi—who would steer Bucky back to us when he tried to run away.

Still, there had to be bars on Bucky's windows, a locked gate for his room, and a variety of restraints that hardly fitted well with a home full of youngsters.

So Bucky went to a school for children with mental retardation in central Massachusetts, a fine institution in its way. But that was not for a youngster with autism. Again, they knew nothing about autism or how to deal with it.

When Bucky reached 21, we were told that he had to be moved. I won't detail the difficulties we had in finding the right place for him, or the complications thrown in our path by one greedy individual who expected us to build a major part of a group home before Bucky could be accepted.

Happily, we found the Eden Institute in Princeton, New Jersey. In addition to getting Bucky started on sign language, Eden placed him in supported employment. With the money he earns there, he has been able to pay for a week at a winter camp in the Poconos *and* another week at a summer camp on the Jersey shore. He has developed a sense of self-accomplishment, and the resulting gains in behavior and control have been significant.

When we take him for drives, which he loves, the detached, vague look on his face disappears—to be replaced by a lucid expression. For fleeting moments we see a normal, extraordinarily handsome young man. I swear to you—he can display keen intelligence. His brain just gets wrong messages.

Yes, and my husband teases me by saying, "There you go, Beverly, playing doctor without a license."

Bucky cannot climb any mountains (unlike his adventurous sister, Muffy). But he has negotiated some fairly steep hills. And his triumphs will continue to mount, thanks to Eden (which plays a part later in this book, through its wonderful director, Dr. David Holmes).

One last high note (as a prima donna, I was entitled to that):

I would not exchange my son for anyone. His triumphs are ours. But those gains only are possible because of the wealth of information now known about autism and how to deal with it. But we can't stop there. The next step is discovering why the many forms of autism occur, and then ways of prevention. I am confident we shall live to see that!

INTRODUCTION

Bernard Rimland, Ph.D.

What a boon this book will be to parents of children with autism, Asperger's Disorder, and related conditions. It contains information that will be immensely helpful, not only to the bewildered parents of newly diagnosed youngsters, but also to the bedraggled parents of the older children, adolescents, and adults with autism.

I am pleased that the editor invited me to tell you, in this Introduction, about my personal initiation to the world of autism, over four decades ago, and about my responses to what I found.

It is a great pity this book was not available in the "bad old days" when very little was known about autism, and most of what was known was wrong. Today, thanks to television, movies, innumerable magazine articles, and dozens of books, one scarcely encounters a high school student without at least some idea of what an autistic child is like. It was not always that way, I can assure you.

I did not learn of autism in high school, nor college, or even in graduate school. To the best of my knowledge, the first time I saw the word "autism" was in early 1958, when I was 29 years old, and that was five years after I had earned a Ph.D. in psychology! Granted, my training in psychology had been concentrated in measurement, statistics, experimental design, and similar areas of research, but I had to take courses, and pass examinations, in such areas as child development, abnormal psychology, and clinical psychology, where a student today would run across the term, "autism," scores, if not hundreds, of times.

I clearly remember the occasion, and the eerie feeling it gave me, when, for the first time, I saw the strange words, "early infantile autism," staring up at me from my wife Gloria's old college textbook. But I'm getting ahead of myself. Let me explain why I had pulled that box of old textbooks off the garage shelf to find the one, the only one, in which autism was mentioned.

Our eagerly awaited son Mark had been born two years earlier, after a picture-perfect pregnancy. Mark was a beautiful, picture-perfect baby, except for the screaming. He started screaming in the hospital nursery and rarely stopped. He screamed so violently that it was difficult to nurse him. The screaming continued, many hours a day, during most of his early childhood. Hard as we tried, we could discern no reason for his crying. Holding him didn't help. He just struggled and cried harder. The only thing that would placate him, we discovered, was placing him face down in his carriage and rolling him back and forth until he fell asleep. I found that by taping a yardstick to the nursery floor and running the carriage back and forth over it, the gentle jouncing would calm him more quickly.

Mark seemed totally oblivious to us, and to others, although he screamed in terror when our kitten approached. He began to rock in his crib constantly, banging his forehead on the headboard until a large, perpetual bruise appeared on his forehead. The crib began to fall apart under the constant banging, so I replaced all the wood screws with nuts and bolts.

During the day he spent hours bouncing incessantly in a jump chair, happily chanting songs in some ancient, unknown tongue, and breaking or wearing out two or three jump chairs over the course of several years. Mark was also extremely intolerant of change, and had violent tantrums when my wife put on a new dress. Only the grandmothers were willing to babysit this extremely difficult child. My wife conceived of a major breakthrough when it occurred to her that she could buy several dresses of the same size and pattern for herself from the Sears Catalog, and buy several larger-sized dresses of the same pattern for my mother, as well as several others, in a smaller size, for her own mother. Mark didn't really care who fed or changed him, just so long as they were wearing that familiar pink-and-gray flowered dress.

Mark began speaking at about eight months, pronouncing, with perfect diction, the words "spoon," "all done," "teddy bear," and "come on, let's play ball." At age two he could repeat anything said to him, with remarkably clear pronunciation. His uncle tried him on "hippopotamus," and Mark replied, "hippopotamus," with no hesitation. (An Italian father once told me a similar event with his two-year-old autistic daughter involving the word "chrysanthemum." If you think chrysanthemum is hard in English, try it in Italian!)

It soon became evident that Mark's speech was like that of a tape recorder—just repetition of words, phrases, sentences, and even nursery rhymes, without any real idea of what they meant. Our pediatrician, a widely respected physician who had spent 35 years in the field of pediatrics, had never seen nor heard of a child like Mark.

One sunny morning, as Mark was wandering through the house with a vacant, staring-into-space expression, repeating words and phrases he had heard in a hollow, monotone, parrot-like voice, Gloria remembered having read in one of her college textbooks almost 10 years earlier about an unusual type of child who walked around the house, staring vacantly into space, while repeating words and phrases in a hollow, monotonic, parrot-like voice.

Before long I had hauled the box of textbooks off the garage shelf, found the one she had mentioned, and found myself looking at, for the first time in my life, the words that would dramatically change my life—the words that have never left my mind for more than a few moments during the ensuing four decades: *early infantile autism.* At last I knew the name of the unseen foe who had seized my child. I vowed not to rest until this enemy was defeated. If it took the rest of my life—so be it.

The textbook provided some references to the medical literature, and I took these to the nearby university library and began to read. I was startled to find, in Leo Kanner's *Textbook of Child Psychiatry,* case histories of children who were *identical* in every respect to my son Mark. There was the "autistic aloneness," the dream world inaccessibility which left him staring into space for hours at a time, taking no notice of those, even his parents, in his environment. There was the insistence upon sameness; the precocious use of words and sentences, without any understanding; the repetitive rocking; the leading of an adult by the hand to the refrigerator, to a toy, or to another object he wanted; the reversal of pronouns, where he would say "you" where the word "I" should be used; the repetition of a question to indicate "yes," rather than the use of the word "yes" itself. There was the strong preoccupation with mechanical objects, which reminded me of the times his loving grandmother stood in the doorway, staring in dismay as her grandchild rushed past her into her house to find the vacuum cleaner, which he towed from room to room by its cord, while he played with the various hoses and nozzles.

At age two, Mark wandered about our house for months, saying "it's all dark outside," even in broad daylight. We finally figured out that the expression was his "word" for window. Gloria had once held Mark near a window and said, "It's all dark outside." Kanner described this phenomenon and labelled it "metaphorical use of language." The resemblance between the children Kanner described as having early infantile autism and our Mark was extraordinary—truly uncanny.

What caused this strange disorder? I went to the *Psychological Abstracts* and to the *Index Medicus* to see what had been written on the topic of autism. I found that "autism" was constantly used by professionals in the field as an alternate word for childhood schizophrenia. I read paper after paper by Kanner, who kept insisting that the children he wrote about constituted a small, unique sub-population of the larger group of children who had been called childhood schizophrenics in the past. He insisted that the children to whom he had given the label "infantile autism" or "early infantile autism" were so remarkably similar to each other in their behavior and speech (if they had speech) that they must be regarded as a unique clinical entity. His pleas were ignored by his colleagues (as they are to this day). The word "autism" sounded better than the term "childhood schizophrenia," which they had used in the past, and thus they applied the term "willy nilly," to use Kanner's words, in referring to children who resembled only remotely those he had labeled as being truly autistic.

I quickly learned that it was almost uniformly believed by authorities in the field that autism (and thus childhood schizophrenia) were emotional disorders which occurred in children who were biologically normal, when the children realized, in some obscure way, that their mothers really didn't love them enough, or loved them too much, or something. I remembered how Mark had screamed implacably in the nursery, even before he was brought home from the hospital, and wondered why these highly trained professionals, psychiatrists, neurologists, pediatricians, and psychologists were so convinced that autism was caused by bad parenting rather than by an unknown biological factor. I read books and articles by Bruno Bettelheim, a psychoanalyst who proclaimed that autistic children had been mistreated by their mothers in about the same way in which Nazi concentration camp prisoners had been mistreated by their guards, thus giving the children (like the prisoners) feelings of hopelessness, despair, and apathy, and leading them to withdraw from contact with reality.

The topic fascinated me. I devoured everything I could lay my hands on that had any connection at all with autism. The trail led into biochemistry, genetics, and neurophysiology.

I took voluminous notes as I read, and began to order from libraries copies of papers on autism and related subjects from faraway lands, even though receiving the papers would require that I find someone who would be willing to translate the paper for me from German, Dutch, Czechoslovakian, Polish, etc., into English. By 1962 I had studied just about everything ever published on autism, in any language, except for the possibility that there might be some articles in Japanese, Chinese, or Russian which were not indexed through the National Medical Library.

My search for the reasons why the professionals believed autism to be a psychogenic (psychologically caused) disorder revealed no compelling evidence whatsoever. Ultimately I came to believe that it was nothing but bias, bigotry, and greed on their part that had led them to the psychogenic conclusion. This angered me greatly, because it was evident that many parents were feeling terrible guilt as a result of these unwarranted professional attitudes. Meanwhile, the professionals were growing richer, and the parents poorer, as the doctors probed, in session after expensive session, for the nonexistent psychic trauma.

By 1962 I had finished a draft manuscript for a book titled *Early Infantile Autism: The Syndrome and Its Implications for a Neural Theory of Behavior.* The book summarized the world literature on autism and related disorders, and presented some sorely needed new ideas on the nature and cause of autism. It also presented some new ideas on how the normal brain might function.

At about this time, a major publisher of college and professional books announced a new manuscript competition for "A Distinguished Contribution to Psychology." I submitted *Early Infantile Autism* and was awarded first place in the competition. As soon as the announcement of my book was released to the press, I began receiving letters from parents of autistic children first from throughout the U.S., then from throughout the world. Critics published rave reviews about this bold new book that would force people to look at autism in "a new light."

They would have to discard their old theories about "refrigerator mothers" causing autism, and view autism as a biological disorder of the brain. Little did I realize what further effects the book would have. Inquiries started to pour in from throughout the world, from parents, professionals, students, and others, and continue to pour in to this day.

At this time, the mid-1960s, there were essentially only two methods used to treat autistic children—psychotherapy and drugs. Both of these methods were universally accepted and deeply entrenched. Autism was viewed as a mental health issue, not an educational problem. When parents brought their children to child psychiatrists or clinical psychologists, they were told, "You caused this problem in your child: your child has only one chance, and that is for you to relinquish control to us, and do as we say." "Treatment" ordinarily involved many years of psychotherapy or play therapy for the children, and weekly sessions with a therapist for the parents. The professional literature was replete with articles discussing the psychoanalysis or psychotherapy of this or that child with autism or childhood schizophrenia (the terms were used interchangeably). The idea that the children suffered from a brain disorder which required specialized methods of teaching was quite foreign.

In the fall of 1965, I decided that the time was ripe for starting a national parents' organization. Without pressure from informed parents, nothing would change. I gathered together the addresses of as many parents of autistic children as I could find. Most were those of parents who had written to me after my book was published. Another list was obtained from Ivar Lovaas, who had received many letters and phone calls from parents as a result of an article on his work that had appeared in *Life* magazine in early 1965. Still more names were gotten from Rosalind Oppenheim, of Chicago, whose article about her autistic son had appeared in *Good Housekeeping* magazine several years earlier.

I was doing a great deal of travelling at the time, some of it as part of my job with the government, but much more as a result of the numerous speaking invitations I received from universities throughout the country, whose students and faculty were very much interested in this strange and little-known childhood disorder called autism, and the (probably) strange fellow who had written a prize-winning book that had revolutionized thinking about the disorder. Whenever I was invited to another city, I would write in advance to all the parents on my list who were within driving distance of that city, tell them I was coming, and ask one or two of them to arrange a meeting at which I could speak to the entire group. At each meeting I gave a talk in which I told the parents how useless were the methods that were now being used to treat their children, and how promising was the new method of teaching—behavior modification—then being pioneered by Ivar Lovaas and a few others. I also told the parents about the new organization we were forming, the National Society for Autistic Children, and suggested that they start a local chapter. This approach proved to be a great success. During the first year about a dozen chapters of the National Society for Autistic Children were formed in various cities. The organization (renamed the Autism Society of America) has grown to approximately 240 chapters throughout the United States as of this writing (June 2000).

Many of the letters and phone calls from parents who had read my book contained information, clues, and ideas that might be of critical importance to researchers studying the cause and treatment of autism. No one was compiling this information, correlating it, or studying it. In response, in 1967, shortly after establishing the National Society for Autistic Children, I founded the Institute for Child Behavior Research (ICBR), which is devoted to collecting information about autism from parents, from researchers, from the medical and scientific literature, and from all other sources, analyzing the data, and making it available to parents and others who need it. ICBR started as a desk and two filing cabinets in the side porch of my home. It has expanded and moved four times since then, and now (with its new name, the Autism Research Institute (ARI)) publishes a quarterly newsletter, the *Autism Research Review International,* corresponds with thousands of parents and professionals throughout the world, and maintains the world's largest database on children with autism.

As an example of the kinds of invaluable information that can be provided by parents, let me mention our experience with the use of high dosage vitamin B6 and the mineral magnesium in the treatment of autism. In the late 1960s, I learned from a number of parents that their children had improved when given much larger-than-usual amounts of certain vitamins. Although I was skeptical at first, I eventually conducted two scientific experiments. Both turned out positive. Other researchers followed our lead, and a number of studies have since confirmed the value of this approach for many children.[1] My

---

[1] *Readers interested in learning more about this research, and other research on autism, are invited to write the author at: Autism Research Institute, 4182 Adams Ave., San Diego, CA 92116.*

years of experience with children with autism have taught me that autistic children vary enormously from one another in numerous ways. It is important for you as a parent to decide for yourself whether this, or any other intervention, is useful for your child.

Before closing, I want to do two things. The first is to provide a brief update on my son Mark, with whose story I started this rather lengthy Introduction. Secondly, I want to give a few words of advice to the parents who will be reading this book.

Mark has just passed his forty-fourth birthday. Even though we were told when Mark was four to institutionalize him as a hopeless case, he has come a very long way, and is now a handsome, pleasant, courteous, and reliable adult who, while far from intellectually gifted, nevertheless has many fine qualities. Behavior modification played a major role in his extraordinary improvement, as did megavitamin B6 therapy. He has been on high doses of vitamin B6 since 1968, when I began working with the vitamins as a means of treating autism. It is clear from the few instances when he has been temporarily taken off the B6 that it helps him immensely. If there is a healthier individual in North America, I would be surprised. Apart from one small filling in one tooth, Mark has not even had any dental work. Mark answers the telephone for us and takes accurate messages when we are not at home, and in general has turned out to be a very fine, if limited, man. At age 22 Mark was discovered to have remarkable talent as an artist. Mark and his paintings have appeared on national television and as illustrations in *The Secret Night World of Cats,* a children's book written by his sister Helen Landalf. Mark says with pride, "I am an artist."[2] Mark has come a long way for a "hopeless child" who at age 8 was still in diapers and never asked a question. Gloria and I are proud of him.

As to my words of advice for the parent-readers of this book: Although there is much valuable and useful information in the ensuing chapters, take all the advice you get from anyone, including me, with a grain of salt. The field is changing rapidly, and much of what is given as gospel truth today may be passé in a few years.

In particular, be cautious about accepting unquestioningly the diagnoses given to your child. Such designations as PDD (pervasive developmental disorder), ADHD (attention deficit hyperactivity disorder), and similar labels change rapidly. The letters and phone calls we get at ARI reflect the confusion engendered in parents (and in profes-

---

[2]*Notecards and prints of Mark's work are available from Autism Research Institute.*

sionals as well!) by the attempts of the American Psychiatric Association to establish criteria for the diagnosis of autism and related disorders. Until the biological bases of autism are more firmly understood, all diagnostic efforts will inevitably be revised. Masking our lack of a complete understanding of autism with fancy diagnostic labels or acronyms really doesn't help very much. Be patient—the professionals are trying their best—but don't be misguided, either.

We have come a long way since the dark ages of the 1950s and before. One of the most important advances is represented by the publication of this book, devoted as it is to informing parents, as intelligent and concerned advocates for their own children, on the state of current thought in the field. We have made great strides since the years when parents were treated contemptuously, and were widely regarded as having caused autism and as the enemies of their children. With a little luck, and a great deal of diligence we will make much larger strides in the years to come.

1 WHAT IS AUTISM?
Michael D. Powers, Psy.D.

▪▪ Introduction

Autism is a very puzzling and painful disorder for parents to understand and deal with. You have a beautiful child who seems totally withdrawn—you reach out with love in your heart and get no response. You are bewildered and hurt. You feel helpless. Autism, however, is not an impenetrable wall; there are things you can do to reach your child and to try to help her. But before you can help her, you need to understand what autism is, how it is diagnosed, and how it is treated. The following true story illustrates how one family first encountered autism in their child:

Robbie was a handsome, blond boy who stopped talking at 21 months of age. His parents had been concerned about him before, but now they were really worried.

Robbie was the older of their two children. There had been nothing unusual about this birth or early months. Robbie stood at six months, said his first word at ten months, walked by his first birthday, and could name about thirty-five objects by the time he was a year and a half old. His parents were proud of his progress and tried to excuse his solitary habits. They noticed that although Robbie usually preferred to be left alone to play with his toys and puzzles, he did smile at family members occasionally and seemed to recognize some of them. That first year, Robbie's generally tolerant nature and lack of fussiness led his parents to con-

sider themselves truly lucky. His excellent hand and finger coordination and early words convinced them that Robbie was a very bright little boy—one who just preferred his own company to that of others.

But as Robbie grew older, other puzzling, disturbing behaviors changed his parents' vague concern into outright worry. For example, sometimes he fell down and scraped his knees or hands but showed no reaction to the pain. Other times he would break into tears for no reason, sometimes crying inconsolably for 20 minutes. He spoke less and less, until there were times when he would go for weeks without saying a word. He would, however, babble, shriek, laugh, and cluck his tongue frequently throughout the day. More and more, his parents suspected a hearing problem or even deafness because he no longer responded to his name. They weren't sure about this, though, because sometimes it seemed as if Robbie would stop whatever he was doing to listen to a train whistle blowing ever so faintly in the distance.

His parents bought Robbie toys they thought he would enjoy. But he preferred to be alone with his trains and cars. He would turn them over and spin their wheels for long periods of time, all the while shaking his hands and babbling as he intently watched them spinning. Sometimes he would arrange them in specific patterns (known only to him) and look at them from different angles. He would also line up his cars and trains by size so that they all pointed in the same direction and would become enraged if anyone disturbed the order while he was away. This insistence on routine and sameness was not just limited to cars and trains. An agile little boy, Robbie soon learned to climb up onto the kitchen counter and open the cabinets to find plates, which he then brought down to the floor to spin. His climbing on the counters was only a preview of more daring feats such as standing on the railing overlooking the stairwell. Unlike other children they had known, Robbie seemed completely unaware of the danger he was in.

Robbie's grandparents were the first to begin to piece together the unusual behavior and lack of social and communication skills. They mentioned the word "autism" for the

*first time when Robbie was two years old. Their daughter
and son-in-law quickly reminded them that many children
are slower to talk. Besides, didn't Robbie's uncanny skill with
puzzles and mechanical toys seem very advanced for his
age? As concerned parents, they had discussed Robbie's
behavior with his pediatrician at his last check-up and had
been told to forget about it. "It was nothing." Robbie's
grandparents were quieted—temporarily.*

*Several months later, however, when Robbie's lan-
guage had not improved, his parents took him to a Child
Development Center at a nearby university hospital.
Robbie's grandparents had been right. Robbie was diagnosed
as having autism.*

■■ What Is Autism?

Autism is a physical disorder of the brain that causes a lifelong
developmental disability. The many different symptoms of autism can
occur by themselves or in combination with other conditions such as
mental retardation, blindness, deafness, and epilepsy. Because children with autism—like all children—vary widely in their abilities and
behavior, each symptom may appear differently in each child. For
example, children with autism often exhibit some form of bizarre,
repetitive behavior called *stereotyped behavior*. Some, like Robbie,
may line up objects and look at them intently. Others may lick their
fingers immediately after touching a doorknob, or stare intently at
particles of dust as they drift downward to the floor in front of a window in the late afternoon sun. The following section introduces the six
major symptoms of autism.

■■ The Symptoms of Autism

What are children with autism like? What makes them different
from children who do not have a disability or from children with other
types of conditions? In understanding autism, it is critical to understand the wide range of symptoms and the wide range of severity of
those symptoms. Each child with autism is unique, with her own individual range of symptoms and behaviors. However, as a result of
extensive study over many years, involving many children with
autism, broad areas of similarity have been identified so that it is now
possible to make some basic general statements about what children

with autism are like as a group. Those symptoms and characteristics are explained in the following section.

Failure to Develop Normal Socialization

The inability of children with autism to develop normal social skills is probably the most noticeable characteristic of autism. Children with autism don't interact with others the way most other children do or simply don't interact at all. Like Robbie, they seem to prefer to be alone most of the time. They appear to live a life of extreme isolation. They have great difficulty understanding and expressing emotion, and show few, or unusual, signs of attachment, the emotional bonding that occurs between people who care for each other. When attachment is observed, it may be stilted, one-sided, or odd. This behavior is very different from the social behavior of most infants and young children.

The child with autism may appear to be very uninterested in other people. She may avoid eye contact or appear to "look through" people. She may seem extremely apathetic and unresponsive, showing little or no desire to initiate contact or to be held or cuddled. Indeed, when she is held she may stiffen or arch her back as if being held is somehow distressing. The social cues of others—a smile, a wave, a frown—may be meaningless to her. She may not develop a social smile until quite late. In addition, she may not play with others. She may use people mechanically as a "means to an end." For example, your child may approach you and take you by the hand to something she wants—like to the refrigerator for juice—without a word or a glance. You are treated just like any other tool.

Most children with autism have extremely limited social skills and seem to live in a world of their own, separate from and unfathomable to outsiders. Social interactions that exist are very idiosyncratic, egocentric, and may have special "rules" associated with them important only to the child. This inability to relate to the world of people is often the strongest clue to autism.

Disturbances in Speech, Language, and Communication

Autism's second major symptom is speech, language, and communication problems. Approximately 40 percent of children with autism do not speak at all. Others have what is called echolalia, a parrotlike repeating of what has been said to them. Sometimes echolalia is immediate, as when your child says, "Do you want a cookie?" after you have just asked her, "Do you want a cookie?" Sometimes echolalia is delayed, and may involve the recitation of TV commercials, advertising jingles, or single words heard several minutes, days, weeks, or even months ago. Your child may have little or no understanding of abstract concepts such as danger, or of symbolic gestures such as waving "bye-bye." She may not understand the proper use of pronouns, particularly "you" and "I," and may reverse them. She may not use speech for communication, and what speech she does use may be repetitive and filled with illogical words or phrases.

Pragmatics—the use of nonverbal and verbal communication for social interactions—is also impaired. Your child may stand too close when speaking to someone, may fail to realize that discussion of a preferred (to her) topic is going on far too long, or may greet every new person by asking about the date and year of their birth. Although the language may be complex, the communication is not functional.

Your child's voice may sound flat or monotonous and she may have no apparent control over her pitch or volume. For example, she may speak in a loud, high-pitched voice in response to your questions but repeat segments of Disney videos with perfect intonation. In addition, she may rely excessively on jargon or use words or phrases out of context. For example, one child said, "Time to be heading home," with great agitation whenever she was asked to do something she did not want to do.

Abnormal Relationships to Objects and Events

Children with autism are usually unable to relate normally to objects and events. For example, remember the way Robbie would constantly spin objects or line things up. Your child may also interact with things or events in this nonfunctional way.

A great many children with autism have what is called a "need for sameness," and may become very upset if objects in their environment or schedules are changed from their familiar placement or pattern. For example, if you ask your child to brush her teeth before her bath instead of afterwards, she may resist the change mightily. This inflexibility can force families into a very difficult and rigid existence as they attempt to follow their child's "rules."

This "need for sameness" can be better understood as a "need for predictability and routine." Your child is less anxious and upset, and better able to organize herself, if she knows exactly what to expect. Some professionals believe that all of the rules the child with autism imposes on the world are actually attempts to control, manage, and predict it. Although the world may be less chaotic and frightening when strict order and predictability reign, the ability to be flexible and to respond to life's unpredictability is an important yardstick for growth and development.

The way children with autism "play" may be very unusual; sometimes children with autism do not play at all. Your child may have no "pretend" play and may start few, if any, play activities on her own. When she does use toys or play materials, she may use them in unusual ways. For example, she may repeatedly drop Lego blocks onto a hard surface, or always arrange her blocks in the same pattern based on size, shape, or color. She may arrange action figures or trains in a particular pattern, then walk away (but insist that they remain undisturbed). Other children will show the beginnings of imaginative play, but their actions will be very immature, idiosyncratic, or focused on only one toy.

These unusual responses to people, objects, and events can and do change. Over time, and with appropriate treatment, children with autism can learn to enjoy using various objects appropriately and can learn to tolerate some change in their world.

Abnormal Responses to Sensory Stimulation

Sensory stimuli are the things in the environment that we touch, smell, feel, see, and hear. While we respond to much of what goes on around us, our brains filter out certain unimportant or unnecessary stimuli, allowing our attention to be focused on the most important information in the environment at that moment. For example, many large department stores use a tone signal to alert store employees. For shoppers, these signals are extraneous noises in the environment. Because they do not communicate a meaningful message to shoppers, most people just filter them out. Store managers attend to and recognize these signals, however. Children with autism have difficulty with this "filtering out" process. They may greatly overreact to sensory stimuli, or have almost no reaction whatsoever. For instance, some children with autism find the tone signals in department stores very distressing. They may cover their ears and throw a tantrum until their parent takes them out of the store. Other children may appear enthralled with sounds they make themselves or with "background" sounds such as distant police sirens. Yet,

except for a strong reaction to only these sounds, they may appear to have no reaction to any other sounds whatever, and indeed may appear deaf at other times. We do not know exactly why sounds affect children with autism in this way, but it appears to be part of the overall tendency of children with autism to *overattend* to some stimuli and *underattend* to others.

As part of her sensory problems, a child with autism may be fascinated with lights, color patterns, logos, shapes, or the configuration of letters and words. She may be preoccupied with scratching or rubbing certain surfaces. She may furiously avoid certain food textures— for example, "rough" textures like toast, or foods of certain colors. For example, one child insisted on all foods being "beige," or she would not eat them.

Your child may respond to motion or pressure in abnormal ways. Some children with autism enjoy being thrown into the air or spinning themselves around and around, never apparently becoming dizzy. Others have an intense fear of "roughhousing" or the movement of elevators. Some will cover themselves with couch cushions, wedge themselves into small spaces, or seek very hard hugs or squeezing in order to obtain the sensory feedback they crave. Others will become distressed by the feel of tugs on their clothing, refuse to wear short pants, or crave the feeling of air blowing at their face from a heater vent.

Generally speaking, children with autism, especially younger children, appear to use their senses of taste and smell more than their senses of hearing and vision to learn and explore. Their reaction to cold or pain may vary from indifference, to oversensitivity, to unpredictable vacillation between the two.

Developmental Delays and Differences

The fifth symptom of autism is the significantly different way a child with autism develops. Children without disabilities develop at a relatively even pace across all of the many areas of development. A child's skills at a given age may be slightly ahead of or behind most other children's and still be well within normal limits. For example, a child may learn to walk sooner than most children, but learn to talk a bit later. For children with autism, however, this development process is not at all even. Their rate of development is quite different, particularly in communication, social, and cognitive skills. In contrast, motor development—the ability to walk, hop, climb stairs, manipulate small objects with the fingers—may be relatively normal or only slightly delayed.

The sequence of development within any one of these areas of development can also be unusual. For example, your child may be able to read complex words and phrases like "Exxon" or "Pirates of the Caribbean" and yet have no understanding of the sounds of particular vowels and consonants.

Sometimes skills will appear in children with autism at the expected time and then disappear. Like Robbie, a young child may appear to develop spoken language, and then at about age two abruptly stop talking. Although a child's abilities in areas such as working puzzles or counting may be normal or even precocious, her language skills may remain far below her age level.

Development is discussed more fully later in this book. Chapter 6 provides an overview of typical child development and explains how you can judge your child's individual development compared to that of most children.

Begins During Infancy or Childhood

The sixth symptom of autism is that it begins during infancy or childhood. Autism is a lifelong disability that one is born with. Generally, parents get a diagnosis before their child is 36 months old, but later diagnosis sometimes occurs. Furthermore, for a variety of reasons, some children may not be correctly diagnosed until several years later. In fact, some parents of children diagnosed with mental retardation and other disabilities like Down syndrome do not learn until their child approaches adolescence or adulthood that she actually has autism. Do not rule out autism in your child just because all of the symptoms of autism are not actually observed until after 36 months, or because she some other diagnosed condition.

Regardless of their age at diagnosis, children with autism almost always exhibit the five other symptoms to some degree throughout their lives. In some children, symptoms become less severe around ages five or six. This change can occur even earlier for some children where highly specialized early intervention programs are available, although the evidence is inconclusive as to exactly which children benefit most from these programs.

Adolescence typically heralds additional changes—some positive, others not—for the child with autism, and the severity of her symptoms may increase. Remember that your child's disorder and diagnosis are features of her personality that signify her need for carefully planned, well thought-out services throughout her life.

■■ Types of Autism

The condition we call "autism" is really one of a set of five closely related conditions. These five conditions, which all share symptoms, fall under the broad diagnostic umbrella called "Pervasive Developmental Disorders" or PDD. "Pervasive" means that the condition affects development extensively and across the board. All of the conditions covered under the term PDD and explained below have this effect on development. According to the American Psychiatric Association's *Diagnostic and Statistical Manual* (DSM), which is the standard reference manual used in diagnosing autism, PDD includes the following conditions:

- Autistic Disorder
- Asperger's Disorder
- Rett's Disorder
- Childhood Disintegrative Disorder (CDD)
- Pervasive Developmental Disorder: Not Otherwise Specified (PDD:NOS)

Regardless of which of the above five types of PDD your child has, there are three primary symptoms they all share and which are used to establish a diagnosis:

1. impaired social interaction;
2. impaired communication; and
3. characteristic behavior patterns.

The specific type of PDD your child has is determined by when these symptoms begin to appear; how quickly or slowly they appear; their severity; and their exact nature or character. The five diagnoses are used by professionals to describe various characteristics common to these disorders, but in varying degrees.

The conditions that fall under the PDD umbrella are called "spectrum disorders." This means that some children are more disabled by their condition than others. Each specific PDD condition runs the gamut from mild to severe, with the majority of children clustering toward the midpoint. However, it is important to remember that

▪▪ TABLE 1. PDD's SYMPTOMS-PROBLEMS

Social Interaction

- Shows little or no interest in making friends
- Prefers own company to being with others
- Does not imitate others' actions (for example, raising arms for "so big")
- Does not interact playfully (for example, participating in "hide-and-seek" games)
- Avoids eye contact
- Does not smile at familiar people
- Seems unaware of others' existence; for example, treats family members and strangers interchangeably

Communication

- Has difficulty maintaining a conversation despite good speech skills
- Reverses pronouns such as "you" and "I"
- Has echolalia—repeats others' words, either immediately or after a delay

each symptom may be present in varying degrees of mildness or severity. In other words, some of a child's symptoms may be milder than others. For example, a child with seriously impaired social skills may have normal or near normal cognitive skills—she may be quite aloof socially, but have no trouble learning to read or solve arithmetic problems. Two children, both diagnosed with one of the PDD conditions, can display communication, social, and behavioral patterns that are very different from each other. Table 1 illustrates the possible range of severity for PDD's primary symptoms—problems with social interactions, problems with communication, and problems with behavior. The mildest symptoms—those closest to "normal" behavior—come first, followed by the more severe symptoms.

Autism professionals use a diagnostic reference book, usually the *Diagnostic and Statistical Manual of Mental Disorders* (DSM), currently in its fourth edition (see Appendix A). In Europe and other countries, the *International Statistical Classification of Diseases and Related Health Problems* (ICD) is more commonly used. Both of these two reference

- Lacks imagination or the ability to pretend
- Does not use symbolic gestures such as waving "bye-bye"
- Cannot communicate with words or gestures

Unusual Interests
- Fascination with facts about specific topics
- Reads words at a very early age, but does not use the words to communicate
- Very intensely interested in mechanical workings of objects
- Lines toys up in neat rows rather than play with them

Behavioral Symptoms
- Is physically inactive, or passive
- Does not respond to requests by familiar people
- Has picky eating habits
- Throws frequent tantrums, often for no known reason
- Behaves aggressively, physically attacking or injuring others
- Injures self with behavior (i.e., head-banging; eye-gouging)

guides are very similar. For parents who live in the United States, the majority of specialists seeing their child will use the DSM.

Autism is one of several different possible diagnoses under the "umbrella category" of Pervasive Developmental Disorders or PDD. In addition to the diagnosis of Autistic Disorder, PDD includes descriptions for Rett's Disorder, Asperger's Disorder, Childhood Disintegrative Disorder, and Pervasive Developmental Disorder: Not Otherwise Specified (PDD:NOS). In the past, parents of children with autism or one of the other PDD conditions would hear different labels used to describe their child. Children who were more severely affected might have been described as having "Classic Autism" or "Kanner's Autism." Other terms like "Infantile Autism," "Early Infantile Autism," and "Childhood Autism" were heard. Today parents are more likely to hear labels like "Pervasive Developmental Disorder," "Autism Spectrum Disorder," "Autistic-Like," or "Pervasive Developmental Disorder: Not Otherwise Specified (PDD:NOS)." *It is important to remember that regardless of their label, the educational needs and treatment of these children are the same.* The following sections describe each of the five types of Pervasive Developmental Disorder.

Autistic Disorder

Autistic Disorder is what is more commonly associated with the term "autism." People with autism have the three major symptoms of PDD discussed above, but in their own unique variety:

- **Impaired Social Interaction.** Children with autism seem to live in their own world. They may not seek out the company of other children or adults, and may relate to other people— even their own parents and siblings—as objects or tools rather than as people. For these children, other people often are a "means to an end." Children with autism have a very hard time sharing the enjoyment of their experiences with others. For example, a child might see several construction vehicles in a parking lot or might find pictures of trains in a book, but would not usually think to share her interest with an adult, using words or gestures. In many ways, children with autism do not understand that their own enjoyment and experience can be made more fun if shared with someone else.

- **Impaired Communication.** Children with autism often do not communicate with the people in their world in typical ways. It can be very difficult to engage them in conversation or to obtain information from them verbally. For example, rather than respond to a question with an answer, they may only repeat the question back verbatim. This is called echolalia. Although many children with autism do learn how to communicate with words and gestures, some cannot; these children often learn to use pictures and symbols to communicate their wants and needs. Those children that do learn to use spoken language may repeat things that are said to them right away (immediate echolalia) or might repeat things they have heard in the past like dialog from a TV show or favorite videotape. They might "invent" words for different things, the meaning understood only by them. Even very capable people with autism have unusual communication. They might be very interested in unusual types of information, and frequently try to work that information into a conversation with someone else. Often they are completely unaware that the other person is not nearly as interested in some of these facts as they are.

- **Repetitive, Stereotypic, or Odd Patterns of Behavior, Unusual Interests, or Responses to the Environment.** Children with autism often have intense interests and preferences that are quite different from other children. Many appear to strongly prefer that their world remain predictable and unchanged. For example, a child might become very distressed if the order of placement of the toys in her room is disturbed by someone; she may become very excited when entering a particular restaurant that has a ceiling fan and stand beneath the fan flapping her hands in a very specific little "dance." Many of these children become agitated by people, objects, and situations that appear benign to the rest of us. For them, however, these benign situations have intense personal meaning. Sometimes accidental interruption of their interests causes great distress, behavior problems, and tantrums. For example, one child becomes very distressed when her mother asks her to put away a small

Thomas the Train. It seems that she wants to carry the
Thomas Train everywhere she goes. Whenever she is asked to
put it away, she tantrums. She does not play with it, drive it,
or use it in more typical imaginative play; she just always
wants to hold it in her left hand. This obviously interferes
with her participation in many activities, but for her, holding
the train is the most important thing.

More boys are diagnosed with autism than girls; in fact almost
four times as many. There are no cultural, social, or economic class
differences, however. There are also no racial differences. Indeed,
autism occurs throughout the entire world in about the same percentage of children. We know for certain that autism is not caused by
something that a mother or father does to their child; children are
born with this disability, even when it does not become obvious until
after a year or two.

Most children with Autistic Disorder also have mental retardation. In fact, approximately 75 percent of people with autism score in
the range of mental retardation (generally an IQ score below 68-70)
on standardized tests. This is one characteristic used to distinguish
Autistic Disorder from some other PDDs. However, the measured cognitive skills of children with Autistic Disorder may not match their
skills in other areas. For example a young child with more severe
autism may be able to read words quite well. Although mental retardation is not a symptom of autism, it does require careful diagnosis in
fully understanding your child's needs.

Although most children with autism also have mental retardation, approximately 25 percent do not. These children are sometimes
referred to as "high functioning;" they are different from children with
other PDDs. Unlike children with Autistic Disorder, males who are
high functioning vastly outnumber females.

Children with high functioning autism must meet the diagnostic
criteria for Autistic Disorder, but certain differences are present. These
children often are able to relate to other people, but use odd responses in social situations. For example, one child recently introduced himself to me by asking the license plate number of my car, and then pro-
ceeded to tell me the license plate numbers of vehicles owned by his
family members. Other children might insist on asking about the
birthdays or ages of people. Some direct conversations into topics like

deep fat fryers or weather phenomenon. Clearly, these children are interested in initiating some kind of social connection with other people, but they do so in odd ways.

The social interaction style of children with high functioning autism is often described as "active-but-odd." This term is used to describe spontaneous social overtures that are one-sided, naïve, or extremely unusual. For children with this interaction style, the social conventions that are so obvious to other people simply escape their notice. Sometimes these conventions involve conversation, but sometimes they involve the nonverbal part of an interaction too. For example, a child might stand too close to another person in a conversation, refuse to look at them when they speak, or flap her hands excitedly while pacing in front of the person she is speaking to. The purpose and quality of the  conversation can also be a problem. High functioning children with autism often become "stuck" on a topic and can be very single-minded in their discussions. For them, the conversational partner is more of a recipient of information than an active participant.

High functioning people with autism usually develop communicative speech, but may have problems understanding gestures and symbolic speech. Some children may have difficulty understanding gestures, while others may be unable to understand phrases like "apples don't fall far from the tree" or "knock it off." For these children, their difficulty understanding the more subtle meaning of language becomes very problematic when they are teenagers and adults. They often seem to miss the point, or they misunderstand something being said to them and act the wrong way. Unfortunately, they do not understand why they have misinterpreted the phrase in the first place.

Children with autism who are high functioning are very interested in routines, predictability, and maintaining the orderliness of things around them. They may arrange their things intricately and precisely. For example, clothes may be hung in a closet grouped by colors, length of the clothing, and season. Everything has a place and there is a place for everything. Disturbing this order might cause a great deal of distress. Many people are like this, but do not have autism of any kind. What distinguishes people with autism who insist on this orderliness is that they become extremely distressed when it is changed and cannot adapt to a different way of organizing themselves readily. When orderliness or predictability is disturbed, people with high functioning autism can become very panicky. They might have symptoms like a rapid heart rate, rapid breathing, and sweaty palms. Their ability to tolerate life's curveballs is very poor.

Some professionals believe that people with high functioning autism need order, predictability, and structure to an excessive degree for the same reasons that very young children with Autistic Disorder insist on things being placed in the same spot over and over again. When the world is kept very predictable, anxiety is reduced. Some professionals (and many parents) believe that their child with high functioning autism craves this structure—called a "demand for sameness"—in order to function. They recognize that their child is more calm, less anxious, and able to learn when her world is very predictable. This approach does not cause a problem generally, unless the child insists on very unusual routines, or her need for sameness interferes with learning. This demand for sameness probably varies with different people with PDDs, but, in all cases, interferes with everyday functioning. Ultimately, the most important thing is for the child to have her needs understood while also learning to handle surprises and change.

Asperger's Disorder

In 1944, Dr. Hans Asperger described a group of four children ages 6 to 11 years, all of whom, despite apparently typical communication and cognitive skills, had significant problems with social interactions. These problems included intense, but very narrow, interests, speech that was unrelated to a conversation's topic, interest in letters and numbers at a very young age, poor empathy, clumsiness, difficulty controlling the volume of their voice when speaking, and trouble adjusting to school. Although Asperger's work went largely unnoticed until the 1980s, the disorder that now bears his name is recognized as one of the PDDs similar to Autistic Disorder.

The DSM definition for Asperger's Disorder is very similar to the definition of Autistic Disorder. Children with Asperger's Disorder have noticeable problems with social interaction and communication and unusual behaviors and interests. However, they tend to develop speech at the right age (although this communication is unusual in many ways), and generally do not score in the range of mental retardation on IQ tests. As with children with Autistic Disorder, people with Asperger's Disorder have the three major symptoms of PDD, but in their own unique blend:

- **Impaired Social Interaction.** Empathy is very difficult for people with Asperger's Disorder. They cannot "put themselves in someone else's shoes" as easily as others might. These children act as if the world revolves around them and their way of thinking and assume that others see things in the same way they do. They have difficulty understanding the more nonverbal parts of social interaction as well. For example, simple gestures of interest such as looking at someone when you talk to them, or lack of interest, such as looking at your watch repeatedly or looking toward the door for escape, are often missed by a person with Asperger's Disorder. People with Asperger's Disorder also have a difficult time understanding the feelings of other people, and can sometimes appear insensitive as a result.

  Although many children with Asperger's Disorder have considerable intelligence and may know a great deal about a particular topic, they have trouble sharing their interest appropriately and engaging other people in those interests. They may be able to look at information and facts in only one way—their way—and may be unable to understand a different point of view. This kind of rigid logic, sometimes expressed as naïve or overly moralistic, is common. As a result, some people with Asperger's Disorder experience social disapproval because of their inflexible opinions.

  People with Asperger's Disorder also have a hard time understanding and responding to affection. They may be able to express their feelings with familiar family members, but may act inappropriately with their peers. Some children are aloof and disconnected emotionally, while others are excessively attentive and affectionate to a fault. Because these children tend to learn their emotional reactions more formally or intellectually (not intuitively by observing others), they often misapply the appropriate social rules. For example, one young man frequently asks his listener, "Did I just say something rude?" in an attempt to learn whether his comments in a conversation were appropriate or not. This young man has learned that: a) he sometimes says rude things; b) he does not always realize he is doing this; and c) he is trying to figure out what other people think of his comments. He asks them specifically in order to learn this. This is hard work! It is easy to see how someone with Asperger's Disorder could be very interested in having friends, in doing and saying the right thing, and in behaving responsibly and appropriately, but fail on all three accounts because they just cannot seem to figure out the social interaction adequately.

▪ **Impaired Communication.** People with Asperger's Disorder also have problems with communication, but these are different from those of children with Autistic Disorder. Children with Asperger's Disorder often are early talkers, sometimes showing a fascination with letters and numbers at a very young age. Single words are heard between ages one and two, and phrases between two and three. However, like children with autism, children with Asperger's Disorder have significant difficulty with the social aspects of communication, including trouble establishing and maintaining eye contact, avoiding the gaze of other people, and standing too close or too far away from others while talking to them. This area, called pragmatics, is concerned with how children use language in social situations.

Compared to children with autism, the problems children with Asperger's Disorder experience with pragmatics are more subtle and less obvious. Their conversations may be one sided, and self-serving or egocentric. Topics of conversations may be quite limited and narrow, often centering around an area of particular and intense interest to the child. For example, one child accumulated a tremendous amount of information about presidents of the United States. Many times in conversations she would bring up facts that she had memorized, even though the topic of conversation was not about presidents of the United States. She worked very hard to steer the conversation in this direction, completely unaware that she was taking over the conversation and had missed the cues that she might be off-topic. Attempts to divert the conversation back to the original topic were generally unsuccessful.

Children and adults with Asperger's Disorder may be very tangential in their conversations, or they might engage in long monologues without recognizing that they are boring the listener. Sometimes people with Asperger's Disorder have trouble shifting topics. For example, some children might switch from one topic to another without warning. Their comments appear unrelated and confusing. Sometimes children with Asperger's Disorder are able to describe the link between topics, but sometimes they cannot. In either case, listeners are often left confused and feeling disconnected from the conversation, and from the person with Asperger's Disorder.

The mechanics of speech are also unusual for people with Asperger's Disorder. Their speech can be monotone and pedantic, almost as if you are listening to a boring lecture from a "little professor." The volume of speech and speed of speaking, and the stress they place on individual words in sentences, may also be unusual. For example, their voice patterns may be high pitched, or their speech may be very rapid. Some children whisper when it is unnecessary. These habits or characteristics not only interfere with understanding what is being said, but they can also be off-putting to others. Unfortunately, children with Asperger's Disorder are often unaware of how off-putting they can be at these times.

- **Repetitive, Stereotypic, or Odd Patterns of Behavior, Unusual Interests, or Responses to Their Environment.** Children with Asperger's Disorder often have unusual and all-absorbing interests or preoccupations. These can occur in any area of interest, such as geography, information about fans, deep fat fryers, different types of water faucets, or airplane silhouettes while in flight. Amassing facts is an end onto itself, not merely a means to better understanding of a subject area. Indeed, more conceptual or abstract understanding of an area of deep interest and intense study is lacking. More often than not, these "splinter skills" stand in contrast to other, less well-developed areas of ability.

Poor motor coordination and clumsiness are more common in children with Asperger's Disorder. This particularly seems to be the case with very young children, although older children can have problems with coordination, handwriting, and self-care skills like buttoning or shoe tying. Play skills involving coordination such as kickball or bike riding, and team sports such as soccer or baseball often are especially difficult. With team sports, the dual problems of motor coordination *and* needing to know the rules of the game and follow them are a real challenge for these children. Finally, children with Asperger's Disorder may be particularly clumsy, gangly, or loose, and may adopt unusual postures or stances. For these problems, evaluation is essential, particularly for understanding fine and gross motor planning and sensory difficulties as well.

How is Asperger's Disorder Different from Autistic Disorder?

- Children with Asperger's Disorder do not have the same level of communication problems children with autism have. Nearly all children with Asperger's Disorder speak and develop language skills roughly when other children do, but their use of social language is very different. In contrast, children with Autistic Disorder are very different in the way they learn to use language, and have more unusual forms of language such as echolalia. Many children with Autistic Disorder never speak.

- Children with Asperger's Disorder usually are not brought to the attention of professionals until after two years of age, and may not receive a formal diagnosis until after age seven or eight. In contrast, children with Autistic Disorder are often identified before their third birthday or earlier, and parents often know that something was not developing correctly for their child even before that.

- Children with Asperger's Disorder usually do not score in the range of mental retardation on standardized IQ tests, while this is much more common in children with Autistic Disorder.

■ Children with Asperger's Disorder have verbal abilities (like vocabulary or factual knowledge) that are generally better than their nonverbal abilities (like reproducing visual designs). The reverse is often true for children with Autistic Disorder.

■ Socially, children with Asperger's Disorder have a basic interest in other people, but often do not have the skills to initiate and maintain social interaction appropriately. Overall, children with Asperger's Disorder have less social disability and less language and communication difficulties than do children with Autistic Disorder. In contrast, children with Autistic Disorder are more likely to be aloof, withdrawn, or passive.

Because Asperger's Disorder has only recently been the focus of study, less is known about exactly how common or rare this condition is. Studies have reported widely differing numbers: One study reported that the incidence is about 3.6 per one thousand people in the general population, while another reported an incidence of one in seven thousand. Unfortunately, such wide variation in reported findings leads to a great deal of confusion for parents and professionals alike. As a result, without larger studies on the prevalence of Asperger's Disorder, it is impossible to speak with any precision on this topic. Although additional research in this area is certainly needed, one thing appears quite clear: Asperger's Disorder occurs more frequently in males than in females, perhaps as much as three times more frequently.

Rett's Disorder

Included under the PDD umbrella is Rett's Disorder (also known as Rett's Syndrome). This genetic condition was first identified 40 years ago by Andreas Rett, an Austrian physician and later by Bengt Hagberg, a Swedish physician. Both physicians saw similar characteristics among girls they studied which included stereotypic motor movements (often hands clasped at the midline in a wringing motion), ataxia (lack of muscle control), cognitive and language limitations, but normal early development. They found that only females appeared to be affected. Although Rett's pioneering work went largely unnoticed for many years, his description of this cluster of symptoms led to the identification of Rett's Disorder as a separate condition in the early 1980s. Previously Rett's Disorder was believed to be a progressive, degenerative neurological disease. However, it is now understood to be a problem of brain development that stops. In 1999 researchers discovered that Rett's Disorder is a genetic disorder. Rett's Disorder is very rare, affecting about one out of every fifteen thousand girls.

Children with Rett's Disorder are both similar and different from children with other PDD conditions. The symptoms of Rett's Disorder develop gradually over time, starting with normal development from birth until approximately five months of age. At that time, head growth may begin to slow through about 48 months of age. At the same time hand skills decline. Social withdrawal begins to occur, and severe receptive and expressive language difficulties follow. Problems with gait and balance emerge, as well as poor coordination of body movements. Stereotypic behaviors like hand clasping or hand wringing appear, and seizures may develop. Because of its significant impact on communication and social interaction, severe receptive and expressive language impairments, and repetitive behavioral patterns, Rett's Disorder is included as one of the PDDs.

Girls with Rett's Disorder are sometimes initially diagnosed with autism, and the differences between these two conditions initially can be confusing. Between one and three years of age, some girls with Rett's Disorder have not yet developed the characteristic stereotypic hand movements, but have experienced a decline in receptive and expressive language as well as social interactions. There are important differences between Autistic Disorder and Rett's Disorder, however. Children with autism generally have better motor skills, both fine motor and gross motor, than girls with Rett's Disorder have. While both groups engage in self stimulatory and perseverative behaviors, children with autism have more skillfulness and complexity in how they use these behaviors.

Girls with Rett's Disorder nearly always wring or clasp their hands at their midline (the center of their body) and are quite insistent about this behavior. Indeed, if their hands are moved away from this position, they will quickly return to it when their hands are released. This is not the case for children with Autistic Disorder. The development of seizure disorders occurs more frequently, and at an earlier age, in children with Rett's Disorder. While children with autism have great difficulties with eye contact, over time children with Rett's Disorder acquire this skill more readily. These girls sometimes become more interested in social interactions in their later elementary school years as well. Mobility problems, seizures, and other neurological difficulties that occur in girls with Rett's Disorder may lead to other health problems when they are older; children with Autistic Disorder experience these problems less frequently. Finally, children with Autistic Disorder have greater range of cognitive and intellectual functioning than children with Rett's Disorder who tend to have more significant cognitive limitations.

Childhood Disintegrative Disorder

Childhood Disintegrative Disorder (CDD) is a very rare PDD, occurring in perhaps one in one hundred thousand children. It is striking because it emerges after an extended period of typical development which often lasts several years. When the developmental regression starts, language skills, social interactions, play, motor behavior, difficulties with toileting, and so on become worse. Once a diagnosis is made, the behavioral symptoms are similar to those seen in children with Autistic Disorder.

For parents, the loss of language and other skills can be a dramatic and very frightening experience. The deterioration can last from several weeks to several months, although a very rapid and abrupt decline sometimes occurs. In as many as three quarters of the reported cases, the developmental deterioration was significant and the recovery of lost skills minimal. From the very limited research into this condition, the ratio of males to females affected by Childhood Disintegrative Disorder appears to be similar to autism.

Compared to other PDD's, identifying Childhood Disintegrative Disorder is reasonably easy. Its symptoms and progression are unlike any of the other PDDs. Compared to CDD in which symptoms appear later and skills regress, symptoms of Asperger's Disorder may appear after two years of age, and cognitive abilities and language skills are better and do not regress. The early and very noticeable changes in motor skills, head circumference, and communication skills seen in girls with Rett's Disorder makes confusion between Rett's and CDD unlikely. And children with Autistic Disorder show significant and very obvious differences from a very early age, in contrast to the later appearance of symptoms in children with Childhood Disintegrative Disorder. There is another condition, Landau-Kleffner Syndrome (acquired aphasia with epilepsy), which might be confused with CDD, but the symptoms and progression are different and can be distinguished during diagnosis.

Pervasive Developmental Disorder: Not Otherwise Specified (PDD:NOS)

"It's like Autism, just not so severe." "It's the same as mild Autism." "It's an easy out for professionals who don't believe parents can accept a diagnosis of Autism." PDD:NOS is a category that has been fraught with misunderstanding and misinterpretation by families and professionals, causing confusion about the nature and extent of services needed by children with this diagnosis. With an estimated prevalence of one in five hundred children, parents need a clear understanding of this diagnostic term.

To understand just what the term PDD:NOS means, and why it is an important diagnosis, think of an umbrella. This umbrella forms a broad canopy over a group of conditions called the Pervasive Developmental Disorders. There are currently four distinct disorders in this group, under the umbrella: Autistic Disorder, Asperger's Disorder, Rett's Disorder, and Childhood Disintegrative Disorder. The defining characteristics of this group of Pervasive Developmental Disorders, described earlier, are:

- impairments in social relatedness and social interaction skills,
- impairments in communication, and
- a restricted range of interests and stereotyped behaviors.

In order to be under the PDD umbrella, all three of these symptoms must be clearly present.

But what if the level of impairment is more mild, or if only two areas are moderately affected but one is not? Although these children have needs that must be addressed, they do not fit neatly into one of the four distinct diagnostic categories under the PDD umbrella. The current diagnostic solution has been to create the category PDD:NOS which allows children with a unique mixture of symptoms a place under the PDD umbrella. Quite literally, the term PDD:NOS refers to children with Pervasive Developmental Disorder who are *Not Otherwise Specified*—not otherwise covered—within the four distinct diagnostic categories.

Given the tremendous variety among children with PDD:NOS and its similarity to other PDD's, it has been difficult for parents to obtain clear information about the condition or a diagnosis for their child. The individual symptoms present in Autistic Disorder, which is far better studied, can be present in a child in mild to severe form. This makes diagnosis tricky. When some or all of these symptoms are absent or very mild, a child might be considered to be developing typically, perhaps somewhat shy or aloof, perhaps somewhat eccentric. This child may have symptoms that might either go unnoticed or might not be seen as symptoms of any condition. As the symptoms become more significant, they begin to interfere with daily functioning, and formal diagnosis becomes possible. Figure 1 provides a visual representation of the three impairments of PDD.

Figure 1

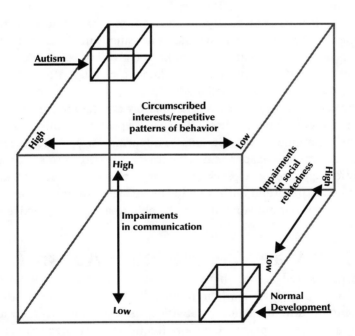

Children with PDD:NOS represent a diverse group of children with a wide variety of difficulties and problems in understanding social interaction, social relatedness, and being able to reciprocate social interactions. Children with a diagnosis of PDD:NOS may have better language skills, but have impairments in social communication (pragmatics), understanding of language, and the use of specific language forms (such as asking questions or making requests). Their interests can be restricted, with more limited imaginative and pretend play. Sometimes ritualistic and stereotyped behaviors are present. In other words, children with PDD:NOS can have the same symptoms present in Autistic Disorder or they can have symptoms that are milder. Some symptoms present in children with Autistic Disorder may be absent in children with PDD:NOS.

Some of the confusion in the use of this diagnostic term and the understanding of its implications comes from the lack of specific criteria or symptoms that distinguish PDD:NOS from the other PDDs. Some physicians, psychologists, or educators using the term may have insufficient experience or understanding of children with milder symptoms, or they may fail to appreciate that children with PDD:NOS can sometimes have a sense of humor, be affectionate, show empathy, or have imaginative or pretend play skills. Often times, children with PDD:NOS who have more mild symptoms are simply under-identified, or misdiagnosed with a learning disability, behavior or conduct disorder, or attention deficit disorder. Only later in childhood or adolescence is a diagnosis of PDD:NOS made.

The diagnosis of PDD:NOS is not merely an academic exercise. Defining and describing precisely the specific profile of abilities and problems for a child allows parents to advocate for specific social, communication, and academic interventions. The key is to seek the diagnostic expertise of a psychologist or a physician with special training and expertise in autism and PDD. Armed with more precise diagnostic information, you will then be able to advocate effectively for your child.

■■ How Many People Have Autism?

In the United States, there are at least 400,000 people with autism, about one-third of whom are children. Autism is one of the most common developmental disabilities; only mental retardation, epilepsy, and cerebral palsy occur more frequently. Although "classic" autism occurs in about 4 to 5 of every 10,000 children, a broader definition including children with less severe but still significant symptoms raises the incidence to about 16 out of 10,000 children. Children with the most severe form of this disorder probably make up only about 2 to 3 percent of children with autism. Again, remember that regardless of the number or severity of symptoms, the treatment for all of these children is basically the same.

▪▪ Do More Boys Than Girls Have Autism?

For reasons we do not yet understand, autism occurs about three to four times more frequently in boys than in girls. For children with more severe cognitive limitations, the ratio is closer to two to one. For the group of children with higher cognitive skills, boys are more frequently represented at a rate greater than four to one. Autism is more common in first-born males, but there have been no conclusive studies to date to confirm this and there is just not enough research available to know for sure. Girls, when affected, are more likely to be more seriously affected by symptoms of autism.

▪▪ Is Autism On the Rise?

To many professionals and parents the number of children with autism seems to be increasing at a faster pace than before. Indeed, some recent research studies of the prevalence of autism suggest that it is twice as high as previous studies had indicated. How can this be?

Two trends have affected the reported incidence of autism. First, the diagnostic criteria for autism and all the PDDs have been refined; currently they are the most stringent and the clearest ever. Because the criteria cover a broader spectrum or range of behaviors, more children are diagnosed correctly. That is, there is greater understanding of the behaviors that are associated with autism and the other PDDs. This leads to an increase in the rate of diagnosis. Second, the increase may be due to the improved sophistication of professionals who diagnose autism. As explained earlier, children diagnosed with autism may also have mental retardation. The reverse is also true: children with mental retardation (or other conditions associated with mental retardation, such as Down syndrome) may also have autism. In the past, these children were usually not given a second diagnosis of autism. Today, however, we are better able to distinguish between different conditions, even when they are present in the same child. The result: more children being diagnosed with autism.

Fortunately, the understanding of the needs of children is changing just as is the precision applied to the diagnostic process. This is leading to a better understanding of the importance of tailoring educational, social, and communication interventions to the needs and strengths of children with autism.

:: Why Does My Child Have Autism?

Scientists do not know why some children have autism. The most important thing you should know about the causes of autism is that *parents do not cause it*. We do not know for sure what causes autism, nor do we know exactly how autism affects brain structure, brain function, or brain chemistry. Studies have found that people with autism have differences in the structure of their cerebellums—a part of the brain. It is far too early, however, to draw any conclusions from this finding or from the other promising research conducted in the area of biological and genetic causes.

While the rates are very low, there is some evidence that autism can be inherited. If you have a child with autism, your overall chances of having a second child with autism are between two and three percent. While this frequency may seem insignificant, it is actually 50 times higher than for parents who do not have a child with autism. Given the low incidence of autism in the general population, however, the risk of recurrence is still very small.

To date, scientists have only identified one specific genetic connection with autism—fragile X syndrome. Fragile X syndrome is a recently discovered form of genetically caused mental retardation. Both sexes are affected by fragile X syndrome, with males usually more seriously affected. The degree of disability caused by fragile X syndrome ranges from severe mental retardation to varying degrees of learning disabilities. Children with fragile X syndrome also can have behavior problems such as hyperactivity, aggression or self-injury, and autistic-like behaviors. Severe language delays and problems are common, as are delayed motor development and poor sensory skills.

This condition, in which one part of the X chromosome has a defect, affects about two to five percent of people with autism. It is important to have a geneticist check for fragile X syndrome in your child with autism especially if you are considering having additional children. For unknown reasons, if a child with autism has fragile X syndrome, then there is a one-in-two chance that boys born to the same parents will also have fragile X syndrome. In addition, there is a greater tendency toward mitral valve prolapse (a kind of heart murmur) in people with fragile X syndrome. It is important to have this condition monitored over time by your child's pediatrician.

∷ A Word About "Cure" and "Recovery"

When it was first identified in 1943, autism was a baffling, severe, and misunderstood disorder to most professionals and parents. Since that time, we have come to understand autism as a brain-based disorder that children are born with. We also understand that the symptoms occur across a broad spectrum and may change for the better with time and appropriate teaching.

Autism and related conditions are caused by genetic, neurological, anatomical, or biochemical differences in the brain. True, these physical differences can be influenced by effective teaching, early intervention, and maturation. Positive, supportive environments help all children grow and develop. However, strictly from a medical or biological perspective, there is no cure for the brain differences found in children with autism.

What then should parents and professionals consider to be progress or even a "cure?" Simply put, reducing the symptoms that led to diagnosis in the first place should be considered progress. Some symptoms may decrease with age and effective teaching. Other symptoms may decrease to the point that they are no longer meet the criteria for a diagnosis of autism. This does not constitute "cure" or "recovery," but rather what is called "habilitation." Habilitation is the process of learning to adapt, accommodate, and cope with one's strengths and limitations. Through hard work—on the part of parents, professionals, and children with autism—much habilitation is often possible.

The emphasis on "cure" and "recovery" from autism is seductive and tantalizing. Which parent would not wish with all their heart for such an outcome? Given our current state of knowledge of the biological, genetic, and neurological nature of this disorder, however, an emphasis on cure and recovery is ill-advised. We understand far too little about which types of children with autism, with what mixture of cognitive, communication, and social skills, benefit from various interventions to bask in smug certainty. The danger is for dedicated parents to give their all and provide what is "best" for their child and to view less than complete recovery as their failure. It is far better to seek habilitation, with all of its hopefulness and reality, and set as a goal the reduction of symptoms to a minimal level, all the while building strengths and honoring diversity.

:: Getting a Diagnosis

Children with autism have been the subject of considerable research in recent years. Much has been learned about the symptoms your child must have in order to get a diagnosis of autism. This section reviews how professionals arrive at a diagnosis of autism and how you participate in that diagnosis.

When you talk with professionals about diagnosing autism in your child, they probably will refer to the American Psychiatric Association's *Fourth Edition of the Diagnostic and Statistical Manual of Mental Disorders* (DSM) (1994). The DSM contains the "official" diagnostic criteria for identifying almost all mental and emotional disorders in children and adults, and is the primary source of this information for medical and mental health professionals throughout the United States. The DSM's diagnostic criteria for each PDD can be found in Appendix A.

The DSM outlines the following criteria for diagnosing autism:

1. Severely impaired social interaction;
2. Severely impaired communication and imagination;
3. Extremely limited interests and activities; and
4. First observed in infancy or early childhood.

If you leaf through the DSM, you will have the same basic vocabulary as the professionals you are working with. Remember, however, that these professionals are working for you, and it is up to them to speak in plain English so that you can understand exactly what is being said. Never feel shy about asking a professional to "say it again, in words I can understand." Professionals say the same thing to each other sometimes!

Differential Diagnosis

When you first became aware that something was different about your child, you probably told your pediatrician about the behaviors that concerned you. Lack of language and a hard-to-describe aloofness were very likely two of those concerns. As various specialists became involved with you and your child, they began the process of deciding what disorder your child has and what disorders she does not have. This process is called differential diagnosis.

The differential diagnosis of autism involves comparing the behavior of your child with the behavior of children with other disorders that might account for the same symptoms—for example, mental retardation or speech-language problems—as well as with medical problems associated with autism such as Phenylketonuria (PKU) or fragile X syndrome. In the differential diagnosis of autism, there are two major disorders from which autism must be distinguished:

Mental Retardation. While children with autism have uneven development—delays in some areas and not in others—children who have mental retardation tend to have delayed development in all areas. Even though approximately 70 percent of children with autism also have some degree of mental retardation, the diagnosis of autism—not mental retardation—is appropriate if a child fits the diagnostic criteria for autism.

Professionals can decide whether mental retardation or autism is your child's condition by carefully evaluating the "unevenness" of your child's profile of development. Children whose primary disability is mental retardation will show a more generalized developmental delay than a child with autism. Figure 2 shows how developmental patterns may differ between autism and mental retardation.

Figure 2, shown below, shows that it is the pattern of development that helps to support or rule out a diagnosis of autism.

Figure 2

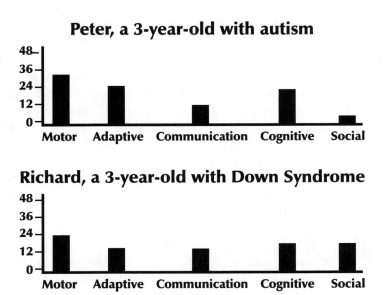

Peter, a 3-year-old with autism

Richard, a 3-year-old with Down Syndrome

Language Disorder. The other condition professionals eliminate in diagnosing autism is a language disorder. This is because children who have only a language disorder do not also have the abnormal responses to sensory stimuli that children with autism have. In addition, children with language disorders typically can use gestures or other methods of communication; children with autism have great difficulty doing this. Finally, the child with a language disorder usually can relate appropriately to people, objects, and events—an ability that a child with autism may not have.

There are two other conditions—each quite rare in childhood—that may be considered in making a differential diagnosis of autism.

Schizophrenia. Schizophrenia, a serious mental disorder, is very rarely diagnosed in infancy or early childhood, whereas autism almost always is. In those rare cases when the disorder does occur in childhood, the young child with schizophrenia has delusions or hallucinations, and uses speech to communicate irrational thoughts. In contrast, the young child with autism does not use speech to communicate.

Degenerative Organic Brain Disorder. In extremely rare cases, children can have Degenerative Organic Brain Disorder. This condition involves progressive deterioration in one or more areas of development. Although many parents report that their child with autism began to lose words and other early language skills at around 18 months, this slide eventually stopped and many of these lost skills were regained with appropriate education. This is not the case for children with Degenerative Organic Brain Syndrome.

Finally, a differential diagnosis must eliminate disorders, such as Tic Disorders, such as Tourette Syndrome, and visual impairments that may have symptoms similar to those seen in children with autism. In these disorders, there may be unusual responses to sensory stimuli, apparent deafness, or bizarre, ritualistic body movements (snorting, grunting, hand flapping). Because many children with autism do not respond to sound normally, deafness is often suspected. Deaf children, however, do not show the overwhelming lack of social attachment that children with autism do.

■■ The Evaluation Process

In establishing a diagnosis of autism, you and your child will likely come into contact with a variety of professionals, each with a special area of expertise. Although these professionals do not replace your pediatrician, who is responsible for the routine medical care of your child, they supplement your pediatrician's information. Often it is your pediatrician who will recommend that you consult specialists. Chapter 3 reviews how to select and work with your pediatrician. This section describes the many professionals you may need to consult to get a definitive diagnosis for your child.

There are two different methods you can use to get an evaluation of your child. The first method is to consult a series of professionals, each of whom separately evaluates your child's abilities and needs in the area of his or her expertise. The biggest drawback to this method is that many times these specialists conduct their evaluations in something of a vacuum. Although they may have read previous evaluations of your child, they may design and perform their evaluation without any actual contact with the other professionals involved with your child. The result is a series of evaluations, each of which addresses only one aspect of your child. This method often fails to provide a unified, comprehensive picture of the "whole child."

A better method of evaluating a child with autism is the *interdisciplinary team approach*. Here a group of professionals, each representing a specialty area—psychology, speech, medicine, special education—develops the assessment. While team members each conduct their evaluations independently, they usually maintain close contact with one another throughout the course of the evaluation. This contact fosters closer collaboration and information-sharing during the evaluation, as well as a more unified interpretation of the team's findings in the final report. While each specialist writes his or her own report, an assigned *case manager* serves as your link to the entire team. The case manager summarizes the team's findings for you in a report which you are encouraged to share with others working with your child, as appropriate. The case manager also oversees implementation of the team's recommendations. If you can use the interdisciplinary team method, do so. It is a better way to get an evaluation of your child.

Interdisciplinary teams come in many shapes and sizes, depending upon the resources of the organization or agency supporting them. For the evaluation of a child with autism, a team should contain at least a *psychologist, pediatrician, speech pathologist, and educational diagnostician*. Other specialists, such as audiologists, community health nurses, geneticists, social workers, psychiatrists, and dieticians, may be included or available for referrals in particular cases.

Locating an interdisciplinary team is not always easy. One important resource is the American Association of University Affiliated Programs (AAUAP) in Mental Retardation and Developmental Disabilities. There are over 60 members of the AAUAP network in 48 states and the District of Columbia, Puerto Rico, and Guam. The addresses and phone numbers for the executive offices of the AAUAP network and the location of each AAUAP facility are listed in the Resource Guide in the back of this book. You can also call the national office or your local University Affiliated Program.

In addition to the AAUAP network, private interdisciplinary teams are sometimes organized by groups of professionals who share an interest in autism and other developmental disabilities. Your pediatrician, local public health (or mental health) department, or local chapter of the Autism Society of America can help you find the private team nearest you. Whether you choose a private team or a hospital-, university-, or clinic-based team, a major factor in your decision should be the recommendations of other parents and professionals and the type of response you get from a team member when making your initial phone inquiry.

The different evaluations of your child may take two to three days to complete. Usually you will get an explanation of the results several days to a few weeks later. You will probably meet with the professionals in what is called a *parent interpretive,* during which the results of the evaluation will be explained to you. At this meeting, the evaluation team should give you its recommendations, and you should have the chance to ask questions. It is crucial that you understand what the evaluation means. Ask as many questions as you want. You probably won't have too many chances to get so much information from so many sources at once. Use this opportunity.

Learning all you can at a parent interpretive is very important because most children with autism require an interdisciplinary evaluation only a few times in their lives, usually at key transition points: once for an initial diagnosis; once after a couple of years of formal schooling; once in adolescence; and once in early adulthood. Of course, some children may require more frequent evaluations, especially if there is a special problem requiring close follow-up.

One of the most important things you can do for your child and your family is to find a professional you trust who has special expertise in the diagnosis and treatment of children with autism. Use this person as your child's case manager and have all reports and evaluations forwarded to him or her. As your child grows older, you will become more and more effective in advocating for your child, locating necessary services, and moving systems and organizations on your own. But having a trusted expert to help you locate resources, to bounce ideas off of, and to provide reassurance can be a great comfort along the way.

Professionals on the Evaluation Team

When you bring your child for an evaluation, you should be aware of what each of the specialists will do, and what information each will contribute to forming the picture of the "whole child." You might encounter a number of professionals, each performing a different part of the evaluation. Which professionals you see will ultimately be based on the needs of your child and family and on your community resources.

Psychologist. A psychologist, a professional trained in understanding human behavior, learning, and how the human mind works, is usually part of the evaluation team. The psychologist will collect a great deal of information about your child, including information about your child's emotional growth, her developmental strengths and weaknesses, her cognitive ability, and her ability to function socially. The psychologist's goal is to get a complete picture of your child with autism. Once the psychologist has this information, he or she will recommend educational and family intervention plans to capitalize on your child's strengths and address her needs.

In order to get the information he or she needs, the psychologist will give your child one or more standardized tests. He or she will observe your child's behavior and ask you a seemingly endless list of questions about your child's development. He or she will conduct a behavioral assessment on your child's special problems—such as severe tantrums—to try to determine their cause. The psychologist also will measure the kinds of "real-world" things your child can do, such as eating with a spoon or using the toilet appropriately. Finally, the psychologist may wish to review any evaluations of other professionals to get clues about other areas of concern.

Physician with a Special Interest in Autism. The psychiatrist, pediatric neurologist, or pediatrician—medical doctors who specialize in treating children—will usually gather information on your child in four main areas:

1. Her general state of physical health;
2. How she reacts to structured and unstructured situations during the evaluation session;
3. How she reacts to attempts at social interaction and her ability to initiate social interactions; and
4. Her general developmental status.

Your physician should review the records of your child's previous evaluations. During the initial office visit, he or she should take a detailed family history and review how your child is progressing developmentally—with language, social, self-help, and motor skills. Some pediatricians perform developmental evaluations using a formal standardized test, while others gather the information informally by direct observation and parent report. The physician will observe your child's response to the office environment, as well as to you and to various structured and unstructured tasks and demands like playing with toys in different ways. Development is discussed further in Chapter 6.

During the physical examination, the physician will check your child's medication history. He or she will look for the presence or absence of seizures and for signs of problems in the function of your child's brain—including motor coordination problems and clumsiness.

Depending on where you live, the medical evaluation may be conducted by a child psychiatrist or pediatric neurologist rather than a pediatrician. Regardless of your physician's specific medical specialty, the most important factor is choosing a physician who has expertise in autism and the medical and health concerns associated with it.

Speech and Language Pathologist. A speech and language pathologist is an essential member of the diagnostic team. Speech and language pathologists can observe your child and evaluate whether her particular speech and language problems are associated with autism or some other condition. The speech and language pathologist assesses your child's skills in the following areas:

1. **Receptive language**—the ability to understand communication.
2. **Expressive language**—the ability to communicate using words, gestures, or written symbols. This area includes word

usage and word combinations—verb-object combinations like "want juice"—and nonverbal communication.

3. **Pragmatics**—the use of words and gestures in social situations. For example, some children express their desire for something by whining or having a tantrum. Others point to the object, or lead their parent by the hand. Still others may use words, either appropriately or inappropriately.

4. **Play behaviors.**

5. **Articulation of sounds.**

6. **Oral-motor functioning**—how well your child can control her tongue, lips, and jaw.

7. **Voice**—resonance, pitch, loudness, and fluency, how smoothly speech flows.

8. **Auditory memory**—your child's ability to immediately recall information she hears.

9. **Attention.**

The speech and language pathologist will observe you and your child together; work directly with your child; give her tests; and review her records. If your child has some language, the speech and language pathologist will probably use more standardized tests than he or she would use if your child were nonverbal. Some children are very resistant to testing. With these children, the professional relies more on direct observations—both yours and his or hers. These observations can give him or her an estimate of your child's abilities and needs.

Audiologist. Since hearing impairment is one of the conditions that must be eliminated in diagnosing autism, an audiologist—a professional trained in evaluating hearing—is often a member of the interdisciplinary diagnostic team. Before getting a diagnosis of autism, parents frequently suspect their child has trouble hearing because she is uncommunicative and unresponsive to sound. In reality, children with autism are no more likely to have hearing problems than the general population. The audiologist on your team will assess your child's hearing using a wide variety of tests. He or she can use tests that require your child's active participation and he or she can use passive tests. Most importantly, the audiologist will observe your child and ask you about your own observations. Often parents are able to supply the clue that demonstrates that there is no hearing loss. At home, for example, parents may notice their child listening to faint, distant sounds that are not present in the audiologist's office.

Audiologists may be found by contacting the American Speech-Language-Hearing Association, listed in the Resource Guide in this book, by checking with local agencies and organizations, and by asking other parents.

Nurse. The nurse plays an important role in your child's evaluation. Working either with the pediatrician or alone, he or she looks at any health problems your child may have and observes her behavioral strengths and weaknesses. He or she attempts to develop a picture of your child as she functions in your family and community.

To get this picture, the nurse will first review records of your child's previous evaluations so that he or she can note the concerns of other health professionals and family members and pay special attention to these issues in the current evaluation. Next the nurse will probably observe your child at home in order to assess your child's behavior in a familiar setting. The nurse will also want to note the problems you are having, your interactions with your child, your child's play behavior, your disciplinary strategies, and the organization of your home environment. Finally the nurse will interview you to learn about a typical day at home for your child; her sleep and play patterns; the degree of structure in her daily life; safety issues; your child's self-care skills such as dressing, toileting, and feeding; and her current state of health. With information from the interview and observation, the nurse can develop a list of major areas of concern to your family and to health professionals.

Social Worker. Interdisciplinary evaluation teams often include a social worker who works to obtain an overall picture of how your family functions. Through interviews with both your immediate and extended family, the social worker will gather information on the roles family members play within your family, the quality of family relationships, your family's ability to cope with challenges, the support of your extended family, the commitment of family members to solving family problems, and your family's problem-solving style.

After developing a picture of your family's strengths and needs both as individuals and as a group, the social worker will direct you to helpful resources such as parent support groups, parent training, and respite care. The social worker may also serve as a service coordinator and liaison with other professionals working with your family.

Many other professionals may also participate in the diagnosis of autism, depending on the resources in your area. For example, educational specialists or dieticians may be part of the diagnostic team. Because these professionals have responsibility for the ongoing care and education of your child, they are described in detail in later chapters. These later chapters also provide information about the treatment of autism that you will find helpful as you prepare to move from the diagnosis stage to the treatment stage. Chapter 3 discusses the medical conditions associated with autism and the medications that are sometimes used to treat the symptoms of autism. Chapter 7 explains how an appropriate educational program can help to minimize your child's autistic symptoms and maximize her potential.

▪▪ A Brief History of Autism

Autism has a long past but a short history. As early as the late eighteenth century, medical texts described cases of children who did not speak, were extremely aloof, and who possessed unusual memory skills. But it was not until 1943 that the condition was given a name. In that year, Dr. Leo Kanner, a child psychiatrist at Johns Hopkins University Medical School, described the common characteristics of 11 children he had studied between 1938 and 1943. These children shared several features, the most notable of which was extreme isolation or withdrawal from human contact beginning as early as the first year of life. So convinced was Kanner that autism was present from birth or shortly thereafter that he adopted the term "early infantile autism." Today professionals rarely use the terms "infantile autism" and "early infantile autism."

In naming this condition, Kanner borrowed the term autism from Eugen Bleuler, a Swiss psychiatrist who had coined the term in 1911. In many ways, this borrowing proved to be an unfortunate choice. In his writings, Bleuler used the term "autism" to describe the active withdrawal of adult schizophrenic patients into fantasy away from social interaction. From the 1940s through the 1960s, many professionals believed that children with autism made a *conscious* decision to withdraw from a hostile, unnurturing human world and were afflicted with a disorder similar to schizophrenia.

Today we know that this is not true. Children with autism do not withdraw because they feel rejected. Unfortunately, however, many parents—and particularly mothers—were labeled cold, ungiving, unnurturing "refrigerator parents" who had in large part caused their child's autism. There were also persistent notions that autism was more common in families of higher socioeconomic status. Needless to say, we now know this is wrong; autism affects children of all classes, nationalities, and races.

Early incorrect beliefs about the causes of autism led to the treatment strategy of removing children from their families for residential treatment, with psychotherapy for the parents. Fortunately, new ways of thinking based on solid research have evolved that support families in raising their child at home and in the community.

Starting in the 1960s, advances in the diagnosis and treatment of autism were made. Researchers identified the particular symptoms of autism that separate it from other conditions and concluded that autism is likely a result of neurological and biochemical causes. Teachers and therapists also began to use more advanced techniques—including applied behavior analysis or behavior modification—to teach important school and life skills to children with autism. Research demonstrated that the techniques of applied behavior analysis were successful in teaching skills to children, and these techniques have become the treatment of choice today. Applied behavior analysis is explained more in Chapters 4 and 7.

Although autism still remains somewhat of a mystery, much progress has been made in understanding how it affects children. More work remains to be done, but today the stereotypes and myths of the past that so hurt parents and families are being replaced by facts.

▪▪ Your Child's Future

Just as children with autism have a very wide range of abilities and skills, so too do adults with autism. Generally, children with less severe cases of autism will have less disability as adults. A few achieve almost normal functioning. Most children with autism, however, continue as adults to be significantly affected by autism, some severely so.

Certain factors—notably the level of cognitive skills, the presence of language, and the availability of intensive, systematic early intervention—are important indicators of a more favorable future. Although there is some disagreement as to the exact cutoff, it appears that children with an initial IQ over 60 to 70 tend to have a better long-term outlook. Children with some spontaneous speech by age five or six also appear to fare better as they grow older. Additional positive indicators include less severe symptoms of autism and a more passive behavioral style.

There are now many more educational and vocational options for children with autism than existed even ten years ago. Part of the reason is the information gathered from research, part has to do with laws mandating an appropriate education for children with autism, and part has to do with society's increased acceptance of children with disabilities. Parent involvement, community integration, early identification and intervention, and systematic teaching all will contribute to a favorable future for your child.

It is impossible to define "favorable future" except to say that more and more children with autism will be growing up with less and less of a disability thanks to constantly improving educational services and a greater understanding of autism. As a result, the future will continue to get better; opportunities for growth and accomplishment will continue to expand. At this time, however, certain limitations are life-long. In most cases, an adult with autism will always require some degree of supervision. Fully independent living and economic self-sufficiency is possible only for a very few. Even when the severity of the symptoms of autism decreases over time, these symptoms usually don't disappear altogether. For example, the adult with autism may appear extremely shy, reclusive, or rigid when faced with variation in routines.

Children more severely affected by autism face a less independent future. In addition, children with autism who develop a seizure disorder by adolescence, who do not develop the ability to play appropriately with toys, or who live in an unstable home environment will likely require more supervision throughout their lives. However, just as the future for those with less severe autism has improved with recent social, political, and educational mandates, so too should the future for those more severely disabled.

∎∎ Conclusion

Your child's autism is due to a combination of neurological and biochemical difficulties that she was born with. Today, with improved testing, more knowledgeable professionals, and more effective teaching techniques, the future of children with autism is far more promising than in the past.

Right now, most children with autism will need supervision on a continuing basis all their lives. But research continues and as the possibilities expand—through research and social acceptance—so do the boundaries expand for people with autism.

Your child's autism is not her sole characteristic. She has a multi-faceted personality like all the rest of us. Keep this in mind when planning her future. You must insist that your child be treated as a learner first, and as a child whose learning is impaired by the symptoms of autism second. You should always work for the best possible educational placement for your child. To do otherwise risks her future life in your community. Remember, the future for those with autism is constantly getting brighter. There is every reason for you to work for, and expect, the brightest possible future for your child.

■■ Parent Statements

Life is never dull with a child with autism.

❧

The pediatrician said, "Have you thought about autism?" He was the first one who had mentioned the word. And we said, "No, it can't be autism. She's too affectionate, too outgoing."

❧

We knew about the stereotype of autism—you know, the self-destruction, the withdrawal—so at first we said, "That couldn't be it; she's just slow." And then we began to see that maybe our pediatrician did have a point. That's when we started looking more into the possibility.

❧

We thought the need for routine was part of his personality. When he went on his daily walk, he had to take exactly the same route he always followed, cross the street at the same point, stop and look at the same sign, and step on the same stone.

❧

She showed no eye contact. You could get right in her face and she'd turn her head either right or left. She made no attempt to interact. Having four siblings one would have thought that she'd have no choice but to communicate in some sort of way, but she did not. My heart told me something was definitely different about my daughter. Friends and relatives tried to reassure me saying, "Every child is different and unique in their own way." No, something was just not right.

❧

We took him to a day care center and the people there said, "Why did you bring us this problem child?" And that's when the wheels started turning.

❧

He went through all kinds of tests to see if he was allergic to different things, but never mental-type tests.

❧

People look at him, and I'm torn between making a sign to hang on him, "I can't help it—I'm autistic," and then handing out pamphlets, or just screaming obscenities at these people, telling them to mind their own business.

❧

I look at Tommy and I treat him as if he's got a label. I don't treat him like a normal kid. I mean, I see his problem and make allowances, or I exert myself more because I figure it's part of his disability I don't care what you call him, just do what's appropriate.

❧

One of the doctors we took Gary to told us, "Well, if he's autistic, he could just snap out of it, like amnesia." I thought to myself, "Don't hold your breath."

❧

When you first understand that your child's been diagnosed with autism, part of the frustration is that people always ask you, "Well, what causes that? What's the cure?" There are no answers. And it's frustrating for us to have to know that initially, but even harder for us to try to explain it.

❧

It seemed as though she was having a conversation with herself in an unknown language.

❧

I knew in my heart that my little angel was beautiful on the outside but lost within herself.

୧୨

Dealing with autism means learning to live in a different culture: it's very overwhelming but at the same time very exciting.

୧୨

There is no one answer! Autism is a puzzle. It doesn't matter if it's a 10 or a 500 piece, address each piece individually. They will eventually interlock.

୧୨

Over time, life with our son has become more complex. As we search for answers to help him, it becomes clearer that autism is an evolving disability. Our recommendation is to give all that you can and let your love for your child drive your unending ambition.

୧୨

Accept that this is the life that has been chosen for you and your family. We are one of the selected few. Try to keep a good sense of humor—it really does help.

2

ADJUSTING TO
YOUR CHILD'S
DIAGNOSIS

Lillian and Joe Tommasone

You've probably spent the first years of your child's life walking an emotional tightrope between hope and despair. On the one hand, you wanted so much to believe the encouraging signs that your baby was perfectly healthy and was making normal progress. On the other hand, you couldn't quite squelch the worry that *something* about him—something you couldn't pinpoint—was a little bit off. In the beginning, you were probably able to explain away some of the fears, but as new fears kept materializing to take the place of old ones, you likely found yourself coming perilously close to losing your emotional balance. I think our experience was fairly typical:

My husband and I came home from the hospital with a beautiful baby. Mike had an impish grin and a mischievous gleam in his eyes. He gurgled and cooed and was fat and healthy. But we held our breaths as our picture-perfect son began to develop. You see, our first child, Jon, was born with a developmental disability, so we waited anxiously to see if Mike would reach his developmental milestones on schedule. We knew what to look for—or at least we thought we did.

I remember coming home from the monthly pediatrician visits during Mike's first year and putting him to the test. I'd make him do all the simple exercises the doctor had done in his office. And Mike could do them. He followed an object with his eyes, reached out to us, looked at our faces, and laughed when we tickled him. He rolled over, sat up, and crawled. Just as you probably did with your son or daughter, we had a sense that all was well.

When Mike was about a year old, however, doubts began to surface. Our child, who had once been so full of expression, now seldom looked at us. Instead he seemed to be looking through us—beyond us—absorbed in his own thoughts. Despite our encouragement, Mike refused to walk, but was content to sit and rock. We rationalized that he was too chubby and was a thinker rather than a doer. Mike also didn't play with toys the way they were meant to be played with; instead he chose to collect them and carry them around. We decided he was feeling insecure. Most worrisome of all, Mike wouldn't respond when we called his name. We knew he didn't have a hearing problem, though, because he always came quickly whenever he heard the rustling of a candy wrapper.

What finally forced us to admit that Mike's problems were not just part of some stage he'd outgrow was his failure to talk. Although Mike whined and made other sounds, he still had not developed any purposeful language by about 24 months. His way of communicating was to throw a tantrum.

Although Joe and I could tolerate and understand an occasional tantrum from our toddler when he didn't get his way, it seemed as if Mike lashed out constantly. He'd throw a tantrum if we tried to read him a story or build a tower of blocks with him. He'd throw a tantrum if we interrupted a favorite pastime such as sitting and rocking, fondling the fringe on his blanket, or looking at his hands. And he'd throw tantrums for reasons known only to him.

Mike's temper tantrums were constant, lengthy, intense, and violent. He'd bang his head against the floor or wall, scream at the top of his lungs, kick and thrash about, and even bite himself. In desperation, I'd rattle off a list of things I thought Mike might want. Sometimes I'd name what he wanted immediately, but more often than not I wouldn't, and the tantrum would go on and on.

Puzzled, distressed, and frustrated, we made an appointment with a neurologist at a large metropolitan hospital. Surely modern medicine and the scientific community could give us some answers. Surely *someone* could fling us an emotional safety net.

▪▪ Getting the News

The sequence of events that led *you* to seek medical help for your son or daughter may have been somewhat different than the one I've just described. For example, you may have been most concerned because your child never smiled or continually flapped his hands, or because he learned to talk, but then mysteriously seemed to forget how. But whatever your worries, nothing could have prepared you for your child's actual diagnosis.

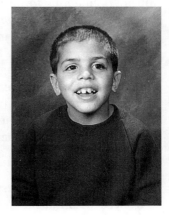

In our case, we were informed after a week of intensive testing that our son was "autistic-like." You may have been told that your child has autism or that he has pervasive developmental disorder or PDD or some other term. However the news is phrased, it is usually a devastating shock to parents already buffeted by months of worry and foreboding. For many parents, this pain is so searing that even years later, the memory automatically causes tears. Very few things indeed are worse than learning that your child has autism. You want to go back in time—to change things somehow. You think that if you could just hold your child and squeeze him, maybe he could be okay. You feel so desperately helpless and overwhelmed that you can't imagine ever laughing or feeling good about anything ever again.

No one would ever claim that adjusting to a diagnosis of autism is easy. There are no secret coping formulas; no magic words that can take away the pain. Still, parents sometimes find that learning to understand and work through their feelings helps get them started back on the path to a manageable, enjoyable family life. This chapter will help you sort out your feelings and then turn your attention to helping your child and the rest of your family.

▪▪ Coping with Your Feelings

Unless you have a background in special education or in medicine, the word "autism" probably meant very little to you the first time you heard it. And in my case, that one word, "autistic-like," was just about all I heard—that and the neurologist's pronouncement that there was nothing the medical profession could do for autism. I remember listening to the doctor explain the disorder afterwards, but I never heard his words.

Usually, it is not until after the seriousness of your child's diagnosis sinks in that your emotions really become overwhelming. While you are floundering toward acceptance, you are likely to be bombarded with feelings that range from rage and resentment to guilt, helplessness, and sorrow. To make matters worse, you may worry that some of your reactions are bad and shameful, and that you must be a terrible person to be having them.

Believe me, you have nothing to be ashamed of. Both your feelings about your child's autism and your feelings *about these* feelings are completely normal. You are going through the same emotions that most parents of children newly diagnosed with autism experience.

Shock

Shock is often the first reaction parents have when their child is diagnosed with autism. You might have felt, as I did, that you had somehow stepped outside of yourself and had physically removed yourself from what was actually happening. Inside I felt nothing at all, although I do recall thinking that tragedies like this happen only in the movies—not in real life, and certainly not to *us*. This inner numbness is a built-in defense mechanism our bodies have for insulating us from traumatic situations. Our minds just naturally shut down until we can begin to come to grips with the reality we face.

Helplessness

Once the shock wears off, you may be paralyzed by a new emotion: helplessness. In the beginning, you feel powerless because you know absolutely nothing about autism or what to expect for your child. You don't have the first idea what you should do, and doubt that you'd have the physical or emotional strength to do it even if you did. Like Joe did, you may feel as if you are falling into a deep, dark hole and that you have to reach the bottom of the pit before you can think of getting up again. And even if you have had experience teaching or working with young children as I had, you may feel completely incompetent to deal with your own child's problems. In desperation, you turn to your doctor for guidance, but each new fact you learn only increases your feelings of helplessness. Eventually the sheer enormity of your child's disability seems to weigh on you like a boulder. You feel defeated and immobilized, even before you've begun.

Guilt

Another emotion parents of children with autism frequently must grapple with is guilt. Each spouse may secretly worry that he or she is somehow responsible for their child's disability. Was it the aspirin I took when I was pregnant? Should I have dropped out of aerobics class sooner? Could it be my genes? Your anguish may become even more acute if you happen to come across out-of-date books written when autism was thought to be caused by cold, unfeeling, "refrigerator" parents.

Soon after Mike was diagnosed, Joe and I read just such a book: Bruno Bettleheim's *Empty Fortress*. According to Bettleheim, parents of children with autism did not give their children either enough love or the right kind of love. His book made us feel that our personalities, parenting skills, and home environment were so defective that they had made Mike autistic-like. His theory, which has now been completely discredited, made it sound as if we had the problems, not Mike.

I admit that we needed direction in bringing up Mike. And we didn't always understand him as well as we should have. But Mike was our child and there was nothing we wanted more than to love him and to watch him grow, learn, and be happy. I knew in my heart that there was nothing wrong with our love for Mike. Eventually my good common sense made me reject the idea that we were to blame for Mike's autism.

No matter what your feelings are now, sooner or later your common sense will also help you overcome any guilt you might have. As Chapter 1 explains, your behavior—either before or after your child's birth—could not possibly have caused your child's autism. And even if a genetic cause is eventually proven, there is currently no test that could have predicted with any surety that you and your spouse would have a child with autism.

Anger

Anger is a natural outgrowth of guilt. You are convinced your child's autism has to be *somebody's* fault—if not yours, then somebody else's. You can't believe that something so unspeakable could just happen to a helpless little kid without someone being to blame.

When Mike was diagnosed, my husband and I were angry with everyone. We were angry first of all at God for allowing this to happen. Our first child was developmentally delayed; hadn't we suffered enough? We were angry with the doctors and medical profession for not finding a cure. We were angry with the educators for not knowing how to make Mike catch up. And we were angry with family and friends whose words of comfort couldn't make the pain go away.

At the time, it just seemed as if no one else in the world understood what we were going through. You may feel the same way now, but believe me, it's not true. I understand your agony, and so do thousands of other parents of children with autism.

Grief

Underlying and complicating your other emotions, you are likely to have a heart-wrenching, bottomless sense of grief. You have lost the ideal, perfect child you once thought you had, along with many of the hopes and dreams you cherished for his future. The idyllic family life you'd once imagined for yourself lies in ruins around you and you don't know where to begin picking up the pieces.

For us the pain and grief of realizing our children had permanent disabilities was shared and separate. Many a night Joe and I would stay up late and talk and cry and talk and cry, trying to find some answer to the question, "Why us?" This only led us to the next question, "Why our sons?" We had many questions, but few answers.

I dealt with my grief in an outward, vocal way. I would cry, yell, moan, groan, and complain until I was wallowing in my own self-pity. I was hurting and I wanted the *world* to know it.

Joe grieved in a more controlled, quieter way. He'd get very quiet, serious, and somber. He wanted to be alone to think. These were the days he needed to go fishing.

There were times we wished our children had not been born— not so much because of who or what they were, but rather because of the problems their conditions posed for them. We worried about the quality of their lives because it seemed there would be so many empty holes that could never be filled. Our older son, Jon, would never know the thrill of hitting a home run or the anticipation of his first date. Mike would never feel compassion for another person or develop lasting friendships. He would always be a taker, never a giver.

At times, you may feel such profound emptiness inside that you may wonder if it might be better if you—or your child—had never been born. Contemptible as feelings like these may seem to you, they are normal, common reactions. They are just a way we have of trying to avoid the reality of our children's autism. With time, your grief, too, will become more bearable.

Resentment

On top of everything else, you may harbor terrific resentment. Why were you, out of all people, singled out to have a child with autism? What did you ever do to deserve this burden? It's just not fair.

Often parents of children with autism find themselves resenting other parents who take the normalcy of their children for granted. For instance, I remember feeling consumed with jealousy as I listened to friends recount stories of their children's latest accomplishments. They just seemed to have it all. I would wish some terrible misfortune would befall their families so they would have a chance to stand in my shoes and feel the pain I felt. Afterwards I hated myself for feeling this way. How could I wish misfortune on my friends? How could I be so cruel?

Some parents also resent their children for having been born with autism. Even though they know their child has no control over his condition, sometimes they can't help thinking that if only he would try a little harder to be normal, everything would be all right. For example, there was a time we thought Mike was acting autistic-like on purpose. We may have felt this way because we were still denying Mike's disability. After all, Mike had a hidden handicap. He was normal in so many ways. He had no physical limitations or distinctions, seemed aware, and was developing within normal limits. Yet sometimes he acted so bizarre in social situations. Couldn't he see that other children were not flapping their hands or getting undressed in public? Why did he act this way? Was it a maneuver to get our attention?

Not until we got a better understanding of the disorder did we realize that Mike's perception of the world was distorted. He doesn't perceive things the way most people do. His view of the world is mixed-up and fragmented. I imagine it's like listening to a static-filled phone conversation. You hear only parts of words and conversations, so you can't understand the total message. As a result, you get a different message than originally intended.

Your resentment of your child's autism and behavior, although understandable, will only build a wall between you and your child if you cling to it too long. Let your resentment go, and you will be able to use your emotional energy to fight your child's disorder in more constructive ways.

Shock, helplessness, guilt, anger, grief, and resentment are all normal reactions to the diagnosis of autism in a loved one. You will probably experience these emotions many times—not only in the beginning, but also later, after you think you have finally adjusted to your child's condition. For example, I still occasionally feel guilty if we're out somewhere in public and a minor inconvenience like waiting in line sets Mike off into a rash of uncontrollable behaviors. I blame myself, even though I know in my heart that I've set the stage for success and have prepared well. It is an unfortunate fact of life, but the healing process is slow and you will always have more stresses and emotions to cope with than other parents will. What is important to remember, though, is that you *will* deal with them. You will adjust.

:: How to Adjust

Address Your Emotions

No matter how strongly you may have suspected that something was wrong with your child, it is still devastating to have your worst fears confirmed. After all, your world has just been turned upside down—it is humanly impossible for you to know which way is up right now.

At first it can be like living in a pressure cooker. All the stresses and strains of everyday life and those worrisome feelings about your child can build to the point where you are ready to explode. You have to release that pent-up emotion somehow. Often the way I coped was to go out into the garden and furiously yank away at the weeds, pulling up flowers and vegetables in the process. Other times I'd go on a shopping spree. I'd buy every toy in sight, reasoning that educational toys were what I needed to "fix" Mike. Sometimes I stored the toys away, thinking that next month he'd catch up and play with them and everything would be okay. Other times I would realize the toys were completely beyond Mike's abilities and interests, so I would return them in despair.

Whatever *you* do, don't try to deny what you are feeling. If you feel like crying, cry. You have a right to cry. If you feel like pulling your hair and screaming at the top of your lungs, pull your hair and scream. You have a right to express whatever emotions you are feeling in whatever fashion seems right to you. Indeed, you *must* come to terms with everything you are feeling before you will

be able to accept your child's condition. After all, if you back away from your emotions now, how will you ever regain enough mental composure to be able to make the best decisions for your child?

Take Time to Heal

This will probably seem like small consolation, but most parents of children with autism go through what you are experiencing, and most eventually come to terms with their feelings. The key word here is eventually. Don't rush the healing process. If the house is a mess and you don't feel like straightening it out, don't. If you don't feel up to going back to work yet, then stay home another day, week, month— whatever it takes. And by all means, don't try to solve all of your child's problems at once. Even if you could, you don't know nearly enough about autism yet to know where to start.

It may take a while, but someday you will wake up and realize that something has changed. Your mind will be clearer and you will feel more optimistic. Without really knowing when, you will have accepted your child's autism and also another momentous fact: that your child is exactly the same person he was before you got a label for his condition. He hasn't lost a single one of the qualities that endeared him to you before his diagnosis; only your perceptions of them have been temporarily distorted. To illustrate, here is how Mike's label made us see him in a different light:

As a baby, Mike was very expressive. His entire face would light up when he was happy. If he saw an airplane in flight, for instance, he just bubbled with excitement. He'd jump up and down, flapping his hands and squealing with delight. He'd follow the plane's path until it was out of sight, screeching and toddling from one end of the yard to the other. For my husband and me, Mike's enthusiasm almost made up for the noisy flight pattern over our home.

Then we learned Mike was autistic-like. Almost at once, we began to see his enthusiasm as a weakness rather than a strength. It worried us that we could never quite predict Mike's response or the intensity of his reaction in any given situation. We felt we always had to be on guard. Now in place of a spirited, alert, happy child, we saw a loud, demanding child who was out of control. Our focus had shifted from Mike to his autism.

Since then, time, training, experience, and exposure have helped Mike get a better handle on his emotions and reactions. And Joe and I have learned to rediscover Mike as a child. Now, although Mike still challenges us, we can once again see him as a happy, lively, vivacious child.

On the day you are able to see your child for himself again, you'll be ready to take positive steps to cope with your child's autism. You will be ready to start educating yourself. You will want to reach out to other parents. You will begin to trust yourself and your instincts again. And most importantly, your early feelings of helplessness, anger, grief, and resentment will begin to loosen their stranglehold on you.

Get the Facts

Once you have begun to cope with your emotions, you will recognize that you can never go back, only forward. And to move forward, you need facts about autism and about disabilities in general. Everyone absorbs information in their own way and at different rates, but be careful not to move too quickly or you may find yourself overwhelmed by the sheer amount of information out there. It is also important to bear in mind that, although you will eventually have to make quite a few decisions about your child's future, you do not have to make these decisions as soon as you read about them. You will likely discover, as my husband and I did, that measured doses of information, as needed, will sustain you best.

The Reading List in the back of this book can help get you started in the right direction. The Autism Society of America (ASA) can suggest books and articles for you to read and provide you with brochures and other information. Your local chapter of The Arc (formerly called the Association for Retarded Citizens) can also recommend reading matter if your child has mental retardation in addition to autism. Finally, to learn more about special education and other issues confronting parents of all special-needs children, you may wish to read some of the journals and magazines listed in the Resource Guide.

▪▪ Your Family and Friends

There is no getting around it. Everyone who is close to you and your child will experience the same emotions that you did when they learn that your child has autism. Brothers and sisters may not yet be able to articulate their feelings and older friends and relatives may not know how to do so in a tactful manner, but the feelings, whether expressed or unexpressed, will be there.

Brothers and Sisters

Most parents find it difficult to break the news of their child's autism to their other children. To begin with, it can be hard to come up with just the right words with which to explain such a complex disorder to young children. Sometimes it helps if you can explain the disorder using experiences your children can identify with. For instance, to explain why your child with autism flaps his hands or bangs his head, you might ask your children to remember the last time they felt like crying, and then tell them that their sibling can't help flapping his hands any more than they could keep from crying. Do not talk down to your children, but do not overwhelm them with an overly technical explanation, either.

Once your children understand that there is something different about their sibling, you should be prepared to help them adjust to their feelings. Your children will probably need to cope with the same emotions that you did. They may wonder, for example, whether they caused their sibling to get sick. They may resent the disruption of their lives and wish that their brother or sister would die. Because your children will not know how normal and acceptable their feelings are, it is up to you to reassure them.

One way to help small children express their feelings is to use play therapy. Using a doll, a television show, or a book to begin the discussion, zero in on the emotions you think your children are struggling with: "Wow, Kelly sure was mad at her brother. I wonder why. Do you know why Kelly was so mad?" Whatever reasons your children give you, reassure them that it is all right to feel that way.

To further help your children understand that they—and their feelings—are normal, you may want to introduce them to other siblings of children with autism or other disabilities. Just as you and your spouse do, your children need to be reassured that there are others in the same boat as they are. Chapter 5 explains how to get your children involved in a siblings' group and also provides additional suggestions to help your children adjust to their sibling's autism.

Grandparents

Most parents of children with autism approach telling their own parents about their child's disability with painfully mixed emotions. They desperately want their parents' support and understanding, but

at the same time they worry about how their parents will take the news. And it's true your parents likely will go through the same range of emotions you did. In their guilt, they may wonder if they passed along defective genes. In their anger, they may try to fix the blame on their son- or daughter-in-law. In their grief, they may mourn the loss of the ideal, super-achieving grandchild they'd had their hearts set on.

Whatever your parents' first reactions, bear in mind that they *are* grandparents. Your child's label no more changes the relationship they had with him before his diagnosis than it changes yours. Chances are that once they have adjusted to your child's diagnosis, their natural grandparents' urge to dote on, and brag about, their grandchild will return in full force. This was certainly the case in my family, although there is no doubt that both grandmothers have felt the strain of Mike's (and his brother's) disability. In fact, in the beginning, they seemed to have double the grief. They grieved over their grandchild's handicap *and* their own child's pain. We talked a lot and cried a lot and were open and honest about our feelings. Now both grandmothers have a special relationship with Mike and are our much-needed extra pair of hands.

To help your parents comprehend and adapt to your child's situation, you will probably need to assure them that their reactions, doubts, and fears are normal and should be discussed openly. You will also have to provide them all the information they need and give them the opportunity to ask questions. Finally, let them help you respond to their grandchild's needs. Then give them time to come around.

Friends

It is all too easy to let your child's autism come between you and your friends. For your part, you may unconsciously push friends away because you feel they cannot possibly understand your pain or because you resent their normal family home life. For their part, friends may avoid you for fear of saying the wrong thing or avoid the subject of your child's autism for fear of seeming impolite. Most friendships that run into trouble probably do so because of actions (or inaction's) on both sides.

From my own experience, I know that it's just about impossible not to feel isolated from friends—at least in the beginning. As a young mother, I felt cut off from my close friends who had had "normal" babies. Their babies learned, grew, and changed every day. My baby seemed to be frozen in time. My friends would chatter and chuckle about the cute and darling things their toddlers were doing. I'd feel so alone and sad because I couldn't contribute to the conversation. I felt that even if I did share one of Mike's achievements, it would have been one that their children had mastered long ago.

I recall an incident when a group of mothers had come together for an evening social. One of my friends shared a story about how her child answered the telephone saying, "She can't talk right now," and hung up quite abruptly. I felt so alienated from this mother; my child had no idea the phone could even ring.

When it comes to friends, have patience and try not to judge the value of their friendship by how they respond to you and your child in the beginning. Give friends time to adjust, to come visit, and to cope with having a friend whose life has just changed. Friends can often help you enormously if you just give them the chance. In my case, it was my sister and her gentle yet forthright pep talks that roused me out of my self-pity and made me do what I had to do. From the start, she helped me steer my anger and pain into more positive directions such as advocacy. With time, she has become the fulcrum that balances my subjective feelings with the realities of the situation. She strengthens me and helps me grow. In short, she is my best friend and my harshest critic.

Although you too may find that autism draws you closer to some friends, don't be surprised if it also drives others away. Maybe your friends can't understand autism or are afraid of illness. No matter. You are bound to make new friends—friends who can sympathize with you and give you advice on how to deal with your problems. You will find these friends at parents' groups and elsewhere in the autism community, and they will do wonders for you and for your perceptions of autism.

▪▪ Your Marriage

Friends and family are important in helping parents cope with their child's autism, but most parents find that their strongest ally is their spouse. My husband and I have discovered that teamwork is vital to both our emotional and our physical survival. Just keeping up with a child with autism can drain you of so much energy that you've got to have a great backup player ready and able to take over if you falter. You and your spouse can also shield each other from some of the pain and sorrow and rally each other's spirits when everything seems to be falling apart. I don't know how many nights there were back in the early days when all my husband and I could do was hold each other and cry. I don't know what I would have done if we hadn't been able to share our anguish with one another.

Before you and your spouse will be able to work as a team, you will both need to come to terms with your feelings in your own way and in your own time. Don't try to hurry your spouse if he or she does not adjust to your child's autism as quickly as you do. Sooner or later you will both reach the point where you feel yourselves ready to go on with your own lives, as well as your family's.

Once you reach this point, your next step is to find out what your spouse has been going through. Both of you need to get your feelings off your chests and to confess your darkest fears. You must try to discuss all issues, especially the big decisions. As Chapter 5 explains, communication is probably the single most important factor in adapting your marriage to the stress of raising a child with autism. Although you and your spouse may occasionally be at a loss as to how to help one another, if you can talk about your uncertainty, you can at least be assured that you both still consider your relationship a top priority.

Some parents suffer from chronic fatigue. Because of their tendency to injure themselves or others if not constantly supervised, many children with autism run their parents ragged during the daytime. Mike, for example, needs constant supervision because he is so impulsive and unpredictable. His high activity level and unpredictability not only wear us down, but on occasion have caused our hearts to stop. For example, one day Mike gave me the slip and wandered out of our fenced-in yard. In my frantic search for him, I suddenly remembered his current preoccupation with swimming pools. I was horrified when I found him walking on the pool cover of a neighbor's in-ground pool. He didn't realize that if the cover gave way, he would drown.

Many children with autism also go through periods when they keep the family up all night by throwing tantrum after tantrum or by repeatedly getting out of bed. Mike went through a stage when he wouldn't stay in his room and would get up every two hours. Naturally he wanted company, dragging out his toys and turning on all the household lights. Since fatigue has a way of robbing you of your ability to cope, try to share night duties equally so that you and your spouse each have a chance to get some rest.

To keep your child's autism from becoming the sole focus of your marriage, try to take some time out for yourselves at least once a week. If at all possible, you should find a reliable babysitter and get out of the house to talk or just to have fun. Don't just go to parent support meetings, either. Go out to dinner or to see a movie. Doing things for yourself—by yourself—can also be very therapeutic. Over the years, I have done craft work, sold cosmetics, and become active in church work. I have also returned to college for my special education teaching certificate, and to graduate school for an M. A. in special education. Like all mothers, I have learned that you have to balance your time and energies between family and self. I have also learned that just knowing that you are going to get out of the house or that you have a outing coming up can boost your spirits tremendously.

Sometimes in spite of all you do, you and your spouse cannot quite manage to cope as a couple. Chapter 5 discusses reasons this may happen and strategies for resolving some typical problems. Whatever your difficulties, however, it is important to realize that your spouse needs you more than ever now, and so do all your children. And believe it or not, having a child with autism just may help you forge a stronger, better marriage than you had before.

:: Reaching Out

Reading books and pamphlets about autism is helpful and necessary, but there's nothing like getting the facts firsthand. By connecting with a parent support group, you can trade questions, concerns, and feelings with other parents who have been there. You learn that you are not alone in your sorrow, anger, and pain, and you also pick up practical advice about meeting the day-to-day challenge of raising a child with special needs. You may even meet someone who is willing to swap babysitting chores with you and allow you some much-needed respite.

To make contact, call your local ASA chapter, affiliate of The Arc, or any of the other parent organizations listed in the Resource Guide at the back of this book. Explain that you have a child with autism and that you would like to talk to someone who can give you some basic information. You won't have to say more—they'll understand. If you don't feel quite ready to share your emotions, nobody in a parent support group will force you to talk. Often just listening to the stories of other parents of children with disabilities can help to dilute your loneliness. It's only a phone call; what do you have to lose?

:: Don't Despair

As later chapters of this book emphasize, it is impossible to predict at an early age just how much your child with autism will achieve. Like all children, children with autism are born with varying abilities and potentials; there is no such thing as a typical child with autism. Do not rule out any long-term goals for your child at present; rather concentrate on the small steps that may eventually help your child reach those goals.

Above all try to keep your perspective and a sense of humor. Inevitably raising a child with autism is going to lead you into some potentially embarrassing situations. If you can somehow manage to see the funny side of these incidents, however, you can often disperse a great deal of tension.

I remember an occasion when my family had gone out to lunch at a fast food restaurant. We were waiting in line to order, when Mike bolted away and sat down with another family. Without a word he reached across the table, snatched a stranger's hamburger, and took an enormous bite out of it. Needless to say, neither my husband nor I particularly wanted to claim Mike as our child. After we'd made our apologies, replaced the hamburger, and were driving home, however, the humor of the situation hit us. "Did you see the look on that guy's face?" my husband asked. The more we chuckled over the stranger's surprise, the less we felt like haggling over whose fault it was that Mike hadn't behaved quite properly.

On another occasion when Mike was in his shoe fetish stage, he took a fancy to an elderly woman's shoes. As she was walking along the sidewalk, Mike began tugging at her heel, trying to remove her shoe. Fortunately I was able to intervene in time to keep the startled woman from falling. Fortunately too she had a good sense of humor and was able to laugh with me over my young son's penchant for women's orthopedic shoes.

I'd be the last person to recommend that you laugh off every awkward situation that your child with autism gets into. Remember, though, that your child *is* a child and all children do funny things. Laughter may not be the best medicine for autism, but it can certainly help to ease some of the pain.

■■ Conclusion

Right now the knowledge that your child has autism may color everything you do. For example, perhaps you can't fully enjoy a good novel or a get-together with your friends without the specter of your child's autism intruding on your pleasure. Maybe you can't even buy a newspaper without wondering if your child will ever learn to read. With time, however, your child's problems will become more of an element in your life and less its main focus. You may still have busy and bad times, but they will no longer seem to swallow you up.

Mike is an adult now. Over the years, there have been ups and downs, good days and bad days, triumphs and tribulations. But Mike has made painstaking strides toward goals Joe and I never dreamed he could reach.

It is really hard to measure what impact Mike and his brother have had on our family life and on our personal growth, but here are a few lessons we have learned:

We have learned to appreciate and treasure the everyday miracles in life—Mike's first word, his older brother's first steps, the way both boys roar with laughter when Daddy imitates animal sounds. We have learned to value another human being despite his problems—to look at our children's strengths, not just their weaknesses. We have learned to be givers as well as takers by helping other families through hard times and pain, by advocating for those with disabilities, and by giving our time, energy, and talents—whether it be chaperoning a teen dance, baking cupcakes for a class party, or giving testimony at a national conference on disabilities. And we have learned we can be happy despite our children's disabilities. We can still laugh at each other's mistakes, lean on one another, and love and care for each other every day.

Eventually you may find that being the parent of a child with autism has completely altered your perception of what matters in life. Most importantly you may discover that you have developed an appreciation for simple things you once took for granted. Former priorities—career advancement, making a killing in the stock market, bowling a perfect game—may pale in importance compared to enjoying the season's first snow, a hug, or an afternoon together with your family. Sometimes just getting your child with autism to smile at a joke and actually *enjoy* an experience is enough to make you feel like King Midas. If raising your son or daughter with autism does nothing more than deepen your appreciation of such simple things, your child will enrich your life many times over.

Your child has autism, and you cannot change that fact. But the autism is not the end of his life, or of yours. There is no denying it: autism *will* affect his life. But it is your challenge to see through the autism to the child underneath, and not to let autism be all you see. I can promise you that there will be days when you glimpse your child at work, at play, or busy with some activity and see just a child...your child.

■■ Parent Statements

There is nothing more devastating than finding out that your physically beautiful child has a disability.

❧❀❧

When you find out, your reaction is that he's still your child. Whatever's wrong with that kid, there are still all these good things. You've already accepted those things. You've already loved them.

❧❀❧

When Scott was first diagnosed, a friend of ours read some articles—not encouraging articles—and I read them and got very depressed. I started seeing Scott in a different light. I had a different attitude, and it was very, very depressing. I developed an object attitude—"There's a Down syndrome kid," "There's an autistic kid." It was as if he was a thing now—not even a human being. It took me about a week and then I said to myself, "Look, Scott hasn't changed. He's still the same person he was a week ago. I can't do this. He's a complicated kid and there's a lot wrong, but he's not these critical studies." His humanness, I think, brought me around and I realized that I can't look at him that way. I have to look at him as him.

❧❀❧

I think possibly—getting real philosophical about it—that denial results from a lack of support.

❧❀❧

I read articles about how it was the parents' fault.

❧❀❧

I kept thinking I must have done something to deserve this.

❧❀❧

I knew I did everything right during my pregnancy. I knew people who drank and took drugs and everything else and had normal kids, and I thought, "What a slap in the face! I did everything right, and I'm the one with the problem."

❧❀❧

I just consider him part of me. When they told me something was wrong with him, it was like they were saying there was something wrong with me. It was really hard to deal with.

❧❀❧

I think the shock was what made the final diagnosis so hard. We'd known in our hearts that something was wrong, but here it was from professionals, saying, "Hey, this is it." And, oh, my God—it's like a ton of bricks hitting you or something.

❧❀☙

I felt grateful that Scott had been diagnosed in a couple of stages and that it wasn't all an instant thing.

❧❀☙

I think we were all secretly hoping that somewhere along the line somebody was going to say, "He's not really autistic. He has a problem and here's a pill that will make it go away."

❧❀☙

The strain on our marriage was a lot worse before we knew what was wrong. Even though we didn't say anything, we were always trying to put blame on each other. Once we knew that we didn't cause the problem, it was easier.

❧❀☙

It is crucial that you don't blame yourself, each other, or anyone else for your child's autism. You need to accept this reality and seek the best course of treatment at the earliest possible age.

❧❀☙

We went from thinking we had a brilliant little boy who could memorize books and videos by heart to thinking we were burgeoning on a lifetime of special education services for a dreadfully disabled child. That's the effect of hearing the "A" word that first time in association with your child.

❧❀☙

I was actually relieved to learn my son's diagnosis. At least now I know and can start to understand him, who he is and where he's coming from.

❧❀☙

For the first year of his life, I woke up in tears from grief. The firstborn son I dreamt of: a popular, ambitious young man, in a sense, had died. The literature said he would never be part of life.

❧

There isn't a day that goes by I don't feel the pain of losing my child to autism. There isn't a day that goes by I don't also see him as a blessing in disguise.

❧

I used to think all autistic kids spent their time spinning in corners or rocking back and forth. Now I realize that many autistic-like behaviors are not stereotypical, and as parents you want to "explain away" these unusual behaviors. People often tell you they once knew someone who did the same things, and now they're fine. You hold onto that and want to believe it so badly, but that pain in your stomach just doesn't go away.

❧

The diagnosis, and all that it entails, is stunning. Today, it seems hard to imagine that not so long ago I barely knew what the word autism meant.

❧

In the beginning, I secretly hoped someone else I knew would have a child with a problem so they would know what it was like. I felt like a monster, wishing it on others. Finally I realized that having somebody else like my son in my circle of friends or family would never change our situation.

❧

When we first received David's diagnosis, we felt like the wind had been knocked out of our sails. Eventually we came to realize those sails would take us on a new course.

3

MEDICAL PROBLEMS, TREATMENTS, AND PROFESSIONALS

Fred R. Volkmar, M.D.

Raising a healthy child is one of the most difficult—and rewarding—challenges any parent can tackle. For parents of children with autism, the rewards are just as great as for other parents. The difficulties, however, can be more daunting because you have to take autism into account in almost all decisions you make about your child's medical well-being. For example, how will your child react to having her teeth cleaned? Can she handle a flu shot? Is it more important to take care of these problems now, or is it better to avoid any additional stress for the present?

All children have a chance of developing any number of diseases or conditions. Parents of "normal" children are rarely informed of all the possible diseases their children might get. But when your child has autism, doctors often tell you the statistics for your child. This may seem insensitive and unfair, but the fact is, children with autism are simply more likely to develop certain medical problems. And because these medical problems can sometimes cause or worsen developmental delays and behavior problems, early detection and treatment are crucial.

As a parent, you can help your child by learning the basic facts about medical conditions so that you can spot problems in the early stages. You can also help your child by learning to ask the right questions and to communicate well with doctors so that you can jointly make important decisions about your child's medical care.

This chapter outlines some of the common medical conditions and potential problem areas you should look out for, and also includes tips on how best to work with medical professionals to ensure optimal care for your child. First, though, because your child's autism and the medications sometimes used to treat its symptoms can contribute to other medical problems or affect the way your child interacts with medical professionals, this chapter discusses the medical treatment of autism itself. It also reviews the medications occasionally prescribed to reduce problem behaviors common in children with autism, and explains their benefits and risks.

■■ Medical Treatment of Autism

Although we do not yet know the causes of autism, medicine has made important strides in treating some of its symptoms. Medications can sometimes be very helpful in reducing or eliminating problem behaviors. Because medications may also produce harmful side effects, though, it is essential to weigh their risks against their benefits. In addition, you should be aware that some treatments are still new or experimental and carefully consider any controversy surrounding them in discussions with your doctor. This section reviews the medications most commonly prescribed for children with autism and the important considerations involved in selecting and using medications.

Medications

The medications used to treat children with autism, like all medications, have their benefits as well as their limitations. Unfortunately no medications have yet been developed that "cure" autism. Rather, medications are sometimes used to treat specific symptoms when these interfere with education or pose a potential danger. For example, medication may be prescribed to treat a self-abusive behavior like severe head banging or to treat behavior like continual hand flapping which can interfere with education.

The medications most often prescribed to treat autism are called neuroleptics, or "major" tranquilizers, and include a number of medications which affect the brain in specific ways. Among the most commonly used major tranquilizers are thioridazine (Mellaril™), chlorpromazine (Thorazine™), haloperidol (Haldol™), and risperidol (Risperdol™).

Do not confuse these major tranquilizers with the "minor" tranquilizers such as Valium™ and Librium™, which adults commonly take to manage anxiety. The "major" tranquilizers act in a different way, and are most frequently used for adults with severe psychiatric illnesses as well as some children with autism. One of the ways they work is by reducing the activity of dopamine, a chemical in the brain that acts as a neurotransmitter, or messenger, between nerve cells. In children with autism, dopamine appears to regulate certain problem behaviors—for example, self injury and stereotyped, or purposeless, repetitive movements. By decreasing these behaviors, major tranquilizers may increase the attention span of children with autism and thus make them more able to learn.

Because each medication has a range of side effects, it is important to balance the potential benefit of the medication against its risks and to be prepared for any side effects you may observe. Whenever medication is prescribed, your child's doctor should review the possible benefits, risks, and side effects with you, other people who help care for your child, and the school staff.

Probably the most common side effect of the major tranquilizers is sedation or sleepiness. A child may become overly sedated after the medication is used and may be unable to benefit from her educational program. In that case, there is little point to using the medications in the first place. Other side effects of the medications include problems in movement. Sometimes children will develop peculiar postures or muscle spasms or stiffness around the head and neck; these side effects can often be controlled by the addition of another type of medication. To some extent, all major tranquilizers produce dry mouth, constipation, blurred vision, and other effects most commonly associated with allergy medications or over-the-counter cold preparations. Less common side effects include changes in the function of the liver, effects on blood cells, restlessness or agitation, sensitivity of the skin to the sun, and true allergic reactions. Often side effects are dose related—they are more common with higher doses of medication—but sometimes individuals have side effects even on low doses of medication.

Sometimes after a major tranquilizer is stopped or has been administered for a long period of time, other side effects may emerge. For example, a child may develop unusual head and body movements, which usually disappear some weeks or months after the drug is stopped. The most worrisome side effect of these drugs, however, is a condition known as *tardive dyskinesia.* Tardive dyskinesia usually occurs only after very long periods of treatment. In tardive dyskinesia, movements of the face—grimaces or tongue protrusion—are accompanied by unusual movements of the body and hands. Probably these movement problems reflect changes in brain sensitivity to neurotransmitters, the brain chemicals affected by the drugs. Because this condition is sometimes irreversible, it is important that the doctor prescribing the medications continue to see your child periodically to monitor the medication.

A new medication, Risperidone (Risperidal™), is called an "atypical" major tranquilizer. It seems to be much more selective in terms of its action in the brain. In general, its side effects seem to be much less than those of other major tranquilizers. Research on this, and related medications, is promising. In particular, it seems that these medications do not have the same potential for causing long-term side effects, particularly tardive dyskinesia. The major problem with Risperidone is weight gain, which can sometimes be significant even on very low doses of this medication.

Given the potential side effects of these medications, it is important that they be used only when necessary. Before starting your child on medications for behavior problems, you and her teachers should review your child's educational and behavioral program to determine whether changes in the environment or program might produce enough improvement to make medication unnecessary. For example, sometimes a change in classroom activities or daily routine may help reduce behavior problems.

When medications are unavoidable, it is essential that they be used sensibly, in the lowest effective dose, and for the shortest possible period of time. This means that your child must be monitored closely while she is taking medication. To make monitoring easier, the prescribing doctor—who may be a psychiatrist, developmental pediatrician, or other specialist—may want to do a physical examination and laboratory studies before starting medication. This enables the doctor to compare behavior before and after medication and to get a "baseline" against which any adverse effects of the medications can be measured. As a parent, you can help monitor your child by providing the doctor with behavioral records from the school and by continuing to observe your child closely. As described later, it is important that you be involved in this process; information you provide is essential for the doctor, who usually sees your child for a short period of time in an unusual (to your child) situation.

The choice of medications and dosages depends on several factors. For example, children who are more agitated do better with a more sedating medication Mellaril™. Otherwise, less sedating medication is generally used such as Haldol™. Typically, a low dose of medication is prescribed to begin with, and then adjusted depending on the child's response. Sometimes children have trouble with one medication, but do well on another. Because of the risk of long term side effects and the need to monitor the usefulness of the medications, you and your physician may decide to reduce or stop the medication during certain periods. In some emergencies, such as when a child's head banging is so severe as to pose the risk of serious injury, higher doses of medications may be prescribed. Once the behavior is under control, the medication can be gradually reduced.

The use of these medications should not be undertaken lightly. Often, though, they can greatly help your child adjust and respond well to an educational program. A good working relationship between you, your child's physician, and the school staff will help to ensure that your child is treated for the shortest period of time with the lowest possible dose of medication.

Aside from the major tranquilizers, there are other drugs available for children with autism, but their usefulness has not been proven as conclusively. In addition, the response of children with autism to other types of medications is more unpredictable than their response to the major tranquilizers or in comparison to the responses of children without autism. For example, stimulant medications are sometimes used for children with attention span problems and "hyperactivity," but when these same medications are prescribed for children with autism with similar behaviors, their behavioral problems often become worse, not better.

Another set of medications has recently been used with children with autism and related disorders. These medications, called selective serotonin re-uptake inhibitors (SSRI), include fluoxetine (Prozac™), fluvoxamine (Anafranil™), and clomipramine (Luvox™). They are prescribed because children with autism have long been known to have high levels of the neurotransmitter serotonin in their systems. Serotonin re-uptake inhibitors work for children and adults with depression and with Obsessive-Compulsive Disorder (OCR). It was the similarity of some of the behaviors in autism to those in OCR that first suggested the use of these medications. A number of studies have shown that in selected individuals, levels of repetitive behaviors and behavioral rigidity in general often decrease. This seems to be more true for adults than for children. Like almost all medications, SSRIs have side effects. One of the most common side effects is called "activation"; when a child becomes easily agitated or upset.

Several other medications have been utilized for the treatment of autism. These include fenfluoramine, naltrexone, other antidepressants, and Lithium. In general, the evidence supporting the use of these medications in large groups of patients with autism is quite limited. However, some children do respond to different medications. Your child's particular history and behavior may guide your physician in choosing a medication. Always ask about the reasons for choosing a particular medication, as well as what the potential side effects and risks may be.

Minor tranquilizers such as Valium™ and Librium™ may sometimes make children with autism more agitated. In addition, the usefulness of some experimental medications remains to be proven conclusively. Some researchers have suggested that special diets or large doses of vitamins and minerals (particularly Vitamin B6 and magnesium) may improve the behavior and functioning of children with autism. These treatments remain controversial, however, since the results of research studies have been rather mixed. At present, it seems possible that some children do respond positively to these treatments, while others respond negatively. Probably the majority of children have little response to them.

In general it is important to realize that education, rather than medication, offers the best chance for improving problem behaviors in children with autism. Parents should not engage in new or experimental treatments if their child's education is adversely affected.

∷ Medical Problems Associated with Autism

As you read about the medical problems that children with autism can have, remember that not every child with autism has the medical problems covered in this section. These conditions are mentioned because of the special difficulties they present for children with autism or because children with autism have higher chances of developing them than children in the general population. It does not mean that your child will have these problems, but that she might. And remember, also, that in medicine, forewarned is forearmed.

The most common medical problems and issues linked with autism are:

1. seizures
2. accidents and injuries
3. infections
4. dental problems, and
5. nutrition problems. This section describes these problems and explains their treatment.

Seizures

For reasons which are unclear but probably related to the underlying cause of autism in the brain, children with autism are more likely than other children to have seizures. Seizures occur in about one in four children with autism, more commonly in those who are mute or have lower IQs. Often, but not always, these seizures do not develop until adolescence.

Seizures are caused by abnormal electrical activity in the brain and disturb the normal functioning of the nervous system. They can produce a temporary loss of consciousness or temporary changes in behavior such as unusual movements, loss of bladder or bowel control, or staring spells. Children with autism can have several of the various types of seizures, depending on the area of the brain where the abnormal activity occurs.

Seizures can sometimes be triggered by environmental factors or stimuli—for example, by rapidly blinking lights (fluorescent lights in particular). They may also be more common in certain situations—for example, when a child has not had enough sleep. In addition, younger children sometimes develop seizures in connection with high fevers, but these seizures usually do not persist.

Seizure disorders are diagnosed by taking a detailed medical history and by doctor examination, as well as by use of an EEG (electroencephalogram). EEGs record electrical activity in the brain and help the doctor pinpoint where the seizures are originating. Their results are not always conclusive, however. Sometimes people with obvious seizures may have normal EEGs between seizure episodes. Similarly, some people with autism who do not have seizures may have abnormal EEG patterns. Depending on the circumstances, your doctor may want a "sleep deprived" EEG (when your child has been kept awake all night) or an EEG while your child is asleep.

Medicine has advanced a great deal in treating seizure disorders, but cannot always entirely eliminate seizures in every child. In treating seizures, a number of different medications, called "anticonvulsants," are prescribed. Depending on the type of seizure, one or more medications may be used. The level of the medication in the blood often is monitored carefully and the dosage adjusted so that as little medication as is effective is used. Since these medications sometimes produce side effects such as drowsiness, changes in the blood, and gum swelling, it is important to work closely with your doctor or a neurologist. It is also important that all medical professionals involved in your child's care know exactly which medications she receives to prevent harmful drug interactions.

Accidents and Injuries

Even if your child did not have autism, you would probably take care to accident proof your home as soon as she was able to get around by herself. You would cover electrical sockets, put locks on cabinets containing poisonous cleaning supplies, and store knives and scissors where prying fingers could not reach them. As the parent of a child with autism, you will need to take these precautions and often much more. Children with autism—and especially younger children with autism—sometimes have a combination of poor judgment and good motor skills which can lead them into dangerous situations or places.

To provide a safe environment for your child, you should periodically check both your home and your child's school for hazards. Check not only for obvious hazards like open stairwells, but also for less obvious hazards like ill-fitting window screens that could easily be jarred loose. In addition, try to keep your child's habits in mind. For example, if your child tends to mouth objects indiscriminately, as many children with autism do, make sure that lead based paint is not used anywhere at home or at school. In addition, some of the precautions you might take with small children without disabilities make good sense for your child with autism. This can include installing plug covers, door latches, and stair gates, placing cleaning supplies and medicines out of reach, and using an intercom to listen to your child when she is in her room.

Because accidents do happen, keep a well stocked first aid kit in your home and make sure that you, your family members, and your babysitter all know how to use it. This should include syrup of ipecac which causes vomiting and is given *on the advice* of a poison control center or physician depending on what was swallowed. As further insurance, post emergency numbers prominently near every phone.

Besides protecting children with autism from unsafe environments, sometimes you must also protect them from their own self injury. Although self injury occurs infrequently, when these behaviors are severe they can cause physical injury or interfere with your child's education. Self injury is most common in children with autism who have more severe mental retardation.

Among children with autism, self injury can range from repeated scratching or gouging of skin and eyes, to self-inflicted bites or severe head banging. Serious damage can result either from the injury itself or from complications like infections. Head banging, for example, can result directly in serious injuries such as skull fractures, while scratching or biting may lead to infections or permanent scars.

Sometimes these behaviors may actually be connected with other medical problems. For instance, head banging may reflect the presence of pain from an ear infection or a toothache. For this reason, you and your child's doctor should search carefully for any underlying problem that may be contributing to your child's behavior. Unfortunately, these problems can sometimes be difficult to treat. A minor skin problem, for example, may lead to scratching, which results in infection, which causes further irritation and more scratching.

As Chapters 1 and 4 explain, a variety of methods, including medicine, protective equipment, or applied behavior analysis (behavior modification) can be used to control self injury. Often two or more of these methods are used together. These methods call for the involvement of parents, school personnel, and physicians. Because multiple methods may be used, it is important that all those included in your child's care work with each other in their treatment.

Treatment of Injuries

The treatment of your child's injuries is much the same as for other children, with a few exceptions. For example, your child may sometimes require casts rather than bandages when it is important that an injury be protected from further damage and when she is unable to leave the injury alone. On the other hand, when an injury is minor, sometimes it may make more sense to avoid extensive treatment; for example, avoiding sutures (stitches) for a wound if they are not really needed. You always need to consider that your child may not do what is in her own best self interest.

Infections

Infections are a natural part of growing up. In children with autism, these illnesses can be harder to diagnose correctly, because your child may not cooperate with the doctor, particularly when she is ill. Furthermore, infections may go unrecognized for some time unless your child is able to complain of pain or discomfort or a dramatic change in her behavior suggests a medical problem. Accordingly, your observations of your child can often be invaluable in helping the physician reach a diagnosis. Signs of infection can include marked changes in your child's behavior or her appearing ill.

Repeated ear or tonsil infections can be a problem. Decisions regarding possible treatments depend on the particular circumstances. For example, with chronic ear infections, tubes can be placed in the eardrum to reduce further infections, but you must decide whether the potential benefits outweigh the risks and stress involved in hospitalization and anesthesia. In general, you will have to weigh the potential benefits of any medical procedure against the risks to your child's emotional well-being. Usually, it is best to make these decisions jointly with a physician who knows your child well and who understands her needs.

Your child, like every child, needs her childhood immunizations, periodic laboratory studies of blood and urine, and other aspects of "routine" medical care. Sometimes medical procedures must be done. You really have little choice but, as this chapter explains later on, you can try to make the procedure as simple as possible. Ask your pediatrician for advice.

▪▪ Dental Care

All children need to take care of their teeth in order to avoid serious problems such as infected teeth and gum disease. Proper dental care may be even more important for your child if she is on one of the seizure medications like Phenytoin (Dilantin™) which sometimes cause gum changes. Unfortunately, achieving good dental hygiene for your child can be especially difficult. She may not be interested in tooth brushing or other aspects of routine dental care. For example, she may not like having things put in her mouth or may resist when you try to brush her teeth. In addition, she may become panicky when visiting a dentist's office.

If your child does not cooperate with the dentist, you may have to interview potential dentists to find one willing to adapt his or her procedures to your child's needs. In choosing a dentist, you may find it helpful to follow the suggestions for selecting a pediatrician given later in this chapter. Asking other parents of children with autism can lead to recommendations. You can also take steps to minimize your child's anxiety and discomfort—chiefly by helping your child to become familiar with the professionals involved. A patient dentist who is willing to take the time needed for your child to feel comfortable is more likely to be successful. In rare instances when your child is very uncooperative and has significant dental problems, general anesthesia may have to be used.

At home, you should take care to teach good dental hygiene along with other skills of daily living. Other professionals, such as occupational or speech therapists, can sometimes provide helpful suggestions. And just as you would with any child, you should use fluoride in the drinking water or in the toothpaste to help prevent tooth decay in your child.

▪▪ Nutrition

Children with autism often have eating habits and other problems that can jeopardize good nutrition. Some are extremely fussy about the foods they will eat. They may eat the same foods over and over again and resist new foods, or may not tolerate certain food textures. In addition, they may have frequent mealtime temper tantrums. Sometimes these problems can approach a self-inflicted malnutrition that causes other health and development problems. For example, a child who refuses to eat dairy products may not develop strong bones and teeth.

In contrast, other children with autism are compulsive overeaters. Since children with autism may also be less physically active than other children, they may gain excessive amounts of weight. In addition, some medications, particularly certain of the major tranquilizers described previously, may encourage weight gain.

Whatever your child's problems with food, you may want to have a dietician do a complete nutritional assessment of your child. By talking with you, observing your child, and analyzing tests and medical records, the dietician can often uncover behavioral and medical reasons, as well as dietary reasons, for your child's nutrition problems. The dietician can also evaluate your child's need for vitamin and mineral supplements, and determine whether she is taking any medication that might affect her appetite or nutritional needs.

After completing the assessment, the dietician will develop a plan to improve your child's diet and her independent feeding skills. By following this plan and the behavior modification suggestions in Chapter 4, you can help to ensure that your child's nutritional needs are met.

▪▪ Balancing Costs and Benefits

Obviously, you want your child to be as healthy as possible. Whenever practical, her childhood illnesses and medical conditions should be treated thoroughly. Because children with autism have special needs, though, intensive treatment of relatively minor problems may not always be appropriate. The saying, "The perfect is the enemy of the good," should always be kept in mind; ask yourself, is the treatment worth its cost to your child and family. For example, the treatment of allergies should depend not only on the severity of the allergic symptoms, but also on the degree to which your child tolerates or resists the treatment. If your doctor proposes desensitizing your child by using multiple injections over a long period of time, but you know that your child finds shots particularly traumatic, the risks involved may well outweigh the potential benefits. In other words, you must sometimes decide whether your child would be better off suffering the symptoms of a medical condition than suffering the cure. To the extent possible and appropriate, your child should always be involved in discussions and decisions about her treatment.

Because medical treatment of children with autism is not always cut and dry, it is vital that you make informed decisions about your child's care. You can best do this by building a strong working relationship with the medical professionals treating your child and by becoming part of the professional team. As the next section explains, your first step is to select professionals who are sensitive to your child's needs and who value your input and opinions.

▪▪ Dealing with Medical Professionals

Dealing with medical professionals can be complicated for any parent. It is even more complicated for parents of a child with autism. While most parents occasionally have trouble getting their children to cooperate with routine medical procedures like examination of the ears, even the most minor procedures can pose major difficulties for the parents of a child with autism. For example, just sitting in the waiting room for a long time can be very stressful for both you and your child. Then, too, because children with autism often need extra time to get used to the doctor, the examining room, and the medical procedures, the usual rather rapid pace of medical care may be inappropriate for your child.

It is crucial to find health care professionals who understand your child's needs and who sympathize with your anxiety about bringing your child to the doctor's office. If you have a good relationship with your child's pediatrician, you can often work together to anticipate problems and keep them to a minimum. For example, to reduce the stress of waiting, you could call ahead to see if the doctor is running late, or have an arrangement where you could wait in an examining room rather than with the other parents and children. And if you develop a particularly strong parent-professional relationship, you may want to ask the pediatrician to be your child's case manager—

that is, to gather information from all the members of your child's health care team and coordinate the various services she needs.

Selecting a Pediatrician

You will probably not be able to pick a pediatrician for your child right out of the phone book. Since autism is relatively rare, many doctors are unfamiliar with the disorder; some may even harbor misconceptions about it. To find out which pediatricians in your area have experience in treating children with severe developmental problems, you will probably have to ask around. Good sources of names are other parents of children with autism, teachers, and school staff, as well as members of your interdisciplinary evaluation team, and local chapters of The Arc or ASA.

Once you have the names of several potential pediatricians, your first step is to call one and request an initial visit. You may or may not wish to bring your child along; discuss this with the doctor or his or her staff when you set up the appointment. Whether you go alone or take your child, your main objectives should be the same: to find out how much the physician knows about autism, to get a sense of how comfortable you are with the physician and his or her office, and to review your child's medical history.

Do not be shy about asking the pediatrician about his or her experience with children with autism. Explain what you are doing and ask him or her whether he or she has cared for other children with autism or what he or she knows about autism. If he or she has not had firsthand experience with children with autism, try to get a sense of whether he or she is interested in learning more about the condition. Also bring up special issues—such as the use of medications for behavior modification—to see how the pediatrician's position compares with yours. Pediatricians are usually willing to discuss these issues with you. If communication problems arise during the initial interview, though, chances are you should continue your search.

Just as important as the pediatrician's knowledge of autism is the way he or she treats you and your child during your child's first visit. If he or she is rushed, your child will likely feel more anxious or frightened. If he or she is prepared to take an appropriate amount of time, particularly during an initial interview, future visits to his or her office may be less traumatic. The pediatrician's sensitivity and tact during the first visit will also provide important clues about his or her suitability as your child's doctor.

While you are interviewing the pediatrician, he or she will most likely be interviewing you about your child's medical history. Bring any copies of previous evaluations that you have. Be prepared also to discuss your child's past medical problems, family history, and responses to medications. Depending on your child's age, medical conditions, and the extent of previous evaluations, the pediatrician may suggest additional laboratory tests or consultations with other medical or nonmedical professionals. For example, the pediatrician may request hearing tests, special kinds of psychological tests, or communication skills tests.

You should always feel free to ask why a specific test or procedure is needed. As a matter of course, your pediatrician should discuss with you why he or she feels another physician should be involved. For example, if he or she is considering prescribing behavior-modifying medication, your child's pediatrician might wish to have the opinion of a psychiatrist or child psychiatrist. Similarly, if your child has seizures, your pediatrician might suggest a consultation with a neurologist. Generally, your pediatrician will supply you with the names of specialists he or she feels would be appropriate.

Specialists may be located in your area or you may have to travel some distance. The first time you meet with a specialist, your pediatrician will probably send copies of medical records or a letter acquainting the specialist with your child. You should also bring your own copies of past evaluations and other records. And just as you do with your pediatrician, feel free to ask the specialist questions—particularly if he or she prescribes any medications. Be sure that he or she provides you and your pediatrician with a report of his or her recommendations and that your pediatrician is kept informed of any new medicine, since it is the pediatrician who will be most involved in your child's care.

The Attitude to Look for in a Pediatrician

The most important quality to look for in a doctor for your child is a desire to try to make your visits easier for everyone. A willingness to make an effort is the key. Because children with autism typically have severe problems in communication, the doctor should spend the first part of every visit asking you about the history of your child's illness and symptoms. The doctor should also try to reduce your child's anxiety by approaching and examining her gradually and slowly. Whenever possible, he or she should start with the least stressful procedures and move on to the harder ones as he or she gains your child's confidence. For example, looking into the ears or mouth may be done after listening to the lungs or heart. This can be very difficult, but it is important that your pediatrician at least try.

Even the best pediatrician may occasionally have to examine or treat your child without her cooperation—for instance, in an emergency, or when your child is too upset to cooperate. Parents sometimes feel uncomfortable being with their child in such cases. If you can be present to reassure your child, then stay. If it is too hard for you to watch, explain your feelings to the physician, and wait outside.

Dealing with Hospitals and Medical Procedures

Hospital stays can be stressful for any child. For children with autism, hospitalization is especially traumatic because of the unfamiliar people, new and highly stimulating environment, and often uncomfortable tests or procedures. Accordingly, my first advice is to avoid unnecessary hospitalizations. Try to treat medical problems in an environment that is less stressful to your child. For some minor surgical or dental procedures, you can either arrange to do them in the doctor's office or, if needed, as an outpatient or as a one day admission so that overnight hospitalization is not necessary. Explore this possibility with your child's doctor.

Sometimes, hospitalization is simply unavoidable. For instance, if your child has acute appendicitis or has an illness that requires administration of medications by vein (IV), then she must be treated in a hospital. In these instances, you can take several steps to ease the stress of hospitalization on your child. For example, to help your child feel more comfortable, you can bring a favorite stuffed toy and see if she can wear her own pajamas. You should also stay with your child as much as possible, or arrange for friends, relatives, or school staff to take shifts with her. Finally, make sure you discuss your child's special needs and problems as well as her strengths and interests with members of the nursing and medical staff. In larger hospitals, a number of physicians and nurses may be involved; if so, find out which physician and nurse have primary responsibility for your child, then introduce yourself and acquaint them with your child's special needs. As with your pediatrician, do not hesitate to ask questions. You should feel that you are working with the staff as part of the team to provide your child with quality health care.

Teamwork is especially important in helping your child cope with unfamiliar hospital procedures like blood tests. To help prevent a crisis, you or the staff should explain to your child in simple terms what will be done. Be honest: well meaning lies ("It won't hurt") usually cause more trouble in the long run than the truth. If your child can, and does, ask whether it will hurt, tell the truth, that it may hurt. You don't have to go overboard with this, but do be honest and straightforward. Try to keep your child's mind off the procedure by suggesting an activity such as counting or listening to a favorite story or talking about a special interest. Often if you stay calm, your child will also be able to stay calm.

If your child cannot cooperate, she may have to be restrained. When this happens, having a number of people on hand helps the procedure go as quickly as possible. Occasionally, although you generally want to avoid sedation or anesthesia since there are risks associated with this, it too may be necessary; if so, ask that your pediatrician be involved in selecting medications appropriate for your child.

Insurance and Managed Care

The current crisis in the American health insurance system has unfortunately reduced both the quality and quantity of care provided to all people with disabilities. Today, unless parents and others are willing to act as strong advocates for obtaining quality care, it is often not provided. In considering insurance, it is important to look for plans that provide for continued care for developmental disorders, as well as for so-called "preexisting" conditions. Some parents have discovered that insurance companies stop providing care if they need or want to switch carriers because the insurance company claims that their child was born with autism. Another unfortunate tactic is for insurance companies to avoid paying for necessary ancillary services such as physical, occupational, or speech and language therapies. They may also attempt to minimize access to more specialized care providers such as pediatric neurologists or child psychiatrists. This is unfortunate because often primary care providers can provide high quality services when they have the option of utilizing specialists for backup. Parents should carefully consider insurance plans and the needs of their child when they consider relocating or switching jobs. Until the time when we have universal health care coverage in this country, these concerns should be central in the minds of parents.

∷ Adulthood

Although this book is focused on children with autism, it is important to say a word about adults with autism. Although autism has been recognized since the 1940s, relatively little has been written on the care of adults with autism. There is a lack of information on the part of many health care providers who typically work with adults. General practitioners and internists often have little or no training in the area of developmental diagnosis or developmental disability. They are sometimes stunned by the lack of cooperation on the part of the adult with autism. In thinking about your child's long-term health care needs, it would be appropriate to begin planning, in her adolescence, for her adult medical care. Sometimes pediatricians are willing to assume continued responsibility for care of a child into early adulthood. This does, however, become less appropriate as the child becomes older. At that time, adults with autism are subject to all the other adult-related medical conditions such as high blood pressure, heart disease and high cholesterol, and diabetes. Depending on your particular state and health care situation, various alternatives may be possible. Some family practitioners care for children with autism when they become adults. Your pediatrician or other health care provider as well as other parents can help you find an appropriate internist for your child as she becomes an adult.

∷ What You Can Do

As this chapter emphasizes, the quality of your child's medical care depends a great deal on you. You can often control not only who cares for your child, but also how, when, and where that care is given. Keep in mind that you are the person who knows your child best and the person who must make sure that your child receives good medical care. The guidelines below summarize the most important ways you can take part in the health care process.

- **Be a careful observer.** You are often the primary source of information about your child's health. If your child has very limited communication skills, the doctor or nurse will have to rely on you for information. Frequently, some change in your child's behavior will be a clue to the beginning of an illness. By being a careful observer, you can provide the physician invaluable information.

- **Ask questions and get information.** While you provide information to your child's doctor, the doctor can provide you with valuable information. Most physicians are sympathetic to your need—and right—to know. They should be able to explain medical terms, issues, and procedures in plain English, but if you do not understand something, ask. Unless you understand your child's medical needs and problems, you cannot be sure she is receiving the most appropriate care.

  You may want to keep a notebook with copies of previous evaluations and past reports from specialists. This information can be helpful to physicians who are unfamiliar with your child. You should feel comfortable talking about the results of past evaluations even if you disagree with some parts of them. By showing the physician that you can discuss differences of opinion reasonably, you encourage him or her to communicate openly with you. If for some reason the doctor resists open discussions with you, however, you should probably consider switching to another physician.

- **Discuss and anticipate your child's special needs.** You should never hesitate to discuss any needs your child has. For example, if your child does not do well in an unfamiliar waiting room, ask if you can arrange to be seen as promptly as possible. Keep in mind, however, that physicians take care of many children and that emergencies and unanticipated problems will happen. By calling ahead you can sometimes schedule the first appointment of the morning or afternoon. Anticipate how you can make your child as comfortable as possible. Bring activities along for your child, for instance, or coax her to play a favorite game. If you suspect that a visit may be difficult, bring other people who can help keep your child calm.

- **Get to know the physician and his or her support staff.** In general, your child will be less anxious about visits to the doctor's office the more familiar she is with everyone who works there. Consequently, it may be best to look for a smaller practice where your child can get to know each of the doctors and nurses individually. It is also a very good idea to take your child to the doctor for routine checkups when she is not ill so she can get acquainted with her pediatrician under less stressful circumstances. While excessive visits to the physician's office should be avoided, occasional routine visits can also be helpful to you and the physician. They give you a chance to talk with the physician in a situation that is less pressured than during sick or emergency visits, and allow the physician to observe your child when she is not ill.

▪▪ Conclusion

Although autism is not yet as well understood as we could wish, the disorder is steadily receiving more attention from the professional community. It is now quite possible for parents of children with autism to find medical professionals who are willing and able to work with them as partners on a team. As a parent, you are still the person who is ultimately responsible for your child's medical well-being, but this is a responsibility you can share with competent, compassionate professionals. You need to select them carefully, then work together toward the best possible medical care and the healthiest, happiest future for your child. I hope the guidelines in this chapter will help you do just that.

▪▪ Parent Statements

Professionals offering services and advice to parents of children with autism should be extremely conscientious about what they say and how they say it, for we are desperately clinging to every word.

◆◆◆

I remember going to see a psychiatrist once, and he was late to begin with, and when he finally came in, he said, "I haven't had a chance to look at Janet's records yet." Later, he was just kind of looking at Janet, and she was trying to read the words off books and boxes and things that were in the office. And I said, "Gosh, she's trying to read." And he said, "Well, she may read, but she doesn't understand a word she's reading." He'd only looked at her for two minutes.

❧

I knew at one year of age that my son was not developing typically. It took me six months to convince my pediatrician that there was indeed a problem. I often think about all the time we lost while I was trying to get past "the overprotective mother" label.

❧

It was frustrating to wait as long as we did—3½ years—before finding the specialist who could give us a diagnosis. Our pediatricians were worthless. When our son was around 18 months old, I started asking questions regarding his speech, but because his articulation was age appropriate, the pediatricians didn't seem to care that he was only reciting episodes of Barney. I became even more resentful when my son was placed in a program at 3½ and I saw 18 month olds receiving early intervention. So much precious time had been wasted all because his pediatricians didn't catch it, and as a first-time parent, I didn't know enough to question the medical establishment sooner.

❧

I said, "Could it be that he's just a late bloomer?" My pediatrician said, "It could be, but I don't think it is." To me that was going out on a limb—saying there was something wrong with my kid. For a pediatrician, that's a very hard thing to do. He steered me in the right direction, and whenever I see him, I always thank him again.

❧

The problem with medication is that about half the professionals I deal with insist that I try different drugs to control Lawrence's hyperactivity and self-stimulating. The other half just as adamantly oppose drugs. I find myself leaning this direction one day and that direction the next— depending mostly on how Lawrence is acting at the time.

❧

Of all the frustrations in dealing with a child with special needs, I think having to be the middle man between the medical community and the insurance companies is the worst. We've had three different companies since Doug was born, and they are all equally bad.

ᴥ

One of Doug's doctors kept ordering all these tests not covered by our insurance. When I objected that they weren't necessary and would cause additional, unneeded trauma to my child, the doctor wrote my pediatrician that I had become "frantic" over the cost of these necessary procedures. Now the name of the game for me is to use my common sense. I know what tests Doug needs, how often, and which doctors will deal openly and honestly with me.

ᴥ

Because our children have autism, we are often advised to take them to doctors who are the best in their fields and, consequently, who charge much more than the insurance companies want to pay for. Some doctors are wonderful when you explain the situation. I've had two that reduced their fees substantially so that they coincided with what the insurance company paid for.

ᴥ

All medications, household cleaners, and toiletries must be kept under lock and key. There was a time when I felt I had a direct line to Poison Control. Our son has eaten plant leaves, tea bags, crayons, cough medicine, and dog biscuits.

ᴥ

Once, Donny got into his medicine and ate five of the pills we give him for his hyperactivity and seizure disorder. We concluded later how very similar in shape, color, smell, and taste the medication was to the bits of candy we were using for reinforcing good behavior.

ᴥ

The seizures are just one small part of his overall condition, but managing them is a major stress and financial burden.

ᴥ

Sometimes it's better for the kid to have a seizure once in a while than to be totally zonked out on medication all the time. You and the neurologist have to agree on the amount of seizure control that's best.

◈

After waiting for what seems like an eternity for an appointment with a specialist, we still have only minutes to relay our case. I often feel that I'm only truly heard when I can exemplify an objective, totally unemotional demeanor. Any sense of urgency or pain I express is frequently judged and misunderstood. Blessed is the professional who can listen, look you in the eye, and stop to "feel" what you feel.

◈

After keeping us waiting for an hour and a half in a room with no toys, the doctor told us our son had autistic-like characteristics. I asked what we could do about this. Instead of talking about different therapies, special schools, diet, or drug therapy, she said there was nothing that could be done. She discounted his whole life and potential value as a contributing member of society in 10 minutes!

◈

Keep all of your child's medical records! I have a 3 ring binder with every specialist's evaluation, progress report from school, prenatal history, and so on. I make a copy of the whole thing and send it to any new team or doctor before we meet with them. This way the doctor knows I am serious about my son's condition and it gives him or her a chance to prepare for our initial meeting.

◈

Many people fear "labeling" a child. We visited a pediatrician, school psychologist, psychologist, neuro-psychologist, psychiatrist, and therapist in the hopes of getting a "label." When our daughter was finally diagnosed with PDD it was such a relief. We found great comfort in learning we weren't alone out there. After six years of searching for an appropriate diagnosis she now is on effective medication, receives appropriate therapy, and has an educational plan that makes her happy to go to school.

◈

I spend a lot of time driving to therapy sessions and hanging out in waiting rooms or in my car. I used to feel sorry for myself and exhausted all the time. Now I bring along a good book and savor the quiet time to catch up on my reading.

4

DAILY LIFE WITH YOUR CHILD

Carolyn Thorwarth Bruey, Psy.D.

When you have a child with autism, every day is a challenge. Every day you are faced with a child who has enormous difficulty communicating with you. Every day you must prepare yourself to reach out to a child who seems emotionally untouchable. Every day you must try again to teach your child a few more of the skills he needs.

At times the challenges you face in the daily care and teaching of your child may seem never ending. This is because of the way autism affects children. Unlike children with other types of developmental disabilities, children with autism have *disturbances* rather than delays in their development. While they may show relative skills in some areas, they will be quite behind in others. Consequently, typical how-to books on child care are difficult to apply to a child with autism. This chapter is a mini how-to book on taking care of your child with autism.

It may seem out of the question right now, but your goal should always be to make your child *part* of the family, not the *center* of it. In other words, do not allow your child's needs to dominate your life. No child benefits from the exclusive attention of his parents, and the rest of the family suffers if this happens. Part of your job of caring for your child and for your family is balancing everyone's needs, including your own. It won't be easy for him, but your child with autism will have to learn to accept this balancing.

∷ Predictability, Structure, and Routine

All children need routine in their lives. If the events of each day were different and unpredictable, almost any child would become anxious and insecure. For children with autism, routine is especially important. In fact, many children with autism have what is called an "insistence on sameness." They become quite upset about even minor changes in their routine or environment. Although this inflexibility can be highly frustrating to parents, it can reveal your child's heightened anxiety and his need for predictability. You must try to give your child the structure he needs, but do not let that need dominate your life.

Providing Structure and Consistency

Establishing a household routine is the first step in providing structure for your child with autism. Regardless of how much juggling of family schedules and commitments it takes, you must try to develop a routine that everyone in the family feels comfortable with, and can follow consistently. If you feel disorganized and flustered, it is likely that your child with autism is feeling the same. Unfortunately, the way your child responds to this confusion may involve a variety of disturbing behaviors such as self-injury and toileting accidents. Therefore, you need to come up with an overall game plan for how each family day will proceed, and then incorporate each day's requirements into it. For example, have relatively set times for when your child bathes, plays, and eats.

If there is one word to stress regarding child care for children with autism, it is *consistency*. Many children with autism have great difficulty learning from the environment. They do not learn well from experience. One way to help them is to make the environment as consistent as possible. This rule applies to almost every interaction you have with your child, ranging from the words you choose when praising his good behavior to how you work to eliminate a behavior problem.

One reason that children with autism need consistency is that they have trouble using the same skills with different people, places, or situations. This inability to use the same skills in different areas is called "poor generalization." For example, although your child may demonstrate wonderful table manners at home, he may be a terror in restaurants. Another child might never have a tantrum when alone with his mother, but may have an average of three tantrums per hour when he is with his father.

Rather than blame anyone or resolve never to go out to eat, realize that poor generalization is a characteristic of autism which can be minimized if everyone responds to your child in the same way. For example, make sure that every family member uses the same phrases when teaching your child, as well as similar verbal and tangible rewards. If everyone is consistent, then your child's behavior will be more reliable regardless of location or the presence of others in the environment. Once a new skill is established, you  can gradually vary the way you present requests or materials. This will help your child become more flexible.

One cause of the problems with generalization children with autism have is called "selective attention" or "stimulus overselectivity." This means that your child may over-focus on one aspect of a situation and not be able to respond unless that particular characteristic is present. Children with autism have difficulty recognizing which characteristics to focus upon. For example, your child might focus on the color of a car in a picture—but not the car itself—and be unable to identify the picture of a car if it is presented in a different color. Or he may overselect on the fact that his mother has blonde hair during a teaching session, and not be able to demonstrate a skill he has mastered with her when working with someone who has brown hair. This leads to many of the generalization problems children with autism have, and can be quite frustrating and confusing for parents. The best strategy to combat this tendency is to make sure that the most important aspects of the teaching situation are constant. Change only some of the more minor characteristics. For example, in teaching your child body part identification, everyone who works with him should use the term "Touch your head" consistently; however, the person teaching the skill as well as the location should vary. That way, your child is better able to recognize that the words "Touch your head" are the important part of the teaching session.

You can introduce the concept of consistency to other people involved with your child by having them read this chapter. Then sit down together and decide how you want to respond to your child. You can set up hypothetical situations and practice on each other. You can discuss past situations and how they could have been handled better. Working together, you should be able to come up with an outline of how you want to act—both individually and as a group.

:: Discipline and Behavior Management

Many parents of children with autism find it difficult to discipline their child. They simply are not prepared to respond to their child's unusual behavior. One reason for this difficulty is that most child care books that cover discipline recommend strategies that would be completely ineffective on a child with autism. To make matters worse, parents must also deal diplomatically with unwanted and uninformed advice from friends, relatives, and even strangers.

There is no magic formula that will ensure that your child always behaves well. But the combined experience of other parents and years of research by professionals has shown that techniques based on *applied behavior analysis* (ABA) are the most effective means of changing the behavior of children with autism. These strategies basically assume that all behavior is learned through events which precede *(antecedents)* and follow *(consequences)* the behavior. If the antecedents trigger or lead to a behavior, your child will likely demonstrate that behavior. For example, the request by a parent or teacher that it's time to come to work may quickly lead to a tantrum by your child. The request to come to work (antecedent) leads to a tantrum in this case because your child most likely wishes to avoid that work. If your child likes the consequences following his behavior, he will demonstrate that behavior again. If he does not like the consequences, he will not exhibit the behavior again. Therefore, problem behaviors can be "unlearned" and appropriate skills can be substituted for them through a process of altering antecedent conditions, and systematically using consequences (rewards for good behavior and punishment for undesirable behavior).

The following techniques and examples should help to clarify these learning principles and increase your effectiveness in managing your child's behavior.

Catch Your Child Being Good

One strategy that is often effective is noticing and rewarding desirable behavior. Most parents feel that their job is to "catch their child being bad," when in reality their goal should be to "catch their child being good." This strategy requires a heightened attention on your part. After all, it is easier to notice when your child is screaming than when he is being quiet. The rule of thumb is to provide ten praise statements—"Terrific, you made your bed!"—for every one corrective statement—"Stop throwing toys."

Studies of children with autism also suggest that parents should be specific when praising their children. Use specific language—"Good, you put on your coat"—rather than general statements such as "Good job." Being specific helps your child understand the exact behavior that is being rewarded. It often helps to provide tangible rewards like food or toys in addition to praise, particularly in the early phases of teaching. Because children with autism do not find social interactions rewarding, using more tangible rewards helps to increase their motivation.

Nip It in the Bud

When your child is misbehaving, you have an immediate problem on your hands. Sometimes it is difficult to decide what to do about misbehavior once it is occurring. For example, it is natural to feel flustered and helpless when your child begins to have a loud tantrum in the middle of the supermarket. Sometimes, however, you can stop the behavior before it really starts. Often parents do not realize that they can plan ahead and develop preventive measures rather than continue to react to each crisis as it occurs. It's easier to prevent problems than to react to problems once they have already begun. Here are some preventive strategies you may find useful:

Change the Environment. There are many ways of changing your child's environment in order to prevent problem behaviors. For example, if your child tears pictures off the wall, you can put up laminated posters or paint a mural instead. If your child has toileting accidents because he cannot unsnap his pants, you can buy him elastic-waist pants.

Although these ideas may sound like common sense, take some time to evaluate your own environment and your own daily routine. With all you have to do each day, it is sometimes easy to lose sight of the simple solution. Ask yourself questions like "How is the furniture placed?" "How accessible are necessities?" "Which breakable items are an 'accident waiting to happen'?" Make changes you think might help, and evaluate whether or not the number of problems decreases. If so, congratulate yourself on having prevented some possible crises. You have successfully altered antecedent conditions so that the problem behavior is not triggered.

Notice Your Child's Cues. All children give subtle clues when they are about to begin misbehaving or when something is beginning to bother them. Some children with autism whine, others tighten their muscles, while still others increase the intensity of hand flapping. Others may actually be extra quiet. Parents tend to assume that escalation— worsening or intensifying of behaviors— is inevitable and actually begin incorporating the "inevitable" upcoming behaviors into their plans: "Let's see, if he begins to scream in five minutes, and his tantrum is over within thirty minutes, I can still get dinner on the table."

Instead of assuming the escalation is inevitable, heed your child's warning signals and redirect him before he escalates. One strategy is to slowly begin giving basic, simple instructions that are familiar and easy for your child: for example, "Please hand me the book" or "Put your hands down." If your child does as you ask, praise him enthusiastically. If he does not follow your instructions, guide him through the task in a nonchalant manner. After your child has followed five to ten instructions independently, an escalation of behavior is unlikely to occur. After all, it is impossible to be "out of control" while following instructions. By providing simple instructions to follow and praising compliance, you stand a fair chance of successfully defusing the situation.

Describe What Is Happening. One factor that often escalates the behaviors of children with autism is confusion. Therefore, you need to explain to your child exactly what is going on in concrete, simple terms. Many parents describe the upcoming activities throughout the day in order to help their child understand. "Okay, now we are on the way to the drug store. That's the big red store near Grandma's. We will only be there for a few minutes." By telling your child what to expect in the near future, he will often feel less anxious and will be less likely to start problem behaviors. You can also show your child pictures of the day's activities to increase his understanding of the daily schedule.

Set Up Clear Consequences. Parents often say that the hardest part about trips into the community is the ever-present fear that their child's behavior will become a problem. In fact, that fear is often more stressful than the dreaded behavior itself.

To prevent problem behaviors from occurring, it sometimes helps to describe to your child the consequences of his behavior before placing him in a potentially problematic situation. For example, if your child usually makes loud demands at the supermarket, talk to him before entering the store. Describe what he will earn if he speaks softly and what he will lose if he screams his demands. It is a good idea to actually have the tangible rewards easily visible during this talk. Then if your child begins to show initial signs of misbehaving, you can point to the desired reward and say, "What are you working for?" Or you can remind him what he is working for by holding up a picture of the desired reward.

These discipline techniques may not work for every child in all situations. Because every child with autism is unique, there are simply no guarantees. Although preventive strategies are not always effective, using them will at least decrease the frequency of crisis situations. You can significantly improve your home life by preventing, rather than reacting to, challenging behaviors. Remember, it is always harder to change a habit than to prevent one from starting.

Use Effective Behavioral Techniques

Using effective behavioral strategies requires first that you clearly understand the behavior in question, and then use that information to guide the development of a treatment plan. The techniques of applied behavior analysis provide the best framework to do this. ABA emphasizes understanding a behavior in the specific situation in which it occurs, and the particular response that the behavior receives from others. Quite literally, very little is left to the imagination. Inference and guesswork are minimized. Teachers and parents do not make assumptions about why a behavior *might be* happening; rather, information is gathered in order to determine those reasons precisely. One of the most important things to remember is that a single behavioral episode does not tell the whole story. Instead, it is absolutely essential to gather several examples of the antecedents and consequences that surround a behavior in order to determine any patterns that might exist. Over time, looking at a series of individual behaviors makes it much easier to see trends, and to begin to understand why a child responds in a particular way.

The first step in using applied behavior analysis is to spend a week or two observing your child and gathering information. The goal of observing is to understand what circumstances promote appropriate behavior and what triggers problem behavior. First create a worksheet for your observations. Draw three columns on a piece of paper, labeled "Antecedents," "Behavior," and "Consequences." Here is how to use this table:

- **In the "Antecedents" column** of the worksheet, write down everything in your child's presence that *immediately* precedes the behavior. For example, write down who was with your child, where he was, what he was doing or being asked to do, whether an ongoing activity was interrupted, the time of day, and any other related information that might shed light on what triggered the behavior.

- **In the "Behavior" column,** write down the undesirable behavior you observe; be very specific in describing the behavior. For example, if you only wrote down that your child was hurting other people, you would not have a very clear idea of how he was doing that. Was he yelling at them? Was he biting or hitting? Or was he hurting their feelings? Failing to be specific increases the risk that you will treat your child's behavior inconsistently, only adding to his confusion. It would be better to be very specific, and describe exactly what the behavior looks like when it is happening. For example, "hurting" would be better defined as hitting with an open hand, with enough force to make noise or leave a mark. This might sound very picky, but it helps to distinquish a soft, gentle touch on the arm from a slap.

:: TABLE 1. ABC ANALYSIS

Antecedents	Behavior	Consequences
▪ everything in your child's presence that *immediately* precedes the behavior.	▪ the desirable or undesirable behavior you observe; be very specific in describing the behavior.	▪ note what happens *immediately* after the behavior.

▪ **In the "Consequences" column,** note what happens *immediately* after the behavior. For example, after hitting someone, your child is sent to timeout for two minutes. A timer is set, and when two minutes has elapsed he is allowed to return to another activity.

After *several days to a week* of recording your observations of your child's behavior, you will begin to see patterns you can use to help improve his behaviors and skills. First, try to identify the situations that tend to "set off" your child's problem behaviors, and the situations that usually lead to good behaviors. Sometimes you may find that something that is innocuous to you can be very troublesome to your child. For example, one family found that having their daughter wear tights prompted her tantrums. She did not have the ability to communicate that tights felt uncomfortable, so she had a tantrum to communicate this feeling. Interestingly enough, when her parents put her in a timeout in her bedroom for tantrums, she usually stripped as part of the tantrum, thus allowing her to remove those darned tights after all! As soon as her parents understood the problem, they stopped having her wear tights and the frequency of her tantrums decreased substantially.

The next step in the process is to look at the antecedents and consequences, to try to determine what *purpose* your child's challenging behavior serves. This step is very important; by assessing the purpose of the behavior, you can more effectively teach your child an alternative, appropriate way of achieving the same purpose. For example, your child may become very agitated and disruptive at 4:30 in the afternoon each weekday. This disruptive behavior might include throwing his toys around, running around in the house, and having a very difficult time settling down. After reviewing the antecedents and consequences to many episodes of this type of behavior, you might recognize that this time of the day is rather unstructured and chaotic for the entire family. You may just have gotten home from work, the children may be hungry, and preparations for dinner may divert your attention away from your children. You might guess that the lack of a clear structure combined with reduced parental attention and possibly hunger might contribute to the disruptive behavior. After looking at the "antecedent" section of the ABC analysis, you might note that on the weekends these types of behavior problems do not occur at the same time. You might also find out that, generally speaking, your family is involved in some type of structured activity at 4:30 in the afternoon on Saturdays and Sundays. This type of information suggests that the lack of structure and parental attention may be antecedents or contributing factors to the disruptive behavior. These assumptions would suggest specific interventions to try.

This type of behavioral assessment is part of a *functional assessment,* and is a very important part of the treatment of children with autism. Evaluating behavior with an ABC analysis is critical. Looking deeply at different situations where a behavior is more likely to occur and less likely to occur; determining with whom it is most likely to occur; deciphering what the behavior might possibly be saying or communicating; and examining other related contributing factors all give more information about what your child is trying to express with his behavior. This information enables parents and teachers to try to manipulate or change the antecedent conditions so the behavior itself becomes unnecessary. It also gives insight into our own reaction to the behavior, and how that reaction might accidentally reinforce the behavior and increase the likelihood that it will happen again.

Understanding why a behavior occurs helps you choose a better behavior or skill to teach in place of the problem behavior. If you do not teach a substitute, appropriate skill, your child may stop the problem behavior but begin a new inappropriate behavior that serves the same function as the original one. For example, if your child hits you to communicate that he is nervous in a new setting, it is important to both eliminate the hitting *plus* teach appropriate ways of communicating this feeling, such as teaching him to say "Go home" or sign "scared." If you never teach the alternative way of communicating anxiety, your child may begin to stop hitting but begin screaming when anxious. Rather than continually eliminating a series of problem behaviors, it makes more sense to teach an alternative, appropriate behavior from the start.

Be skeptical when you hear of an intervention which is touted as the "best way" to eliminate a specific problem behavior for all children. For example, using timeouts in response to physical aggression is sometimes offered as a blanket response. The problem with this type of approach is that children may become aggressive for many different reasons. One child may become physically aggressive at being told "no," while a second child may become aggressive at being asked to set the table. If this second child is in a timeout while the table is being set, his aggression is reinforced because his behavior has successfully allowed him to avoid setting the table. Instead of using one type of response to one type of behavior, it makes more sense to match the strategy to the *purpose* of the behavior, as described below.

Matching Purpose to Intervention. The purpose of most behaviors of children with autism is communication. They serve one of four possible functions: 1) to gain attention; 2) to obtain some type of sensory stimulation; 3) to avoid a less preferred activity or task; or 4) to try to obtain a desired item. Once you determine which of these purposes is *usually* the reason for the challenging behavior, develop a matching intervention strategy, following these guidelines:

- **For attention-getting behaviors:** Strategies such as time-outs and planned ignoring are useful when the behavior is an attempt to gain your attention. Stop giving your child any attention whatsoever when he shows the problem behavior, but give lots of praise and attention when he shows alternative, appropriate ways of getting your attention. Of course, if your child begins to escalate the behavior to the point where someone may get hurt, do what you need to do to keep everyone safe. It is also useful to teach your child how to obtain your attention in appropriate ways (such as by saying your name, tapping your shoulder, or signing "play" or "help").

- **For sensory stimulation behaviors:** Many children with autism exhibit unusual body movements such as rocking, hand-flapping, making perseverative sounds, and even self-injury because they provide desirable sensory input. Many people call this type of behavior *self-stimulatory*. The two ways of approaching these kinds of behaviors is to either prevent the stimulation from occurring (for example, by putting gloves on a child who scratches his skin to the point of bleeding), or provide an alternative way of allowing sensory stimulation (such as rocking in a rocking chair). Self-stimulatory behaviors can be difficult to eliminate, and at times parents have to focus on teaching their child to discriminate when and where the behavior is allowed (for example, "You can only handflap in your bedroom").

- **For avoidance or escape behaviors:** All children have tasks they dislike , and will usually let you know of their disinterest through language (for example, "No! I don't want to!"). Due to their difficulties with language, it is not uncommon for children with autism to communicate their disinterest through problem behaviors. Many parents respond to the behavior by lessening their demands, which in fact reinforces the maladaptive behavior. For example, if your child tantrums when asked to clean up his toys and you end up cleaning up the toys yourself, you have "taught" him to tantrum in order to avoid cleaning up. It is important for you to give your child the message that escalating his behavior will not lead to getting "off the hook." At the same time, it is important to teach your child acceptable ways of communicating disinterest (for example, simple negotiation skills or pointing to a sign that says "No thanks"). Then when the task is truly optional and your child communicates disinterest in an appropriate fashion, try your best to go along with his request.

- **For behaviors that communicate the desire for something which has been denied:** Children generally do not like the word "no," and children with autism are no exception. At times children with autism will "up the ante" by worsening their behaviors in an attempt to get you to change your mind and say "yes." Again, it is important to not give in because this will teach your child to escalate his behavior in order to get what has been denied. The appropriate, alternative behavior which needs to be taught is to accept "no" for an answer through whatever means is within your child's capabilities (such as saying, "Okay, Mom," nodding his head, or just walking away quietly when told "no"). You can then also teach him when this particular item *will* be available at some later time, perhaps using a picture schedule of activities.

Using Consequences Effectively. If you are faced with behavior that is already a habit, you have to decide whether it is acceptable behavior. If it is not, then it is up to you to try to change it. It will take a lot of work and you may not always succeed, but in many cases you will. The following is a summary of some procedures that have proven effective in eliminating problem behavior. The strategies are listed in order from least to most punishing. Unless your child has a problem behavior which places him or others in significant danger, try less punitive techniques first before going on to harsher ones. And consult a professional for more detailed information and advice.

Rewards. As discussed earlier, one method of changing behavior is to systematically reward your child for any and all appropriate behaviors. That is, make sure that you praise your child every time you notice him doing well. Another method is to reward him for a *specific* appropriate behavior which is incompatible, or the opposite of, the undesirable behavior. For example, you can reward your child for being quiet if you are trying to break him of the habit of screaming, or you can reward him for playing with his toys instead of flapping his hands. As your child is rewarded for substitute behaviors, he will be more likely to show them in the future and less likely to exhibit the undesirable problem behavior. Instead of merely "catching your child being good," you should carry out these strategies in a formalized manner—for example, by setting up a schedule of how often your child will be rewarded or by making a chart with stars earned for substitute behaviors.

Extinction. An "extinction procedure" is the technical term for the strategy of ignoring your child completely when he misbehaves. When you try this technique, you should consciously remove all of your attention whenever your child shows the problem behavior.

Avoid letting your child know that you are even aware that he has displayed the problem behavior. Look away, appear distracted by something else, and make no reference whatsoever to the fact that the behavior occurred. Take care that you are not responding to his behavior in subtle ways like tightening your muscles or sighing.

Extinction is used for behaviors that are primarily attention getting. It is based on the assumption that if you remove your attention, your child will be less motivated to display the behavior in the future. For example, if you have determined that your child screams to get your attention, begin to ignore each and every scream. Do not make eye contact or in any other way acknowledge that the behavior is occurring.

When trying an extinction procedure, remember that children's behavior often gets worse before it gets better. Your child will often escalate his behavior to try to get your attention. For example, if you decide to ignore your child when he whines, "Mommy Mommy!" he may begin to scream or cry very loudly. Your job is to continue to ignore the behavior (as long as no one is in danger), giving the strong message, "I'm really not going to pay attention, no matter how high you 'up the ante.'" After a while, your child will finally realize that his efforts are in vain, and will find more appropriate ways of getting your attention.

Timeout. If your child is misbehaving and your attempts to change his behavior have not worked, then try a timeout. Physically remove your child from the problem situation. For example, you can put him in his room whenever he has a tantrum. Or you can have your child sit in a chair facing the wall whenever he hits someone.

Remember, sometimes your child will misbehave because he wants to get out of something you have asked him to do. In this case, timeout would be the wrong response, because it just gives your child what he wants: escape from your request. In these situations, you should first require that your child comply with your request, or have the task waiting for him when the timeout is over.

It is important to plan ahead by making sure the timeout room is nearby; you do not want to make things worse by having to drag your child to the timeout area. Be sure to watch your child unobtrusively during timeout, but do not talk to him or even make eye contact. You can watch him through a peephole to make sure he is safe. Timeouts should not be prolonged nor should they be used when the problem behavior is potentially dangerous. For small children, the timeout should not last more than five minutes; for adolescents, the timeout should not last more than 15 minutes.

Response Cost. In the response cost method, your child earns desired treats like stickers or pennies when he behaves well, and he loses some of these items when he misbehaves. Sometimes it helps to have your child earn items like tokens or points which can be exchanged for tangible rewards like food or toys. When using a response cost, make the give-and-take procedure as simple as possible to make sure that your child clearly understands how the system works. Also provide plenty of rewards so that you never reach the point where your child misbehaves but has no more tokens, points, or other rewards to lose.

Aside from the methods discussed above, there are other common ways to change behavior. The publications in the Reading List in the back of this book provide a more comprehensive review of the strategies you may find useful in eliminating your child's problem behaviors. Should a dangerous or disruptive behavior persist, even with your best efforts, it is best to seek out a professional who has expertise in treating behavior problems in children with autism. You can ask your pediatrician or case manager for the names of appropriate professionals.

General Rules When Using Behavior Reduction Procedures

Children with autism often have unusual responses to discipline techniques. Regardless of the particular behavior reduction procedure you use or the specific problem behavior you are attempting to eliminate, keep the following suggestions in mind:

- **Ask yourself, "What Do I Want to See Instead?"** Rather than focus exclusively on decreasing a problem behavior, you also need to choose and teach an appropriate behavior to take the place of the problem behavior. For example, if your child hits you to get your attention, it is important to eliminate the hitting and spend time formally teaching appropriate ways of getting your attention. For instance, you can teach your child to say, "Watch, please," to sign "Help," or to tap you lightly on the shoulder.

  As mentioned earlier in this chapter, if you do not teach a substitute, appropriate skill, your child may stop the problem behavior but begin a new inappropriate behavior which serves the same function for him as the original one. For instance, in the example above, using a behavior reduction procedure alone may help your child stop hitting; however, if he is never taught an appropriate way of gaining attention, he may then begin to scream loudly for attention. Rather than continually eliminating a series of problem behaviors teach alternative, appropriate behaviors to take their place.

- **Do Not Assume That Your Child Feels Punished.** One characteristic of autism that especially frustrates parents is that many children do not find traditional "punishments" to

be punishing. For example, although most children dislike being sent to their room, many children with autism prefer being alone. Therefore, using a timeout procedure where a child is sent to his room every time he has a tantrum may decrease tantrums in most children, but may actually increase the frequency of tantrums for some children with autism. Unfortunately, parents often inadvertently reward their child when they think they are punishing him.

The only way to determine if your discipline technique is effective is to notice its effect on the particular misbehavior. If that behavior decreases or is eliminated, then the technique is a punishment for your child. If the behavior increases in frequency, however, then you should develop a new strategy because the technique may actually be encouraging the problem behavior. For example, if your child loses a snack each time he tears paper, and his paper tearing subsequently decreases, you have chosen an effective punishment. However, if the tearing stays at the same level or increases in frequency, then, for whatever reason, your child finds losing a snack to be neutral or even pleasurable. If you determine that you have chosen the wrong punishment, do not give up; instead consult professionals or the Reading List for some new ideas.

- **Ignore It If You Can.** Unless your child's inappropriate behavior places him or others in danger, it is usually best to pretend that the behavior never occurred. Your child with autism will often display unusual behaviors as a way of getting your attention. Rather than inadvertently rewarding your child by paying attention to him, simply ignore the behavior and try to wait for an appropriate behavior to occur. As soon as your child behaves appropriately, praise him enthusiastically. That way, your child learns, "I get attention for appropriate behavior and not for inappropriate behavior."

- **Watch Your Own Behavior.** Because children learn by imitating other people's behavior, it is important to monitor your own behavior. Do you show, or "model," behaviors you do not wish to see in your child? Picture a parent screaming, "Stop yelling!" Or another parent spanking his child while saying, "No hitting!" While all children have trouble accepting the concept, "Do as I say, not as I do," children with autism are especially confused by contradictions. Therefore, be cautious when choosing behavior reduction procedures and make sure you do not accidentally model behaviors you do not want your child to imitate.

▮▮ Teaching Throughout the Day

The thought may seem overwhelming, but every interaction you have with your child is a teaching situation. Even the briefest encounters can provide learning experiences. For example, when you give in to your child's demands, he is learning that he is capable of manipulating you. When you only give him what he wants when he asks for it in a clearly articulated manner, he learns that he only gets desirable items through speech. Therefore, try to interact with your child in ways that best help him learn. The guidelines below will help you capitalize on these learning situations.

Make Your Instructions Clear and Simple

Clear and simple instructions help your child understand what you want from him. Phrase your instructions according to the following guidelines:

- **Make sure your child is paying attention to you before you give an instruction.** Often parents misinterpret a child's nonresponse as noncompliance when in fact the child never realized that an instruction had been given.

- **Allow at least three seconds of silence before beginning the instruction.**
- **Use brief phrasing.** Give enough information for your child to understand what you expect, but do not overload him with too many words. For example, you should say, "Look at me," not "Look" or "Lookee-lookee at mommy with your big blue eyes."
- **Use familiar phrases.** In other words, use the exact wording that has proven effective in the past rather than change how you speak. If "Hands down" has worked in the past, do not switch to "Place your hands at your side."
- **Be specific.** Tell your child exactly what you want him to do. Using vague phrases such as "Cut it out" or "Be a good boy" will only confuse him.

Prompt As Needed

If your child does not respond to your instructions, you must prompt or guide him to try to at least approximate the desired response. There are four major types of prompts. First, you can prompt through *environmental prompts*. For example, you can place an empty cup immediately in front of your child as a way to get him to say "I want milk, please." You can also use *gestural prompts*—nonverbal signals such as pointing. At times it may be necessary to provide *verbal prompts* such as saying "Start with the sheets" when you have asked your child to make the bed. Finally, if other more subtle prompts fail to produce a response, you may want to attempt a *physical prompt* and physically guide your child to respond.

To provide effective prompts, keep the following in mind:

- **Prompt after one command.** Do not keep repeating yourself over and over again, waiting for your child to respond. If you do, he will learn to ignore your initial commands.
- **All prompts should be effective.** Once you prompt your child, he must at least approximate the desired behavior even if you have to guide him through the entire action. If not, your child will learn to avoid your prompts—for instance, by pulling away.
- **Provide as little guidance as possible.** If you can get a correct response by merely gesturing, this is better than providing hand-over-hand guidance. Graduated guidance is

especially important with children with autism because they tend to become what is called "prompt-dependent"; that is, they will rely on prompts rather than respond independently. For example, your child may not respond to a command, but wait for you to guide him through the use of gestures, verbalizations, or physical prompts.

- **Don't prompt too soon.** Give your child five or six seconds to begin to respond before prompting.
- **Phase out prompts as soon as possible.** You can do this by gradually making your guidance more and more subtle. For example, you may begin to teach speech by pronouncing the entire word; in time you can reduce your guidance until you only vocalize the first syllable of the desired word, then the first sound. Finally, merely shape your mouth as if you were going to say the word.

Provide Corrective Feedback

At times your child may attempt a response but still respond incorrectly. At that point you need to explain both what was wrong with his response and also describe the correct response. In providing corrective feedback, remember:

- **Be specific.** Tell your child exactly what he did wrong. "No, that's putting the bread on the chair. Put it on the *table*."
- **Use a neutral tone of voice.** Yelling only serves to let your child know he has "pushed your button."
- **Be brief.** Do not give lengthy explanations. A short sentence rather than a long-winded correction is best.

Reinforce Appropriate Behavior

It is essential that you reward your child for appropriate behavior. Unfortunately, parents often have a hard time deciding what to use as rewards for their child because traditional rewards are often ineffective. Although choosing rewards for some children is more difficult, it is never impossible. All children are "reinforceable."

To determine what is rewarding for your own child, watch him closely. What does he make an effort to obtain? What items or activities interest him for longer periods of time? Consider the sensations (such as sight, sound, taste, touch) your child seems to prefer. Choose items or activities that provide feedback to those sensory channels.

You can set up a smorgasbord of foods, toys, and household items on the table and then make a list of what piques your child's interest. It may turn out that you need to use relatively unusual objects like string and pieces of tin foil as rewards.

Regardless of what you actually provide as a reward, remember the following:

- **Reinforce all correct behavior with praise.** Whenever possible, provide physical contact—hugs or pats on the back—as well. Even if you use tangible reinforcers such as food, pair it with praise so that your child learns to appreciate praise.
- **Give behavior-specific praise.** Tell your child exactly what he did to earn the reward: "Good, you said your address" or "Great, you picked up the red block."
- **Be enthusiastic.** When praising, make sure your tone of voice is significantly different from other times. Sometimes your child will be able to identify praise simply by the change in tone alone.
- **Give praise first, then tangible rewards, if necessary.** This makes it easier for you to phase out the tangible reward in the future. For example, while you may initially have to provide food each time your child uses full sentences, make sure that you say, "Good talking in sentences!" *before* you provide the food. By having the praise so closely linked with the correct speech, your child will eventually learn to talk in full sentences merely to gain your praise.
- **Provide reinforcement immediately** after your child's response so that he can easily associate the two.
- **Allow your child to choose the reward.** This will help him be more interested in earning the reward. For example, you can offer your child two toys. When he chooses one, offer it to him *after* you see the behavior you are trying to teach.

Being told that every interaction with your child is a potential learning situation can be intimidating. With time and practice, however, you will be able to both teach your child and get on with the rest of your life. You goal should be to "teach wittingly," not unwittingly—to control your life with your child, rather than to be controlled by him. By incorporating the above suggestions into your daily life, your child's skills will improve through your teaching and your daily life will be more manageable.

▪▪ Mealtimes

Mealtimes can be very discouraging to parents of children with autism—especially if their child's food preferences are very limited. Although not all children with autism demonstrate limited food preferences, it is not uncommon for children to insist on eating only a small variety of food. If the only foods your child will eat are bananas and pancakes, it is difficult to feel creative during meal preparation. In addition, parents often respond to this problem by allowing their child to eat his preferred foods in order to prevent any escalation of problem behaviors. Unfortunately, this only prompts new worries about nutrition.

To help your child eat a balanced diet, slowly introduce new foods during meals. At first, you may put a tiny piece of cheese on the plate and insist that he eat the cheese before he can have any preferred foods. Once your child gets used to the cheese and eats it, you can gradually increase the type and quantity of foods. Whenever your child eats something outside the "preferred list," praise and reward him enthusiastically. Encouraging a balanced diet can be a complicated process. For professional help consult a dietician as described in Chapter 3.

Another potential problem at mealtimes may be your child's inability to sit still for the entire meal. Parents sometimes resort to feeding their child through many "mini-meals" rather than expecting him to sit through a full-length meal. Sooner or later, however, your child will have to learn to sit at a table and finish a meal; otherwise, he will greatly limit family life and outside activities such as visits to restaurants or Thanksgiving dinner at Grandma's.

It may be helpful to teach the concept of "sitting still" first. Spend 20 to 30 minutes per day instructing your child to sit still during a seated activity like eating a snack or playing with toys. Initially, reward your child when he sits for a few seconds. Then gradually increase the length of time he must sit still in order to receive a reward and praise. As he learns to sit still during these "formal" teaching sessions, you can begin to expect longer sitting at the mealtime table.

▪▪ Toilet Training

It is common for children with autism to be delayed in toilet training. Approximately 70 percent of children with autism also have mental retardation and therefore may learn toilet training more slowly. It is also often much more difficult for your child to understand the toileting behavior that is required or for you to find suitable rewards for proper toileting. Despite the challenges, however, toilet training cannot be put off; changing diapers when your child is five or six years old can be tiring as well as expensive.

Your major tool in toilet training is knowledge of the times your child normally relieves himself. Although some books recommend taking your child to the bathroom every five minutes throughout the day, this can be exhausting, if not impossible, for many families. Therefore, first try to mark down every time that you notice your child has soiled or wet his diaper.

After a few days of charting, you may have a relatively clear idea of your child's toileting pattern. When you have found a stable pattern, set up a rigorous toileting schedule during the times when your child is most likely to require toileting. For example, if you find your child usually urinates during the hour after dinner, take him to the toilet every ten minutes during that hour. The rest of the day, merely encourage visits to the toilet on a less rigorous schedule.

During visits to the toilet, praise your child for remaining seated, and reward him with tangible items and praise whenever he urinates or has a bowel movement in the toilet. If he has a toileting accident during other times of the day, guide him in cleaning up the mess. As your child begins to use the toilet reliably, you can gradually begin to lengthen the intervals between visits to the toilet to every 15 minutes, then 20 minutes, 30 minutes, and more. Most importantly, create and follow a predictable routine for toileting that includes eliminating, wiping, flushing, pulling up clothing, and washing up.

Another problem which sometimes arises when teaching toileting skills to children with autism is smearing or eating feces. This can be especially distressing to parents from both a health standpoint and the inconvenience involved. Yet many parents accept the mess and repeatedly clean up after their child. Guide your child through verbal or physical prompts to clean up his own toileting messes. Otherwise, you are penalized for his inappropriate behaviors, and he does not learn that the natural consequence of his behavior is to clean up the mess. At times your prompting may involve hand-over-hand guidance; regardless, it is better that your child realize that there are unpleasant consequences to smearing feces. If your child eats feces, it may be necessary to monitor him during toileting, while reinforcing him frequently if he doesn't eat feces.

When it comes to toileting, many parents put off the inevitable rather than focus on their child's needs. However, with consistent effort and energy, toilet training can be accomplished. It may help to read the "how-to" books in the Reading List or to seek professional help.

∷ Bedtime

Many children with autism have unusual sleeping patterns, such as staying up very late or wandering around the house during the night. Parents are often up half the night chasing their child or listening for any signs that their child has awakened. Such nighttime activities can only leave the parents feeling exhausted and discouraged. Consequently, the very word "bedtime" can become anxiety-provoking.

Various strategies can help lessen this problem. First, decide what time to designate as bedtime and then stick to this decision. Your child may scream, cry, or rock in bed for hours when you insist that he go to bed on time, but do not allow this to convince you that it would be easier to let your child decide when to go to bed. Otherwise, you may inadvertently teach your child to scream, cry, or rock whenever he wishes to have his own way.

When enforcing a consistent bedtime, remember that you can force your child to go to bed, but you cannot force him to go to sleep. Therefore, your only goal is to teach your child to stay quietly in his bedroom during the night. If he tends to wake up in the middle of the night, provide toys next to his bedside. Or, buy a mat which sets off a buzzer whenever your child goes through the bedroom doorway. It is essential that he learn that wandering around the house is forbidden. If this lesson is not learned, you will have trouble sleeping at night for fear that he is drinking drain cleaner, turning on the stove, or placing himself in other potentially dangerous situations.

Regardless of periodic nighttime wandering, set a daily sleep schedule and do not allow your child to benefit from sleepless nights. For instance, allowing your child to stay home from school because he is tired only encourages more sleepless nights. Stick to your schedule and discourage napping regardless of how little he has slept the night before. It may also be useful to contact teachers to let them know that they should not lower their demands just because your child would not sleep the night before.

If sleep problems persist, it will be important to find a professional, often a psychologist specializing in autism, to help you resolve the problem. In some cases, it may be necessary to consider the use of medications to help your child sleep through the night. Chapter 3 provides information on this.

▪▪ Babysitting and Respite Care

Getting time away from your child is difficult, but essential. You have a life, too. You have many roles—not just the role of parent to your child with autism. For your own sanity, you must find ways to get some time off.

Unfortunately, it can be very difficult to find a competent, loving babysitter for children with autism. Consequently, many parents either never leave their child or only leave him with relatives. This limits their lifestyles unnecessarily.

Fortunately, more and more agencies and organizations are realizing the need for specialized babysitting for children with developmental disabilities. Some agencies provide training for babysitters in specific techniques that are effective with children with autism. Contact your local resource centers—chapters of the Autism Society of America or The Arc or ACL—to find out if these kind of services are available in your area.

If there are no specialized babysitting services in your area, there are various solutions nonetheless. Do not assume that you will never be able to go off on your own. Although it may be difficult at first to leave your child with someone else, you need to do so for your own mental health.

If you cannot find a specialized babysitting service, one possible solution is to contact teachers at local special education schools that serve children with autism and other developmental disabilities. Local college students who are studying to be special education teachers also make good babysitters. Not only are they not distressed by any unusual behaviors, they are often trained in behavior management strategies. It is essential that you feel confident in your child's babysitter so that you do not worry the entire time you are out of the house. Special education students can give you that confidence.

In addition to specialized babysitting services, respite programs have been developed in various states. Although the programs differ from state to state, many pay for up to 40 hours per month of respite care. The service goes beyond babysitting, however; many programs provide parent training as a part of the service. Therefore, not only do you gain time to do things without your child, you also learn strategies that will help you feel more competent when the respite worker is not in your home. Ask your local chapters of the Autism Society of America or state agencies about the respite programs that are available in your area.

Whether or not your community provides respite programs, specialized babysitting, or any other type of child care, you should set aside time for yourself. Focusing only on your child with autism while limiting your own experiences and relationships can only be detrimental to yourself, your child, and your family.

▪▪ Conclusion

Having a child with autism is a tremendous challenge. Never forget, however, to treat him as a *child first* and as a child with autism second. Providing clear routines, expectations, and standards will help your child reach his full potential and enable him to become a part— and not the center—of your family's life.

Remember to take time for yourself. If you are exhausted, or stressed, you will be unable to notice the gradual progress that your child demonstrates. It is through the awareness of these tiny improvements—and the knowledge that your teaching helped to bring them about—that you will find true enjoyment in your child.

▪▪ Parent Statements

We often avoid social situations that are too busy, unstructured, or unpredictable, and gravitate more to small groups, simple itinerary with, preferably, a physical component.

❦

Even if all goes well and as planned, the anticipatory stress of knowing that something could happen can cause you to avoid social situations rather than participate.

❦

We used to be able to just pick up and go to the mall or anywhere else without planning the route, worrying if there will be a big crowd, or what will be available to eat. Now we have to wonder about all of that, not to mention, does our son even want to go or will he throw a tantrum?

❧❀❧

We supported our son in discovering areas of interest in the community. Swim team was made successful through adaptation and piano lessons built on his good ear for music. We let him bargain for independence and granted it whenever he displayed appropriate behavior and skills.

❧❀❧

People look at you as if to say, "My God, are you ever a horrible parent. Can't you control that child? What's wrong with you? Spoiled rotten brat. If he were mine, boy, would I...."

❧❀❧

At the grocery store, my daughter would want candy and make a huge scene, screaming and kicking, because she couldn't verbally ask for it. Nearly every time, someone would embarrass me by commenting. I felt I had to come right out and tell them "She's autistic." That's one of the day-to-day things that makes life difficult.

❧❀❧

My husband and I often joke about the golden rule of autism: "I WANT EVERYTHING TO STAY THE SAME!" Moving a lamp or a book on a shelf has caused many a tantrum. Slight variations in food temperature or presentation have ended many a meal. The phrase "you can get used to it" has been very useful for us.

❧❀❧

My son and I have a routine we follow every morning. I have tried letting him set the pace, the order of what we do, tried rewards, but no matter what, he fights me. When other moms tell me how hard their morning rush hour is, I just nod my head and say, "I just can't imagine" while really thinking, "Try my world for a week!"

❧❀❧

What's punishment? With an autistic kid, sometimes it's hard to tell. We've found a few negative consequences that work but we use a lot more positive reinforcement.

❧

The discipline we used with our other child was completely inappropriate for Lawrence. We found ourselves using no discipline at all with him. With the help of Lawrence's teachers and a class in behavior modification, we are now trying to impose some limits on his behavior.

❧

I help him go in the little grocery store down near the day care center. I send him up to the counter to get experience dealing with the salespeople. It's been embarrassing at times, but then, I'm sensitive.

❧

Being out in the community with him where people know him can be a really positive experience. They know what to expect and they know what not to expect, and they know how to talk to him—to be very direct and helpful.

❧

With everything else involved in raising an autistic child, I tend to give the least emphasis to his diet. I figure a lot of normal kids survive on rotten diets and I have only so many hours in a day. There's just no time to force-feed Lawrence every meal.

❧

I do not and will not tolerate tantrums from any child, autistic or not. Distraction from whatever caused the tantrum usually seems to help.

❧

At home we have some basic rules. Although it may take hand-over-hand manipulation and a lot of extra time, my son finishes out his morning routine as independently as possible. Even though it would have only taken me two minutes to complete the chores myself, the extra effort pays off in the end.

❧

I find it more comfortable to be friends with other parents of children with disabilities. They don't sit in judgment of me when my child is disruptive or refuses to share his toys. I don't have to constantly explain his behavior.

✦❀✦

Something that has helped me greatly is having a friend who is also the mother of an autistic child. Though our children are at different places in the spectrum, it's so nice to be able to share anecdotes about our kids and hear on the other end of the phone, "That sounds just like what happens at my house!"

✦❀✦

I have one family member and one true friend who truly understand the daily trials and tribulations our family endures. Others are understanding but they just don't get it: my son will not just wake up one day and be cured.

✦❀✦

I have been accused by various professionals at my son's school of being "too hard" on him. I fear that the next person who gives me that patronizing smile and begins a sentence with, "Even typical kids do that..." will find me lunging for his or her throat. Yes, of course all children exhibit maladaptive behaviors at some time or another, choose not to say hello, choose not to play with others, exhibit rigid behaviors with a preferred food or toy, for example. With a child with autism, it's a matter of degree and frequency.

✦❀✦

Behavior modification works best when your child knows that making mistakes is normal and that you still love him when he does.

✦❀✦

My son's autism is and will always be the greatest test in my life. The complexity of his daily challenges makes mine seem relatively simple. I am grateful to Michael. He has taught me so much about life.

5

CHILDREN WITH AUTISM AND THEIR FAMILIES

Michael D. Powers, Psy. D.

Finding out that your child has autism may well be the most devastating experience of your life. It is not, however, the end of the world, nor is it the end of your family. True, having a child with autism can be very stressful and can strain families to the limit at times, but there are ways to cope. Your family will face the challenge of coping in its own way, but right from the start you should know that it can be done. Thousands of families have proved that.

Most parents worry about what having a child with autism will do to their families. In particular, they often worry whether their child will fit into the family. Parents ask, "Will our child's behavior be so abnormal and disruptive that everyday family life will be destroyed? Will her behavior wear me down and ruin her siblings' childhood? Will normal family life come to an end forever?" These are just some of the questions that reflect common concerns of parents of children with autism.

A major part of the worry that you feel is fear of the unknown. But remember, other parents have confronted the same fears and worries. They can tell you that raising a child with autism forced significant changes in their lives that involved hard work and tremendous adjustment. But they can also tell you that they survived—and, what's more, that having a child with autism enriched their lives in unexpected ways.

∷ Being the Parent of a Child with Autism

The single most important thing for a child with autism—more important than good education or proper table manners—is that her family stay together. If you allow your child's autism and her needs to destroy your family or drive family members away, everyone loses. But the biggest loser by far will be your child with autism. Therefore, in setting your priorities, dividing your time, balancing everyone's needs, and deciding just how much you can take, never allow your child's needs or your devotion to her to jeopardize your family life. Raising a child with autism should not become a choice between her and your family.

Being the parent of a child with autism does require more attention to your own attitudes, hopes, fears, and expectations. How you approach family life will have a profound effect on your child with autism, your other children, your marriage, and, of course, yourself.

Feeling Good about Yourself as a Parent

There are no two ways about it: having a child with autism can be a tremendous blow to the self-confidence and self-esteem of parents. Even parents who have already raised children without autism lose confidence in their ability to be parents of a child with autism. What causes this sudden self-doubt? First and foremost is the mystery that is autism itself. Parents are faced with totally unfamiliar behavior and unique demands. They are simply unprepared for this type of parenting, however capable they had felt before as "ordinary" parents. Second, along with autism usually comes a battalion of well-meaning professionals to advise you on the daily care, education, integration, and medical treatment of your child. In a sense this book is part of that—professionals telling you how to do things you had previously considered instinctive. Having professionals inject so much thought and planning into every aspect of raising a child can undermine the self-confidence of any parent. Third, you lack information about what autism is like and what to expect. If your child with autism is your first, you may not have even had the chance to gain confidence from previous successes as a parent.

If you have other children, take some time to consider your successes. Remember that you are a good, loving parent who is both capable and caring. Having a child with autism changes your life, but it does not render you inept. Other parents can tell you that the same skills that help with "normal" children apply in raising a child with autism. Some parents actually decide to have additional children  to help reassure themselves that they can have "normal" children. Parents who were planning to have more children should not let having a child with autism change their plans except possibly if their child has fragile X syndrome (see Chapter 1).

One terrific method to bolster your parental self-confidence is to tally all the many things you do yourself for the care, education, and health of your child with autism without either thinking about it or getting paid for it. Every day you are your child's doctor, nurse, therapist, educator, and advocate, as well as her parent. You know more about her than anyone else. But because you are not labeled a "professional" you don't get credit. Make sure you give yourself that credit. You really are an expert (or fast on your way to becoming one), and you are clearly not helpless without professional help. Demand a working relationship in which your involvement, ideas, and concerns are respected. Some parents go one step further: They take on some of the jobs of professionals, either because professional services are not available in their area or because they are too expensive.

The more you learn about your child's disorder, the more your confidence will grow. In the beginning, few parents are prepared for the "scenes" that can happen when their child with autism is momentarily out of control. Most parents of children with autism come from family environments that are more tranquil than their own, and are just not prepared to deal with outrageous behavior at first. In fact, the unusual behavior and tantrums of children with autism probably do more than anything else to undermine a parent's feeling of competence. As you learn how to tolerate some of your child's more extreme behavior and how to stop it, however, you will find your self-confidence rebounding on its own.

Besides feeling incompetent, some parents also feel that they are constantly scrutinized as a parent. They feel that they cannot be seen getting annoyed, frustrated, or mad at their child with autism. After all, she is helpless to prevent her behavior. In addition, they feel that their friends and family do not understand just how trying a child with autism can be every day. For example, people who do not have to live with a child with autism may not understand why a parent may lose his or her temper over a seemingly small event, such as the child spinning the squeaky wheel of a toy, bouncing a ball, repeating herself, or dropping food on the floor. If these behaviors happened only occasionally—roughly the frequency a friend may witness them—they would be tolerable. But parents of children with autism must tolerate behaviors like these every day, sometimes every minute. Friends or professionals who don't live in your shoes shouldn't judge you when you've had it with your child with autism. You should not judge them, either. The feeling that nobody understands what you are going through does, however, make parents feel isolated. This is only one of the many reasons why sharing experiences with other parents of children with autism is so important to your emotional equilibrium.

** Family Life

First You Are a Family

Families of children with autism and families of children without a disability are more alike than different. And parents of children with autism and parents of children without a disability are more alike than different. Having a child with autism changes your life, but does not change you. You are still the same person you were before your child was diagnosed.

All parents experience some feelings of guilt, incompetence, frustration, and tension. All brothers and sisters are jealous, angry, and embarrassed many times over the course of their childhoods. From time to time, most grandparents disagree with their children about the best way to raise their grandchildren. And almost every married couple has occasional (and not-so-occasional) arguments. We wouldn't be human if we didn't experience these emotions, and we wouldn't be human if we didn't express them. Having a child with autism does not change these basic facts of family life.

Feelings, conflicts, and problems are usually intensified by the demands of being a parent, sibling, grandparent, aunt, or uncle of a child with autism, but they are still normal responses that are felt by most people. Remember, even if you did not have a child with autism, you would still have these occasional problems.

This is not to say that having a child with autism doesn't change your family—in some families, the change is profound. Every single family member is affected in some way, but so is the family as a unit. For example, remember how it was before your child with autism was born. The family probably had a set of "rules" (usually assumed or informally stated) that everyone tried to follow. These rules could be as simple as: "Daddy takes care of the car and Mommy plans the meals." They could be more complex rules like: "Mommy decides I have been good today and can watch television. Daddy thinks my grades are too low to go out for Little League." By and large, the rules were understood and everybody obeyed them—at least usually. This made family life predictable, organized, and secure. If sudden changes came up—if, for instance, your younger brother moved in with you—family members tried to readjust and cope. Sometimes these adjustments were successful and sometimes they were not. Nevertheless, your family tried to cope together.

After your child with autism was born, all the stresses and changes you had previously grappled with paled in comparison to how you felt. Your ability to manage your time, or to be the kind of parent you knew you were capable of being, was drastically altered. Your family had to revise its "rules" in order to cope with the extraordinary demands of your child with autism.

Whether you call it coping or adapting, you have probably already changed your lifestyle to accommodate the new demands and stresses caused by having a child with autism in the family. For example, you may have stopped going to restaurants as a family, or changed your grocery shopping habits because your child can last only 15 minutes.

Whatever your feelings about these changes may be, don't blame your child for causing them. Blame the autism. It is an unfortunate fact that your child has autism. But this fact is not one she would have chosen for herself or her family.

You can count on two things always being true: Your child with autism will grow and change and your family will too. Your child with autism and your family will often change in reaction to each other. Sometimes they will change together and sometimes the change will look like a constant series of adjustments and reactions. For example,

as your child learns to communicate with you more effectively, some of the "guesswork" you have relied on to understand her will diminish. You might then begin to make more demands for even better communication from your child, because your expectations have risen. Your child will react to this. She may rise to your challenge, or she may rebel and resist. Either way, you and your child will struggle with these changes together, and continue to grow. It may appear chaotic, but it is what social scientists call "dynamic," the never-ending process of growth *all* families and all people experience. It is a constant part of life for all families. However, you can anticipate, plan for, and manage this constant change.

As you learn to understand your child's autism—her preferences, fears, communication strategies—you will begin to anticipate those things that might be difficult or easy for her, and you will help her through them as best you can. Helping your child cope with her own family might be one of the most important (and rewarding) things you do with your child when she is young.

How Families Adapt through Time

There is no absolute "right" way to integrate your child with autism into your family. Most families work hard to secure the future independence of their child with autism through education and training at home and in school. They also try to maintain the mental and physical well-being of all members of the family. You can strive for this balance, too.

Just because your family faces unusual stress does not mean that the common sense approaches to family life no longer apply. Indeed, because the stress of having a child with autism can shake even the strongest family's foundation, it is especially important for you to ground your family life on solid values. This means that love, respect, communication, and hard work—all the elements that help other families run smoothly—are also the keys to your own family's survival.

Chapter 2 discussed dealing with the emotional impact of your child's diagnosis and with the immediate changes autism may cause. After the initial adjustment—after some of the shock wears off—most families settle into a stable routine. Responsibilities are understood. Each family member's involvement with the child with autism is established. And time commitments are set. For example, you have decided who has the responsibility for supervising your child Saturday mornings, or who will take her for her haircut.

Because all families grow and change over time, these commitments and responsibilities must also change. What worked before—the division of work, sibling responsibilities, or discipline techniques—may cease to work. As old, comfortable methods of coping become less effective, the family must find new ways to adapt. In the life cycle of the family of a child with autism, there are several important transition points where change usually occurs. Negotiating these transitions successfully requires flexibility and hard work from each member of your family.

Early Years: From Diagnosis to School Age

Moving from the initial shock of their child's diagnosis to coming to grips with the implications of her disability is often the first transitional crisis families face. Suddenly you have to find special therapeutic and educational services, as well as physicians, dentists, and babysitters who understand and can work with your child. In addition, you have to change your own schedules or other commitments in order to devote more time to your child. For instance, you or your spouse may have to change jobs or quit working completely; one or both of you may have to postpone plans for further education. And there may be even more personal worries.

Parents who worry about the risks of having another child with autism may struggle to balance their desire for more children with the slight (approximately three percent) but real risk of a second child with autism. The realization of the additional efforts a child with autism requires can terrify parents into forgoing future children. The personality of your child with autism can also influence a parent's outlook.

Some young children with autism are very aloof, or refuse to allow anyone to hold them. Others are more tolerant, sometimes even briefly engaging, with parents. It can be very hard to "connect"—to establish that two-way bond—with a young child with autism. Mothers and fathers often question themselves, or their parenting skills at this time. "Am I doing something wrong? Why doesn't my baby want me to hold her? Why is she rejecting everything I try to do to make her happy?"

None of us likes rejection, least of all from our baby or toddler. It is essential to remember that your child is not rejecting you; she just cannot understand what or why you're doing, and her lack of understanding makes her retreat to avoid the fear of this confusion. As your toddler gets to know and understand you, and you come to understand her, the avoidance and rejection will diminish.

Grandparents, aunts and uncles, other relatives, and friends all might want to know about your child: how she is doing, what the diagnosis means, why she won't talk, or why she tantrums when she wears short pants or when she cannot have "beige" colored food. So many questions and so little time, or so few obvious explanations. As your child grows older and teaches you, you will have better answers to some of these questions. For now, however, informing others and explaining everything can be a lot of work (especially if Aunt Sue or Uncle Joe disagrees with you, or with the diagnosis). As a result, some parents offer only a little information, while others give a lot. How your family handles it will depend on many factors. What is important, however, is that information and answers be available to those who need and want it. This will help them become part of the solution instead of an added, sometime annoying, burden.

In the early years, many parents try to find meaning to their child's autism. "Why did this happen to us?" "We don't have the kind of temperament that our daughter needs." These types of questions are very common, and they are a very normal part of coping. It helps many families to find a satisfying answer to the early "why me?" questions. Being able to discuss these with your spouse, or siblings, or friends will help you clarify your own personal beliefs about autism, and give you a frame of reference for future decision making. For example, you might decide that your child grow up to be "one-of-the-kids" in the neighborhood, and you will become an ardent supporter of integration or inclusion. Or you might decide that the best path for your child begins with intensive, early educational intervention, and you will become a strong proponent of intensive applied behavior analysis (ABA) teaching (described in Chapter 7). The important point is that you obtain as much information as you possibly can, use it thoughtfully, and keep moving forward.

No question about it: autism changes a family. When your child is young, these changes can be overwhelming, and may come on fast and furiously. Just remember to hang on. Dealing with change, transitions, and your child's needs gets easier as you get to know her better, and as she grows and learns. You and your family will establish new patterns of interaction that support your child's fullest participation. You can then identify those high priority family functions, such as family vacations, parental "alone time," getting everyone off to school and work in one piece, and then establish new family routines to carry on those functions.

Because autistic behaviors often are more severe when your child is between the ages of two and four, your family's coping abilities may be stretched to the limit during these early years. Fortunately, however, a variety of strategies can help your family weather this stormy developmental period. You can actively seek out information about autism and learn as much as possible about ways to help your child. You can explore services available for children with autism in your community, and seek advice from professionals. And you can enlist the support and understanding of other parents of children with autism who have already gone through what you are going through now.

School Years (3-12)

When your child with autism enters school, your family must shift gears once again to accommodate her needs. Family members need to adjust their schedules to create a predictable structure and routine for your child's day, and must also teach important daily living skills at home. For example, it will no longer be appropriate for a parent or older sibling to completely dress your child with autism. To do so would work against her future independence. Teaching her to dress herself and resisting the urge to help out and make it easier will be just one important adaptation during this phase. Independent toileting and remaining with the family on outings are two additional skills your child will need to learn.

Early in this transitional period, you may experience added anxiety if you are not certain that your child has received the best educational placement possible. Once you have found an appropriate school, however, you will probably feel more optimistic about your child's progress. Just having their child out of the house for some time each day helps parents tremendously. Working with teachers gives parents new ideas and techniques for handling their child when she is at home. Especially if parent training services are available, you will likely have more energy to work with her. Finally, during these school years, you will have opportunities for on-the-job advocacy training at school planning and placement (or IEP) meetings. Your participation is essential, because you know your child best. The skills you acquire in effective communication, compromise, and consumerism will help you and your child long after she graduates. Chapter 7 discusses these and other aspects of your child's educational program in detail.

During the middle childhood years, parents become more and more aware that their child's needs are unrelenting. These needs—for supervision, toileting, and eating properly, to name but a few—demand enormous amounts of time from parents. Unfortunately there are only 24 hours in a day, and the time you devote to your child's needs is automatically subtracted from the time you have for other activities. Leisure activities and time alone are often the first to be sacrificed. Some families obtain respite care assistance when they realize that the balance has tipped too far in their child's direction. Locating community resources for child care, respite care, and extracurricular activities and arranging for your child's participation without your supervision can help reduce the relentless barrage of demands for your time.

Parents with primary caretaking responsibilities frequently feel lonely and unable to relate to parents of children without handicaps. They may feel trapped, helpless, or overwhelmed. In such cases, if the other spouse can relieve some of the burdens of child care, provide companionship, and share the process of integrating the child into the community, the primary care-giving parent's feelings of isolation can be reduced. It is very important to reach out to others for support wherever possible at these times. Establishing (or re-establishing) support networks for yourself may help you find the perspective and energy to push ahead. This is a perfect time to call on the support and help of your extended family as well.

One final hazard that families need to guard against during these school years is stagnation. In a well-functioning family, members mature and take on new and different responsibilities. When there is a child with autism in the family, however, the change process may be brought to a screeching halt, because you may be reluctant to change management strategies as your child matures. When this happens, adaptation ceases and there is little role flexibility—that is, family members may become unable or unwilling to switch individual responsibilities for their child. For example, one parent may always end up with the responsibility for morning supervision (dressing and toileting).

Given the extraordinary demands that having a child with autism places on a family, the loss of flexibility and opportunities to grow can be crippling. Fortunately it doesn't have to be this way. As long as you are aware of the possibility of stagnation and alert to its dangers, you can talk about what to look out for and how to avoid it. If you notice yourself becoming unnecessarily short-tempered with your spouse or children, or that you are avoiding certain responsibilities, discuss these concerns with your spouse or family members. Try to arrive *first* at a clear definition of the problem, and *then* a solution.

Adolescence

By the time your child is 13, you will be an expert on autism. You will also be older, and perhaps a bit less energetic in dealing with your child. This is understandable. During their child's adolescent years, many parents begin to shift focus and start to consider the long-term future. Issues such as vocational training, financial security, and independent living arrangements for your child may occupy more of your thinking. Often parents channel their energies into establishing or securing these things.

Even as they concentrate on the future, however, parents must continue to cope with the present. They must, for instance, confront more directly the differences between their child with autism and her peers. While other young people are hurtling toward adulthood, the adolescent with autism usually remains indifferent to social events, career plans, or the struggle for independence. The parents of a 16-year-old daughter with autism may watch with sadness while her peers begin dating and forming those early relationships that often are the foundations for marriage and children.

With the physical and emotional changes of puberty may come concerns about emerging sexuality. Most people with autism are unconcerned about developing intimate long-term relationships with members of the opposite sex. Many, if not most, however, respond to the biological, hormonal, and physical changes to their bodies each in his or her own way. The lack of good judgment, social understanding, or poor social interaction skills may lead some children into situations embarrassing to them, parents, or siblings. Although the risks of sexual abuse are a concern to any parent of a child with a developmental disability, the dangers of HIV/AIDS and other sexually transmitted diseases cause even greater concern for some parents.

At this stage, parents of a child with autism must also deal with differences between their own marriage and those of others. For example, while other husbands and wives have the chance to reconnect as couples when their teenagers leave home, the parents of a child with autism may be denied that opportunity by their child's continued dependence on them. Adjusting emotionally to the chronic, lifelong demands of autism requires work. Even the solution to this crisis—consideration of community-based living options—may precipitate its own crisis. For example, you may find that there are no suitable living options near your home and that you must consider options in other, more distant communities.

The main task of the family of an adolescent with autism is to foster the adolescent's independence in every way possible. Chapter 10 discusses this in greater detail. In addition, the family must come to terms with issues of separation, and parents must begin to redefine their own roles as parents of grown children. With careful financial planning, vocational preparation of their child, and the selection of an appropriate community living setting, most families are able to negotiate this phase of the life cycle successfully.

∷ What Helps

The preceding sections have described how families with children with autism grow and adapt over time. But how do you handle the thousand and one minor crises that daily plague the family of a child with autism? How does a family cope with the stress of raising a child with a disability day in and day out without falling apart under the strain? Coping formulas vary, but, in general, four ingredients are essential to success: positive parental attitudes, communication, support, and family empowerment.

Parents' Attitudes

Parents are the key to how well a family adjusts to having a child with autism. Children, other family members, and friends all follow the parents' cues. Because the way you act toward your child sets the pattern for the whole family right from the start, you must take care to treat her with love and acceptance, to set high, but reasonable goals for her, and to encourage her individuality and independence in every way possible.

Love and Acceptance. Autism is a very difficult condition for parents to deal with because of the way it affects their child. The diagnosis usually comes as a shock, and parents often grieve for some time. It is important to remember, though, that your child is not any less a person now that she has a label. She is still a child—your child. And provided you accept her as she is, she can still be just as much a part of your family as anyone else.

Accepting your child does not mean that you should ignore her autism; rather, you need to love her the way she is and see through her autism to glimpse the child underneath. Although this can often be quite a challenge, it is essential to enabling your family to adjust and cope.

All parents of children with disabilities feel some sense of loss for both that "perfect" child they could have had and for themselves. It *is* sad to think how autism will affect your child's life. But for your child's and your family's sakes you must accept her autism as a fact of her life and of yours. All that you will accomplish by denying your child's condition will be to place a wall between you and her. In contrast, if you accept your child's autism and are comfortable with her, she can learn to fit into your family. The goal is always to nurture your family; accepting your child and her autism is the first step.

A necessary step in accepting your child is to evaluate carefully just how many of her problems—and yours—are directly attributable to autism. Parents sometimes attribute *all* problem behavior to autism, whereas in reality autism is responsible for only *some*. For example, when a child refuses to eat dinner or hits her sister, it is easy for the parent of a child with autism to blame this misconduct on autism. Yet parents whose children do not have autism will tell you that these things happen in their families, too. In addition, children who do not have autism may be unin-

quisitive or socially aloof—characteristics associated with autism. Therefore, although autism does make your life more difficult, it is not the cause of all the problems you may experience with your child.

Acceptance should *never* be confused with resignation or capitulation. Accepting your child does not mean surrendering your child to all of autism's potential effects. Many parents are able to transform their anger at their child's autism into a determination that helps fuel a fierce desire not to let autism win every time. If you channel this determination properly, you can use it to protect your child's interests and to push her to achieve her potential. In addition, you can sometimes convert determination into the energy needed in confronting uncaring professionals or callous neighbors.

Expectations. Just like other children, children with autism are born with a wide variety of physical and intellectual abilities. True, autism will limit your child's abilities, but it is impossible to predict any child's full potential at an early age. In fact, to set limits now on what you think your child will be able to accomplish may actually prevent her from reaching her maximum potential. This is because the expectations that both you and other family members have can affect your child's achievements.

Because you are likely to spend more time with your child than anyone else is, it is essential that you project an optimistic attitude about your child's ability to master new skills. For example, if you always dress or undress your child or help her too much with dressing, she may never learn to dress herself. If your other children stop trying to play with her because you give them the impression that your child with autism will always be in her own little world, she may never learn how to act with her peers. In both cases, your child may fail because you have unwittingly not given her the chance to succeed.

Of course, expecting too much can sometimes be as frustrating as expecting too little. Just because you work hard to *teach* your child with autism basic life skills does not always mean she will *learn* them. But not trying ensures that she won't. It is far better to *expect* your child to learn— no matter how slowly—than it is to deprive her of the opportunity to try.

Do not form your expectations in a vacuum. Talk to doctors, teachers, therapists, and other parents of children with autism. It takes information and exposure to set realistic expectations. More importantly, try not to look too far into the future. Focus on the next skill; set short-term goals. After all, every small success your child enjoys today paves the way for a successful tomorrow.

Just as important as setting realistic expectations for your child is setting realistic expectations for yourself. Parents sometimes fall into the trap of feeling that their child with autism needs, and therefore deserves, every free moment of their day. They feel that without their constant work, their child with autism will not learn and that an hour not spent teaching a new skill is an hour wasted. The guilt that accompanies this belief is dangerous. You can't possibly do everything that *might* benefit your child with autism. No parent can. And feeling guilty about not using every spare moment doesn't help your child either. Strive for balance. Accept *your* limitations: do not feel guilty if you are not able to turn every event or free moment into teaching opportunities. For example, parents often feel that every mealtime is a potential clinic for teaching independent feeding skills. But if they are occasionally not up to the messes and tantrums that can result, parents should not feel they are failing their child. Sometimes just getting through mealtime is all any parent can manage.

Independence. It is natural to feel that your child is particularly vulnerable because she has autism. It is a natural reaction to feel sorry for your child and to want to protect her. But if you allow your child to remain too dependent on you for too long, she will eventually come to dominate your whole family's life. For the sake of your child's future as well as for your family's, you need to encourage her to function as independently as possible.

As Chapter 7 explains, one of the first steps to independence is to enroll your child in an educational program specifically geared to her needs. Just as important, though, is the atmosphere you create at home. You and your family should *expect* your child to learn self-help skills like dressing and feeding herself. You should not rush to help her before you have given her the chance to try something on her own, and you should reward her when she asserts her independence in appropriate ways. For example, you should praise your child lavishly if she picks up her shoe and hands it to you when you are dressing her, but not if she gets out of bed in the middle of the night. The first is an appropriate display of independence, while the second is not.

What should you aim for in working toward independence? One suggestion is to work for skills that make it possible to take your child with autism out with you in public. The skills necessary to take your child to the store, a restaurant, or other public place—following simple directions, avoiding inappropriate behavior, and not throwing tantrums—are important in freeing a family from being trapped at home by their child.

Communication

Although parents can often ease their family's adjustment to a child with autism by working to maintain positive attitudes, open and honest communication is also essential. Remember, raising a child with autism is a new experience for everyone involved. Not only is it important for family members to exchange information about what works and what doesn't work, but it is also important that they share their feelings about having a child with a disability in the family.

You should encourage everyone in your family to vent his or her emotions and to listen to what others have to say without judging. Set an atmosphere of acceptance and allow family members to express negative feelings such as hate, anger, fear, worry, and guilt, as well as positive ones. If you share and acknowledge these feelings, you can often work through them together.

Occasionally family members—especially children—feel so guilty about the anger and frustration the child with autism arouses in them that they suppress their emotions completely. If this happens, reassure them that it is normal to feel as they do, but that it is also healthy to express themselves. Especially with your children, try taking the lead by explaining that *you* are mad or frustrated at times;

honesty on your part will create a climate for honest communication from all of your children.

You can urge your children (or arrange for them) to meet with other siblings of children with autism or other disability to work through their feelings. Organizations in your community may sponsor a sibling group, or you can form your own informal group with children of members of your parent support group.

Whatever you do, do not ever accept silence from family members merely because you are afraid they may voice the same negative feelings you are experiencing. Nothing you can do can prevent these feelings, and left to fester, they may breed serious long-term problems. Sharing emotions with members of your immediate and extended family is the first and most important step in nurturing the supportive environment your family needs in order to grow and thrive.

Support

You will also want to reach out to other parents of children with autism for support. As mentioned earlier, there are few experiences that can make you feel quite so alone as having a child with autism. The isolation can be overt—for example, when friends and family don't visit as often—or it can be subtle—for example, when parents feel that friends and family can't understand what life with a child with autism is really like. In any case, nothing can shatter the isolation quite like talking to parents who have already been there. Not only can you draw strength and inspiration from other families' stories, but you can also gain a great deal of practical information on coping and on the resources in your community. And you may even find a friend.

For help in locating a parent support group, call the local affiliate of the Autism Society of America listed in the Resource Guide in the back of this book. They can direct you to a variety of publications about autism and to the resources and people in your area who can help you. In addition, the Resource Guide lists other organizations you can contact for information about parent groups.

Your child's teacher and professionals such as the psychologist and social worker described in Chapter 1 can also be a tremendous source of support. Because their advice is based on the collective experience of many children and families, they can help you confront and resolve your questions and worries, and also suggest ways for you to cope with your feelings. Nothing works better to relieve worry about a problem with your child with autism than solving that problem. Often just knowing there is someone you can count on to help solve problems can calm your anxiety.

Embarrassment, fear of rejection by extended family or community members, or the realistic needs inherent in managing a child with autism may limit the social contacts of a family. In its most debilitating form, the family members see themselves only as a part of a "family of an autistic child," and restrict social contact solely to other families with children with autism or to activities revolving around the child's needs. In addition, it is not uncommon for families of newly diagnosed children with autism to reduce their contacts with extended family members, friends, and neighbors. This normal response to such a crisis permits the family to adjust to and assimilate the disability. However, when temporary isolation becomes permanent entrenchment, the family is at risk for overidentification with the child with autism or for scapegoating the child.

Families with children with autism must work to maintain their social networks because these networks serve as informal support systems. For example, your friends can be a source of information about child development and about local educational and medical resources. In addition, friends can often be an outlet for family concerns considered too personal to discuss with professionals. By helping your family avoid isolation, you will bring additional opportunities to your child with autism, as well as everyone else.

Even with the support of family, friends, and professionals, there still may be times when communication fails and the stress of raising a child with autism completely overwhelms you. If this happens, you should not hesitate to turn to a psychologist or other mental health professional for help. A counselor will be able to reassure you that your feelings are not only real, but justified, and can also provide you with some of the coping skills you need to regain your emotional balance.

Family Empowerment

Feeling a sense of control over your and your child's destinies helps tremendously in adapting to a child with autism. That control is called "empowerment." Empowerment for families of children with disabilities means that they are full partners in all decisions affecting their lives and the lives of their children. In all dealings with professionals—medical and educational professionals—parents should be treated with respect for the information and insight into their child only they have. Building empowerment takes work and time. You gain it by becoming very well-informed about autism and effective teaching and management strategies. You especially gain it by understanding *your* child, and helping others understand her strengths and difficulties. In a nutshell, the way to build empowerment is to become the best-informed consumer for your child that you can be. All family members need to work together to achieve this, and expect the same from professionals. Information and knowledge are keys to empowerment for parents, and informed parents can operate with mutual respect from the professionals serving their child.

▪▪ What Hurts

Some of the ways that families of children with autism try to adapt do more harm than good. Almost invariably, these are "errors of the heart"; the result of good and loving, if misguided, intentions. The three common traps that parents of children with autism should beware of are overinvolvement, overprotectiveness, and rejection.

Overinvolvement

Sometimes one parent gets so wrapped up in the child's need for extra supervision and attention that he or she spends almost all his or her waking hours trying to care for, stimulate, and teach the child. Ironically, this overinvolvement may result in a relationship that actually encourages dependence, not independence. The parent may become so skilled at anticipating the child's every need that the child has no incentive to learn appropriate communication skills or good behavior. For example, recognizing that a tantrum after awakening from a nap is a request for juice, and then always providing the juice when the tantrum occurs, will never help your child learn a more appropriate way to request juice.

Overinvolvement is not only self-defeating, it may also threaten your marital relationship or make your other children feel neglected. After all, when one parent becomes consumed with the needs of a single family member, little time or energy may be left over for his or her spouse, other children, or him- or herself. Occasionally neglected family members may direct pent-up anger and resentment at the overinvolved parent or at the child with autism, who is seen as the cause of parental overinvolvement. If you think you may be neglecting your spouse or other children, check it out with them. Establish an open line of communication so that you—and they—have permission to discuss potential overinvolvement. If their complaints persist, it may be that you are not achieving the proper balance, and that professional assistance may help you regain it.

Overprotectiveness

It is a natural impulse for parents to want to shield their children from potential harm. Sometimes, though, parents can go overboard. They may come to view their child with autism as too disabled to do anything for herself, and may rush to satisfy her every whim.

Even though this overprotectiveness is usually motivated by concern and affection, the results can be disastrous. The child with autism may develop into a little tyrant who rules the family with an iron fist, throwing a tantrum at every limit or demand placed upon her. In addition, the overprotected child with autism often makes her parents feel very inept whenever they ask her to do something and she fails to comply.

If you feel your child is in danger of developing into a little tyrant, now would be a good time to talk to other parents who have "been through it all" and made it to the other side without a little tyrant. They may have tried-and-true suggestions, or can perhaps recommend a professional who was especially helpful to them.

Rejection

Most parents find autistic behaviors like self-stimulation and self-injury very upsetting to watch. To cope with the distress this behavior causes them, some parents may pull away emotionally and physically from their child, ignoring both the child's problems and needs. In its most extreme form, this detachment becomes outright rejection. This hurts both the parents and the child by interfering with the development of the parents' sense of competency and self-esteem. Professional assistance to help the parents regain control of the situation is often very helpful.

⁑ Keeping Perspective

Having a child with autism does not magically transform you into "Supermom" or "Superdad," with boundless energy, miraculous teaching abilities, or infinite patience. In addition to all you face with your child with autism, you still have to earn a living, eat, sleep, take care of your other kids, and clean the house. Like everyone else, you have good days and bad days. Many parents of children with autism, however, lament that the world no longer sees them as the mortals they really are, but regards them as somehow gifted. This can set up a very high standard that can haunt parents with guilt. Helen Featherstone, in her fine book, *A Difference in the Family: Life with a Disabled Child*, perhaps states this paradox best:

> Suppose I, an ordinary person, am walking alone beside an icy isolated river and see someone drowning. I have two options: I can jump in and try to save him (risking death myself), or I can agonize on the shore. In the first case I am a hero; in the second a coward. There is no way I can remain what I was before—an ordinary person. As the mother of a profoundly retarded child, I felt I was in the same position: I had to look like a hero or a coward, even though actually I was still an ordinary person.

Even though being the parent of a child with autism may require superhuman effort at times, you are still the same person you were before. Set your own goals, standards, and rules. Never forget that what matters is what you think of yourself, not what other people may think.

▪▪ Brothers and Sisters of Children with Autism

"As close as brothers." "Sisters under the skin." Expressions like these reflect the special bonds of love and loyalty that inextricably draw siblings together in the best of relationships. When your children were small, you may have cherished the hope that they would develop one of these relationships, or, at the very least, that they would become fast friends. Now that your child has been diagnosed with autism, however, you may worry more about the negative effects she may have on her siblings' lives.

Your child's autism will definitely affect the way she relates to her brothers and sisters and the way they relate to her. Do not assume, however, that all these ways will be bad. Far from it. Having a sibling with autism is stressful and enriching, exasperating and fun, distressing and rewarding. In other words, it is not much different from being the brother or sister of any other child. This section reviews the effects—both good and bad—that children with autism have on their siblings, and focuses on what you, the parent, can do to encourage healthy relationships.

Children's Feelings

As soon as they begin to take an interest in the world around them, your other children will have thoughts and feelings about their sibling. At first, they will notice only that their brother or sister takes longer to learn basic skills like talking, playing with toys, and toileting. Gradually, however, they will begin to understand that their brother or sister has a disability. What follows is a summary of the thoughts and emotions typically experienced by siblings of children with autism.

Preschool Years. Young children are very perceptive, so you can expect them to pick up on your anxiety about your child with autism. They may recognize developmental differences and try to help teach skills, but they will not be able to understand what autism is. They may ask questions. They may also resent the time you spend in home-teaching or early intervention programs with their sibling. In response to this resentment, the nondisabled sibling may regress in order to gain your attention, or to convince you that they, too, are developmentally immature and deserving of special treats or toys. Sometimes young siblings begin to talk less maturely or to bed-wet even though they have been toilet trained for months. Preschoolers tend not to discuss openly their feelings about having a brother or sister with autism. Because they have not yet learned to be judgmental, however, they will accept your child with autism as she is. Best of all, they will likely fall in love with their sibling.

School Years. Somewhere between the ages of three and six, your children will probably begin to wonder what is "wrong" with their sibling. They may worry about catching autism, or wonder whether there is something the matter with them, too. In addition, they may feel guilty about any negative thoughts they have toward their sibling. For example, the envy they feel about the extra time you spend with your child with autism can arouse feelings of guilt. Sometimes children attempt to make up for their sibling's problems by trying to be especially well behaved. They may become excessively helpful and obedient beyond limits that are good for them, for your family, or for the child with autism. Other children may respond by deliberately misbehaving as a way to draw your attention to themselves and away from their sibling.

For most of their elementary school years, your other children will have conflicting emotions about their brother or sister with a disability. One moment they may feel good about being needed by their sibling with autism, and the next moment they may think she is a pest. When other children tease their sibling, they may defend her, and then again, they may not. They may resent having to do chores that their brother or sister is unable to do, or complain that you are unfairly babying your child with autism.

Adolescence. More than anything, most teenagers want to conform—to fit in with the right crowd. They become acutely aware of even minor differences between themselves and others. As a result, your teenaged children may be embarrassed by their brother or sister with autism when friends and dates come to the house or when you are all out in public together. Although they still love their sibling and want to help care for her, they may be torn by a natural desire for freedom and independence. They may resent all responsibilities imposed on them, not just responsibilities for their sibling with autism. In addition, they may begin to worry about their sibling's future, and what effect it may have on their own.

Dealing with Your Children's Emotions

Obviously, being the sibling of a child with autism can be just as stressful as being her parent. By and large, your other children will try to follow your lead in coping with this stress, but their adjustment may be complicated by conflicting emotions. They may feel ambivalent, for instance, about helping a sibling who is so disruptive and takes up so much precious parent time. They may at times feel unloved, rejected, embarrassed, or neglected, but attempt to hide their feelings or act them out in inappropriate ways. This means that before you can help your children deal with their emotions, you must first decipher what they are feeling. To do this effectively takes patience, observation, and listening.

Information. Parents do not have a monopoly on fear of the unknown. Brothers and sisters of children with autism also worry about the ways in which having a sibling with autism may affect them and their family. They may wonder whether they will always have to walk their sibling to school, for example, or worry that they may somehow cause her autism to continue or to get worse. As they grow older, they may begin to worry about having a child with autism of their own, or about caring for their sibling in the future.

The best way for you to anticipate and deal with such concerns is to provide your children with as much information about autism as they can absorb. Try to be as honest with your children as possible, but be sure that you present the information in a way that respects their ages and cognitive development. For example, don't tell your five-year-old son that his sister has a problem with social interactions. Tell him instead that his sister doesn't know how to play and has trouble learning. Timing is important too. A lot of information all at once can overwhelm your child. Try to recognize those times when just a little information now will plant a seed for more detailed information later. And whatever your children's ages, be prepared to correct the erroneous information they will undoubtedly pick up from classmates and adults.

Balance. Always remember that your child with autism is only part of your family, not the center of it. Even though your other children may not demand the emotional and physical resources their sibling does, they still have needs that should not be ignored.

It can be quite a juggling act, but it is important that you balance the many demands on your time so that all your children get their share of parental attention and have their fair share of responsibility. Otherwise siblings may become extremely jealous of the time you spend with your child with autism and resent her ability to obtain special treats for doing things they are expected to do automatically.

In addition to dividing your attention equitably, you need to impose a fair balance of household responsibilities. Children will not long tolerate being the servant of a sibling with autism without developing resentment. Everyone in the family should have to pull some weight, each according to his or her abilities. The key is to have expectations—to make your child with autism help in some way. It is almost more important for your children to feel you have expectations than it is for your child with autism to do a great deal.

An important part of balancing family responsibilities is to avoid turning one or more of your nondisabled children into a "parental child" by giving him or her too much responsibility. On the one hand, you should encourage brothers and sisters to take an active part in their sibling's educational and therapeutic programs—many parents find that doing so actually strengthens the bonds between their children. On the other hand, take care that responsibilities do not interfere with the emotional growth and development of the nondisabled sibling. For example, when a 16-year-old sister does not socialize with friends because she feels her mother depends on her to help with her brother with autism, it is not a healthy situation. Even if children seem ready to take on parental roles, they will resent being asked to grow up too quickly.

Balancing goes one step further: It is common advice—advice even given in this book—to celebrate the small victories of your child with autism. And this is good advice; parents of children with autism need to focus on small gains. You should remember, however, that your other children deserve the same treatment. They too have small victories of their own, and need to be noticed. Don't take their development, growth, education, or other achievements for granted. Celebrate everyone's victories—accomplishments are accomplishments regardless of whose they are.

Organization. It is all very well to stress the need for balance in your life, but how can you possibly cope with the seemingly endless demands on your attention? After all, there is only so much of you and only so many hours in the day. For many parents, the key lies in organizing their time. Having a child with autism can make this rather complicated, but it is worth the effort.

Of course, even the best-laid plans can be disrupted. Children do not conveniently schedule their crises. They scrape their knees, have nightmares, and fight with one another without advance notice, and when they do, they need your immediate, undivided attention. Barring unforeseen circumstances, however, there are many ways to manage your time so that your family runs more smoothly. Here are some ideas:

- Keep track of how much time you spend with each child. Try to spend some time alone with each child and your spouse.

- To prevent your other children from feeling neglected, try to schedule the periods that must be spent exclusively with your child with autism for times when siblings are not around.

- Encourage group play among all your children when they are at home.
- Keep your children busy. Schedule play times, chores, and outings.
- Enlist the help of others. Organize carpools and play groups and trade baby-sitting chores with other parents.

Individuality. One of the constant threads running through this book is that you should treat your child with autism as an individual. The same holds true for your other children. They need lives outside of the family. If their identity is not to be limited just to being the brother or sister of a child with autism, they need friends, social acceptance, and nonfamily responsibilities. Encourage them to try out many roles—athlete, artist, musician, astronomer—wherever their interests and talents lie. When children feel good about themselves as individuals, they are more likely to feel good about being part of a family with a member with a disability and to support both you and their sibling with autism.

Specialness. Besides encouraging your other children to be individuals, try to give them a sense of their own specialness. Help them to understand that having a sibling with autism also makes them special—in the positive sense of the word. Point out ways they make an important difference in their sibling's life, for instance, or ways they help keep the family running smoothly. Praise their compassion, their coping abilities, and the extra responsibilities they take on. In short, let your children know that they are needed by you and their sibling with autism, and that their contributions are appreciated.

At the same time you are praising your other children's specialness, you need to recognize that, just like you, they may from time to time yearn to just be ordinary. Being the sibling of a child with autism sometimes brings with it unwanted distinction outside the family and a lack of attention in the family. Helen Featherstone writes:

> Listening to normal brothers and sisters talk about family life, I am struck by a paradox about disability. In the world outside the family, in school and in the neighborhood, children long to fit in, to resemble everyone else. In these contexts...a sibling's disability stigmatizes them as different. Inside the family, however, each child wants to be special. Each needs assurance that he occupies a unique place in the

family circle. Here disability confers a certain advantage, a passport to special attention, recognition, and privileges. In consequence, many able-bodied brothers and sisters remember a childhood tinged by jealousy and resentment.

There is no foolproof advice for overcoming this dilemma. Common sense, however, dictates that parents give their typical children the chance to be special when they want that and the chance to be just like everyone else when they need that.

Dealing with Problems

No matter how carefully you follow the suggestions in the preceding pages, having a child with autism in the family will inevitably create problems for your child's brothers and sisters. Other children may wound them with teasing or cruel remarks about their sibling, and adults, too, may sometimes confuse them with insensitive comments. As peer acceptance and social interaction become more important to your children, they are likely to be increasingly embarrassed by their sibling. Furthermore, at some point in their lives, your children are bound to resent the added responsibilities that go with having a sibling with autism, and they may fervently wish that their family were not "different."

Although your first instinct may be to try to heal your children's emotional pain yourself—to set things right by telling off everyone who makes your children feel bad about having a sibling with a disability— you should fight the urge to rescue. Instead teach your children to cope with their feelings themselves. Acknowledge your children's hurt and confusion, but also let them know that you have confidence in them and their ability to handle those hurts. Share with them hurtful experiences you have had, and explain how you responded. And by all means make sure your children understand that the autism is to blame for their sibling's behavior, not the sibling herself. Not only is it healthier for your children to turn their anger and resentment away from their sibling and toward her autism, but it can also help to reduce their feelings of guilt.

Remember, no parent can solve every problem for his or her children. Even attempting to do so can often do more harm than good. Just as you can adversely affect the development of your child with autism by trying to do too much for her, so too can you prevent your other children from learning to cope on their own. If you keep the lines of communication open and reassure and support your children with information and understanding, they will develop their own effective methods of coping, and without losing their love for their sibling or the friendship of their peers.

If your children have a great deal of trouble adjusting to their sibling with autism, you may want to consider counseling for them. Talking to an objective, caring professional can be just as helpful for children as it is for adults. Do not deny your children this help because you think that all problems need to be solved within the family. They don't. To seek help for your children is not an admission of failure, but an expression of love and concern. Sometimes giving your children room to adjust with the help of a counselor can accomplish what you cannot.

■■ Your Child with Autism and Your Marriage

Every marriage is unique; every relationship, a highly original blend of shared and divergent values, interests, and experiences. Regardless of each spouse's individual strengths and weaknesses, though, having a child with autism tends to create certain predictable problems in most marriages. All couples, for example, find that coping with their child's needs reduces the time they have to devote to one another. Relationships are further complicated by the strong, conflicting emotions each partner must deal with as the parent of a child with autism. And all couples are beset by worries about their child's future and the long-term effects her continued dependency may have on their marriage.

In general, if your relationship with your spouse is strong, your marriage can withstand the added stress that goes with having a child with autism. Some parents even feel that their child has drawn them closer together. Whether having a child with autism will have a positive effect on *your* marriage depends on the support you and your spouse give each other.

As discussed earlier, one of the best ways to support one another is to openly share your feelings about your child with autism. Remember, it is normal for your emotions to run the gamut from love to hate; from hope to despair. In most cases, if you share and acknowledge these feelings, you can sort them out together, or together you can seek someone to help you cope.

If one or both of you falls into the trap of misdirected anger, however, it may be somewhat harder for you to rescue one another emotionally. As Chapter 2 explained, parents often become angry after learning that their child has autism. They may fume at God, the obstetrician, or at the genetic counselor who did not recommend against having another child. They may also be angry at the child for all the expense and sleepless nights she costs the family. It is *absolutely* normal for parents to experience anger and frustration temporarily in resolving their feelings about their child and their new circumstances. But it is when a spouse's anger continues over time and becomes directed at his or her partner that it is most damaging.

Sometimes one parent will blame the other for the child's autism—"If you hadn't drunk so much wine during your pregnancy, this never would have happened" or "This is all due to the marijuana you smoked in college." If the accused spouse believes the charges are true, he or she may feel tremendous guilt, while the accusing spouse may withdraw emotionally and leave the guilt-ridden spouse feeling even more angry and alone. In another scenario, a husband or wife may be furious at the child with autism for disrupting career and future plans. Because the husband or wife feels very guilty about being angry at a little child with a severe disability, however, he or she turns that anger on his or her spouse. Constructive communication breaks down, and emotional withdrawal follows.

Some couples manage to avoid the pitfall of misdirected anger, but still find themselves drifting apart because the demands of raising a child with autism leave them so exhausted. As Chapter 2 discussed, the key is not to find time for each other, but to *make* time. As mentioned before, everyone in your family suffers if your child with autism destroys your marriage, and the biggest loser would be your child with autism. Staying together should be your highest priority, even if that affects the time you can spend teaching, training, and working with your child with autism.

You may also want to investigate opportunities for respite care in your community. Respite care is skilled child care provided by people trained to work with children with disabilities. It can be for a few hours each week, or for a weekend. Some agencies provide care in your home, while others have the child brought to a respite worker's home. Public and private agencies generally provide this service. Check with local chapters of the Autism Society or The Arc (formerly called the Association for Retarded Citizens) or ACL in your area for availability. Sometimes, parents find that a few hours or a weekend alone goes a long way in restoring energy.

Sharing the responsibility for caring and working with your child with autism is a very useful way for couples to cope with the added stress. No spouse should feel that he or she has been consigned to endless daily care. Allow each spouse to have successes inside and outside the family. It is important that each spouse retain the self-image he or she had before your child with autism was born. In some marriages, it is helpful for spouses to attend separate support groups. This allows each to voice concerns and feelings they may hesitate to confide to their spouse.

One final stress that you, like all parents of children with autism, must cope with is your uncertainty about your child's future. Whether you express your concerns or not, you and your spouse probably worry constantly about your child's education, her future prospects for employment, and her ability to live independently. Although you will want to find more information about these subjects later, in the meanwhile you must learn to live one day at a time. Concentrate on the small gains your child makes, and rejoice in her personal triumphs. And whatever you do, don't spend so much time thinking about getting your child to her destination that you forget to enjoy the parts of the ride that truly are fun.

Single-Parent Families

Sadly some marriages fail. Although there may be a number of reasons for marriage failure, a child with autism obviously puts a great deal of stress on any relationship. Sometimes a marriage—already teetering—will topple under the weight of this extra stress. When this happens, one parent is left with the major responsibility for raising the child with autism. Of course, single-parent families with children with autism can also result from a variety of other causes.

A single parent raising a child with autism experiences the same range of reactions and needs that couples do. Coping, however, may be considerably harder because the single parent must make important decisions alone. You may be able to lessen the burden somewhat by asking someone you trust to serve as your sounding board. You could turn to a close friend, a member of the clergy, your brother or sister (but *not* the siblings of the child with autism), a therapist, or a social service worker. What matters is that you have someone to talk to who will be available on a consistent basis—someone who will offer you support, but who will not be afraid to question your decisions, either. Often just knowing that there is someone with whom you can discuss your concerns can help reduce some of the overwhelming feelings of being on your own with your child every day.

■■ Conclusion

The secrets to adapting to a child with autism are really not secrets at all, but just common sense. Just as in any family, hard work, love, acceptance, communication, and support can all help. If you try to see your child with autism as a child first, and then as a person with autism, you can go a long way toward normalizing family life. True, your child with autism has needs and strengths that are probably very different from the needs and strengths of other family members. But she is still an individual, with her own unique contributions to make to your family. With hard work and encouragement, she can become a vital part of your family. And with your loving, educated leadership, your family can become a team.

The realization that a child's autism will not go away is a severe blow for many families. It may seem incredible to you right now, but most families survive. They also work, play, laugh, cry, fight, and grow—just like other families. But for the family with a child with autism, there is much more. Having a child with autism in the family teaches lessons of a higher order, lessons other families may never have the chance to learn: love, commitment, mercy, contentment, sacrifice, and dignity. In short, in my experience working with families, I have found that having a child with autism often ennobles parents and siblings. Clara Claiborne Park, in her outstanding book, *The Siege*, says it well:

> This experience [raising a child with autism] we did not choose, which we would have given anything to avoid, has made us different, has made us better. Through it we have learned the lesson that no one studies willingly, the hard, slow lesson...that one grows by suffering....I write now...that if today I were given the choice to accept the experience, with everything that it entails, or to refuse the bitter largesse, I would have to stretch out my hands—because out of it has come, for all of us, an unimagined life.

■■ References

So much of what I have learned about families has been learned from the best of teachers: the families of the children with autism in New

Jersey, New York, Maryland, and Connecticut who have opened their lives to me. I owe them a debt of gratitude. In addition to my own work, I must acknowledge the debt to others whose writings I have incorporated into this chapter.

Featherstone, Helen. *A Difference in the Family: Life with a Disabled Child.* New York: Viking, 1980.

Harris, Sandra L. *Families of the Developmentally Disabled.* Elmsford, NY: Pergamon, 1983.

Park, Clara Claiborne. *The Siege: The First Eight Years of an Autistic Child with an Epilogue, Fifteen Years Later.* New York: Little, Brown, 1982.

:: Parent Statements

My relatives spent the first four years thinking my son's autism would disappear with lots of work and effort. They would fax me articles, tape TV shows, call doctors, anything that might give us the "cure". Now that they know it's not going away, they've stopped expecting as much from him. He gets away with stuff he wouldn't at home. They don't realize my son has to work twice as hard as their kids do.

⋅⚘⋅

I share things I learn about autism with my group, or I go and read differ-ent things about autism, or I talk to my intimate friends. But my husband and family don't want to hear these kinds of details because they don't want to deal with that term. They want to hear about Tommy's progress.

⋅⚘⋅

Having a child with autism makes a strong marriage just slightly weaker. I'm afraid to think what it would do to a weak marriage.

⋅⚘⋅

Our family has had its fair share of challenges with three boys, ages five, nine, and four years. Our two older children are currently non-verbal and still in diapers. The additional stresses of an unemployed spouse and a non-supportive, budget-driven school administration, that detoured us into litigation, were more than our marriage could withstand.

⋅⚘⋅

Prior to having children, my husband and I had a life full of the average trials and tribulations. These struggles helped build our love, strengthen our bond, and increase communication. Having a child with autism has tested our relationship and made it even stronger.

❧

Lawrence has had a positive and negative effect on our marriage. On the positive side, he forced two extremely independent people to lean more on each other. Before we had Lawrence, we both felt we could handle anything life threw our way—even without each other. After Lawrence, we changed our minds in a hurry. On the negative side, raising Lawrence leaves us very little time or energy to devote to each other.

❧

The rewards of parenting a child with autism can be many. Our son doesn't call us Mommy or Daddy unless asked to, but the love and affection he shows us makes up for that.

❧

Our two daughters have been able to accept him as he is, but his brother has had a very difficult time. We should have had family counseling when we started down this road, but I put up this shield all around us and vowed to take care of everybody. It was a huge mistake.

❧

At one point our daughter would only eat crunchy foods. Later, only mushy foods would do. My other children had to sit at the dinner table and eat the nutritional food I served while their sister ate ice cream. It was difficult to explain to them why only she could have sweets for dinner. But now the kids know exceptions have to be made for their sister with autism. They realize there are a lot of things they get to do that she cannot.

❧

I don't feel that Michael has affected my relationship with his older brother at all. As with any family, every child is different. I have always treated my kids equally, being conscious of who they are and what needs they have.

❧

We are a family, and that means we do things together as much as possible. If there is something Pete physically cannot do, he stays home *just for that activity. You can't restrict your other children's lives because of one child. It feeds resentment.*

❧

Our daughter seems to take Lawrence's handicap in stride. So far she's managed to enjoy a normal, active life. And I think it's done her some good to be exposed to Lawrence and to the kids in his school. She's very comfortable around kids with disabilities, while most of her peers are frightened of them.

❧

Janet was out one day and one of the kids pushed her. Janet just kind of stood there, and her sister, Becky, went up and pushed the other kid. It was like she was saying, "You don't push my sister." So, it's kind of automatic for her. I think they just know, you don't do that, not until they can push back.

❧

The significance of our son's life has never been overshadowed by the significance of his disability. Each day he wakes smiling, ready to face new challenges. His goodness is sincere and true. He's taught us to focus on the small blessings. They are there, you just may have to look harder.

❧

The other day I was chatting with a woman I had a nodding acquaintance with at the gym. I was telling her about my family and she said how lucky I was to have three children and a husband I loved. She said she wished she had my life, that it was what she had always wanted. I was about to tell her one of my children was autistic, and my life wasn't so perfect but I stopped myself. Whose life is perfect anyway?

❧

There's nothing more wonderful than visiting extended family members who have not seen my son in months or even years and to witness their delighted shock when they see how he has improved.

❧

Four of my five children always get to go to relatives' houses to spend the day or even sleep over. Elisa never gets invited. I have to remind myself that it is not because they do not love her but because they're afraid. I understand their fear but it still hurts.

❧

My brother means a lot to me. I worry that people will pick on him and he won't be able to defend himself.

❧

Sometimes I get confused and angry with him because he doesn't listen. He has to get his own way or I have to give in.

❧

Siblings have to know how much you appreciate the help and sacrifices they make.

❧

My mom spends more time with him than me, but I know it's because of his autism.

❧

We still hug. We still give kisses and love.

6

YOUR CHILD'S DEVELOPMENT

Sandra L. Harris, Ph.D.

Mothers and fathers the world over delight in watching their children grow and learn. After all, sharing in a child's achievements—his first faltering steps and first garbled words—is one of the greatest rewards of parenthood. What makes this complex process of growth and change, called *development,* especially exciting for parents is the knowledge that each new skill their child learns takes him further along the road from dependency to maturity.

In observing their children's development, most parents cannot help comparing their children's achievements with other children's. This is a natural impulse. It is also natural for parents to feel proud and elated when their child progresses faster than normal; fearful and discouraged when he lags behind. As the parent of a child with autism, you may find this process of comparison disheartening indeed.

If your child has just been diagnosed with autism, a little knowledge about the ways this disorder affects development may calm some of your anxiety. To begin with, it can help you to learn what lies in your child's future and what his needs will be. And it can help you even more to learn that your child, like every child, is going to grow and change in the years ahead, and that you can do a great deal to help him reach his maximum potential.

This chapter provides you with some of the information you will need in order to influence your child's development most effectively. It will introduce you to the basics of human development and help you to understand not only how autism affects your child's development, but also how a good educational program and consistent, loving care can make a critical difference in your child's life.

As you read this chapter, bear in mind that autism affects different children in different ways. Some children with autism have average or above average intellectual ability, while others have varying degrees of mental retardation. Some children with autism are profoundly withdrawn, while others are more sociable. And some children with autism have seizures or other physical disabilities, while others do not. As this chapter explains, all of these factors can affect a child's long-term development.

** What is Development?

Before you can put your child's development into perspective, you need a basic understanding of human development in general. Actually, you may already know quite a bit about typical development—it was probably the differences in your child's development that led you to seek help to begin with. For example, if you have older children, you may have realized that your child with autism was not developing in the same way as the others did; if you did not have other children, you may have seen that your child was different from nieces, nephews, or neighbor children. Perhaps you noticed that your child was not babbling or did not seem to be forming an emotional attachment to you. Then again, you may have seen some odd behaviors like handflapping, body rocking, or resistance to change in routine. In short, because you had some idea of how children typically develop, you knew that your child was not progressing normally. What you didn't know was why.

No one knows exactly why children with autism develop as they do. But we do know that all human development depends largely on biological programming—that is, your child's genetic makeup lays the foundation for the way he grows and acquires skills, or develops. Other factors—environmental, psychological, and cultural—also play roles in human development.

Because so many variables are involved, no child's developmental profile is quite the same. For example, one child may say his first words several months earlier than another child, but learn to stand several months later. One child may move step by step through the sitting-crawling-walking sequence, while another may skip the crawling stage completely. In other words, no child progresses at exactly the same rate or in the same sequence as any other.

For the most part, however, children tend to develop from top to bottom. That is, they can suck before they can grasp, and sit before they can stand. A child will be able to use his hands before he can control his legs. Children also become increasingly refined in their movements the more they develop. For example, when a baby is excited, his whole body wiggles with delight, while an older child may simply smile.

The development of all children can be divided into six areas: 1) gross motor; 2) fine motor; 3) cognition; 4) language; 5) social; and 6) self-help. Some working definitions follow:

Gross Motor. In gross motor development, your child learns to control his body by using his large muscles, including those in his legs, arms, and abdomen. Rolling over, sitting up, crawling, and walking are all basic gross motor skills. More advanced gross motor skills include running and climbing. These skills give your child the tools to explore his world and are the foundation for growth in other areas.

Fine Motor. In fine motor development, your child learns to make precise, detailed movements with smaller muscles, such as those in the fingers and hands. Skills like picking up small objects, using the index finger to poke and probe, and squeezing soft objects are all important fine motor skills. So too are control of eye muscles, and facial and tongue movements.

Communication. Development of communication is usually divided into two areas: the acquisition of receptive language and the acquisition of expressive language. Receptive language is the ability to understand words and gestures. Expressive language is the ability to use gestures, words, and written symbols to communicate. In most children, the understanding of a word—its receptive use—usually precedes its expressive use, but in children with autism this is not always the case.

Cognition. A good working definition of cognition is the ability to reason and solve problems. In the early stages of your child's cognitive development, he comes to understand that objects do not cease to exist when they are out of sight (the concept of object permanence); grasps the principle of cause and effect; and learns to draw conclusions from experience. Mastering these skills enables your child to understand how the world works and how he can manipulate his environment.

Social. Your child's social development affects his ability to interact with people. From birth onward, children learn how to respond appropriately to themselves and others. For example, they learn to take turns, share their toys, form attachments to other people, and assert their independence. These are important skills that help children develop into functioning members of society.

Self-Help. In this area of development, your child learns how to take care of himself. He progresses from total dependence on you for his survival to being able to look after himself. Some important self-help skills include dressing, feeding, and toileting.

A seventh area, *sensory ability*, is not usually considered a separate area of development itself, because it is so closely tied to development in all the other areas. In sensory development, your child acquires the ability to process sensations like touch, sound, light, smell, and movement. These skills are refined as your child grows, and they affect all areas of development. A good example of sensory differences of some children with autism is their discomfort with cuddling. Hugs, which bring such pleasure to typical children, may be physically unpleasant for children with autism. Another common sensory difference is the over-or underreaction to sound some children with autism have. For example, your child may cover his ears in response to a sound typical children would ignore or find interesting.

The sensory problems common to children with autism may not only be unpleasant for your child or appear odd to bystanders, they may also limit some of your child's developmental opportunities. For example, a child who is upset by certain noises or who cannot tolerate certain kinds of touch may avoid those experiences and be reluctant to go places in the community where those kinds of stimulation are present. Similarly a child who engages in a great deal of self-stimulatory behavior, such as handflapping or light gazing, may be regarded as odd by other people who may tend to avoid him.

Because these areas of development are all controlled by genetic and environmental factors, a problem in either a child's genetic makeup or in the environment can disrupt the normal process of development. For example, it is possible to inherit a genetic defect which will lead to differences or problems in physical growth. The person we call "dwarfed" stays physically tiny even as other areas of development proceed normally. In contrast, a person might be born with the genetic potential for normal physical development, but fail to reach full height because of an environmental factor like inadequate nutrition.

Fortunately, environmental factors do not always have a negative effect on development. In fact, when positive environmental factors are deliberately optimized, development can be dramatically enhanced. For example, speech and language therapy can help a child with a severe speech problem develop communication skills; physical therapy and a rigorous exercise program can help a child with weak muscles gain better control of his movements. Particularly when a child has a developmental disability like autism, *intervention*—direct, intensive involvement in development—can make a critical difference.

∷ How Do Children Develop?

In human development, there are no hard-and-fast age limits for the achievement of basic developmental skills such as walking and talking. Children can achieve these skills—called "milestones"—at different rates and in different sequences and still be considered "normal." For example, some "normal" children may sit up much earlier than other "normal" children, or say their first words later. Because children do develop within a fairly broad range, the realization that a child has a developmental disorder may sometimes be delayed. Physicians and parents may expect a child to "outgrow" a problem or may explain away a delay with statements like: "He's a boy and boys are slower to talk," or "He's just lazy because all his older sisters and brothers do things for him." When a physician reassures the parents of a "normal" child that "He'll outgrow this," he or she is often right. Unfortunately, this is seldom the case for the child with autism.

To give you a yardstick to measure your child's development against, we will look first at how "normal" children develop in several

:: TABLE 1. SOME NORMAL DEVELOPMENT MILESTONES

Age	Social	Communication	Motor
10 Mo.	Waves bye-bye	Says mama, dada + one word	Sits indefinitely
12 Mo.	Cooperates with dressing	2 words	Walks with hand held
18 Mo.	Hugs a doll	10 words	Walks fast Scribbles
24 Mo.	Asks for toilet Puts on simple garments Parallel play	3 word sentences Uses I, me, you Refers to self by name	Walks up & down alone Imitates vertical strokes
36 Mo.	Feeds self Pours from pitcher	Uses plurals Tells sex	Alternates feet on stairs Rides tricycle
48 Mo.	Washes & dries hands & face	Names colors	Throws over-hand

key areas. Some typical achievements in the areas of cognitive, communication, social-emotional, and motor development are summarized in Table 1, and discussed in more detail below.

:: Cognitive Development

The term "cognition" refers to our ability to know or understand our environment. For an infant, this means acquiring information about the most basic aspects of life and about his relationship to the rest of the world. In the first year of life, for instance, a baby learns that objects have weight, size, taste, and feel, and that people look and sound different. Between 18 and 24 months, the young child begins to develop an imagination and can pretend, for example, that a doll is alive. From about two years to seven years, the child becomes adept at thinking in abstract terms and no longer needs to see or touch an object in order to learn about it. The young child also learns to devise solutions to problems, but is still limited by an inability to take many different dimensions of a problem into account at once. In later childhood, the "normal" child becomes more skilled at thinking in abstractions, and, by adolescence, can manipulate mathematical equations, understand that there may be several different explanations for the same event, and speak in metaphor (for example, "this room is a pig sty"). All through childhood, cognitive development has a profound effect on development in other areas, but particularly on a child's ability to use language.

■■ Motor Skills

Typically, the development of gross and fine motor skills goes hand in hand. For example, during the first eight months of life while a baby is learning to use his large muscles in turning over, sitting, and crawling, he is also learning to control smaller muscles by following movements with his eyes, reaching, and transferring objects from hand to hand. By 24 months of age, the fine motor skills of the typical child are so highly developed that he can pick up objects as small as a crumb, and his gross motor skills are so refined that he can walk upstairs with two feet to a step. These motor behaviors continue to grow more complex through early childhood as the child learns to throw, catch, skip, jump rope, and run in a smoothly coordinated fashion. By adolescence the human body has developed into a beautifully coordinated mechanism that moves with speed and grace.

■■ Communication

The development of communication skills parallels the child's growing motor abilities. At 28 weeks, most babies play with vowel sounds ("ah-ah-ah," "uh-uh-uh"); by 32 weeks, they have added consonants ("da," "ha," "ma"); and by 36 weeks, they will imitate sounds like coughs or tongue clicks and also respond to their names. At 40 weeks, the typical baby uses "mama" and "dada" to refer to those very important people in his world, and will probably have another word in his repertoire as well. At a little over a year, most babies say three or four words and demonstrate an even greater receptive (understanding) vocabulary. By 18 months, they point to objects when requested and have a vocabulary of perhaps ten words.

Over the next six months, the average toddler makes an enormous leap forward in language abilities. He adds about 200 words to his speaking vocabulary, learns to string two or three words together in simple sentences ("want juice"), and begins to use "what" questions. These skills develop so rapidly that by age three, he talks in three-word sentences, asks "where" and "who" questions, and has a speaking vocabulary of perhaps 500 words. By six, the child knows 1500 to 2000 words and has mastered very complex sentence forms. As he grows, the youngster becomes fully fluent, while continuing to develop an increasingly sophisticated and technical vocabulary that reflects his individual interests.

:: Social-Emotional Development

Normally, a baby's emotional and social development follows a fairly predictable pattern. By as early as two months, a baby will smile back if you talk and nod to him, and will follow your movement with his eyes. At 16 weeks, he recognizes his bottle and smiles when people approach. By eight months, the child is so skilled at recognizing family members that strangers may frighten him. This distress usually disappears by about 12 months of age, to be replaced by another kind of emotional concern—that of separation anxiety. In this phase, the toddler may be reluctant to be without his mother or father, but may be quite content and secure as long as one or both parents is nearby.

During the preschool years, the "normal" child begins to learn important things about self and feelings. He learns how to distinguish gender (am I a boy or a girl?), how to deal with strong emotions, and how to recognize feelings in other people. As he begins to explore his immediate world and his relationships within it, he may often react with shyness, fearfulness, aggression, or anger. The preschool child plays jointly with other children and may act out the roles of his mother, father, or teacher in pretend play.

After he enters school, the typical child begins to form special friendships. Peer relationships gradually take on more and more significance, while the family begins to decline as a source of influence. By late adolescence, the child is well on the road to emotional and social self-sufficiency.

:: Development of the Child with Autism

Children with autism follow a developmental course similar to other children. They walk before they run and use single words before sentences. However, their development is often uneven. For example, your child with autism may be at age level in gross motor skills, but well behind in social development. This is even more true of children with more severe symptoms than those with milder symptoms. The areas of communication and socialization are most vulnerable to this delay. However, even in  the area of motor ability, children with autism may show some differences from other children. For example, they are less likely to be consistent in preferring either their right or their left hand.

As the parent of a child with autism, you know that your child deviated in troubling ways from the usual patterns of cognitive, communication, and social-emotional development. Your child's *motor* skills, on the other hand, may have developed right on schedule, or just a little slower than normal, unless some kind of physical disability affected his motor development. Indeed, watching your child learn to roll over, sit up, and walk on time may have reassured you that all was well. Perhaps it was not until more complex social and communication skills failed to emerge that your child's growth really began to worry you.

Most parents of children with autism do not begin to be seriously concerned about their child's development until late in the first year, although in retrospect they will recall problems from an early point. Videotapes of children with autism show that they behave differently at their first birthday party when compared to other children. Typically, a child's autistic symptoms increase gradually through the second year, peak between the ages of two and four, and then improve somewhat.

It is encouraging to know that children diagnosed with autism today have a somewhat better long term outlook than children diagnosed 10 or 15 years ago. This may be especially true for their language and cognitive skills, but less true for their social skills. The more limited a child's skills at an early age, the less progress he is likely to make over time. The degree of spontaneous improvement your child will make depends on the severity of his symptoms: less impaired children who receive appropriate intervention may experience such a dramatic decrease in abnormal behaviors that they may no longer seem autistic by the time they reach school age; children whose problems are very severe from an early age will probably continue to have problems. In any case, if you have a very young child with autism, you can expect his behavior to change for the better in the next couple of years. Early and intensive intervention can make a big difference.

Table 2 summarizes some of the developmental differences and difficulties that autism can cause. You may wish to refer to this table for a brief overview of some of the problems in language, social, and other developmental areas that may arise for your child with autism. The following sections discuss these developmental difficulties in more detail and also offer you some practical advice about helping your child overcome problem behaviors.

** Cognitive Development in Children with Autism

Even among normally developing people, there is wide variation in cognitive or intellectual abilities. Although most of us can be described as "about average," there are some people who are very bright and others whose ability is well below average. People with below-average intellectual abilities are said to have "mental retardation." These cognitive abilities can be measured by IQ tests, as well as by how people cope with daily life.

Most children with autism have intellectual abilities that are well below average. In fact, about 70 percent of these youngsters have mental retardation, while only 30 percent are of normal to above average ability. Children whose abilities are within the normal range can often master much of the material in a regular school curriculum, but still show the symptoms of autism.

Many parents find the distinction between autism and mental retardation a confusing one. It may be helpful to recall that most children who have mental retardation develop language and social skills that are consistent with their intellectual abilities, while the child with autism typically has language and social skills that fall below his skills

:: TABLE 2.   EARLY SYMPTOMS OF AUTISM
(NEWBORN TO 5 YEARS)

Newborn to 6 Months
- May be "too good"
- May be irritable, easily distressed
- Does not reach to be picked up
- Does not babble
- Lack of social smile
- Lack of eye contact
- Motor development may appear normal

6 Months to 12 Months
- Does not cuddle, may be limp or rigid when held
- Relative indifference toward parents
- Does not play simple social games ("Peek-a-boo," "Bye-bye")
- Does not begin to use words
- Does not seem interested in baby toys
- May be fascinated with own hands
- Uneven or delayed motor development
- May not chew or accept solid foods

2 Years to 3 Years
- Interpersonal interest still limited; may show some improvement
- Uses other people as "tools"
- Limited eye contact
- May sniff or lick objects
- Does not cuddle, may be limp or rigid when held
- Relative indifference toward parents

4 Years to 5 Years
- If speech develops, there may be echolalia (Repeats in rote fashion what others say, either immediately or later)
- Odd voice quality (high-pitched or monotone, for example)
- Very upset by changes in routine
- Eye contact still limited; may show some improvement
- Gradual increase in affection, but still limited
- Tantrums and aggression continue, but may gradually improve
- Self-injury
- Self-stimulation

in other areas. A young person with autism who does not have mental retardation may be quite proficient at many basic academic subjects, but still speak in a peculiar fashion and be very limited in his ability to negotiate the emotional world of childhood. And although he may learn to follow a set of rules which govern social interaction, his interactions usually lack the smooth, spontaneous quality which marks most people's relationships. By contrast, a child with autism and mental retardation will typically learn more slowly, have more limited speech, and less awareness of other people than will a child with autism without mental retardation.

Regardless of whether your child with autism is among the majority who show some mental retardation, or that smaller percentage who have higher skills, you will want to ensure that your child is exposed to a wide range of opportunities to learn from the environment. Repeated opportunities to celebrate holidays, go to the grocery store, watch children's programs on television, and learn the cause-and-effect relationships among the many routinely occurring events at home and in the community will help your child collect a fund of knowledge about the world and about how to cope with day-to-day activities. Children with lower intellectual abilities will need more repeated exposure in smaller chunks, but every child with autism can learn over time. As they enter adolescence most young people remain stable in intellectual ability, a small group show an increase in IQ, and an even smaller group a decrease in IQ.

Language Development in Children with Autism

Probably one of the first symptoms of autism you noticed in your child was a failure to begin talking. In fact, studies of children with autism suggest that their language development may be abnormal from as early as two months of age. Babies with autism may not babble at all, may show less variety in their sounds, or may make primarily high-pitched squealing sounds.

Delays in language development are usually readily apparent by 12 months of age. While typically developing infants generally know "mama," "dada," and one other word by this time, babies with autism will generally not have learned any words, nor can they be coaxed into imitating their parents' nonsense sounds. At two, when normal toddlers are surging ahead in their language development—learning to speak in three-word sentences and constantly carrying on imaginary conversations with themselves—your child with autism may actually lose the use of those few words he has previously acquired.

Between the ages of four and five, the child with autism finally begins to make slow progress in language development. He may learn some words by rote, but will probably have only a limited ability to use them to communicate. At four years of age, only about a quarter of children with autism use speech meaningfully, and then only to express an immediate need—to ask for juice, for example. More than half of all children with autism still have no useful speech by this age, while an additional 25 percent are *echolalic*— they can parrot other people's words, but without understanding. Having some useful speech by two years of age is a favorable sign for future development.

Over time, all children with autism do make gains in language development. Even young people who are so severely impaired that they never develop functional speech acquire at least some skill in understanding language. Other young people with autism may eventually develop near-normal speech, and find their ability to communicate hampered only by a lack of voice inflection that makes their speech sound somewhat mechanical. Most children with autism fall somewhere between these two extremes.

Regardless of the severity of your child's autism, there are ways you can help him develop his language skills to the fullest. These techniques are best learned under the direction of an experienced speech therapist or teacher, and include such strategies as using simple language with your child, insisting that he use the language he has, and providing reinforcing responses to your child's attempts to communicate.

Social Development in Children with Autism

Next to your child's language delays, you probably found his lack of progress in social development most alarming. Although most children with autism (roughly two out of three) do not actually begin to withdraw until around two years of age, parents usually notice other problems in social development long before that. In the first few months, for instance, it may have bothered you that your child would not reach to be picked up as other children do, or that he never smiled. At one year of age, your child may have stiffened when you held him and seemed completely uninterested in playing typical baby games like waving "bye-bye." Also in contrast to "normal" children, your child probably showed little or no separation anxiety when left alone or with strangers.

Despite these early differences in social development, you—like most parents—were still probably caught off guard by the new problems that began to surface around your child's second birthday. When your child began to withdraw from the outside world and engage in self-stimulation behaviors like hand flapping, whirling, or staring, you may have tried to link the change to some major event in your child's life—an illness or the birth of a sibling, perhaps. In fact, there is no reason to believe that these experiences help trigger a child's withdrawal. As explained earlier, autism is caused by biological factors, and certainly not by child-rearing practices.

As with other developmental areas, the amount of progress your child will ultimately make in social development is related to his cognitive abilities. Children who are more intellectually impaired usually show fewer changes, while children who are less impaired make more progress. Be assured, though, that your child *will* make strides in social development. Many children will be less aloof as they get older, although they also seek less comfort from others.

Usually, the social behavior of a child with autism takes a turn for the better beginning around the age of four. For instance, your child may continue to engage in self-stimulation or self-injury, but may also begin to show some affection toward family members. And although he may still become very upset at changes in routine, the frequency and intensity of his tantrums may decrease. Preschool peer relationships, however, remain a problem; children with autism have limited peer relationships because they enjoy little if any interactive play and may show little imagination in their play.

As they enter adolescence, most young people with autism become more flexible in how they respond to their environment and pose fewer behavior management problems, although a small percentage of teenagers with autism show an increase in the need to maintain constancy in their environment. The child whose need for routine limited his activities in earlier years may become more able to tolerate some change, while the child who had tantrums when frustrated may have developed the communication skills to diminish the need for this disruptive behavior.

Teenagers with milder forms of autism may develop an interest in other people; but may have trouble approaching them and interacting with them in satisfying ways. It is very rare for a youth with autism to develop a truly intimate friendship. For some young people with autism, this can be a source of distress as they begin to recognize the gap between themselves and others. Other adolescents and adults with autism who function at a lower intellectual level may remain profoundly withdrawn, but perhaps show more attachment to their family than they did when they were younger. Whatever their cognitive abilities, young people with autism typically remain very limited in their ability to be sensitive to other people's feelings. The subtle cues that would tell us we had offended another person, or that someone was pleased or annoyed with us, may not be picked up by the person with autism. As a result, even those people with autism who can hold jobs in the regular work force may need help in managing their relationships with peers and supervisors.

What about other problem areas in social development—aggression, tantrums, and self-injury? Do these change with age? We know that for a small group, hyperactive behavior, aggression, destruction, and self-stimulation tend to worsen as the child gets older. Because these behaviors may not improve with age, it is very important that they be thoroughly treated in childhood. After all, aggression that is tolerable in a five-year-old would be unbearable in a 20-year-old.

In general, it is not as easy to influence the social development of a child with autism as it is to influence his language development, but there are still many ways you can help your child grow. One of the most useful steps you can take is to ensure that your child is exposed to a range of social experiences. Although your child may not at first seem interested in or responsive to other people, it is nonetheless important that you keep trying. Keep the social contact short so that your child does not find the experience too unpleasant, but do not give in to your child's desire to remain alone. Do not rely only on the classroom for providing opportunities for socialization. The experience of learning to be with others needs to extend beyond school to the world outside the classroom.

Other Developmental Problems

Along with social and language problems, children with autism often experience developmental delays in acquiring self-help skills. Learning to use the toilet, for example, may be an especially large stumbling block for many children. While most typically developing children are toilet trained between the ages of two and three, nearly half of all children with autism are still not toilet trained by the age of four. In addition, many children with autism have trouble acquiring good feeding habits. As infants, they may refuse to chew or eat solid foods; later on they may binge for months at a time on one particular food.

A third problem area for many children with autism is developing normal sleeping patterns. Particularly between the ages of two and three, many children with autism resist going to sleep and wake up frequently during the night. Although it is not unusual for a normal preschooler to climb into his mother's or father's bed when he has been frightened by a nightmare, the child with autism may not be able to sleep alone until well into childhood. Sleep disturbances are covered fully in Chapter 4.

As Chapters 1 and 4 explain, parents can fight these self-help problems with a variety of behavior modification (applied behavior analysis) strategies. Some of these techniques may help your child and some may not; some may help him sometimes and not other times. Do not be surprised if you do not immediately discover a strategy that works, but do not be discouraged either. It may take a lot of hard work from you and your child, but eventually you *will* see gratifying improvement in your child's self-help skills. It may also be wise to give your child more time to mature before you tackle hard problems like toilet training. For example, if your child does not respond readily to training at three years of age, wait until he is four.

▪▪ What to Expect for Your Own Child

You undoubtedly have serious concerns about what your child's current developmental differences mean for the years ahead. Will he ever start to speak? Will the self-stimulation that is so much a part of his daily routine ever decrease? Will your child's resistance to change ever diminish to the point where your family can lead a more normal life? When will he be toilet trained and sleep in his own bed?

No amount of general information could possibly set your mind at ease about your child's specific problems. Still, the information presented in this chapter about the general development of children with autism should help you make an educated projection of the long-term course of your child's development.

As Chapter 1 discusses, an expert in human development and autism such as a clinical child psychologist, pediatric neurologist, or other specialist can make an even more informed judgment. Since it may be helpful to that expert if you have records of your child's development, you may want to keep track of some of your child's unusual behaviors in a notebook.

▪▪ TABLE 3. BEHAVIOR CHECKLIST

- Eating pattern (for example, only eats a few foods or will not use utensils)
- Sleeping pattern (for example, wakes often at night or has trouble falling asleep)
- Toileting problems
- Self-stimulation (for example, rocks, waves fingers, or flips an object in front of eyes)
- Resistance to change
- Self-injury
- Tantrums
- Withdrawal (is not responsive to other people)
- Aggression (injures other people when frustrated)
- Echolalia (repeats in rote fashion what others say)
- Pronoun reversal (for example, says "you" for "I")
- Jargon in speech (makes up words that may not have obvious meaning to others)

Some common problem behaviors to look for are listed in Table 3, on page 171. If you copy this list into your notebook, then each time you notice one of these behaviors, you can simply jot down the date you first observed it. For instance, if your child starts refusing to stay in bed when he is two, you should make a note of it under "sleep disorders." You should also record observations about the ways your child's problem behaviors change over time. For example, if your child does a lot of body rocking between the ages of three and four, but then stops the behavior, you should make a note of both the date it starts and the date it stops. If you use special procedures like rewarding quiet sitting or appropriate play to help your child learn self-control of the behavior, put that in your notebook, too.

Besides keeping a record of your child's autistic behaviors, you should also get into the habit of describing your child's developmental achievements in a notebook. By referring to Table 4 below, you can make four charts: one each for recording your child's cognitive, com-

** TABLE 4. DEVELOPMENTAL MILESTONES

My Child's Cognitive Skills

- Searched for an object that was moved out of sight
- Recognized himself in mirror
- Counted to six
- Drew a picture of a person including a head, body, and arms or legs
- Remembered the main facts in a short story
- Printed letters or words with small and capital letters
- Named the days of the week
- Knew multiplication tables
- Did long division
- Read the newspaper

My Child's Communication Skills

- Babbled
- Said "Mama" and "Dada"
- First words
- Put 2 words together
- Put 3 words together
- Used name to refer to self
- Used "I," "Me," "You"
- Used plurals
- Named colors
- Asked questions
- Described pictures
- Talked about feelings of self and others

munication, social-emotional, and motor development. Then, whenever your child reaches one of the developmental milestones listed in Table 4, write down the date and a few examples of the new skill. For instance, the first time you notice your child using a two-word sentence, note the date, as well as exactly what he says.

When you compare your child's achievements with those on the normal developmental chart, do not be surprised if you find that your child is reaching the milestones not only at different ages, but also in a different order from the normal sequence. Some children with autism acquire skills in a different order than other children, while others may simply be slower, but pass through the same general patterns of development. In this respect, children with autism are just like any other children. Because each child has his own individual learning style, strengths, and weaknesses, it is normal for one child to develop differently than any other.

My Child's Social-Emotional Skills

- Reached to be picked up
- Waved "bye-bye"
- Cooperated with dressing by inserting arms or legs into clothing
- Hugged doll
- Pulled off shoes and socks
- Parallel play (played near another child on individual task)
- Used basic utensils such as spoon and fork
- Poured from pitcher
- Washed and dried hands and face
- Cooperative play (played with another child on single task)
- Dressed and undressed without help

My Child's Motor Skills

- Sat alone
- Crawled
- Walked with one hand held
- Walked well
- Scribbled with crayon
- Walked up and down stairs alone
- Copied vertical line
- Alternated feet on stairs
- Rode tricycle
- Copied circle
- Threw overhand
- Copied cross
- Skipped
- Copied triangle

▪▪ What Can You Do to Help?

First and foremost, you can shower your child with every bit of developmental help you can round up. Children with autism are eligible for publicly funded early infant education through local school districts. In these programs—described in Chapter 7—children receive early, intensive intervention aimed at maximizing their potential. Intensive early treatment is very important to the young child with autism, and you should be a firm advocate on behalf of your child in seeking these services.

Over the past decade, applied behavior analysis has been developed as an early treatment technique. The use of applied behavior analysis to structure the learning of a very young child with autism may have a significant impact on development. A number of recent studies have shown an increase in cognitive skills, adaptive behavior, and social skills among preschool-aged children with autism who receive intensive treatment for 30 to 40 hours per week. This treatment begins by increasing the child's compliance with simple directions and gradually moves to more complex skills, including speech, play, academic readiness, and social interaction. In the hands of a skilled treatment team, applied behavior analysis has the potential to shift the developmental path of some children. It is not, however, a panacea, and many children will continue to exhibit serious problems in spite of high quality treatment.

Where can you find these services? In addition to public school services, you may be able to make use of private teachers and therapists—especially if your medical insurance covers their services. Local organizations, advocacy groups, and other parents of children with autism will also gladly help you locate developmental aid for your child.

Finally, do not underestimate the enormous difference a supportive home environment can make in your child's life. Even though your child's autism is a biological disorder and his developmental progress is tied in some ways to that biology, taking the time now to teach your child social, language, and self-help skills will pay off in big ways later. The more time you spend with your child the better, but even 30 minutes a day devoted to home teaching as a supplement to school based instruction adds up to thousands of hours across the childhood and adolescence of your child. Work with your child as much as you can, and remember, it is not how *soon* your child learns a particular skill that matters, but how *well* he is eventually able to do it.

Given the value of early, intensive treatment, parents should work to ensure that their child is receiving appropriate services from a young age. One helpful resource is a book I have written with my colleague, Mary Jane Weiss, explaining some of the strategies for obtaining early treatment services. The book is *Right from the Start: Intensive Behavioral Intervention for Young Children with Autism.*

▪▪ Conclusion

There is no one "right way" for children to develop. All children are born with different potentials and grow and learn according to their own unique timetables. Because of the way autism affects your child, however, you can expect that he will develop more slowly than most children and have trouble mastering cognitive, communication, social, and self-help skills. Fortunately, you can help offset some of these developmental delays by providing good early intervention and educational programs and a supportive home environment for your child. Children with autism *do* acquire self-care skills, master basic academic concepts, develop at least the rudiments of communication, and learn to cooperate in group settings. With your help and encouragement, your child will master these skills that much faster and more thoroughly.

▪▪ References

Brodzinsky, D., Gormly, A., & Ambron, S.R. *Lifespan Human Development.* New York: Holt, Rinehart & Winston, 1987.

Burack, J. A. & Volkmar, F. R. "Development of Low- and High Functioning Autistic Children." *Journal of Child Psychology and Psychiatry and Allied Disciplines* 33 (1992): 607-16.

Cornish, K. M. & McManus, I. C. "Hand Preference and Hand Skill in Children with Autism." *Journal of Autism and Developmental Disorders* 26 (1996): 597-609.

Dalrymple, N. J. & Ruble, L. A. "Toilet Training and Behaviors of People with Autism: Parent Views." *Journal of Autism and Developmental Disorders* 22 (1992): 265-75.

Eaves, L. C. & Ho, H. H. "Brief Report: Stability and Change in Cognitive and Behavioral Characteristics of Autism through Childhood." *Journal of Autism and Developmental Disorders* 26 (1996): 557-69.

Freeman, B. J., Rahbar, B., Ritvo, E. R., & Bice, T. L. "The Stability of Cognitive and Behavioral Parameters in Autism: A Twelve-year Prospective Study." *Journal of the American Academy of Child and Adolescent Psychiatry* 30 (1991): 479-82.

Gillberg, C. "Outcome in Autism and Autistic-like Conditions." *Journal of the American Academy of Child and Adolescent Psychiatry* 30 (1991): 375-82.

Harris, S. L. & Weiss, M. J. *Right from the Start: Intensive Behavioral Intervention for Young Children with Autism.* Bethesda, MD: Woodbine House, 1998.

Osterling, J. & Dawson, G. "Early Recognition of Children with Autism: A Study of First Birthday Home Videotapes." *Journal of Autism and Developmental Disorders* 24 (1994): 247-57.

Rogers, S. J. & DiLalla, D. L. "Age of Symptom Onset in Young Children with Pervasive Developmental Disorders." *Journal of the American Academy of Child and Adolescent Psychiatry* 29 (1990): 863-72.

░░ Parent Statements

We noticed there was something wrong with Ray at two. He wasn't chewing. And we asked the pediatrician, "Why isn't he chewing?" And she said, "Well, he'll chew when he gets ready. Just don't give him anything he can choke on."

◄❃►

Doug simply could not handle any food with texture—he gagged, turned blue, threw up—from six months on. Yogurt became a God—send to us. I never gave up. Now that he's three and a half, we've just started going to fast food restaurants and he happily sits in a high chair eating french fries, chicken nuggets, and milk shakes.

◄❃►

At six months he wasn't turning over, and the pediatrician said, "He's a big boy—he'll learn." You take what you're given at this point. I mean, he was our first child; we didn't know any different.

◄❃►

He had terrible tantrums at 15 months of age. If one block fell off a pile, he would throw the whole pile and scream. The pediatrician said that children who have temper tantrums before 18 months are usually very bright!

◄❃►

At three and a half, Doug can use some picture communication, but has never said one word. All my friends and relatives tell me of dreams they have where Doug is talking. I've never had such a dream, and when I try to envision him speaking, I really can't.

◄❃►

We were trying to teach Donny the response to the common question, "How are you?" The answer we were looking for was "fine." It didn't take long for him to catch on to the idea and to use the response appropriately. Shortly afterwards, while recovering from a virus, Donny overheard my husband and me comment on how the virus had made him look so pale and white. Donny had not totally recovered from the virus when I asked him how he was feeling. He answered, "White." We were delighted because he had spontaneously learned a word to tell us he was not yet well.

❧❀❧

He's seven, going on eight—someday he's going to be fifteen, going on sixteen—and if we hadn't done what we've done so far, he might be at the developmental stage of seven going on eight when he's fifteen going on sixteen. There could be a lot of repercussions when he's twenty going on twenty-one.

❧❀❧

When your child can't talk as well as the other kids can, you start to feel like you still have a baby while the other parents have a little companion.

❧❀❧

Ryan's first love is the alphabet. He can recite it backwards just as fluently as forwards. He sees letters in everyday objects: hold a candy cane upside down and he calls it a "J," take a bite out of a Ritz cracker and it's a "C."

❧❀❧

He will repeat whatever he either heard or read last, when he is stressed or being silly. Sometimes it's a fragment of a conversation, a commercial, or words written on a bathroom wall!

❧❀❧

You have no idea how excited we become when Brian says a word we thought he didn't know. Of course, then he turns into a parrot and keeps saying it. It may be echolalia, but it's still music to our ears!
By the time he was two, he had lost the five or six words he had previously had. Every time I asked the pediatrician about this, his response was the same: "If he can hear, it doesn't worry me." A few months later, he was diagnosed as having autistic behavior.

❧❀❧

I get an evil satisfaction out of observing "typical" children who misbehave. I know many who tantrum, who can't sit still, and who have poor social skills. My son, now, has better social skills than most kids his age, can sit and work quietly better than most of his kindergarten classmates, and virtually never tantrums. It was not always this way.

❧

What amazes us is the dynamic course of this disability. Some earlier symptoms have subsided, others remain, and new ones have cropped up.

❧

When your child begins to show signs of progress—be they the tiniest steps—you want to sing for joy, but you'd feel like an idiot doing so. So I share these tiny-yet-momentous triumphs with my husband. He understands how incredible it was the first time our son had an extended conversation on the phone with his uncle. He understands the significance of our son asking what a word meant. He got tears in his eyes when our son allowed a younger neighbor into his room and dragged out his box of trains for the child to play with. You see, "typical" kids do this stuff all the time, but other parents take it for granted. I don't believe we will ever take our son's achievements for granted.

❧

Well, I guess it's another year without the proverbial "visions of sugarplums" dancing in our son's head. He's six and doesn't understand the concept of Christmas. We will all get our full Christmas Eve's rest, but would trade it in a heartbeat to watch him, just once, experience the excitement of Santa Claus.

❧

The holidays have come and gone with Ryan not understanding any concept surrounding them. I remember using the holidays as kind of a gauge of his progress. Each Halloween I would say, "Next year he will get this." Now I don't bother guessing when and if that will happen. Still, on each holiday, I get a twinge in my heart and a tear in my eye; however, it passes quickly because I realize that Ryan's happiness is measured in the everyday moments.

❧

The most significant lesson I've learned recently is to not assign an intent to an observed behavior. We have a 12-year-old son with PDD:NOS and seizures. When he yells, is aggressive, or says seemingly rude or inappropriate statements, we are learning to step back and remind ourselves that it doesn't necessarily mean that his motive was bad, or that his feelings were hostile. Rather, the behaviors are coming from his challenging needs. His actions toward us are not maliciously motivated or intended to be taken personally. This process is really helping us be more objective, regardless of how painful it can be.

❧

One day I said to my son, "Daniel, don't eat that stuff. It's unhealthy!" He responded, "You're joking?" You don't know how we celebrated those two words!

❧

Having typically developing children has really helped us become better parents for our child with autism. When your only experience is parenting a child with special needs you don't realize that all 18-month-olds throw food on the floor and most 2½ year olds have temper tantrums. I know what to react to and what not to overreact to because I can differentiate between being autistic and being a kid.

❧

I explained to the kids in our new neighborhood about Peter's disabilities. One of them said to me, "Well he's still a kid, right?" It's true! My son likes videos, wrestling with his dad, and riding down the hill on his Big Wheel, just like all kids.

❧

I now have a kind of radar for developmental delays in other children, and secretly reproach their parents, who are probably aware of these disabilities but are afraid to face them. My tough, probably quite unattractive, attitude is, "Yep, our kids have issues. It sucks for us, it sucks for them. You ought to stop wringing your hands and deal with it."

❧

How frustrating that my son can't retain language for any stretch of time, especially since his intelligence is above average. He gets emotionally torn up inside because he wants so badly to be able to communicate.

7

FINDING THE RIGHT EARLY INTERVENTION AND EDUCATIONAL PROGRAMS

Andrew L. Egel, Ph.D.

▪▪ Introduction

In theory, you may already know that the surest route to a fulfilling, independent future for your child is through the right behavioral and educational program. In practice, however, you may be at a loss as to how to find the best placement for her. This is understandable because there are a bewildering number and variety of programs available, many with different, even contradictory philosophies.

This chapter is designed to ease your entry into the world of early intervention and special education. It presents an overview of common placement options in special education programs, and reviews the evaluation and eligibility process. The professionals likely to have roles in your child's education are introduced as well as skills you might expect your child to learn in early intervention and school. Finally, to help you obtain the best possible educational program for your child, this chapter offers guidance on what to look for in a program, what questions to ask, and how to evaluate the information you receive.

▪▪ What Is Special Education?

Special education is instruction designed to meet the unique needs of a child with special needs. It is provided by professionals trained in helping children overcome the learning problems associated with their disabilities. When your child is very young, you may have these professionals come to your home. As children reach the age when they attend school, services will be provided in a variety of other settings, such as public or private school classrooms or hospitals. Children with disabilities will also receive the related services necessary in order to benefit from an educational program. The intensity and type of related services will vary according to the child's needs. Speech therapy, occupational and physical therapy, social services, psychological services, and transportation to and from school are just some of the related services a child with autism might receive. Your school system may offer your child a half-day or full-day program depending on her age. Parents of very young children may find that a full-day program is too much for their children to handle. By age two and a half to three, however, many children with autism will benefit most from a full school day of five to six hours.

▪▪ Early Intervention

Early intervention is a term used to describe a variety of comprehensive services that focus on infants, toddlers, and their families. These children have disabilities or are at risk for developing developmental disabilities. Services can include:

- family training and counseling;
- speech and language instruction;
- occupational and physical therapy;
- health services to enable your child to benefit from other early intervention efforts;
- assistive technology;
- transportation needed for your child and your family to receive early intervention services; and
- psychological evaluation and counseling.

The level of service provided depends on your child's needs as identified in her Individualized Family Service Plan (described in detail in Chapter 8).

Early intervention can be provided in many different forms. The goal, however, is always the same: to minimize the effects of disabilities that can delay development in infants and toddlers. Early intervention specialists use specific educational and therapeutic techniques to help children with disabilities master skills they are having trouble learning; they also teach parents how to help their child learn these skills and maintain them over time.

Children with autism are excellent candidates for early intervention services because they have a range of developmental problems. All can benefit from early and intensive training in communication, cognitive, and social skills, and the sooner children with autism begin work to overcome behavioral problems such as tantrums and self-injury, the less likely these behaviors are to interfere with future learning.

Types of Early Intervention Programs

The Individuals with Disabilities Education Act specifies that early intervention programs be provided, to the maximum extent possible, in a child's "natural environment." Thus, the primary location of educational programming for children with autism can vary with their age. For example, very young children with autism are typically provided services in their homes. In traditional home-based programs, members of an early intervention team come to your home to work with you and your child. They may all visit together or they may come separately during the week. How many teachers or therapists visit and how often they visit will vary depending on your child's needs and the services available in your area. Home-based services usually are provided up to age three. Some school systems may also provide instruction both at home and at a school. Teachers in these programs would spend some time at school working with your child in individual and group settings, while also providing services in your home to help foster learning and generalization.

During a home visit, the teacher will work with your child, focusing on the different areas of development. Particular emphasis should be given to the areas presenting the greatest difficulty to children with autism: socialization, communication, and cognitive skills. The teacher will try various activities with your child, and may want you to try them too. He or she may work with your child alone, with you alone, or with you and your child together. At the end of the session you should have a clear idea of what skills were emphasized, what was learned (by you and your child), and how to help your child build upon her progress. The teacher may leave you with suggestions of activities to try with your child until the next session.

Home visits are also a good time to discuss your child's problem behavior. Many children with autism have trouble sleeping through the night; others have frequent temper tantrums. Discussing these problems with your child's teacher will help her focus on the areas of greatest importance to you and your family. It will also help you learn techniques to manage challenging behaviors at home and in the community.

The type of home-based services provided for your child will help determine whether they continue past age three. Traditional home-based services that provide a few one-hour visits each week cannot (in most cases) adequately meet your child's need for socialization and communication training. School-based programs are usually recommended for older children because they enable staff to provide more teaching time and much more intensive programming than is available in traditional home-based early intervention programs. Alternatively, home-based programming may continue until age four or five if your child is receiving the intensive one-to-one instruction discussed previously. Socialization goals in that type of program are typically addressed by splitting instructional time between home and settings that have children without disabilities (for example, preschools, daycare centers, neighborhood parks).

Programs for children with autism who are of preschool age are typically located in public schools or private facilities. Some programs are "segregated," serving only children with autism, or both children with autism and those with various disabilities. Other programs are "integrated," in which children with autism receive instruction in the same classroom attended by children without disabilities for at least a portion of the day. Children in that type of program may also receive instruction in a segregated classroom when they are not integrated. Finally, some programs may be described as "included" or "inclusive." That term means that the homeroom for children with autism is the same as for typical children and that most if not all instruction occurs with their typical peers at neighborhood schools.

Classrooms should be staffed by teachers who have special knowledge about working with children with autism or other developmental disabilities. The student-to-teacher ratio is also very important. A ratio of three children to one staff member is often appropriate, but the ratio should generally be determined by the child's needs. For example, extremely challenging children may initially require a smaller ratio of one to one or two to one, while more self-sufficient children may do better with less supervision (with a ratio such as six to one). Too much supervision may prevent more competent children from learning the skills needed to become independent; too little supervision of more challenging children may mean insufficient opportunities to practice skills, as well as insufficient teacher time to intervene with behaviors such as tantrums, perseveration, or self-injury.

Classrooms in school-based programs for children with autism ages three through four usually resemble those for other preschool-age children, with toys, a housekeeping area, and materials to stimulate large and small muscle development. In addition, a variety of toys and materials appealing to the sensory interests of children with autism might be available. The classroom should also contain areas for large group activities such as circle time, small group instruction, and free-play. Children with autism in this age range may be provided with intensive one-to-one programming in their classrooms (or at home) using Applied Behavior Analysis (explained below and in Chapter 4). Classrooms using this model may look just like traditional classrooms (for example, housekeeping area, circle time, and stimulating toys), differing only in how instruction is presented.

Like staff in home-based programs, school-based teachers often involve the parents in their child's education. Frequently parent education services are provided to teach parents how to help their child use skills or behaviors at home that she has learned in school. For example, parents may be taught to toilet train their child following a program used at school.

❚❚ Programs for School-Aged Children

Just as there are different types of special education programs for younger children with autism, so too are there different types of special education programs for children five and older. Some programs are provided within the public school system, others by private schools. Public school programs may be located within elementary or secondary schools that also have classes for students without disabilities, or in centers just for children with special needs (and in some cases, just for children with autism). For both preschool and school-aged children, you may find that some schools provide an educational program throughout the year (12 months), while others are in session only for the regular school year—typically September through June—with extended year services provided based on the needs of an individual child.

There may also be considerable differences between programs for school-aged children and those for younger children. For example, older students are likely to spend more time in structured activities. Furthermore, many of the curriculum goals may differ because they should be related to the older children's "next environment," the next setting to which they will be transitioned (for example, elementary school to junior high). More teaching will also occur in nonschool settings, especially as children reach adolescence.

The type of program that is best for your child will ultimately depend on her needs, but some information about these different program types may help you make your decision. In all cases, the characteristics of appropriate programs described later in this chapter will help you sort out the pros and cons of any program you are considering.

Whether a public or private school will be most appropriate for your child often depends on where you live. Some public school systems have made special efforts to create educational programs that meet the specific learning and behavioral needs of children with autism. In other areas of the country, private schools have taken the lead because the public schools have not. In these cases, public and private schools often have agreements that children with autism from a particular town or county will be referred to the private school because it provides a more appropriate educational experience.

Occasionally parents may find that they cannot properly meet the needs of their child with autism on a day-to-day basis. In these cases, a residential program may be considered. These programs tend to be private and they are more expensive than a typical school based setting. However, if the school system determines that the child's behavior in school or at home is preventing her from benefiting from a typical school program, then the local school system and the state education agency will pay for the residential program that

is most appropriate given your child's needs. Sometimes there is no question that the home situation is hurting a child's educational progress, but more often some degree of advocacy and legal assistance is needed before the school district will agree to pay for residential services. Even in the most obvious situations, a great deal of information and documentation must be gathered, and it is critical that you maintain communication with the school and the local education agency. Chapters 8 and 9 will help you understand your legal rights in this kind of situation, as well as how to exercise these rights to obtain the best services for your child.

▪▪ Curriculum: What Your Child Is Taught

We know that children with autism have needs in many developmental areas, particularly in social interactions and communication. Naturally it is important that your child's educational program address these two critical areas. But your child's curriculum, or teaching program, must cover other areas as well. For young children with autism, these include cognitive skills, self-help skills, gross and fine motor skills, and behavior problems. As your child enters adolescence, the emphasis of instruction may shift to teaching functional living skills in areas such as community (for example, bus riding), leisure-recreational (for example, video games, bowling), domestic (for example, preparing foods, personal hygiene), and vocational (for example, answering a supervisor's questions, learning specific job skills).

There is no one curriculum for all children with autism. Like all children, they have strong and weak points when it comes to learning. For example, some children with autism have more trouble learning communication skills than they do learning cognitive skills. In autism, this "discontinuity," or tendency to progress at different rates in different developmental areas, is one of the reasons that autism is so puzzling. Moreover, there can be uneven performance within a single area. For example, some children with autism have unique, and very highly developed visual perceptual skills and can read almost any word. Although this particular cognitive skill may be well above average, the same child may be completely unable to comprehend what she has read.

Because each child with autism is unique, your child's curriculum will have to be tailored to her unique needs. In general, however, you should expect that your child will receive instruction in each developmental area in which she has learning needs. Lists of skills children with autism may need to be taught are provided below. These lists are furnished merely as examples. The order in which skills are listed is not necessarily the order in which they would or should be taught to your child. Remember, it should always be clear why your child is learning a particular skill and how this skill fits with some ultimate goal.

Cognitive Skills. Cognitive skills can be thought of as the "building blocks" of learning. They include such basic "thinking" skills as the ability to tell the difference between two objects, as well as such complex skills as abstract reasoning. Many children with autism have problems with the most basic cognitive skills and need to be taught them methodically. Others have both strong and weak skills in this area, so that a graph of their cognitive abilities looks like a series of peaks and valleys. Some early cognitive skills that often require attention are discriminating among different people, objects, and events, and imitating the actions of other people. Additional cognitive skills that your child may be taught in school include:

- matching identical objects, identical pictures, and pictures to objects;
- identifying colors, shapes, letters, and numbers;
- telling the difference between "big" and "little;"
- identifying and writing her first and last name;

- reading basic and more advanced words, depending on cognitive abilities;
- spelling simple words.

Social Skills. In determining that your child has autism, the professional making the diagnosis paid special attention to your child's social interactive skills. He or she probably noted that your child lagged behind in the development of both elementary and complex social skills. An example of an elementary skill is the "social smile" that most babies without disabilities develop by two months of age. A more complex social skill would be understanding what to do when you see that a stranger has inadvertently left her wallet at a store counter. Children without disabilities learn many elementary and complex social skills simply by observing and imitating other people. Most children with autism, in contrast, do not learn social skills this way, and must be taught formally. Some examples of social skills that are taught to children with autism include:

- engagement, the ability to remain focused and interactive (responsive) to a person or object;
- responding to peers when they initiate social interactions;
- initiating social interactions with peers;
- asking peers for assistance;
- independent play skills;
- waiting turns;
- following directions from a co-worker or supervisor.

Communication. This is the other developmental area that professionals observed very carefully when examining your child. As Chapter 6 explains, it takes two separate skills to communicate. It takes expressive language—the ability to express yourself through gestures, words, or symbols—and it takes receptive language—the ability to understand what is being communicated to you through gestures, words, or actions. Children with autism often experience problems with either or both of these skills, and receive extensive training from teachers and speech and language therapists to help them learn to communicate better.

But there is more to communication than just sending or receiving messages; communication is also part of a social interaction. For instance, have you ever felt that your child was communicating something to you, such as a request for juice, but that she just was not "there" with you, and that you could just as well have been some stranger capable of meeting her need? She was communicating with you, but without any social recognition or eye-contact. Professionals identify this type of problem as one of "social communication," and it represents an important area for teaching children with autism.

Here are some examples of communication skills that may be taught to your child:

- basic attending skills (for example, making eye contact in response to her name);
- imitating others' (for example, peers) actions, words, and sounds;
- using objects, action words, or both;
- using one-, two-, or three-word sentences;
- mastering the concepts of recurrence ("more"), negation ("all done-gone"), and affirmation ("yes");
- using an alternative communication system such as sign language, picture communication system, or computerized communication system.

Self-Help Skills. These skills represent those activities of daily living that all people need to participate as fully and independently as possible in their families, communities, and schools. Many children without disabilities learn self-help skills—washing themselves, using the toilet, and eating with a spoon and fork—by imitating other children and their parents. Learning through watching and imitating is very hard for children with autism, so these skills often must be taught systematically. It is sometimes tempting to expect that all children will learn self-help skills on their own, but this is a big mistake if your child has autism. To acquire these important skills, children with autism require consistent teaching—teaching that should take place both at home and in school in the context in which they occur naturally. For example, the best time to teach your child to put on her coat is each time she wants to go outside. Examples of self-help skills that might be taught in school include:

- dressing and undressing;
- using the toilet;
- grooming and personal hygiene;

- caring for one's own belongings (for example, making the bed, washing clothes);
- cooking and meal preparation skills.

Motor Skills. You may have read or been told that children with autism usually have motor abilities that are typical of children of their chronological age. Although children with autism generally have far less difficulty in this area than in communication or social skills, some do have trouble with fine or gross motor skills. For example, some children with autism may have trouble picking up small objects between their thumb and forefinger or gripping a pencil correctly. Others may have problems with gross motor skills such as walking with a steady gait or riding a tricycle. Examples of motor skills that might be taught in school include:

- riding a tricycle;
- catching and throwing a ball;
- cutting with scissors;
- placing coins in vending machines;
- applying make-up;
- shaving

Vocational Skills. As your child gets older, more emphasis should be placed on teaching domestic, leisure and recreational, community, and vocational skills. These skills become particularly important because your child needs them in order to ultimately function as independently as possible. Significant attention has been focused recently on preparing people with developmental disabilities for the eventual transition to the world of work. In the past, adults with autism rarely were considered as candidates for any "real" job. That is now changing thanks to programs that are demonstrating that, with sufficient support (for example, a job coach), many people with autism can be employed in a variety of jobs. These jobs have included library assistant, food service worker, file clerk, printer, and cable operator.

Preparation for the transition to work must begin long before your child is ready to leave school. Vocational training, if your child is under 18 years old, should provide her with various work experiences in different types of jobs. The types of jobs should be narrowed as she grows older so that preparation can focus on a particular job placement. Of course, this requires teachers (or transition specialists) to survey the community to identify types of jobs that are available and the skills most employers require for a particular type of job. Chapter 10 discusses vocational options for young adults with autism in more detail.

Behavioral Problems. By now you have undoubtedly noticed that your child repeats certain actions such as throwing tantrums, being aggressive to teachers, peers, or herself, hand flapping, spinning objects, or lining up toys more often than other children. These behaviors can present problems in school because they may interfere with learning. For example, if your child is more interested in spinning the wheels of an overturned car than in rolling the car back and forth to a classmate, the likelihood that other children will want to play with her decreases. Such behaviors can be problems at home, too. They require attention wherever they interfere with learning or participating fully in the family or community.

There will also be behaviors your child might be expected to have mastered by a certain age, but has not. These can include playing appropriately with toys, maintaining interest in an activity for more than a few seconds, or using social language (such as "hi"; "bye").

Individual children with autism have their own unique set of behavioral issues that can affect how well they engage in the learning process. These problems should be addressed at school or home whenever they interfere with learning or participation in family and community activities.

❚❚ How Your Child Is Taught

Over the past 25 years, much information has been collected about how children with autism learn best. As noted previously, numerous experts have suggested that an approach based on the principles of Applied Behavior Analysis is by far the most effective for presenting instruction for children with autism.

Applied Behavior Analysis (ABA)

ABA assumes that the reasons why a behavior does or does not occur can be found primarily in the environment. It is based on the knowledge that behavior is acquired through interactions with the environment, and that altering environmental events can change behavior. Programs using ABA monitor and evaluate a child's progress and behavior carefully in order to establish a clear understanding of the relationship between instructional strategies used and the changes in the child's learning and behavior. ABA involves systematically breaking down a skill to be learned into small steps, and reinforcing a child for each step as she demonstrates it correctly. Simple responses are typically taught first and then expanded into larger, more

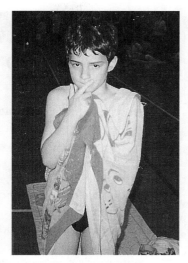

complex, age-appropriate behaviors. Students are initially prompted or guided to engage in the appropriate responses while minimizing opportunities for errors.

Teaching trials are repeated many times to provide enough opportunities for learning. Depending on the goals of a behaviorally based classroom, these sessions may occur in a one(teacher)-to-one(child) or group instructional format, or with individual students during naturally occurring activities throughout the day. Skills taught during one-to-one instruction will be practiced and reinforced in less structured, more typical settings to help the child generalize the skill.

Here is how an ABA approach might work: A child with no speech might be taught to make the "mmm" sound for "more," in order to obtain more of a preferred item. Initially the teacher might accept an approximation of "mmm" before offering the item the child had selected. Later she would expect a more clearly pronounced "mmm" sound. Over time this sound would be shaped into the sound for the word "more." When this is successful, the child would be taught to use the word "more" whenever she wanted something repeated. Eventually she would learn the labels for preferred items (like milk, cookie, and train), and would be taught to chain together these two words into a more complex request such as "more cookie." She would then be taught to use this response in different, more natural situations (like at the lunch table) to help her generalize. Additional teaching objectives might include teaching her to use an "I want" phrase with "more" and the name of the item, to form a more

:: ABA SUMMARY

Applied Behavior Analysis and Children with Autism

1. Based on scientific principles to teach appropriate behaviors and reduce problem behaviors with over 50 years of research.
2. Focuses on teaching small, measurable components of behavior in a systematic manner:
   - everything is broken down into small steps,
   - appropriate responses are followed by a consequence (reward) that reinforces the behavior,
   - prompting is provided as needed to help the child learn
3. Includes Systematic Instruction Procedures
   - Positive reinforcement
   - Discrete trial instruction
   - Task analytic instruction
   - Incidental teaching procedures
   - Prompting and prompt fading
   - Shaping
   - Chaining
   - Choice and preference
   - Quick pacing of sessions
   - Functional analysis of problem behaviors, and teaching socially appropriate alternatives
   - Many teaching opportunities are provided in the initial stages of acquisition of a new skill

complete sentence ("I want more milk").

Recently, many teachers and therapists have been providing very intensive instruction to young children with autism using the methods of ABA in a one(teacher)-to-one (child) teaching format. Most often, this type of instruction is presented in the home by a rotating team of teachers and therapists for 30-40 hours per week. The location of instruction is expanded to the community and schools usually after six months to one year, although the actual time period is determined for each child individually. Some schools also provide intensive ABA programs for young children of a similar nature. In these cases, it is essential for teachers to work very closely with parents to ensure that consistent teaching happens at both school and home.

Regardless of the specific approach used, a good behavioral teaching program must satisfy several requirements. First, there must be a clear description of the goal to be achieved (exactly what will be learned, or what problem behavior will be decreased). This should include the level or rate of the behavior that will be considered acceptable, and the point at which the teacher will determine that the behavior has been learned. For example, a teacher may require your child to complete an addition worksheet with 90 percent accuracy over three consecutive math sessions before she will consider the skill acquired. Second, the teaching procedure must be clearly stated with each step listed so that it can be followed by anyone using it. Third, consequences used to encourage the behavior being taught must be specified, and must be meaningful to your child—that is, they must be something for which she will respond consistently. These consequences are referred to as reinforcers and may include praise, stickers, foods, additional recess, or access to preferred toys. There are an unlimited number of stimuli that may be reinforcing to a child; it is important to remember, however, that

---

:: ABA SUMMARY (CONTINUED)

- Skills learned are systematically embedded in natural routines for generalization of treatment gains.
4. Emphasizes making learning fun.
5. Teaches students to discriminate among many stimuli.
6. Inappropriate behaviors are not reinforced. Systematic analysis used to determine exactly what events function as reinforcers for those responses.
7. The student is guided to engage in appropriate responses while minimizing opportunities for errors.
8. Teaching trials are repeated many times (initially in rapid succession).
9. Data are collected according to specific criteria, and graphed to provide a picture of the student's progress.
10. Timing and pacing of sessions is important. Practice opportunities and consequences are determined on an individual basis.
11. Emerging skills are practiced and reinforced in less structured situations.
12. Simple responses are built systematically into typical age-appropriate ones. Children are taught how to learn from their natural environment.
13. Professionals are trained in behavioral teaching principles in order to implement programs effectively.
14. Consistency is very important in order to maintain treatment gains.

whether or not something is a reinforcer depends entirely on whether it causes your child's behavior to increase. Fourth, the effectiveness of the teaching program must be frequently evaluated using data collection. By keeping track of your child's response to a teaching program, the teacher can quickly determine whether the program is achieving the desired results, and make changes at once if it is not. Finally, the program should specify how the skill just taught would be transferred to other people and places. This is called "generalization," and it is an extremely important part of any teaching plan. Without it, your child may learn how to do something very useful in one place—school, for instance—but nowhere else.

The name of the teaching approach a program uses is less important than its use of proper teaching strategies. All teachers who provide educational programs for children with autism should be able to tell you exactly how they teach, what they teach, their reasons for using those techniques, and the specific way they evaluate the effectiveness of their teaching. What they do, how they do it, and how they tell whether it works should be open to everyone for review, and should be judged by professionals to reflect the best practices for educating children with autism. If a program is unwilling or unable to meet these standards, then you should look for another program for your child.

:: Evaluation and Eligibility

Knowing that your child is entitled to early intervention and special education services is just the first step in securing those services. To receive services, your child must first be evaluated, and her need for special education services must be determined.

This evaluation and eligibility process begins with a referral (from you, your pediatrician or another professional, or teachers) to the special education division or department of your local school system. Typically your child will be assigned a case manager who represents the school system's placement committee and is responsible for obtaining all of the information required by the committee in order to recommend appropriate programs. The case manager gathers this information by interviewing you, observing your child, and reviewing reports from previous teachers and support personnel, pediatricians and other doctors, and any other professionals who have worked with you and your child. When additional information is required, the placement committee will request that the appropriate professionals conduct further assessments. As a result, you and your child may see a speech-language therapist, educational specialist, occupational therapist, physical therapist, or any of the professionals described in Chapter 1 who may have been involved in your child's diagnosis. Some of these professionals may continue to work with your child after she begins her early intervention or special education program if it is identified as an area of need.

The speech-language therapist is trained to evaluate how your child communicates using words, gestures, and symbols and also specific speech disorders (for example, articulation problems, and problems with voice quality, pitch, and loudness). The former is most likely to be assessed in children with autism. The speech therapist will also work directly with your child and your child's teacher in the context of classroom activities. It is especially important for the speech therapist to consult with the early intervention or special education staff. In so doing, the therapist can ensure that the teaching staff are using the same techniques to build communication skills throughout the day.

To assess your child's communication abilities, the speech-language therapist usually will observe your child interacting with others. The evaluation may include an assessment of your child's ability to: 1) understand language (for example, identify objects upon request, follow directions, answer questions); 2) initiate communication using words, gestures, or symbols (for example, getting someone's attention and making a request, identifying objects and actions in the environment); and 3) use communication in interacting with others (for example, playing a game, turn-taking, requesting and sharing information). The speech-language therapist and the classroom teacher will, based on the assessment information, develop programs that address those areas of need. For example, the assessment may show that your child with autism does not interact with her peers. As a result, the teaching staff and the speech-language therapist may provide specific cues to help your child know when to interact and provide reinforcement for the initiation.

Your child might also require evaluation by an occupational therapist (OT) or a physical therapist (PT). An OT specializes in assessing and improving the development of fine motor skills such as holding a pencil or tying shoelaces and the relationship between motor input and output. OTs can also be helpful if your child has problems with feeding and eating because they are trained to provide treatment for problems with oral-motor control—the use of muscles in and around the face. An OT may use standardized tests as well as direct observation to evaluate your child for problems with movement and perception. A physical therapist will assess your child for problems involving gross motor skills such as mobility (walking), posture (sitting), and balance.

Finally, to develop an overall picture of your child's educational needs, an educational specialist may examine your child. The educational specialist (sometimes called an educational diagnostician or child development specialist) will determine your child's abilities in a number of areas using information gathered from you, standardized tests, observation, and direct interaction with your child. Areas the educational specialist may assess include communication skills; readiness for educational instruction (for example, the ability to sit still, make eye contact, and follow directions); pre-academic and academic skills in language, math, and reading; play skills; and self-help skills such as washing, dressing, and clothing selection. After placement, recommendations developed by the educational specialist will be included in the special education teacher's curriculum for your child.

Once your child's evaluations have been completed, the school placement committee (sometimes called the Child Study Team) must hold an eligibility hearing to decide whether your child should receive special educational services. Throughout this process, you, as parents, have certain important rights. These are outlined in Chapter 8. Of all the rights you have, the most important one is the right to appeal almost any decision including eligibility that you feel is incorrect.

Assuming that your child is found to be eligible for special education services, the next phase of the process is to determine placement. The same team that determined eligibility will probably also recommend placement options to you. Some teams may recommend several programs for you to visit; others may have only one choice to offer. Certain parts of the country are more sparsely populated than others, have fewer children with autism, and fewer programs to serve them. Nevertheless, it is the responsibility of your public school system to provide an appropriate program (public or private) for your child even if your child is the only one with autism in the school system. Your child cannot be put into an inappropriate program because she is the only one with this condition, no teacher trained in working with children with autism is available, or because your child lives too far from the school. If your child has been declared eligible, then she must be provided an appropriate educational program.

Programs for students with autism must have certain characteristics if they are to be successful. As a parent, information about these characteristics will be helpful in identifying the right program for your child. The following section explains how to gather information about potential programs and how to then check this information against the characteristics of an appropriate program.

Gathering Information

Your school district's special education placement office should provide you with a list of the programs being considered for your child. If at all possible, try to visit all of these placement options before the formal placement meeting is held. You can obtain the information you need to make a fully informed decision about a specific program from several sources. The school principal, for example, is important to meet because she can provide you with information such as:

- The philosophy of the program—for example, how does the program promote inclusion with peers who do not have disabilities? Try to determine if there is a philosophy and whether you agree with it.
- The availability of an extended-year program.
- Current staff-to-student ratio and, equally important, whether that ratio is likely to change in the near future.
- The availability of services such as speech and language therapy, occupational therapy, and physical therapy.

Weigh each of these issues carefully. For example, a student-teacher ratio of two to one might be excellent for your child; however, the classroom might not be appropriate if that ratio changes unpredictably. The program should have the ability to change the ratio depending on student needs.

Another important source of information is the speech-language therapist. You need to know how language and communication services are provided to other students in the class. In the past (and to some extent currently) students were typically removed from the classroom in order to work with the speech-language therapist. This practice has serious drawbacks because it does not promote the transfer of communication or language skills to settings outside of the speech-language room. Skills are more likely to transfer to other environments if the therapist conducts training as part of an ongoing instructional activity in the classroom (as opposed to "pull-out" services). For this method to be effective, the therapist must work with teachers to ensure that all instructional programs are designed to increase a child's language and communication.

As important as it is to talk to the educators involved in the program, you should spend the majority of your time observing actual classroom activities. Before visiting, call the school office and ask for the classroom schedule so that you can decide on the most informative time to observe. Try to see as many different activities as possible in order to determine whether the teacher and the assistants have consistent reactions to students' attempts to communicate and respond to instructions. In addition, observe if the teaching staff behave in a similar fashion when students exhibit problem behavior such as tantrums. Ideally, spend some time observing during the morning and afternoon hours so you can develop an understanding of what your child's day would include. This is important because many teachers schedule more intense teaching time for morning, and concentrate on activities such as art, music, and physical education during the afternoon. Parents who have limited time to observe could perhaps schedule more than one visit at different time periods.

■■ Characteristics of an Appropriate Program

Educators, researchers, and advocates have thoroughly debated the features of appropriate classrooms for children with autism and other disabilities and have reached a general consensus from an educational standpoint. Knowing these features will be one of your primary resources as you begin the evaluation process. The order in which they are discussed does not reflect the importance of one over another. Ideally, parents would find a program or many programs that contain all of the features described below. Unfortunately the ideal is rarely available; therefore, parents should seriously consider programs that have a majority of the ingredients discussed while continuing to advocate for the ideal.

Functional Activities. One of your major goals in evaluating programs should be to determine whether the skills taught and the materials used are functional. The skills emphasized should be those the students need in order to function as normally as possible in the real world. Furthermore, they should be skills that are appropriate for the students' ages. For example, learning to play with three-piece puzzles may be a functional leisure skill for a child in preschool, but would not be for a student in junior high.

You should expect to see in classrooms for older students more emphasis on community-based instruction and other functional living skills, such as street crossing, bus riding, shopping, and cooking.

In general, you can determine whether skills are functional by asking yourself three questions:

1. Does it appear that the skills being taught are immediately useful to the students?
2. Are the materials used likely to be found in the students' everyday environment?
3. Will learning a particular skill decrease the probability that someone else will have to do it for her in the future?

Affirmative answers to these questions are critical if the skills your child acquires are to be used in situations outside the classroom. Suppose, for example, you observe a ten-year-old girl with autism learning coin identification using play money. Although the skill may be functional, the play money would be considered nonfunctional because the child would not use it outside of the teaching session. As a result, it is very unlikely that she will be able to select the correct coins when asked to get two quarters from a pocket full of change in order to buy a soda. Teaching the same student to identify geometric shapes on a form board would be considered nonfunctional because that skill is not immediately useful or likely to be required in the real world.

Whether or not a skill is taught in a functional manner can also be determined by observing the sequence in which it is taught. For example, it is functional to teach toothbrushing following a snack or lunch, zipping and unzipping as students are putting on or taking off their jackets, or clothes folding after getting the clothes out of the dryer. Some students will need additional practice outside the natural sequence, but you should try to determine through observation and discussion with the teacher whether natural sequences are emphasized.

Chronological Age Appropriateness. As you observe the program, notice whether it is based on the concept of age appropriateness. This means that curricula and materials used within a classroom should suit the students' chronological, rather than developmental, ages. Age appropriateness may be less of an issue with preschool-aged (or younger) children because the gap between chronological age and developmental level may not be as pronounced as it is likely to become later. For example, having a morning circle and singing nursery rhymes may be chronologically age appropriate as well as appropriate to the developmental level of a three-year-old, but teaching the same skill to a high school student would be inappropriate regardless of the child's developmental level. Similarly, you should notice whether the physical environment of the classroom is designed with age appropriateness in mind: posters of Barney the Dinosaur and the Muppets are expected in classrooms for preschool and some primary-age children, but are not appropriate in junior and senior high classrooms.

The importance of age appropriateness cannot be overemphasized, especially considering how hard it can be to get children with autism to use skills outside of the classroom. If the materials used and the skills taught are not age appropriate, there is even less chance they will be useful to students outside of the classroom. For example, interactions typical of high school students might include sharing video games, going to dances, or just "hanging out" and talking or listening to music. If students with autism are to fit in with other students, they must be taught skills that are appropriate to the age group and setting. Teaching them leisure skills more appropriate to their developmental level would shut them out of their peer group.

Punishment. The use of punishment has historically concerned parents of children with special needs. By definition, punishment refers to a process in which the consequence for a behavior reduces the probability that the behavior will occur in the future. In other words, whether or not a teacher is punishing a child depends strictly on the child's behavior. A procedure that does not decrease behavior is not punishment, no matter how much a teacher wants it to be. In the classroom, a teacher might try to reduce a problem behavior by: reminding a student not to engage in that behavior; teaching an alternative behavior that produces the same result (for example, teaching a student to raise her hand to get attention rather than just calling out); or removing a child from an activity for a brief period of time following the behavior ("time out").

Among educators, there has been considerable concern over whether or not to use punishment to curb behaviors that interfere with learning. This has been fueled by reports that some programs have used "aversive" procedures (for example, pinching, slapping, ammonia inhalants) to reduce problem behaviors. Some professional organizations (for example, TASH) adopted resolutions calling for the prohibition of aversives, while others (for example, ASA) have condemned the use of abusive procedures.

Because of the controversy, you may encounter professionals who believe punishment is never justified, professionals who believe punishment is a necessary component of every program, and professionals who stick to a more middle ground. Where your child is concerned, be sure to obtain sufficient information from your observations and discussions with classroom staff to determine if punishment procedures are used, and if so, whether you think they are appropriate. When interviewing teachers or principals, ask whether the school has standards governing the use of punishment procedures. The following guidelines should help you determine the answers to the following questions:

- Under what conditions will punishment procedures be considered?
- Who is involved in making the decision (for example, parents, teachers, principal, psychologist)?
- Are there reinforcement procedures in place to teach appropriate, alternative behaviors?
- Who will monitor and evaluate the administration and effectiveness of punishment? At the least, parents, classroom staff, and the principal should be involved.
- How often will this evaluation occur (no less frequently than every three days) and what data will be used to support the continued use of punishment?
- Are parents required to provide informed consent before punishment is used? If not, you should question the appropriateness of the program very seriously.

If you see a punishment procedure used in the classroom, ask whether previous attempts have been made to reduce the behavior using methods other than punishment. The teaching staff should be committed to teaching alternative, appropriate behaviors before using punishment procedures. For example, it would be more desirable to teach students to get attention by raising their hands rather than to punish tantrums that serve the same purpose. Some exemplary programs for children with autism may very occasionally use punishment under certain conditions; however, they will always concurrently teach another skill to replace the behavior to be reduced, and will also be able to provide you with satisfactory answers to the above questions.

Data-Based Instruction. You have probably experienced the variability of your child's behavior. One day your child completes a task; another day she appears not to understand what is being asked. The same type of problems occur in the classroom, and the only way teachers can judge student progress accurately is to record and chart each student's performance consistently. Data collection that occurs prior to and throughout an instructional program enables a teacher to identify a student's entry skill level, monitor the effectiveness of a teaching program, and, if necessary, modify the course of instruction.

You will discover that many programs assess students' progress only at the beginning, middle, and end of the year using standardized tests. Because so much time passes between assessments, it is difficult for teachers to determine how well or if a student is progressing and whether changes might be needed in the educational program. They are more likely to plan effective programs if they record how a student actually does throughout the course of instruction.

Ask the staff how often data are collected, charted, and reviewed, and also observe whether any data collection occurs during your visit. Teachers may report that data collection as described above does not occur because it is too time-consuming, interferes with actual instruction, and is unnecessary in determining a student's level of performance. However, there are many ways that teachers can reduce the burden of data collection (for example, use timers, counters, and stopwatches to help them count or to signal the time to observe; schedule data collection for three times per week rather than every day) and still obtain information that is much more valuable than that provided by tests given at six- and twelve-month intervals. Finally, in most situations, teachers of children with autism and other severe disabilities cannot judge student performance accurately unless they collect data regularly.

Instruction in Nonschool Environments. As you gather information about programs, you should ask for a copy of the weekly schedule to determine how much instruction takes place outside the classroom (in grocery stores, homes, and libraries). This information is important because, until recently, children with autism were taught almost exclusively in the classroom. Instruction in the community was accomplished through "educational" field trips. Unfortunately, children with autism are not likely to learn skills by being exposed to the community only once or twice a week.

Over the past ten years, many professionals have argued that children with autism need frequent and systematic teaching outside of school in order to learn how to respond appropriately to the wide range of cues and consequences in the real world. For example, students taught to shop in supermarkets are more likely to learn how to respond to cues found there—placement of aisle headings or location of cashiers—than are students taught only in the classroom. In addition, instruction outside of school increases the probability that students will learn important skills such as street crossing that are not needed in a classroom.

Although community-based instruction will become more important as your child gets older, all programs should provide some instruction outside of the classroom. For example, young children can be taught age-appropriate skills such as accompanying their parents to stores and libraries without engaging in tantrums or other disruptive behavior. Older children might learn skills such as locating and selecting items in a supermarket, checking out library books, and riding a bus. You should look for instructional goals that reflect this type of teaching strategy and, for older children, a classroom schedule that permits frequent trips in the community.

Social Integration. As discussed earlier, educational programs for children with autism are now typically found in public schools serving children without disabilities. This important trend in special education, called "inclusion," has resulted in many children with autism attending the same schools and classes as their neighbors and peers without disabilities. Although some parents may be concerned about how their child will be treated by children and staff without disabilities in an inclusive school, these placements provide many advantages not available when children with autism attend segregated programs. The primary advantage is that peers without disabilities are more likely to encourage any attempts at social behavior by children with autism. Conversely, because segregated classrooms typically serve other children with equally poor social skills, it is doubtful that peers will respond appropriately to social behaviors such as greetings, sharing, and interactive play. As a result, children with autism are not as likely to learn or maintain social behavior in segregated programs. Inclusion also provides the opportunity for students without disabilities to gain a better understanding of children with autism or other disabilities. Finally, as several programs for preschool children have shown, inclusion can help children with autism develop social interaction, cognitive, and communication skills.

As you visit programs, you may be exposed to different methods of inclusion, depending on the age of your child. At the preschool level, inclusive programs usually provide instruction to children with autism and those without disabilities in the same classroom, with the typical children receiving training in how to interact with, and be a tutor for, the children with autism. For older students, inclusion may involve providing all instruction for a child with autism in a classroom with typical peers (full inclusion). Alternatively, some public school systems may locate classrooms for children with autism in regular public schools, and provide systematic instruction with typical children at different points during the day (for example, calendar time, math, physical education, lunch, recess, and after-school activities) depending on a child's abilities. In both cases, parents should check carefully to ensure that the program does not just provide opportunities for children with autism to have contact with typical students without also teaching them the skills they need to interact with their peers. There is clear evidence that nearness or physical integration alone does not promote interaction between children with autism and those without disabilities. Locating the classroom near the students' chronological age-appropriate peers, and devising a classroom schedule that allows students with autism to be at student gathering places at appropriate times, will make it easier for staff to provide systematic instruction. How well a classroom provides for structured inclusion and the support that it receives in the school are critical tests of the appropriateness of a program.

Extended-Year Programming. As this chapter emphasizes, one of the most important features of an appropriate program is classroom instruction that continues beyond the traditional nine- or ten-month school year. It will be very difficult to ensure that your child with autism maintains the skills she has learned in the past school year if she does not receive instruction during the summer. In addition, valuable teaching time will be spent in the fall re-teaching those skills lost over the vacation. Therefore, if at all possible, you should insist on a year-round program for your child.

Parent Involvement. The opportunity for parents and other family members to become actively involved in the education of their children is an important part of all appropriate educational programs. This has been shown to be especially true for parents of children with autism, and should be recognized by the staff in any classroom you visit. Teachers should realize that you know your child best because you spend significantly more time with her, and that you can make classroom instruction easier by continuing to work at home on skills taught in school. In other words, the parent-professional relationship must be a two-way street: You can learn various teaching strategies from the classroom staff, while they can learn about you and your family and how your child interacts with her environment. Never forget that you and your child have very specific rights under the law and you must be prepared to ensure that they are not violated.

Parents should also have the chance to be involved in other ways. For example, programs should provide parents with the opportunity to receive training in teaching their children new skills, practicing skills previously acquired, and controlling problem behavior at home and in the community. Furthermore, parent training programs should be flexible enough to serve both parents who want intensive training and those who just want assistance teaching a specific skill, such as learning how to accompany parents successfully when they are grocery shopping. An appropriate program will offer parents the type of systematic training that best serves the needs of their family.

There are additional ways for you to determine the extent to which a program encourages family participation. For example, programs that include a system for daily or weekly contact with parents (for example, through school-to-home notes and journals) and have a flexible visitation policy promote parent involvement. In contrast, a classroom policy that restricts contact unreasonably may indicate a program that discourages involvement.

■■ Conclusion

The guidelines discussed above are based on a review of recommendations provided by professionals over the past 15 to 20 years. Although programs that satisfy all or most of these requirements exist, finding an appropriate placement for your child is never an easy task. Being an informed parent, however, is the first step toward ensuring that you are an active and knowledgeable participant in the placement process. As you review various programs, remember that it is important that you keep the ideal classroom in mind—one that incorporates all of the features discussed above. The ideal classroom may be difficult to find, but it is well worth your effort to keep looking. In the end, a program that includes a majority of these characteristics is more likely to effectively address the needs of your child and of your family.

■■ References

Browder, D. & Snell, M.E. "Functional Academics." In *Instruction of Students with Severe Disabilities*. Edited by M. E. Snell. NY: Prentice-Hall, 1999.

Carr, E., Levin, L., McConnachie, G., Carlson, J., Kemp, D., & Smith, C. *Communication-Based Intervention for Problem Behavior: A User's Guide for Producing Positive Change*. Baltimore: Paul H. Brookes, 1994.

Harris, S. & Handleman, J. *Preschool Education for Children with Autism*. Austin: PRO-ED, 1994.

Harris, S. & Weiss, M. J. *Right from the Start: Behavioral Intervention for Young Children with Autism*. Bethesda, MD: Woodbine House, 1998.

Koegel, R. L., Rincover, A., & Egel, A.L. *Educating and Understanding Autistic Children*. San Diego: College-Hill Press, 1982.

Kohler, F., Strain, P. & Shearer, D. "Examining Levels of Social Inclusion within an Integrated Preschool Program for Children with Autism." In *Positive Behavioral Support: Including People with Difficult Behavior in the Community*. Edited by L. Koegel, R. Koegel, & G. Dunlap. Baltimore: Paul H. Brookes, 1996.

Maurice, C., Green, G., & Luce, S.C. *Behavioral Intervention for Young Children with Autism: A Manual for Parents and Professionals*. Austin: PRO-ED, 1996.

Schopler, E. "Editorial: Treatment Abuse and Its Reduction." *Journal of Autism and Developmental Disabilities* 16 (1986): 99-103.

Scott, J., Clark, C., and Brady, M. *Students with Autism: Characteristics and Instructional Programming*. San Diego: Singular Publishing Group, 2000.

Simpson, R.L. "Children and Youth with Autism in an Age of Reform: A Perspective on Current Issues." *Behavioral Disorders* 21 (1995): 7-20.

Simpson, R.L. and Myles Smith, B. *Educating Children and Youth with Autism: Strategies for Effective Practice*. Austin: PRO-ED, 1998.

Snell, M. and Brown, F. "Instructional Planning and Implementation." In *Instruction of Students with Severe Disabilities*. Edited by M. Snell. NY: Prentice-Hall, 1999.

Zager, B. *Autism: Identification, Education, and Treatment*, 2nd ed. Mahwah, NJ: Lawrence Erlbaum Associates, 1999.

■ Parent Statements

Early intervention was a very negative experience for me. At the time, we didn't know Lawrence had autism. I was surrounded by little babies with Down syndrome smiling and learning how to throw balls and stack blocks while Lawrence wouldn't even look at the toys. I'd always ask myself, "Why are these kids learning and making progress while Lawrence is doing absolutely nothing?" No one mentioned autism to me.

❦

Even in Special Education, the term "autistic" turns people off.

❦

All our friends now are in Special Education. All we do is Special Education.

❦

Donny tried two early intervention programs, but neither one did him much good. The teachers tried very hard, but Donny just didn't seem to sit and attend. His behavior interfered with whatever the staff tried to do. They were not equipped to deal with a child like Donny. He cried and tantrummed a lot and barely made any gains. He just didn't seem to fit in with the other kids.

❦

You can't afford to alienate anybody. You have to be nice to the administrators, you have to be nice to the classroom teacher—you have to learn to be a politician.

❦

A physical therapist came to our house to work with our daughter. I was so amazed by what bouncing and rough play did for her physical and verbal skills. That was the first time she strung words together to from a sentence. I had never seen her smile and laugh so much. It wasn't until then that I realized how much more there was for me to learn in order to help her.

❦

Initially, a component of Donny's school program required my active participation at home. Being an active participant in Donny's play and behavior management helped restore my self-worth.

❧

What bothers me most about some educators and professionals who work with my son is their assumption that he understands far more than he demonstrates. To me, that is like approaching a typically developing three year old, rattling off commands in Latin, then becoming frustrated when the child fails to respond. Mistaking my son's lack of response for non-compliance seems unfair.

❧

If anyone offered a twelve-month program, I'd jump at it. Lawrence needs a continuous program. And I think I need it more than he does.

❧

He comes home from school fairly often and it's not so hard to take anymore. We go back to our old way of living temporarily. But he's always glad to go back to school. He does so much better with the 24-hour structure, which certainly doesn't exist at home.

❧

"We teach during the day—part of our job is not to educate parents, it's only to educate kids. Find that someplace else," was the message I was getting from teachers. "You're taking too much of my time. I don't have time to do that."

❧

When I first heard about full-day school and long bus rides for a two-year-old, I cried. But he loved it right from the beginning. And once he started school, he progressed so quickly!

❧

Four hours of testing for a three-year-old? Give me a break! When you get bitter and frustrated you tend to react to these sort of things.

❧

Applied Behavior Analysis works! Any child would benefit from one-on-one intensive therapy. However an hour of music therapy or therapeutic horseback riding never killed anyone. ABA fanatics might argue it cuts into the time your child could be recovering. When and if my child recovers I want him to have something to do besides look at flashcards in his spare time.

❧

There are a few teachers out there who are masterpieces, who will give that extra mile. Sometimes they give an extra 500 miles. There are some real champs out there who will spend the time.

❧

They shouldn't try to do all of the testing at one time. After the first half hour or 45 minutes, the child gets frustrated, and he just doesn't want to be there anymore. They shouldn't try to cram everything into two or three days, because that's really not enough time and you can't get the child to perform his best.

❧

Applied Behavior Analysis has changed our lives. It's a lot of work but it empowers you to help your child learn. Behavioral intervention prevents household chaos. It is the single greatest factor in keeping my family from coming apart.

❧

Know what is available in your town and neighboring towns with respect to education and recreation programs. Attend board of education meetings in order to stay on top of what's happening in your town.

❧

My son David was supposed to be receiving speech and language services at school. The therapist presented herself to be interested in my son's progress and welfare. When I became suspicious and checked on whether he was receiving services, I was shocked to discover that he was only getting partial services. It is disheartening to discover that people you trust with your son's education deceive you.

❧

The teachers at my child's school insist that he is learning; however, when my husband observed in the classroom, our son was staring into space 100 percent of the time. He was not disruptive but he was not engaged.

❧

I am a professional. People don't call me constantly, begging me to do my job well. Why do I have to constantly hound my child's teachers to get them to do their job well?

❧

One of the single greatest sights I ever witnessed was when my son's entire classroom was sitting on the floor eagerly looking through his picture symbol communication book. There were 15 children busily looking at the symbols, asking questions, sentence-stripping requests, and marveling at our son's "language." He benefits from their example and the other children benefit from his presence as well. It is a win-win situation.

❧

My child is fortunate to have well-intentioned teachers, but the bottom line is I don't believe that public school is going to prepare him as well as his intensive behavioral preschool program. Am I steeling myself for second best in the name of socialization?

❧

When it was time for David to transition to middle school, I took him for private visits in order to introduce him to the teacher, classroom, building, and all the facilities he would be using (bathrooms, water fountain, cafeteria, gym, office). By September, everyone knew David and Mom. After the first week of school, his teacher told me he had made a smooth transition!

❧

Always look at your child's whole program, never just one piece.

❧

No one program has the "miracle cure," and you may have to do some shopping around before you find the program that serves your child best.

LEGAL RIGHTS AND HURDLES

James E. Kaplan and Ralph J. Moore, Jr.

∷ Introduction

As the parent of a child with autism or other pervasive developmental disorder (PDD), it is important to understand the laws that apply to your child and you. There are laws that guarantee your child's rights to attend school and to live and work in the community; laws that can provide financial and medical assistance to your child; and laws that govern long-term planning for your child's future.

Knowledge of your child's legal entitlement can help to ensure that your child receives the education, training, and special services he needs to reach his potential. You will also be able to recognize illegal discrimination and assert his legal rights if necessary. Finally, if you understand how laws sometimes create problems for families of children with disabilities, you can avoid unwitting mistakes in planning for your child's future.

No federal laws deal exclusively with autism or PDD. Rather, the rights of children with autism or PDD are found in the federal laws and regulations for children and adults with disabilities generally. In other words, the same laws that protect all persons with disabilities also protect your child. It would be impossible to discuss here the law of every state or locality. This chapter, however, reviews some of the most important legal concepts and laws you need to know to enable you to exercise and protect your child's rights effectively and fully.

For information about the particular laws in your area, contact the national offices of the Autism Society of America (ASA), The Arc (formerly the Association for Retarded Citizens) or the Association for Community Living (ACL) in Canada and some U.S. communities, your local or state affiliate of the ASA, The Arc, or ACL, or your state Parent Training and Information Center (PTIC). You should also consult with a lawyer familiar with disability law if and when you have questions or need specific advice.

:: Your Child's Right to an Education

Until the middle of this century, children with disabilities were usually excluded from public schools. They were sent away to residential "schools," "homes," and institutions, or their parents banded together to provide private part-time programs. In the 1960s, federal, state, and local governments began to provide educational opportunities to children with disabilities; these opportunities have expanded and improved to this day.

Perhaps nothing has done more to improve educational opportunities for children with autism than the Individuals with Disabilities Education Act ("IDEA"). This law, originally enacted in 1975 and amended extensively in 1997, used to be called "The Education for All Handicapped Children Act of 1975" and was better known as "Public Law 94-142." IDEA has vastly improved educational opportunities for almost all children with disabilities. Administered by the U.S. Department of Education (DOE) and by each state, the law works on a carrot-and-stick basis.

Under IDEA, the federal government provides funds for the education of children with disabilities to each state that has a special education program that meets the standards contained in IDEA and regulations issued by DOE. To qualify for federal funds, a state must demonstrate that it provides all children with disabilities a "free appropriate public education" in the "least restrictive environment" that meets IDEA's standards. At a minimum, to receive federal funds under IDEA, a state must provide approved special educational services, opportunities for participation in the regular curriculum (inclusion), and a variety of procedural rights to children with disabilities and their parents. The lure of federal funds has been attractive enough to induce all states to provide special education for children with disabilities, including children with autism.

IDEA is limited. The law establishes only the *minimum* requirements in special education programs necessary for states to receive federal funds. In other words, the law *does not* require states to adopt an ideal educational program for your child with autism or a program that you might feel is "the best." Because states have substantial leeway under IDEA, differences exist from state to state in the programs or services available. For example, the student-teacher ratio and the quality and quantity of teaching materials vary widely among the states.

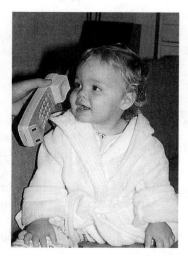

States *can* create special education programs that are better than those required by IDEA, and some have. Check with the placement or intake officer of the special education department of your local school district to determine exactly what classes, programs, and services are available to your child. Parents, organizations, and advocacy groups continually push states and local school districts to exceed the federal requirements and provide the highest quality special education as early as possible. These groups need your support, and you need theirs.

What IDEA Provides

As already mentioned, IDEA has been amended several times since its enactment in 1975. Today IDEA consists of a large volume of laws and regulations. The Resource Guide at the end of this book tells you how to obtain copies of these laws and regulations from the U.S. Senate, House of Representatives, DOE, or national organizations. The summary below highlights the provisions most important for you and your child.

Coverage. IDEA is intended to make special education available to all children with disabilities, including children with autism, mental retardation, learning disabilities, speech or language impairments, attention disorders, and multiple disabilities. Autism is listed in IDEA and the regulations as a condition meeting the disability requirement.

In most cases, a diagnosis of autism is enough to establish that IDEA applies to your child. Regardless of how your child's intellectual or physical impairments are labeled, he qualifies for services if his condition hinders learning.

Before your child is formally diagnosed or evaluated and "labeled" by your school district under IDEA, he may be eligible for services under the law. Infants and toddlers under age three are eligible for early intervention services if they are found to be "at-risk of experiencing a substantial developmental delay" if services are not provided. And if your child is between ages three and nine, states may, at their option, provide services if he is experiencing undiagnosed developmental delays.

"Free Appropriate Public Education." At the heart of IDEA is the requirement that children with disabilities receive a "free appropriate public education" in the least restrictive environment. Children with autism are entitled to receive an education at public expense that takes into account their special learning needs and abilities and their right to attend school with their nondisabled peers. This section examines more precisely the meaning of the elements of "free appropriate public education." Following sections explain the term "least restrictive environment."

"Free" means that every part of your child's special education program must be provided at public expense, regardless of your ability to pay. This requirement is often satisfied by placement in a public school, but the school district must pay the cost of all the necessary services your child receives there. If no suitable public program is available, the school district must place your child in a private program and pay the full cost. Remember, IDEA does not provide for tuition payment for educational services for your child *not* agreed to by the school district or other governing agency (unless, as explained later in this chapter, the decision of your school district is overturned). As a result, if you place your child in a program the school district has not approved for your child, you risk having to bear all the costs of that program.

It may be difficult for parents to accept that the "appropriate" education mandated by IDEA does not guarantee the best possible education that money can buy. IDEA, however, requires states to achieve "educational success," as measured by performance goals for children with disabilities that lead toward economic independence, community living, and employment as adults. Thus, IDEA attempts to hold school districts accountable for providing effective special education services. The nature and extent of services provided typically depend on the nature and extent of the need. The law in this area is constantly evolving. Check with your local office of the ASA, The Arc or ACL, or your state PTIC for information about the current state of the law regarding an "appropriate" educational program.

Only you can assure that your child receives the most appropriate placement and services. Under IDEA, parents and educators are required to work together to design an individualized education program (IEP) for each child. If you are dissatisfied with the school district's placement for your child, you must demonstrate to school officials not only that your preferred placement is appropriate, but that the placement approved by the school district is not. The goal is to reach an agreement on the appropriate placement and services. If agreement cannot be reached, procedures exist for resolving disputes. These procedures and IEPs are discussed later in the chapter.

"Special Education and Related Services." Under IDEA, an appropriate education consists of "special education and related services." "Special education" means instruction specifically designed to meet the unique needs of the child with disabilities, provided in a full range of settings, including regular education classrooms, separate classrooms, home instruction, or instruction in private schools, hospitals, or institutions. Regular education teachers, special education teachers, therapists, and other professionals—all provided by the school district at public expense—are responsible for delivering these educational services. In addition, supplementary aids and services are provided if necessary to enable a student to participate in regular education classrooms.

"Related services" are defined as transportation and other developmental, corrective, and supportive services necessary to enable a child with disabilities to benefit from special education. "Related services" are often a critical part of a special education program. Services provided by a trained speech or language therapist, occupational therapist, physical therapist, psychologist, social worker, school nurse, aide, or other qualified person may be required under IDEA as related services. Some services, however, are specifically excluded. Most important among these exclusions are medical services ordinarily provided by a physician or hospital. For example, immunizations may not be provided as related services under IDEA.

Because communication and speech problems often result from autism, appropriate and adequate speech-language therapy should be part of your child's special education program. Parents should demand that their child receive the related services he needs; these related services are your child's right under the law.

"Least Restrictive Environment." IDEA requires that children with disabilities must "to the maximum extent appropriate" be educated in the *least restrictive environment*. This requirement influences all decisions about your child under IDEA, and, since IDEA's enactment, has become a major emphasis of the law due to the efforts of parents who have advocated for their children to be educated with their peers.

The least restrictive environment is the educational setting that permits your child to have the most contact possible at school with children who do *not* have disabilities and with the regular general education curriculum. In other words, your child should have the opportunity to learn the same subjects in the same classrooms as other children his age. IDEA expresses a strong preference to integrate children with disabilities, including children with autism, in the schools and classes they would attend if they did not have a disability. IDEA is specifically intended at least in part both to end the practice of educating children with disabilities in separate schools or classrooms and to open the doors of neighborhood schools to those children. Once the door is open, IDEA requires your school to find ways to truly integrate your child into a typical student's educational life at school while he receives the additional services and support he needs to succeed.

Some school officials might assert that your child with autism or other PDD should be educated in a separate special setting. Most children with autism, however, can receive their instruction with typical peers, so long as proper in-classroom supports and therapy are provided. In some localities, all children with disabilities are educated in regular classrooms at all times.

Over the 25 years since IDEA was enacted, a wide range of placement options has developed and is supported by the law. Many children spend all their time in regular classrooms with teachers or aides who can adapt the curriculum to their needs and help them with the regular education curriculum. Others spend most of their time in regular classrooms, but receive special education services in certain subjects in separate classrooms. Still others spend most of their time in separate classrooms, but have opportunities for inclusion in school activities such as assemblies, physical education, sports teams, music, and lunch and recess. The extent of your child's inclusion depends on a variety of factors and will be set forth in your child's IEP.

IDEA also recognizes that public schools may not be suitable for all educational and related services required for some children. In these cases, federal regulations allow for placement in private schools, or even residential settings, if the school district can demonstrate that this placement is required to meet the child's individual educational needs. When placement within the community's regular public schools is determined to be not appropriate, the law still requires that he be placed in the least restrictive educational environment suitable to his individual needs, which can include some participation in regular school classroom programs and activities. Even a student whose parents enroll him in a private school without school district approval or funding may still receive some services at public expense if the services would otherwise have been required at the public school.

Neither your child's autism itself nor his developmental delay is a sufficient reason for a school district to refuse to provide opportunities for your child to learn with his peers. Some of the most important learning in school comes from a student's peers and from modelling typical behavior. Thus, in each IEP, the school district must explain how much each child with disabilities will or will not be included in regular education classes and why.

When Coverage Begins under IDEA. IDEA requires all states to begin special education services at the age of three. In addition, IDEA also includes a program of grants to states that create an approved program for early intervention services to infants with disabilities from birth until age three.

Some form of early intervention services under IDEA is available in each state. But there is wide variation in what services are provided, how and where those services are provided, and which agency provides them. You should check with your local school district, the state education agency, your local office of the ASA, The Arc or ACL, or your state PTIC about the availability of early intervention services, which can include speech-language, physical, or occupational therapy to help infants and toddlers with autism to maximize their early development. Chapter 8 discusses the types of early intervention services your child may receive. You may be required to pay for some of the early intervention services your child receives. The law seeks to have insurance companies and Medicaid cover some of the costs.

Under IDEA, special education services must continue until children reach at least age 18. A state that offers education to all students until age 21, however, must offer special education services until that age for students with disabilities.

Length of School Year. Under IDEA, states must provide more than the traditional 180-day school year when a child with disabilities requires year-round instruction as a necessary part of a "free appropriate public education." In most states, the decision to offer summer instruction depends on whether your child will "regress," or lose substantial progress made during the school year without summer services. If this so-called regression exists, summer services must be provided at public expense. Because some children with autism can regress without year-round services, you should not hesitate to request year-round instruction, but you and school staff must be prepared to document your child's need for this service.

Identification and Evaluation. Because IDEA applies only to children with disabilities, your child with autism must be evaluated before he is eligible for special education. The law requires states to develop testing and evaluation procedures designed to identify and evaluate the needs and abilities of each child before he is placed in a special education program. All evaluation and re-evaluation procedures are required to take into account your input.

For parents of a child with autism or other PDD, identification is somewhat simpler. School districts almost uniformly recognize that children with autism need at least some form of special education or related services. A medical diagnosis of autism or other PDD should therefore be sufficient for identification under IDEA. Your challenge will not be convincing a school district that your child needs services, but rather obtaining the needed services as early as possible. Doctors, organizations, and—most importantly—other parents can be extremely helpful at these initial stages.

Do not be deterred from seeking services if your child's condition is not fully understood, diagnosed, or "labelled." If your child is an infant or toddler (ages birth to three), your state may provide early intervention services for him if he is considered "at risk" for experiencing developmental delays. In addition, if your child is between ages three and nine, IDEA specifies that states *may* provide services to children who experience some form of developmental delay, but do not have a formal diagnosis of disability. States are not required, however, to accept the "developmental delay" label to establish eligibility for special education services, and can limit the age range for which the "developmental delay" label applies to less than the full span of ages three through nine. Contact your state Board of Education to determine your city's, county's, or state's policy about the "developmental delay" label.

"Individualized Education Program." IDEA recognizes that each child with a disability is unique. As a result, the law requires that your child's special education program be tailored to his individual needs. Based on your child's evaluation, a program specifically designed to address his developmental problems must be devised. This is called an "individualized education program" or, more commonly, an "IEP."

The IEP is a written report that describes:

- your child's present level of development in all areas;
- your child's developmental strengths and needs;
- both the short-term and annual goals of his special education program;
- the specific educational services that your child will receive;
- the date services will start and their expected duration;
- standards for determining whether the goals of the education program are being met;
- the extent to which your child will participate in regular education programs;
- any behavior intervention programs that will be used to enable your child to participate in regular education classrooms without impeding his or other students' learning; and
- parent concerns.

Under federal regulations, educational placements must be based on the IEP, not vice versa. That is, the services your child receives and the setting in which he receives them should be determined by your child's individual needs, not by the availability of existing programs. "One size fits all" is not permitted by IDEA.

A child's IEP is usually developed during a series of meetings among parents, teachers, and other school district representatives. Your child may be present at these meetings. School districts are required to establish committees to make these placement and program decisions. These committees are sometimes referred to as Child Study Teams, Pupil Evaluation Teams (PET), or Administrative Placement Committees.

Writing an IEP is ideally a cooperative effort, with parents, teachers, therapists, and school officials conferring on what goals are appropriate and how best to achieve them. Because of IDEA's emphasis on inclusion, regular education teachers are required to be on the IEP team. Preliminary drafts of the IEP are reviewed and revised in an attempt to develop a mutually acceptable educational program.

The importance of your role in this process cannot be overemphasized. IDEA requires the IEP team to consider "the concerns of the parents for enhancing the education of their child." This means that your goals for your child's education must be taken into account in drafting your child's IEP.

You cannot always depend on teachers or school officials to recognize your child's unique needs. To obtain the full range of services, you may need to demonstrate that withholding certain services would result in an education that would *not* be "appropriate." For example, if you believe that a program using augmentative communication methods is necessary for your child, you must demonstrate that a program without these services would not be appropriate for your child's specific needs. And if you want an academic-oriented program for your child, you must demonstrate that a program that emphasizes only vocational or functional skills is not appropriate given your child's skills, abilities, and needs.

IEPs should be very detailed. You and your child's teachers should set specific goals for every area of development, and specify how and when those goals will be reached. Although the thought of specific planning may seem intimidating at first, a detailed IEP enables you to closely monitor your child's education and to make sure he receives the ser-

vices prescribed. In addition, the
law requires that IEPs be reviewed
and revised at least once a year,
and more often if necessary, so
that your child's educational program continues to meet his changing needs. Parents can also request
a meeting with school officials at
any time.

Because your child has special needs, his IEP must be developed and written with care.
Unless you request specific services, they may be overlooked.
You should make sure school officials recognize the unique needs
of your child—the needs that
make him different from other children with disabilities and even from
other children with autism.

How can you prepare for the IEP process? First, explore available educational programs, including public, private, federal, state,
county, and municipal programs. Observe classes at the school your
child would attend if he did not have autism to see the different programs and placements offered. Local school districts and local organizations such as the ASA and The Arc or ACL can provide you information about programs in your community. Second, collect a complete set of developmental evaluations to share with school officials—obtain your own if you doubt the accuracy of the school district's evaluation. Third, give thought to appropriate short-term and
long-term goals for your child. Finally, decide for yourself and
request the placement, program, and services that are necessary for
your child. If you want your child educated in his neighborhood
school, request the services necessary to support him in that setting,
such as supplementary aids. If no program offers enough of what
your child needs, you should request that an existing program be
modified to better meet his needs. For example, if your child would
benefit educationally from learning sign language or using an augmentative communication system, you should request the service
anyway even if no program currently offers that option.

To support placement in a particular type of program, you should collect "evidence" about your child's special needs. Evidence to support a particular type of placement as appropriate can include letters from physicians, psychologists, therapists (speech-language, physical, or occupational), teachers, developmental experts, or other professionals, and the like. This evidence may help persuade a school district that the requested placement or services are the appropriate choices for your child. A few other suggestions to assist you in the process are:

- Do not attend IEP meetings alone—bring a spouse, lawyer, advocate, physician, teacher, or whomever you would like for support, including, of course, your child;
- Keep close track of what everyone involved in your child's case —school district officials, psychologists, therapists, teachers, and doctors— says and does;
- *Get everything in writing;* and
- Be assertive and speak your mind. Children with unique developmental challenges need assertive and persuasive advocates during the IEP process. To be sure, school officials are not always adversaries, but you are your child's most important advocate. You know him best.

"Individualized Family Service Plan." Parents of children from birth to age three develop a plan that is different from the IEP used for older children. States receiving grants to provide early intervention services must draft an "Individualized Family Service Plan" (IFSP). This plan is similar to the IEP, but has an early intervention focus. Unlike an IEP, which focuses primarily on the needs of the child, an IFSP emphasizes services for the family. In other words, the law recognizes that families with young children with special needs often have special needs themselves. Consequently, IFSPs do not simply specify what services are provided for the child with autism. They also describe services that will be provided to: 1) help parents learn how to use daily activities to teach their child with autism, and 2) help siblings learn to cope with having a brother or sister with autism. The procedures and strategies for developing a useful IFSP are the same as described above for the IEP. IFSPs are reviewed every six months.

One important recent change to IDEA requires that early intervention services be provided to children and families to the "maximum extent appropriate" in the child's "natural environment." This requirement means that services should be provided at the child's home or a place familiar to the child rather than at a separate center, and reflects IDEA's strong preference for inclusion.

As your child approaches age three, IDEA requires a written plan for your child's transition into preschool services. This transition process can begin six months before your child turns age three. Parents, teachers, and a representative of your local school district are required to participate. The plan must contain the "steps to be taken to support the transition of the toddler with a disability to preschool or other appropriate services" to ensure "a smooth transition" into preschool services.

Disciplinary Procedures

When IDEA was amended extensively in 1997, Congress added provisions to govern how children with disabilities were to be disciplined in public schools. These provisions restrict school actions in situations in which a child would be suspended from school. In general, schools must continue to provide a free appropriate education in the least restrictive environment even if a child is suspended. Schools that have previously failed to address behavior problems with appropriate functional behavior intervention cannot then suspend a child for that behavior. Functional behavior analysis is explained in Chapter 4. If the school already has a behavior intervention plan, school personnel must meet to review and, if necessary, revise the plan. And if a long suspension of ten days or more is considered (or if a series of shorter suspensions amounts to more than ten days), the school must present to a neutral hearing officer for approval the plan and the proposed interim placement. The school must also demonstrate that the behavior was not a manifestation of the child's disability and that the IEP was appropriate for the child at the time. In addition, parents have the right to appeal all disciplinary actions. Parents should closely monitor how these new provisions in the law are implemented to make sure public school districts do not use "discipline problems" to routinely exclude children with disabilities.

Resolution of Disputes under IDEA

IDEA establishes a variety of effective safeguards to protect your rights and the rights of your child under the law. Written notice is always required before any change can be made in your child's identification, evaluation, or educational placement. In addition, you are entitled to review all of your child's educational records at any time. Your school district is prohibited from making decisions without first consulting or notifying you. Further, your school district is required to inform you of your rights under IDEA at each step of the process.

Despite these safeguards, conflicts between parents and school officials can arise. Disputes over your child's educational or early intervention program should best be resolved *during* the IEP or IFSP process, before firm and inflexible positions have been formed. Although IDEA establishes dispute resolution procedures that are designed to be fair to parents, it is easier and far less costly to reach agreement if possible during the IEP or IFSP process or by informal discussions with appropriate officials. Accordingly, you should first try to accomplish your objectives by open and clear communication and by persuasion. If a dispute arises that simply cannot be resolved through discussion, further steps can and should be taken under IDEA and other laws to resolve that dispute.

First, IDEA allows you to file a formal complaint with your local school district about *any matter* "relating to the identification, evaluation, or educational placement of the child, or the provision of free appropriate public education to such child." In other words, you may make a written complaint about virtually any problem with your child's educational or early intervention program. Parents have successfully used this broad right of appeal in the past to correct problems in their children's education programs.

The process of challenging a school district's decisions about your child's education can be started simply by sending a letter of complaint. This letter, which should explain the nature of the dispute and your desired outcome, typically is sent to the special education office of the school district. IDEA requires that you notify your local school district or your state education agency with specific information about your complaint. You have the absolute right to file a complaint—you need not ask the school district for permission. For information about starting complaints, you can contact your school district, your local office of the ASA, The Arc or ACL, your state PTIC, local advocacy groups, or other parents.

IDEA encourages parents and school districts to resolve disagreements without hearings and lawsuits. Under IDEA, the school district must present you with the option of mediation, but you are not required to pursue that option. Mediation is a process of negotiation, discussion, and compromise. In mediation, you and school officials meet with a neutral third party and try to reach a mutually acceptable solution. If you decline the school district's request to mediate, you may still be required to meet with a neutral party to discuss the benefits of mediation.

If you decline mediation or mediation does not produce agreement, the next step in the complaint process is an "impartial due process hearing" before a hearing examiner. This hearing, usually held locally, is your first opportunity to explain your complaint to an impartial person, who is required to listen to both sides and then to render a decision. At the hearing, you are entitled to be represented by a lawyer or lay advocate; present evidence; and examine, cross-examine, and compel witnesses to attend. Your child has a right to be present at the hearing. After the hearing, you have a right to receive a written record of the hearing and the hearing examiner's findings and conclusions.

Just as with the IEP and IFSP processes, you must present facts at a due process hearing that show that the school district's decisions about your child's educational program are wrong. To overturn the school district's decision, you must show that the disputed placement or program does not provide your child with the "free appropriate public education" in "the least restrictive environment" required by IDEA. Evidence in the form of letters, testimony, and expert evaluations is usually essential to a successful challenge.

Parents or school districts may appeal the decision of a hearing examiner. The appeal usually goes to the state's education agency or to a neutral panel. The state agency is required to make an independent decision upon a review of the record of the due process hearing and of any additional evidence presented. The state agency then issues a decision.

The right to appeal does not stop here. Parents or school officials can appeal beyond the state level by bringing a lawsuit under IDEA and other laws in a state or federal court. In this legal action, the court must determine whether there is a preponderance of the evidence (that is, whether it is more likely than not) that the school district's placement is proper for that child. The court must give weight to the expertise of the school officials responsible for providing your child's education, although you can and should also present your own expert evidence.

During all administrative and judicial proceedings, IDEA requires that your child remain in his current educational placement, unless you and your school district or the state education agency agree to a move or a hearing officer agrees to an interim change of placement for disciplinary reasons. As already explained, if you place your child in a different program without agreement, you risk having to bear the full cost of that program. If the school district eventually is found to have erred, it may be required to reimburse you for the costs of the disputed placement. Accordingly, you should never change programs without carefully considering the potential cost of that decision.

Attorneys' fees are another expense to consider. Parents who ultimately win their dispute with a school district may recover attorneys' fees at the court's discretion. Even if you prevail at the local or state level (without bringing a lawsuit), you likely are entitled to recover attorneys' fees. You may not recover attorneys' fees for a mediated settlement, and attorneys' fees are reduced if you fail to properly notify the school district or state education agency of your complaint. A word of caution: A court can limit or refuse attorneys' fees if you reject an offer of settlement from the school district, and then do not obtain a better outcome in the end.

As with any legal dispute, each phase—complaint, mediation, hearings, appeals, and court cases—can be expensive, time-consuming, and emotionally draining. As mentioned earlier, it usually is wise to try to resolve problems without filing a formal complaint or bringing suit. When informal means fail to resolve a dispute, formal channels should be pursued. Your child's best interests must come first. IDEA grants important rights that you should not be bashful about asserting vigorously.

IDEA is a powerful tool in the hands of parents. It can be used to provide unparalleled educational opportunities to your child with autism. The Reading List at the end of this book includes several useful guidebooks about IDEA and the special education system. The more you know about this vital law, the more you will be able to help your child realize his full potential.

▪▪ Programs and Services When Your Child Is an Adult

Many parents of children with autism share the hope that their children with autism will grow to live independently or semi-independently as adults. To achieve community living and employment skills, your child will likely need some special services. These services include employment, job-training, and residential or community-living programs. Regrettably, these services are often unavailable because very few federal laws require states to offer programs for adults with disabilities and few states offer these programs on their own. The programs that exist typically are underfunded and have long waiting lists. As a result, many parents must provide the necessary support and supervision on their own for as long as possible. Thousands of children receive education and training intended to equip them to live independently and productively, only to be sent home when they finish schooling with nowhere to go and nothing to do. Although more emphasis has been placed in recent years on community living and employment, the progress to date is woefully inadequate.

Now is the time to work to change this sad reality. The unemployment rate for people with disabilities is appallingly high, especially for young adults. As waiting lists for training programs grow, your child may be deprived of needed services, and, consequently, of his independence. Programs sponsored by charities and private foundations are limited and most families do not have the resources to pay the full cost of providing employment and residential opportunities. The only other remedy is public funding. Just as parents banded together in the 1970s to demand enactment of IDEA, parents must band together now to persuade local, state, and federal officials to take the steps necessary to allow adults with disabilities to live independently and with dignity. Parents of *children* with disabilities should not leave this job to parents of *adults* with disabilities; children become adults all too soon. One worthwhile avenue for involvement is to begin to work with groups like the ASA and The Arc or ACL.

Vocational Training Programs

A federally funded educational program available to most adults with autism provides money to eligible states for vocational training and rehabilitation programs for qualified people with disabilities. As with IDEA, states that seek federal funds under this program must meet the standards established in the law. These laws set forth procedures—similar to those under IDEA—to review decisions affecting the services provided to individuals with disabilities.

Adults must fulfill two requirements to qualify for job-training services: 1) they must have a physical or mental disability that constitutes a "substantial handicap to employment"; and 2) they must be expected to benefit from vocational services. In the past, some people with disabilities, including people with autism, were denied vocational training services because it was believed that they could not satisfy the second requirement of eventual full-time or part-time employ-

ment. The law now requires that services and training be provided to people with disabilities whose ultimate goal is "supported employment," which means employment dependent on services such as a job coach or special training that allows the person to work productively.

The state Departments of Vocational Rehabilitation, sometimes called "DVR" or "Voc Rehab," are charged with administering these laws. Adults who apply for Voc Rehab services are evaluated, and an "Individualized Plan for Employment" (IPE), similar to an IEP, is developed. The IPE sets forth the services needed to enable a person with a disability to work productively. The law requires that IPEs be developed in partnership between the individual and his vocational rehabilitation counselor so that the individual can make informed choices about his vocational training.

You should contact your state DVR or your local office of the ASA or The Arc or ACL for specific information on services available to your child when he is an adult. Despite limited federal and state budgets, some states, communities, and organizations offer their own programs, such as group homes, supported employment programs, social activity groups, continuing education, and life-skills classes. Other parents and community organizations likely will have information about these local programs.

■■ Developmentally Disabled Assistance and Bill of Rights Act

Under a federal law called the Developmentally Disabled Assistance and Bill of Rights Act, states can receive grants for a variety of disability-related programs. Important among them is a protection and advocacy (P&A) system. The P&A system advocates for the civil and legal rights of people with developmental disabilities. P&A offices have been leaders in representing institutionalized people seeking to improve their living conditions or to be placed in the community. In addition, P&A offices may be able to represent persons who cannot afford a lawyer for an IDEA due process hearing or a discrimination suit. Because some people with autism may not be able to protect or enforce their own rights, state P&A systems offer necessary protection. Contact the National Association of Protection and Advocacy Systems (in the Resource Guide).

■■ Anti-Discrimination Laws

State and federal laws exist to protect children, adolescents, and adults with disabilities from being denied opportunities or otherwise discriminated against solely on the basis of their disability. This section reviews the highlights of the landmark Americans with Disabilities Act and the Rehabilitation Act of 1973, both federal laws which prohibit discrimination against your child with autism and all people with disabilities.

The Americans with Disabilities Act

The Americans with Disabilities Act (ADA), enacted in 1990, prohibits discrimination against people with disabilities, including children and adults with autism. The law is based on and operates in the same way as other well-known federal laws that outlaw racial, religious, age, and sex discrimination. The ADA applies to most private employers, public and private services, public accommodations, businesses, and telecommunications. We focus here on the employment and public accommodation provisions of the law.

Employment. The ADA states that no employer may discriminate against a qualified individual with a disability "in regard to job application procedures, the hiring or discharge of employees, employee compensation, advancement, job training, and other terms, conditions, and privileges of employment." In other words, private employers cannot discriminate against employment applicants or employees who have a disability. The law defines "qualified individual with a disability" as a person with a disability who, with or without reasonable accommodation, can perform the essential functions of a job. "Reasonable accommodation" means that employers must make an effort to remove obstacles from the job, the terms and conditions of employment, or the workplace that would prevent an otherwise qualified person from working because he has a disability. Accommodations can include job restructuring, schedule shuffling, modified training and personnel policies, and access to readers or interpreters. Failing to make reasonable accommodations in these respects is a violation of this law.

The law does not *require* employers to hire people with disabilities or to make accommodations if an "undue hardship" will result for the employer. Rather, employers may not refuse to employ qualified people with disabilities solely because of the existence of the disability. For example, if a person with autism applies for a job as an office assistant, the employer may not refuse to hire him if he is as qualified as or *more* qualified than other applicants to perform the job's duties and the employer's refusal was based on the applicant's autism. The employer is not required to hire a qualified person with autism, but may not refuse to hire a person because of his disability. The employer may not either inquire whether the applicant has a disability or fail to make some reasonable accommodation to enable a person with autism to work productively. The employment section of the ADA applies only to companies that employ 15 or more persons.

The ADA specifies procedures for people with disabilities who believe they have been the victim of employment discrimination. A person must file a complaint with the federal Equal Employment Opportunity Commission (EEOC), the agency responsible for resolving employment discrimination complaints. If the agency does not satisfactorily resolve the dispute, a lawsuit may be brought to prohibit further discrimination and to require affirmative action. The ADA allows an award of attorneys' fees to a person with a disability who wins a lawsuit. Your local office of the ASA or The Arc or ACL may be able to provide basic information about how to challenge discriminatory employment practices, but a lawyer likely will be required.

Public Accommodations. One of the most stunning and potentially far-reaching provisions of the ADA is the prohibition of discrimination in public accommodations. Mirroring the approach of the civil rights laws of the 1960s, the ADA bans discrimination against people with disabilities virtually *everywhere*, including in hotels, inns, and motels; restaurants and bars; theaters, stadiums, concert halls, auditoriums, convention centers, and lecture halls; bakeries, grocery stores, gas stations, clothing stores, pharmacies, and other retail businesses; professional offices; airport and bus terminals; museums, libraries, galleries, parks, and zoos; nursery, elementary, secondary, undergraduate, and postgraduate schools; day care centers; homeless shelters; senior citizen centers; gymnasiums; spas; and bowling alleys. Any place open to the public must be accessible to people with disabilities, unless access is not physically or financially feasible. No longer can businesses exclude people with disabilities just because they are different. The excuse that people with disabilities are "not good for business" is now unlawful thanks to the ADA.

Like other civil rights laws, the ADA also requires integration. The law bans the insidious practice of "separate but equal" programs or facilities that offer separate services to people with disabilities, rather than access to programs offered to everyone else. The law prohibits the exclusion of people with disabilities on the grounds that there is a "special" program available just for them. For example, a recreation league (public or private) cannot uniformly exclude people with disabilities on the ground that a comparable separate league is offered. Similarly, a theater, restaurant, or museum cannot exclude people with autism from their establishments, cannot restrict their use to certain times or places, and cannot offer them only separate programs, unless equal access would impose an unreasonable expense to the establishment. The end result is that the new law does not merely prohibit active discrimination, but rather imposes a duty to open our society to all people with disabilities.

People with disabilities who are the victims of discrimination can file a lawsuit to prohibit further discrimination. And if the U.S. Department of Justice brings a lawsuit to halt a pattern and practice of discrimination, monetary damages and civil penalties may be imposed. Again, your local office of the ASA, The Arc or ACL, and your state P&A office will be able to provide information and assist in a discrimination complaint.

The ADA protects rights and opportunities for people with autism. By prohibiting discrimination and requiring reasonable accommodation, the ADA stands as a true Bill of Rights for people with all disabilities, including autism.

The Rehabilitation Act of 1973

Before the ADA was enacted, discrimination on the basis of disability was prohibited only in certain areas. Section 504 of the

Rehabilitation Act of 1973 continues to prohibit discrimination against qualified people with disabilities in *federally funded programs*. The law provides that "No otherwise qualified individual with handicaps in the United States . . . shall, solely by reason of his handicap, be excluded from the participation in, be denied the benefits of, or be subjected to discrimination under any program or activity receiving federal financial assistance. . . ."

An "individual with handicaps" is any person who has a physical or mental impairment that substantially limits one or more of that person's "major life activities," which consist of "caring for one's self, performing manual tasks, walking, seeing, hearing, speaking, breathing, learning, and working." The U. S. Supreme Court has determined that an "otherwise qualified" handicapped individual is one who is "able to meet all of a program's requirements in spite of his handicap." Programs or activities that receive federal funds are required to make reasonable accommodation to permit the participation of qualified people with disabilities. The law covers programs like day care centers, schools, and jobs in programs receiving federal funds.

Section 504 has been used to enforce the right of children with disabilities to be integrated in their school district, to challenge placement decisions, and to assert the right to special education services for children who do not qualify for services under IDEA. Even if a child functions at a level that disqualifies him from services under IDEA, his right to services may be enforceable under Section 504. This may be important for parents of very high functioning children with autism or PDD who may somehow not qualify for services under IDEA. Every local education agency is required to have a Section 504 Coordinator to answer questions. As with other legal issues, you should consult a qualified lawyer to explore claims under Section 504. Section 504 permits the recovery of reasonable attorneys' fees if you prevail in your challenge.

Fair Housing Laws

Federal fair housing laws prohibit discrimination against a person with a "handicap" in the sale or rental of housing. As defined by federal law and regulations, the term "handicap" includes autism. Under these laws, landlords cannot refuse to rent to a person with autism or a family with a member with autism because of his disability. In addition, landlords may not isolate people with disabilities in one part of a building or deny them access to any common facilities available to other tenants. They must also make "reasonable" accommodations for all people with disabilities. This law is enforced by the federal Department of Housing and Urban Development (HUD) where discrimination complaints can be sent, filed by telephone, or even sent over the Internet.

■ Health Insurance

The mere fact of a child's disability can cause serious problems for families in finding and maintaining health insurance that covers the child. Insurance companies often do not offer health or life insurance at a fair price, or sometimes at any price, to children or adults with autism. This practice results from the belief that these children and adults are likely to submit more insurance claims than others. Until they become adults, children who are covered from birth by their parents' insurance face fewer problems, but coverage depends on the particular terms of the insurance.

About half the states have laws against discrimination that prohibit insurance companies from denying coverage based on a disability like autism. The drawback to all of these laws, however, is that insurance companies are allowed to deny coverage based on "sound actuarial principles" or "reasonable anticipated experience." Insurers rely on these large loopholes to deny coverage. In short, the laws often are ineffective in protecting families of children with disabilities from insurance discrimination. Even the ADA does not prohibit these same "sound actuarial" practices that frequently result in denied coverage.

A few states have begun to lessen the health insurance burdens on families with children with disabilities. These states have passed insurance reform laws that prohibit exclusion of children with disabilities from coverage or prohibit exclusion of pre-existing conditions. Other states offer "shared risk" insurance plans, under which insurance coverage is offered to people who could not obtain coverage otherwise. The added cost is shared among all insurance companies (including HMOs) in the state. To be eligible, a person must show that he has been recently rejected for coverage or offered a policy with limited coverage. The cost of this insurance is usually higher and the benefits may be limited, but even limited coverage is usually better than no health insurance at all. Some state laws also cover people who have received premium increases of 50 percent or more. In addition, Medicare,

Medicaid, and other federally funded programs aimed at improving health care for children (discussed below) may be available to help with medical costs. Check with your state insurance commission or your local office of the ASA or The Arc or ACL for information about health insurance programs in your area.

:: Planning for Your Child's Future: Estate Planning

Although some children with autism grow into independent adults, many can never manage completely on their own. This section is written for parents whose children may need publicly funded services or help in managing their funds when they are adults.

The possibility that your child may always be dependent can be overwhelming. To properly plan for your child's future, you need information in areas you may never have considered before. Questions that deeply trouble parents include: "What will happen to my child when I die? Where and with whom will he live? How will his financial needs be met? How can I be sure he receives services he needs to assure his safety, health, and quality of life?"

Some parents of children with autism delay dealing with these issues, coping instead with the immediate demands of the present. Others begin to address the future when their child is quite young, adding to their insurance, beginning to set aside funds for their child, and sharing with family and friends their concerns about their child's future needs. Whatever the course, parents of children with autism need to understand certain serious planning issues that arise from their child's disabilities. Failure to take these issues into account when planning for the future can have dire consequences both for your child and for other family members.

There are three central issues that families of children with autism need to consider in planning for the future. These are:

- possible cost-of-care liability;

- the complex rules governing government benefits; and

- your child's ability to handle his own affairs as an adult.

The disabilities of children with autism may affect planning in a number of other ways as well. For example, more life insurance may be needed, and the important choice of trustees and guardians may be more difficult. Issues about insurance coverage and financial management face most parents in one form or another. Cost-of-care liability, government benefits, and the inability to manage one's own affairs as an adult, however, present concerns that are unique to parents of children with disabilities.

■■ Cost-of-Care Liability

Many adults with autism receive residential services of some kind paid for in part by the state. Most states require the recipients of residential services to pay for the services if they have the funds to do so. Some states impose liability for daytime and vocational services as well. Called "cost-of-care liability," these requirements allow states to tap the funds of the person with disabilities to pay for the services the state provides. States can reach funds owned outright by a person with disabilities and funds set aside in improperly written trusts. A few states even impose liability on parents for the care of an adult with disabilities. This is an area parents need to look into early and carefully.

You should understand clearly that payments required to be made to satisfy cost-of-care liability do *not* benefit your child. Ordinarily they add nothing to the care and services your child will receive. Instead the money is added to the general funds of the state to pay for roads, schools, public officials' salaries, and so on.

It is natural for you to want to pass your material resources on to your children by will or gift. In some cases, however, the unfortunate effect of leaving a portion of your estate to your child with autism may be the same as naming the state in your will—something few people do voluntarily, any more than they voluntarily pay more taxes than the law requires. Similarly, setting aside funds in your child's name, in a support trust, or in a Uniform Transfers to Minors Act (UTMA) account may be the same as giving money to the state—money that could better be used to meet the future needs of your child.

What can you do? The answer depends on your circumstances and the law of your state. Here are three basic strategies parents use:

First, strange as it may seem, in a few cases the best solution may be to disinherit your child with autism, leaving funds instead to siblings in the expectation that they will use these funds for their sibling's benefit, even though they will be under no *legal* obligation to do so. The absence of a legal obligation is crucial. It protects the funds from cost-of-care claims. The state will simply have no basis for claiming that the person with disabilities owns the funds. This strategy runs the risk, however, that the funds will not be used for your child with autism if the siblings:

1. choose not to use them that way;
2. suffer financial reversals or domestic problems of their own, exposing the funds to creditors or spouses; or
3. die without making arrangements to safeguard the funds.

A preferable method, more often, in states where the law is favorable, is to leave funds intended for the benefit of your child with autism in what is called a "discretionary" special-needs trust. This kind of trust is created to supplement, rather than replace, money the state may spend on your child's care and support. The trustee of this kind of trust (the person in charge of the trust assets) has the power to use or not use the trust funds for any particular purpose as long as they are used for the benefit of the beneficiary—your child with autism. In many states, these discretionary trusts are not subject to cost-of-care claims because the trust does not impose any *legal* obligation on the trustee to spend funds for care and support. In contrast, "support" trusts, which *require* the trustee to use the funds for the care and support of the beneficiary with a disability, can be subjected to state cost-of-care claims.

Discretionary special-needs trusts can be established during your lifetime or at your death under your will. As with all legal documents, the trust documents must be carefully written. It is generally wise, and in some states it is essential, to include provisions stating expressly that the trust is to be used to supplement rather than replace publicly funded services and benefits.

A third method to avoid cost-of-care claims is to create a trust, either during your lifetime or under your will, that affirmatively describes the kind of expenditures that are allowable for your child with autism in a way that leaves out care from state-funded programs. Like discretionary trusts, these trusts—sometimes called "luxury" trusts—are intended to supplement, rather than take the place of, public benefits. The state cannot reach these funds because the trust does not allow trust funds to be spent for care provided by state programs.

In determining what estate planning techniques to use, you should consult an attorney who is experienced in estate planning for parents of children with disabilities. Individualized estate planning is essential because each state's laws differ and because each family has unique circumstances.

■■ Government Benefits

People with disabilities may be eligible for any of a number of federal, state, and local benefit programs. These programs provide a wide variety of benefits and each has its own eligibility requirements. Some of these programs provide income while others provide specific benefits for persons with disabilities. The principal programs that provide income, apart from work programs, are SSI and SSDI, described below, but these are not the only programs of this kind; income is also provided for disabled survivors of federal employees and railroad employees, for example. Other programs, such as housing assistance, provide benefits that supplement income. Perhaps the most important benefit programs are those that pay for medical care—Medicare and Medicaid. These programs are also described below.

In planning for the future, it is useful to take these programs into account. For obvious reasons, it is important to avoid arrangements that will interfere with eligibility. A key point to know about eligibility is that some but not all of these programs are "means-tested." That is, the programs are available only to people without substantial financial means. SSI and Medicaid are means-tested, while SSDI and Medicare are not. Housing assistance is means-tested. If it may be important for your child with autism to qualify for one of these programs, funds should not be given to him directly, either now or under a will when you (or his grandparents) die. Instead, you should consider one or a combination of the three planning strategies described above to avoid cost-of-care liability: disinheritance, or more commonly, a discretionary special-needs trust; or in some states, a luxury trust. In addition to avoiding cost-of-care liability, each of these strategies is intended to minimize interference with eligibility for the important means-tested benefit programs.

The principal features of four of the most important of these program—SSI, SSDI, Medicaid and Medicare—are described in more detail below.

SSI and SSDI

There are two basic federally funded programs that can provide additional income to people with autism who cannot earn enough to support themselves. The two programs are "Supplemental Security Income" (SSI) and "Social Security Disability Insurance" (SSDI). SSI pays monthly checks to children and adults with serious disabilities (along with senior citizens) who lack other income and resources. SSDI pays a monthly check to adults who are too disabled to work who have either acquired Social Security coverage based on their own past earnings, or whose disability began before age 18 and who are the children of deceased or retired persons who earned Social Security coverage. Both SSI and SSDI are designed to provide a monthly income to people with disabilities who meet the programs' qualifications. Both program are administered by the Social Security Administration (SSA).

SSI. As of 2000, SSI pays eligible individuals $512 per month and eligible couples $769 per month. These amounts are reduced by other income of the recipient. If the recipient lives at home or is otherwise provided with food, clothing, and shelter by others, the benefit is generally reduced by about one-third.

To establish eligibility on the basis of disability, an individual must meet both a disability test and certain tests of financial need. To qualify as "disabled," an adult applicant's condition must be so disabling that he cannot engage in "substantial gainful activity." This means that he cannot perform any paid job, whether or not a suitable job can be found. The test of disability for minor children is different: whether the child's condition "results in marked and severe functional limitations." SSA regulations prescribe a set of tests and functional criteria for making these determinations. The criteria include:

1. Your child's cognitive ability, as measured by standardized IQ tests;
2. Your child's behavior patterns, including his ability to adapt to different environments; and
3. Your child's communication ability.

In making an eligibility determination SSA is required to consider all the factors that can affect your child's ability to work (or the equivalent criteria for children under age 18). Both the symptom (such as behavior) and its intensity are considered as part of a functional analysis.

SSI's eligibility requirements do not end with the disability test. Eligibility is also based on financial need. To establish need, one must satisfy both a "resource" test and income tests. An applicant is ineligible if his assets ("resources") exceed $2,000 for an individual or $3,000 for a couple. The income of an SSI applicant or recipient also affects eligibility. The SSI rules allow a $20 "disregard" for monthly income of all kinds and an additional $65 "disregard" per month for earned income. Unearned income in excess of the $20 disregard reduces SSI benefits dollar for dollar. Earned income in excess of the disregards reduces SSI benefits $1 for every $2 earned, under a statutory work incentive program. In calculating an applicant's income, SSA also disregards certain impairment-related work expenses. In addition, under the PASS program (Plans for Achieving Self-Support), an SSI recipient can receive additional income or assets if they will be used to make it possible for the recipient to work in the future or to establish a business or occupation that will enable him to become gainfully employed.

In these determinations, SSA "deems" the resources and income of the parents of a child under age 18 who lives at home to be resources and income of the child. Thus, children with disabilities under age 18 who live with their parents are eligible only if their parents are very poor. When a child is 18, however, the attribution ("deeming") of parental resources and income to the child stops, and eligibility is determined on the basis of the child's own resources and income. Thus, many people with disabilities become eligible for SSI on their eighteenth birthday. To be eligible, however, they cannot have excess resources or income. If a child reaches his eighteenth birthday with more than $2,000 in assets in his own name, he will not be eligible for SSI unless and until he disposes of the excess assets.

People with autism can work. Finding a job for a child with autism is a goal most parents strive hard to achieve. It is unfortunate that earning a salary can lead to a reduction or elimination of SSI benefits, because SSI is intended to provide income to people whose disabilities prevent them from working. Most significantly, in many states the loss of SSI may lead to a loss of medical coverage under Medicaid, discussed below. At this writing, Congress is considering additional work incentives to provide continued Medicare or Medicaid coverage for people who work their way out of SSI (or SSDI).

SSDI. People with disabilities may also qualify for SSDI—disability benefits under the Social Security program. The test for disability is the same as it is for SSI. People do not have to be poor to qualify for SSDI, unlike SSI, however; there are no financial eligibility requirements based on resources or unearned income, although earned income is severely limited. To be eligible, an applicant must qualify on the basis of his own work record for Social Security purposes, or he must be unmarried, have a disability that began before age 18, and be the child of a parent covered by Social Security who has retired or died.

As with SSI, your child's employment can cause serious problems. The work incentive program under SSI does not apply to people on SSDI, who lose eligibility if they earn more than $700 per month, because they are then deemed not to be disabled. This rule places an unfair burden on recipients of SSDI by forcing them to make a choice between work and financial security (and medical insurance). SSDI rules allow recipients to work for only a limited trial period without losing eligibility. Although most people with disabilities that are severe enough to meet the SSA tests become eligible for SSI at age 18, they may become eligible for SSDI on their parents' work record when their parents retire or die, thus subjecting them to the SSDI rules described above. However, if SSDI rules reduce benefits below SSI levels, SSI generally will make up the difference.

Medicare

Medicare is a federal health insurance program that helps pay for the medical expenses of people who qualify. People who are eligible for SSDI benefits, either on their own account or on a parent's account, will also be eligible for Medicare, starting at any age, after a waiting period. These persons will automatically receive Part A (hospital) coverage, and they can elect Part B (medical) coverage, for which they pay a premium. If a person can also qualify for Medicaid, discussed below, Medicaid may pay the Medicare Part B premium. In some cases, children or adults with disabilities who would not otherwise be eligible for Medicare may qualify if a third party—parents, relatives, charities, or even state and local governments—pays into Medicare. Called "third party buy-in," this works very much like purchasing private health insurance. Check with your local SSA office for details.

Medicaid

Medicaid is also important to many people with autism. It pays for medical care for people who do not have private health insurance or Medicare and lack sufficient income to pay for medical care. It also provides certain benefits that are not covered by Medicare, including prescription drug coverage and financial aid for the purchase of wheelchairs. In many states, under so-called "Medicaid waivers," it pays for residential services for many people with disabilities.

Because Medicaid is funded by both federal and state governments, there are differences among states in the range of benefits offered. For example, some states provide "optional" services such as dental care, speech or language therapy, and occupational therapy. Consequently, parents must check with their state or local SSA office to make sure they are receiving the maximum range of Medicaid benefits available in their state.

Medicaid is funded partly by the states and partly by the federal government, and is administered by the states. In most states, if your child meets the eligibility criteria for SSI, he will qualify for Medicaid when he reaches age 18. Because eligibility is based on financial need, however, placing assets in the name of your child can disqualify him.

Early and Periodic Screening, Diagnosis, and Treatment Program (EPSDT). Under this Medicaid program, states provide periodic medical and developmental assessments of children under the age of 21 whose parents qualify for Medicaid, and provide the services—medical and otherwise—needed to treat any diagnosis. These services can include physical, occupational, and speech therapies, immunizations, assistive devices, and vision, dental, and medical treatment. Your state or county department of health services should have an EPSDT contact who can help you determine if your child is eligible for services under this program. Your county or state P&A office can also help you obtain EPSDT services.

It is important for you to become generally familiar with the complex rules governing SSI, SSDI, Medicare, and Medicaid. You can contact your local SSA office, or call their national toll-free number (800/772-1213). Again, we repeat the importance of avoiding a mistake that could disqualify your child from receiving needed benefits by implementing one of the basic strategies described in this chapter.

Children with Special Health Care Needs Program

Under a program of grants administered by the Maternal and Child Health Bureau of the U.S. Department of Health and Human Services, states receive funds to pay for wide variety of health-related services to children of low income families. Services can include evaluations, clinic visits, hospitalization, surgery, medications, physical, occupational, and speech therapy, dental care, and genetic testing. Each state sets its own financial eligibility requirements based on a family's annual income. Unlike Medicaid, however, your child's assets do not affect eligibility. States can select the conditions that will be covered. This list is generally very broad; children with autism should qualify for services if their parents are eligible financially. There is also variation among states in the age at which these services cease to be available; generally between age 18 and age 21. Each state has a coordinator for this program typically at the state departments of health or human services. Your local office of the ASA or The Arc or ACL can help you locate the state coordinator.

Children's Health Insurance Program (CHIP)

In 1997, Congress enacted a new health insurance program, the Children's Health Insurance Program (CHIP), to provide free or low-cost health insurance to children whose parents' income is too high to qualify for Medicaid and too low to be able to afford private family insurance. In most states, uninsured children age 18 and under in families with an income of less than $32,900 qualify for coverage under CHIP. Most states currently participate in this program and offer a wide range of coverage for children, including checkups, immunizations, doctor visits, prescription drugs, and hospital care. Applications for coverage under the CHIP program can be obtained from state or local health and human services departments.

■■ Competence to Manage Financial Affairs

Even if your child with autism may never need state-funded residential care or government benefits, he may need help in arranging his financial affairs. Care must be exercised in deciding how to make assets available for your child. There are a wide variety of arrangements that can allow someone else to control the ways in which money is spent after you die. Of course, the choice of the best arrangements depends on many different considerations, such as your child's capacity to manage assets, his relationship with his siblings, your financial situation, and the availability of an appropriate trustee or financial manager. As an adult, your child will deserve to be consulted regarding decisions that affect him; you should arrange for that.

Choosing trustees and financial managers is harder for a person who will need assistance all his life than it is for a minor child who can take charge of his own affairs when he becomes an adult, because the trust or other arrangements must last so much longer after parents die. Consequently, particular consideration must be given to mechanisms for changing trustees after the original trustees can no longer serve. Each family is different. A knowledgeable lawyer can review the various alternatives and help you choose the one best suited to your family.

Need for Guardians

Parents sometimes ask whether they should take steps to be appointed guardian for a son or daughter with autism when the child becomes an adult. There is no general yes or no answer to the question. It depends on the child's circumstances, and whether guardianship will meet some need.

Guardians have the legal power to make decisions for the "ward"—the person for whom the guardianship is established. There are two kinds of guardians: guardians of the "person," and guardians of property (sometimes called guardians of the "estate"). A guardian of the person has the legal power to make personal decisions for the ward—for example, to authorize and consent to medical treatment, determine where the ward will live, have access to the ward's records, authorize police to bring a wandering ward home, and matters of that kind. A guardian of property manages the ward's property for the benefit of the ward and has legal power to determine how to invest the ward's assets and what kind of expenditures to make for the ward. The same person may be guardian of both the person and the property of a particular ward, but different persons can also be appointed for these two different jobs.

In general, guardians for adults (persons over 18 years of age) can only be appointed by a court. Parents are the "natural" guardians of the person of their minor children without court appointment in many states, and in some states the deceased parents of a minor can appoint guardians of the person of that minor by will, without court appointment. In many states, on the other hand, court appointment is necessary to establish a guardianship of the property of a minor.

Under the laws of almost all states, parents can nominate guardians for their minor and adult children with disabilities in their wills. Courts that are asked to appoint a guardian for such a person will honor the parents' nomination, unless it is affirmatively shown not to be in their son's or daughter's best interest, or unless the son or daughter is deemed to have sufficient judgment to choose a guardian for himself or herself. It is therefore prudent for parents of persons with autism to nominate the persons they want to serve as guardians if guardians are ever needed. If a guardian is needed and appointed, the preferences stated in a parent's will usually will be respected.

Should parents seek their own appointment by a court as guardians of their son or daughter with autism when the child becomes an adult? Circumstances may require appointment of a guardian if the person with autism has funds that need management. A guardian of the property may be required, although in some states it may be possible and preferable to put those funds in a special needs trust. These situations arise where the person with autism recovers damages for personal injury, or (for families who have not been properly advised) inherits funds directly from a deceased relative, or becomes entitled at age 21 to funds in a Uniform Transfers to Minors Act account.

Other circumstances may dictate appointment of a guardian for the person or property of an adult with disabilities. If health care providers require consent for medical treatment and will not accept the consent of the patient, a guardian of the person will be needed to give consent unless the state has a "surrogate" consent law. Similarly, if the person with autism refuses to give consent for needed medical treatment, appointment of a guardian of the person with power to give consent may solve the problem. If program providers or health care providers refuse to let parents see records of an adult son or daughter with autism, the parents may need to secure their own appointment as guardians to solve the problem. If the person with disabilities has a habit of wandering off and police will not return him to his home unless a guardian tells them to, guardianship provides a solution. If a person with disabilities is victimized by some person to whom he gives away his funds, or starts making large and imprudent purchases, appointment of a guardian may give the guardian power to invalidate the transactions and seek the return of the funds.

Guardianship has its disadvantages, and many persons with autism will never have any real need for a guardian. Guardianship entails a loss of decisionmaking power for the ward. In some states guardianship may entail loss of rights to contract, vote, or marry. Some courts routinely grant petitions for the appointment of guardians for a person with disabilities, but other courts will not do so in the absence of a demonstration that a guardianship will meet some genuine need. Moreover, securing appointment of a guardian involves expense and some bother. Parents who petition for the appointment of a guardian usually will need a lawyer, and in many states, the court will appoint another lawyer to represent the proposed ward. There may be a hearing in court, even if the ward does not object to the proposed appointment. Court proceedings may be humiliating to the ward. In addition, in most states guardians must account or report to the court once a year; indeed, a guardian of property will be required to account to a court (in addition to the Social Security Administration) for SSI or Social Security benefits. That may be a mere nuisance, or it may involve unnecessary expense, particularly if a lawyer must prepare or file the reports.

Consequently, there is no one "right" answer to the question of whether parents of persons with autism should secure their appointment as guardians for their son or daughter. The right answer requires balancing these conflicting considerations. It may be worthwhile to discuss the pros and cons with a lawyer who is experienced in these matters.

Life Insurance

Parents of children with autism should review their life insurance coverage. The most important use of life insurance is to meet financial needs that arise if the insured person dies. Many people who support dependents with their wages or salaries are underinsured. This problem is aggravated if hard-earned dollars are wasted on insurance that does not provide the amount or kind of protection that could and should be purchased. It is therefore essential for any person with dependents to understand basic facts about insurance.

The first question to consider is: Who should be insured? Life insurance deals with the *financial* risks of death. The principal financial risk of death in most families is that the death of the wage earner or earners will deprive dependents of support. Consequently, life insurance coverage should be considered primarily for the parent or parents on whose earning power the children depend, rather than on the lives of children or dependents.

The second question is whether your insurance is adequate to meet the financial needs that will arise if you die. A reputable insurance agent can help you determine whether your coverage is adequate. Consumer guides to insurance listed in the Reading List of this book can also help you calculate the amount of insurance you need.

The next question is: What kind of insurance policy should you buy? Insurance policies are of two basic types: term insurance, which provides "pure" insurance without any build-up of cash value or reserves, and other types (called "whole life," "universal life," and "variable life"), which, in addition to providing insurance, include a savings or investment factor. The latter kinds of insurance, sometimes called "permanent" insurance, are really a combined package of insurance and investment. The different types of insurance are described in more detail in the consumer guides to insurance listed in the Reading List of this book.

People with children who do not have disabilities try to assure that their children's education will be paid for if they die before their children finish school. Many people use life insurance to deal with this risk. When their children are grown and educated, this insurance need disappears. Term insurance is a relatively inexpensive way to deal with risks of this kind.

On the other hand, people with autism may need supplemental assistance throughout their lives. That need may not disappear completely during their parents' lifetimes. If the parents plan on using life insurance to help meet this need when they die, they must recognize, in deciding what kind of insurance to buy, that term insurance premiums rise sharply as they get older. Consequently, they should either adopt and stick to a savings and investment program to eventually replace the insurance, or consider purchasing whole life or universal life.

Whether you buy term insurance and maintain a separate savings and investment program, or instead buy one of the other kinds of policies that combine them, you should make sure that the insurance part of your program is adequate to meet your family's financial needs if you die. A sound financial plan will meet these needs and will satisfy savings and retirement objectives in a way that does not sacrifice adequate insurance coverage.

Finally, it is essential to coordinate your life insurance with the rest of your estate plan. This is done by designating the beneficiary—

choosing who is to receive any insurance proceeds when you die. If you wish any or all of these proceeds to be used for your child's support, you may wish to designate a trustee under your will or the trustee of a separate life insurance trust as a beneficiary of your insurance. Upon your death, the trustee will receive the insurance proceeds and use them for the benefit of your child in accordance with the trust. If you do not name a trustee, but instead name the child with autism as a beneficiary, your child's share of the proceeds may be subject to cost-of-care claims, or may interfere with eligibility for government benefits, described earlier.

∷ A Guide to Estate Planing for Parents of Children with Autism

More than most parents, the parents of a child with autism need to attend to estate planning. Because of concerns about cost-of-care liability, government benefits, and competency, it is vital that you make plans. Parents need to name the people who will care for their child with autism when they die. They need to review their insurance to be sure it is adequate to meet their child's needs. They need to make sure their retirement plans will help meet their child's needs as an adult. They need to inform grandparents of cost-of-care liability, government benefits, and competency problems so that grandparents do not inadvertently waste resources that could otherwise benefit their grandchild. Most of all, parents need to make wills so that their hopes and plans are realized and the disastrous consequences of dying without a will are avoided.

Proper estate planning differs for each family. Every will must be tailored to individual needs. There are no formula wills, especially for parents of a child with autism. There are some common mistakes to avoid, however. Here is a list:

No Will. In most states, the children (including a child with a disability) of a married person who dies without a will are entitled to equal shares in a portion of the assets the parent owns at death. The entire estate of a single parent who dies without a will must be divided equally among the children. The result is that your child with autism will inherit property in his own name. His inheritance may become subject to cost-of-care claims and could jeopardize eligibility for government benefits. These and other problems can be avoided with a properly drafted will. Do not ever allow your state's laws to determine how your property will be divided upon your death. No parent of a child with autism should die without a will.

A Will Leaving Property Outright to the Child with Autism. A will that leaves property to a child with autism in his own name is often just as bad as no will at all, because it may subject the inheritance to cost-of-care liability and may disqualify him for government benefits. Parents of children with autism do not just need any will, they need a will that meets their specific needs.

A Will Creating a Support Trust for Your Child with Autism. A will that creates a support trust (described above) presents much the same problem as a will that leaves property outright to a child with autism. The funds in these trusts may be subject to cost-of-care claims and jeopardize government benefits. A qualified lawyer experienced in these issues can help draft a will that avoids this problem.

Insurance and Retirement Plans Naming a Child with Autism as a Beneficiary. Many parents own life insurance policies that name a child with autism as a beneficiary or contingent beneficiary, either alone or in common with siblings. The result is that insurance proceeds may go outright to your child with autism, creating cost-of-care liability and government benefits eligibility problems. Parents should designate the funds to pass either to someone else or to go into a properly drawn trust. The same is true of many retirement plan benefits.

Use of Joint Tenancy in Lieu of Wills. Spouses sometimes avoid making wills by placing all their property in joint tenancies with right of survivorship. When one of the spouses dies, the survivor automatically becomes the sole owner. Parents try to use joint tenancies instead of wills, relying on the surviving spouse to properly take care of all estate planning matters. This plan, however, fails completely if both parents die in the same disaster, if the surviving spouse becomes incapacitated, or if the surviving spouse neglects to make a proper will. The result is the same as if neither spouse made any will at all—the child with autism shares in the parents' estates. As explained above, this result may expose the assets to cost-of-care liability and give rise to problems with government benefits. Therefore, even when all property is held by spouses in joint tenancy, it is necessary that both spouses make wills.

Establishing UTMA Accounts for Your Child with Autism. Over and over again well-meaning parents and grandparents open bank accounts for children with disabilities under the Uniform

Transfers to Minors Act (UTMA). When the child reaches age 21, the account becomes the property of the child, and may therefore be subject to cost-of-care liability. Perhaps more important, most people with disabilities first become eligible for SSI and Medicaid at age 18, but the UTMA funds will have to be spent or financial eligibility for these programs will be lost, thus making the state and federal governments the indirect beneficiaries of funds the family has set aside. Parents and relatives of children with autism who are likely to need government-funded services or benefits should *never* set up UTMA accounts for their child with autism, nor should they open other bank accounts in the child's name.

Failing to Advise Grandparents and Relatives of the Need for Special Arrangements. Just as the parents of a child with autism need properly drafted wills or trusts, so do grandparents and other relatives who may leave (or give) property to the child. If these people are not aware of the special concerns—cost-of-care liability, government benefits, and competency—their plans may go awry and their generosity may be wasted. Make sure anyone planning gifts to your child with autism understands what is at stake.

Children and adults with autism are entitled to lead full and rewarding lives. But many of them cannot do so without continuing financial support from their families. The *only* way to make sure your child has that support whenever he needs it is to plan for tomorrow today. Doing otherwise can rob him of the future he deserves.

▪▪ Conclusion

Parenthood always brings responsibilities. Substantial extra responsibilities confront parents of a child with autism. Understanding the pitfalls for the future and planning to avoid them will help you to meet the special responsibilities. In addition, knowing and asserting your child's rights can help guarantee that he will receive the education and government benefits to which he is entitled. Being a good advocate for your child requires more than knowledge. You must also be determined to use that knowledge effectively, and, when necessary, forcefully.

▪▪ Parent Statements

By the time we were finished with the due-process procedures, I was tired of a school system that I felt was unresponsive to youngsters who are severely disabled. We moved to a county we knew had more

*options for autistic children, and so far we've been happy here.
In regard to the laws pertaining to people with disabilities: Know them,
learn them, and quote them if you have too!*

⊷❀⊷

*Since the diagnosis, my husband and I have added a new item to our
household budget: money to retain a lawyer each year.*

⊷❀⊷

*You never get to talk to the school administrators, so you just get a
lawyer. And the lawyer knows what to say. So, it costs you $500,
because it usually doesn't go to a hearing, because the lawyer knows
what the law really is and what they have to do.*

⊷❀⊷

*When we called the attorney, she wasn't really very receptive. Her atti-
tude was, "Well, try and get it on your own and save your money," and
that kind of thing.*

⊷❀⊷

*I think what's hardest for me to understand about IDEA is that
"appropriate" doesn't necessarily mean "best"—at least not to the
schools, it doesn't.*

⊷❀⊷

*We've been taking estate planning really seriously because we feel that it
shouldn't be up to our other children to provide for Carl later on. I
mean, if they want to, fine, but we're not going to make them feel as if
they have to.*

⊷❀⊷

*When it comes to understanding the ins and outs of IDEA, there's noth-
ing like having another parent who's already dealt with the system
explain everything to you.*

⊷❀⊷

*When I first started working with the school, I thought nobody there
would be able to recognize an appropriate program for Bobby if it fell
on them—but I was wrong. For the most part, the school's been very*

receptive to my suggestions. You can't ever rest, though. You've got to be constantly monitoring your child's progress.

❧

My only advice is that you plan the best you can. You sit down with a good lawyer and draw up a will. You try to decide who will best look out for your child's needs and his well-being. You pick a good back-up for that person and then you stop worrying about the "what ifs:" what if the person you've left in charge has an accident and is sued; what if the person you've left in charge is widowed and remarries and he or she runs off with the money? You cover every track you can think of, you pray it will be okay, and then you stop agonizing about it because there's nothing else you can do.

❧

The law guarantees an "appropriate" education, not a "quality" education. What nagged me was that although I knew what my child needed, I didn't know how much was appropriate to ask the school system to provide. How am I to know what "appropriate" means? After all, I've never been through this before, and I don't have any way of knowing what others are asking for and getting.

❧

The IEP team seems to respect that my position is based on authoritative sources, not just parental emotions. Knowing what's reasonable has enabled me to request all the recommended services with confidence. I've found that asking for more than you really expect to get is an unsuccessful ploy.

❧

Study the IEP format and make sure you understand how it works. Never go into an IEP meeting without an outline or agenda, and use it! It's also a good idea to tape record the meetings. Afterward, go over the IEP with a fine toothed comb. Make sure every detail is written out. Send a follow up letter on your understanding of the meeting.

❧

The department of education in my state has published a document on educating children with autism. It gave me a pretty good idea of what the state (not me, not the town, not someone I'm paying) considers to be appropriate. Look for something like this from your state—it carries a lot of weight!

❧❧❧

Bring a large picture of your child to IEP meetings. It helps keep the focus on your child instead of everyone's political agenda.

❧❧❧

I enlisted the services of a parent advocate who attends many IEPs and knows what other parents in the state are asking for and getting.

9

BECOMING AN
ADVOCATE

Bernice Friedlander

■■ Introduction

Do not be intimidated by the title of this chapter. Contrary to what you may have heard, you do not need a law degree to be an advocate for your child or to understand the principles behind advocacy. Some advocates are lawyers, but many more are teachers, mental health and medical professionals, or concerned parents and citizens like you. Some advocacy does take place in the courtroom, but much more takes place in schools, hospitals, at the local supermarket, in front of a computer, and at home. Advocacy is accomplished through sworn testimony, but also through letter-writing campaigns and phone calls, talking to neighbors, professionals, public servants, and officials. Modern technology has created a powerful new tool for the citizen-advocate—the Internet. It brings your message to thousands of people—whether you are transmitting information, seeking remedies, asking questions, or alerting other parents about proposed legislation or regulations that might impose hardships on parents, families, and their children.

What then is advocacy? Simply put, to advocate means to plead someone's cause. In the disability arena, this usually involves working to change how society views children with disabilities, and working to obtain needed services and benefits for them.

This chapter provides an overview of some of the ways advocacy is used to help children with autism and other disabilities. It describes how people and organizations can work to achieve educational, legislative, and other reforms, and leads you step by step through the advocacy process. Most importantly, this chapter explains how you, the parent, can get involved in advocating for your child in order to ensure that her future is as fulfilling as possible.

** The Need for Advocacy

A variety of state and federal laws are intended to guarantee your child important rights—in education, training, employment, and access to health care, for example. A legislative cornerstone for children with disabilities and their families is the Individual with Disabilities Education Act (IDEA).

IDEA exists in part because thousands of parents of children with autism and other disabilities fought for the right of their children to be educated in the public school system. It is probably safe to say that parent advocates have played critical roles in the passage of all recent legislation benefiting children with disabilities. The reason for this is simple: Since elected officials seldom have time to keep up with every issue affecting people with disabilities, they rely on experts to tell them what legislation is needed.

In many instances, the "experts" who can best convince officials of the need for improved services are parents like you who have first-hand experience in raising children with disabilities. Parents can not only persuade officials to propose new legislation, but they can also play major roles in clinching the support needed to pass a particular law. For instance, when a bill is being debated before a crucial vote, members of Congress or the state legislature frequently refer to messages of support they have received from parents. They reflect on the conversations you and other parents had with them over the Internet or in person. They put a lot of trust in your views as an "on-the-job" parent and advocate for your children. They correctly assume, "who knows the situation better than the parents?"

Besides urging legislators to pass new legislation that will help the entire category of children with disabilities, parents may find that they must practice another kind of advocacy—directed advocacy—on behalf of their own children. Because children with autism usually have communication problems and cannot speak out for their own rights, you may find yourself using this brand of advocacy often. This does not mean that you should expect to see your child's rights trampled at every turn, but rather that there may be times when someone else's ignorance of your child's unique needs prompts a decision that is not in your child's best interests.

Here is how directed advocacy can work: You may feel that your child is not receiving the services you think she needs. Even though IDEA specifies that parents and educators are supposed to work together to develop each child's Individualized Education Program (IEP), it is up to you to convince the educators that your child needs additional services to help her maximize her potential. Though there has been much progress in the last ten years, school officials are often simply unaware of the special needs of children with autism, so *you* must ensure that your child's IEP will meet those needs. For instance, delayed speech requires therapy involving various language stimulation techniques, but unless you advocate that your child be given this therapy, she may not receive it. Your advocacy may include providing medical and clinical information to document your request, or involve testaments from experts in education, training, medical science, or psychology. Using the collection of knowledge already compiled, networking with other parents of children with autism, and accessing assistance through the Internet, puts very significant tools at your disposal for making a compelling case.

∷ Advocacy in Action

The principle behind advocacy is simple: "the squeaky wheel gets the grease." However, there is an important caveat. Being "squeaky" and getting recognized is a vital first step. When you get the attention of an official, you must be prepared to describe the problem concisely and the proposed solution you are seeking. You must be able to answer critical questions about the problem during your meeting or afterward in a follow-up memo in order to be effective. You are in a world of a thousand issues, each having a constituency and each doing its best to capture the attention of the powerful and influential. So when you step forward, follow the Scout motto: "Be prepared."

Let us say you have concerns about the treatment your child is or is not receiving. This is most important for your child and your family. You *will* get results provided you attract the right people's attention. Sometimes you can resolve the problem on your own. Particularly in cases where you feel that a specific situation is adversely affecting only your child, a phone call to an elected official or a well-worded letter to the editor of the local newspaper may work wonders. Other times, the best strategy may be to band together with other parents to advocate for change. It is usually most effective to work with a group when attempting to get changes made that will benefit all children with autism or all children. There is strength in numbers.

In past years, both individuals and groups have enjoyed considerable success in advocating for children with autism. In the account below, Lillian Tommasone, the co-author of Chapter 2, describes how she and her husband obtained needed educational services for their child:

> Our personal involvement in advocacy began at a PTA meeting. We heard that a Pennsylvania court had ruled that a 12-month education program was sometimes necessary to meet the needs of a child with disabilities. According to the court, a ten-month program did not always adequately fulfill the child's right to a "free and appropriate education," as provided in IDEA. In such cases, an extended school year could help maintain a child's appropriate skills and behaviors, and, more significantly, help prevent him from losing those skills.

> We had mixed feelings about the 12-month program. Although we were thrilled about our toddler's steady gains and proud of his hard-won struggles to master simple tasks, somehow we felt sorrowful and cheated. It didn't seem fair to send Mike to school during the summer. But as we saw the consequences of regression, we decided it would be a good idea to replace our usual summer activities with added instruction for Mike.

> At once, we set out to get Mike into an extended program. Being novice advocates, we thought a simple verbal request to the Supervisor of Child Study in our local school district would be sufficient. The supervisor, however, told us that our request was not in keeping with current Board of Education policy. At first we were shocked and angry, but we learned that he was absolutely correct: there was no local or state policy for extended school programs. The board was not required by law to provide one. On the other hand, there was no law that said it couldn't be done, either, if the board should choose to do so.

In the beginning, we felt powerless and frightened at the thought of questioning or making recommendations to the authorities. Then we realized that what we needed to do was to show the board that the extended school year was necessary, easy-to-implement, and cost-effi-cient—in short, the best solu-  tion for everyone involved. To do this, we needed more information, preparation, and a systematic plan.

We began to learn all we could about autism and the law. We attended workshops and seminars on advocacy to familiarize ourselves with the procedures for obtaining services. We contacted the state protection and advocacy office and asked questions about things we didn't understand. We spoke with "seasoned parents" who told us about some of the pitfalls in dealing with the Child Study Team (CST). We attended local Board of Education meetings to identify key players sensitive to children with disabilities and requested documentation of Mike's needs from his teachers and school administrators. Finally, we kept a diary of the regression that took place on days Mike was not in school.

Bolstered by the confidence that our thorough preparation had given us, we now began to advocate in earnest. We wrote letters to the CST, the Superintendent of Schools, and Board members, documenting Mike's needs and request-ing funding for an extended school year. We arranged for a conference to explore together the possibilities of securing services. We also continued to attend Board of Education meetings, where we expressed our concerns and explained that surrounding states were offering 12-month services.

By contacting local and state legislators—especially those on the Appropriations and Education Committees—we developed a feeling for what was going on. Several legisla-tors hinted that a mandate concerning the provision was on the horizon. The need, however, hadn't been demonstrated *in our state and a bill had yet to be written on the subject.*

Then we learned through the Education Committee that grant monies were available to communities who wanted to participate in the development of innovative approaches to special education.

Our research, planning, and persistence were beginning to pay off! We contacted the CST and told them about the exciting new opportunities to obtain funding. Surely the Board wanted to be a model for other communities to emulate, we said. Then, striking while the iron was hot, we offered to make trade-offs. If the School Board would pay tuition for Mike's summer schooling, we promised that we would provide transportation. We also suggested that we could all sit down together at the end of the first summer and evaluate whether or not the program was helping Mike.

When the Board agreed to our proposals, we were ecstatic. True to our word, we kept the Board informed about the program and Mike's progress. A show of good faith, a cooperative partnership, and Mike's continued development were instrumental in his receiving both tuition and transportation the following summer.

Our story is not a dramatic one. By gathering needed information, developing a systematic plan, and being both assertive and persistent, we succeeded in building a working partnership with "those on the other side of the fence."

By following a few simple steps, you too can become an effective advocate:

1. **Become informed**—*Read, read, read.*
2. **Explore all avenues**—*don't leave any source unturned: parents, legislators, educators.*
3. **Be patient, yet persistent;** *it pays off.*
4. **Identify the key players**—*those sensitive to special needs.*
5. **Stay objective.** *Being emotional can be disastrous—it clouds objectivity and diplomacy.*
6. **Save copies of correspondence** *and make notes of phone calls to keep the memory fresh.*
7. **Make compromises and develop partnerships.** *Remember, a slice of the pie is better than none.*

8. **Share your experiences** *with other parents.*
9. **Say "thank you"** *to those who helped.*
10. **Believe in yourself, and your child.**

One final piece of advice: In working to help your child today, remember that advocacy does not just involve children. Some of the most important advocacy work for parents is longer term. For example, there is much to advocate for in vocational training, supported employment, community living options for adults, and availability of other programs. All of these are, and will continue to be, subjects of advocacy by concerned parents. Being an advocate for your child is good training for being an advocate in the future.

There is a lot you can do as an individual. We know! We did it ourselves. But sometimes the job can be done better, faster, and more completely by an organization. That is why the Autism Society of America (ASA) can be so important to all of us.

▪▪ The Autism Society of America

One of the primary purposes of the Autism Society of America (ASA) is to advocate on behalf of people with autism and their families. From its early beginnings, the ASA has been an active force on Capitol Hill, pushing for the rights of individuals with autism on a national scale. As the largest autism organization in the United States, the ASA can be more effective than a single parent or even a small group of parents. The organization has the resources to monitor legislation, reach out to the media, and keep large numbers of people informed on the issues. Most importantly, of course, the ASA monitors and acts when governmental programs and legislation are not adequately serving the needs of people with autism. The following is a good example of how the ASA works:

In the last few years, the ASA's most successful, prominent advocacy effort has involved the reauthorization of IDEA, also known as the Individuals with Disabilities Education Act, and the subsequent attempts to amend and weaken it.

IDEA, originally called the "Education for All Handicapped Children Act" or "Public Law 94-142," guarantees individuals with dis-

abilities the right to a free, appropriate education. IDEA is the most important federal law governing the educational rights of people with autism age under 21.

In 1997, IDEA was reauthorized and strengthened. However, during this process, various forces arose to threaten and undermine the law's protections. An issue that became part of the public debate then and continues to present day involves the handling of students with disabilities who require disciplinary action. In 1997, proponents of increased disciplinary measures tried to introduce amendments to IDEA on this issue. One of the initial challenges involved the "cessation of services" as a disciplinary measure for individuals with disabilities. These provisions would have entitled school districts to withdraw all educational services to students with disabilities who have been suspended. Provisions such as these were unacceptable to the ASA and others in the disability community. Over the course of 1997, the organization issued a call to action to its members and members of the general autism community, asking them to call, write, and e-mail Congress on this issue. ASA issued e-mail Action Alerts, Fax alerts, and released special announcements to its members. In addition, the organization actively lobbied Congress with the same message: "Reauthorize IDEA without amendments." The consistent, large-scale lobbying effort worked—in 1997, IDEA was successfully reauthorized without the damaging provisions.

Since then in 1998 and 1999, various attempts have arisen again to introduce measures to weaken the law for individuals with disabilities. ASA has been a vigilant force in keeping these forces at bay. The organization has organized Call-in Days to Congress, faxed information to every member of the House of Representatives, and, at critical points during the legislative year, asked autism advocates to contact their legislators directly to help defeat any and all measures. In 1999 and 2000, individual members of ASA's Board of Directors visited members of Congress to further advocate on this issue and others important to the autism community.

As individuals, parents and family members can do much to advocate on behalf of their loved ones. Working with a group like the Autism Society of America, parents can have a much larger impact. The ASA, which keeps its fingers on the pulse of issues important to autism, is an important advocate on behalf of all individuals with autism and their families.

ASA has a large national network consisting of 225 chapters in 46 states. It maintains an award-winning World Wide Web site, "http://www.autism-society.org," a toll-free number, an alert government relations team, and a bimonthly magazine that connects its 20,000 members. ASA and sister organizations such as Cure Autism Now and the National Alliance for Autism Research use technology to expand the constituent base, and share information and contacts between tens of thousands of concerned citizens, experts in the field, and government officials.

Advocacy organizations like ASA can accomplish a great deal on the national level. The key to effectiveness is building upon a base of concerned and informed parents and other people. The most effective organization is the one in which the "trickle up" of experiences, information, and data is continuous. Unless parents keep the ASA informed, the ASA cannot possibly keep track of all the local issues that affect children with autism. And the ASA cannot influence public policy without proof—in the form of your letters, telegrams, phone calls, internet correspondence—that thousands of citizens support its positions and are alert to those in power who are making decisions that will affect the lives of children with autism.

The Autism Society of America concentrates its advocacy on national issues. Matters of concern to parents on local and state levels can most effectively be addressed through local ASA chapters and other parent and advocacy groups. In the past several years, many ASA chapters have developed statewide lobbying organizations in state capitals, hired professional staffs, and established networks with other disability organizations. This is the newest sign of effectiveness brought about by parents and other concerned citizens pooling their resources to battle the common enemy of ignorance and prejudice in the struggle to gain important rights for our kids.

The next sections are designed to provide a step-by-step guide for you and your parents' groups to help you become effective advocates.

:: At the Legislative Level

Know Your Issue

In recent decades, parents and other citizen-advocates have played crucial roles in enacting federal, state, and local legislation benefiting millions of Americans with disabilities. There is still a Herculean amount of work to be done if we are to improve existing laws and secure the passage of new initiatives. Protecting IDEA from weakening amendments, and advocating for reauthorization of the Developmental Disabilities Assistance Act, are two priorities that require constant vigilance by advocates. Obtaining designated funding for autism research, epidemiology, and education at the Centers for Disease Control and Prevention and at the National Institutes of Health is an important goal that could lead to advances in research. Both of these efforts must continue during the coming decade to nourish progress. And there is little dispute about the continuing need for public funding of community-based living options and employment programs for adolescents and adults with disabilities.

As the parent of a child with autism, you will undoubtedly want to keep abreast of all pending or proposed legislation that may affect the welfare of your child. One of the simplest ways for you to find out about important issues is to write, phone, or e-mail the ASA national office and ask that your name be added to the ASA ACTION ALERT list. ASA will notify you of any legislative developments affecting children with autism.

With a membership in ASA comes a subscription to *The Advocate*. It will keep you up-to-date about new regulations affecting your child, legislative activity, coalitions with other concerned parents of children with disabilities, information about recent publications and resources, plus state and local notices of interest such as regional leadership meetings. The "Watching Washington" column gives the most recent information about federal activity.

Other sources of information include other parents, community newspapers, and radio and television stations. When an issue rouses you to action, remember first to do your homework. You must get all the facts straight, marshal rational, irrefutable arguments, and make sure that you understand the issue inside and out. After all, if you are going to sway a public official's opinion, your command of the issues will have to be as good as his or hers, if not better.

The following section explains how to get involved with legislative matters before United States Congressmen and Senators. However, these suggestions are equally applicable when you are devising a strategy for lobbying or advocating before state legislators, county government officials, city council members, or any other elected representative.

Position Paper

In the process of getting to know your issue, you may find it useful to develop a position paper detailing exactly where you stand. These are some points to include:

- **Know the formal name of the bill, act, or public law that is affected by the legislation you support and be able to refer to it properly.** For example: Who are the sponsors of the measure in the Senate and House? Which Committee(s) was the measure referred to for consideration? Which Subcommittee(s) is charged with considering the bill within each Committee?

- **Categorically refute all major arguments being used against the measure you are supporting.** Frequently objections will involve cost or "local rights." When no cost or low cost is involved, this is something you will want to state clearly and often in all of your communications with public officials. If there is real cost involved, justify it. What price is the official placing on your child's lifetime opportunities?

- **Utilize important phrases** like "children's rights," "parents' rights," "the right to a free and appropriate education," or "in order to bring justice to our children" in your arguments. Issues involving the preservation of basic rights, justice, and the welfare of children often cut across partisan and ideological lines and can be supported by most legislators.

- **List or refer to organizations, special interest groups, coalitions, and influential members of your community that support your point of view.** Use Internet sites for additional information or examples to illustrate your point.

- **Cite newspaper or magazine editorials that agree with your stand.**

Although putting your position in writing may seem like busy work at first, it actually serves several useful purposes. To begin with, it forces you to look objectively at issues that may arouse your deepest emotions. In addition, the process of writing down your thoughts can help you pinpoint any logical inconsistencies in your own arguments, as well as in those of your opponents. And, more importantly, detailing your stand in writing will help you feel confident about your grasp of the issue.

Know Your Elected Official

Once you have a good grasp of the issue, the next step is to gather information about your elected official. Your goal here is to learn enough about the official's background to help you determine the angle to use in asking for his or her support. For example, if the official has small children, you may want to appeal to him or her as a father or mother. If your elected official made campaign promises about increased funding for special education and then failed to deliver, you may want to remind him or her of that fact. In general, your background investigation should cover the following:

Personal Profile. This includes family background, education, occupation, and social, community, and religious affiliations. You can usually obtain a formal biography by requesting it from your Congressman or Senator. Since each member of Congress and the Senate maintain pages on the World Wide Web, it should be relatively easy to access the information. Your local newspaper office can provide appropriate background on local office holders. Many state legislators and city council members also maintain web sites.

Political Profile. This includes current and past political offices held, party affiliation and participation, special interest group constituencies such as school boards, educators, and medical societies, and names of key advisors and staff aides. Make an analysis of votes cast by the legislator on issues targeted by ASA or your local ASA chapter. Be sure to jot down his or her campaign promises. It is very effective to confront an elected official with his or her own words in support of your issue.

Base of Political Support. From whom did your legislator receive his or her greatest financial and voting support? It is important to determine whom the elected official owes both financially and politically. This information can make it easier for activists to contact people sympathetic to their position when a crucial vote is at stake.

A complete list of all contributors of $250 or more to any candidate for federal office is available from the Federal Election Commission. Their web site, "http://www.fec.gov," contains a complete list, which you can print out, of all contributors to every Congressional and Senate candidate. States that offer public funding for state elections also have public access to contributor records. Check with the Office of the Secretary of State of your state to identify the appropriate Internet site. You may see the name of someone you know listed as a contributor. Be sure to contact that person, as he or she may become an important ally to your cause.

Contact Your Elected Officials

After you have gathered the pertinent background information about the issue and the elected official, it is time to contact the elected official and let him or her know where you stand and what you want.

If you are like many first-time advocates, you may begin to get cold feet when you reach this stage of the advocacy process. You may worry that you are not "important" enough to disturb your Senator or Congressman or that he or she will not be interested in what you have to say. Nothing could be further from the truth.

Senators and Congressmen do not make laws in a vacuum. They want to hear from constituents who would be affected by pending legislation. Since a third of the Senate and all members of the House of Representatives are up for re-election every two years, elected officials are always anxious to please the voters back home. So when you contact your Senator or Congressman, you are not imposing at all, but actually doing him or her a service.

Article I of the U.S. Constitution guarantees every American the right "...to petition the government for a redress of grievances." This is what you are doing when you seek to meet with any elected official. Remember that any elected official who refuses to meet with you or respond to you is endangering his or her political future. It is in his or her best interest to listen to your point of view. To obtain his or her support, you will have to emphasize the merits of the issue and your personal interest in seeing it favorably resolved. You should indicate that you intend to pursue this matter until it is favorably resolved.

What follows is a description of how to go about contacting your elected officials through writing, visiting, telephoning, or the Internet. Always remember: your message should be clear and you must remember to follow through after each stage of the contact.

Write Your Elected Officials

One of the most effective ways to contact your elected officials is to write them a letter. Whether you use surface mail or electronic mail, each letter received on a particular issue is presumed to represent 20 to 30 other people who did not write. Therefore, when a Congressional or Senate office receives ten or 15 letters on one subject, you can be sure the topic will get the attention of a senior staff member.

Many Congressmen personally review their mail each day. Most Senators find this impossible since they receive mail from an entire state. Legislative assistants keep counts of the mail received on each subject and bring these reports to the Senator's or Congressman's attention when specific legislation is pending.

Both Congressional and Senate offices put a high priority on quick responses to constituent mail. Congressmen usually respond within a week to snail mail. Senators respond within two to three weeks. Electronic mail is usually answered more quickly.

Here are some guidelines to keep in mind when writing to elected officials:

- Know the issue and state your position clearly and concisely. One-page letters or three to four paragraph e-mails are preferable. It is sometimes difficult to handle a complex topic in such a brief form and it is better to cover the subject adequately.

- If it is a letter, write legibly in your own handwriting or typewrite, and be sure to sign the letter in your own handwriting. Always identify yourself as the parent of a child with autism.

- Limit your remarks to one or two issues per communication.

- Refer to pertinent legislation by the proper bill or public law number or title.

- If possible, include materials such as recent editorials or articles supporting your position. If you cannot actually include an article, make reference to it. Articles from local newspapers are especially effective because the official will know that many people back home have probably seen the article too.

Occasionally you and your group may want to conduct an extensive letter-writing campaign in a relatively short period of time—for example, right before a bill is to be debated in Committee or

Subcommittee, or just prior to final consideration of a bill in either House of Congress. Electronic mail is something each person can handle personally. It will be most effective if all of the e-mails are sent within a set period of time—five to seven days. Coordinate your efforts for maximum effectiveness.

Another way to organize this communication initiative is to hold a letter-writing party. Invite ASA members and other supporters to an informal gathering at someone's home. Ask your guests to bring personal or business stationery. Instruct everyone to write their messages in their own words, taking care to state clearly what your group supports as well as the proper titles and numbers of the bills involved. Because individually written messages are usually more effective, try to avoid preprinted messages unless time is of the essence. If you feel you must use preprinted letters or cards, however, make sure everyone signs clearly and includes his or her return address.

At the end of the letter-writing party, all letters and cards should be completed, stamped, and ready for delivery to the mailbox or post office. Unless time dictates immediate delivery, stagger the mailing over several days so that the letters are not all received at once.

Remember: Send a copy of all letters, e-mail, or other messages you send to your elected officials to the ASA national office and any other coalition with whom you are associated. This will enable that organization to follow up with the member(s) you contacted and remind them that their votes are being monitored and will be reported back to the membership.

Visit Your Elected Officials

As a parent-advocate, you can accomplish a great deal through visits with your elected representatives or their legislative aides. You can get a clear idea of your representative's legislative priorities and educate him or her about the needs of people with autism. You can also get immediate feedback about your concerns.

In planning your visits to Congressional offices (or your state or local legislative offices), be sure to call or write in advance requesting an appointment. If you are unable to plan that far ahead, call as soon as you know when you will be in Washington, DC Congressmen and Senators maintain offices in their districts so if you find it easier to visit a local office, your appointment can be arranged for a time when the Congressman or Senator is in your area.

You may wish to visit alone or with a small delegation. If you assemble a delegation, try to include a cross section of the community, including politically influential citizens who support your views and someone who may have been politically supportive of the Congressman or Senator in the past.

If you visit Washington on a special lobbying day or day of legislative activity on your issue, be sure someone or a delegation from your group visits influential members of the House and Senate Appropriations Committee and the relevant Subcommittees. Even if your local Congressman or Senator is not on the Committee, you should seek out a meeting with either the Chief of Staff on the Committee or the legislative counsel. Appropriations are crucial for our issues and the members must know you were there and what you are thinking. Bring a legislative packet for each of the staffers you meet with (there are Republican and Democratic lead staff for each Subcommittee in each body).

An important part of your visit is the presentation of an issue packet to the legislator. The issue packet should include:

- A cover letter urging support of specific legislation.
- Copies of editorials or similar written endorsements.
- One to three pieces of factual background information about the bill you are supporting.
- A fact sheet about autism. This can be obtained from the national ASA office.
- A list of organizations, interest groups, national figures, and local leaders who support your position.

You should present a second copy of the same issue packet to the legislative assistant who handles disability issues.

You will probably have only a limited amount of time to speak with your representative, so you will want to make every word count.

During your meeting, try to accomplish the following:

- Summarize the contents of the issues packet so your legislator can understand exactly what you want him or her to do about specific proposals that are being brought before his or her committee or House of Congress.

- Listen to explanations by the legislator or his aide about his philosophy or past record on similar issues. Listen also for any reservations he or she may express about the legislation or appropriation.

- Where appropriate, try to correct any misconceptions or misunderstandings the legislator or aide may have about pending legislation or about autism in general.

- Do not hesitate to use your personal experience to explain the everyday problems faced by children with autism and their families.

- Give the legislator some idea of the larger group of voters you or the delegation represents. (How many members are in your ASA chapter? How large is the support group that favors your bill back home? Which national coalitions or other organizations have expressed their support?)

- Make sure you meet the assistant who handles disability issues because he or she will be the key contact person for you in the months to come. Let the representative as well as the staff person know that you or your chapter would be happy to keep the office informed about new developments, new information about the specific measure, and autism in general.

Remember: Staff members can be valuable resources, as many elected officials rely on them both for their political judgment and their knowledge of issues. If you ever find yourself in disagreement with a staff person, be diplomatic. *NEVER* threaten to go over the staff person's head. You always retain the right to contact the member directly when he or she is back in the home district or state. Avoid stepping on anyone's toes because that could cut you off from further meaningful contact with the office thus hurting your efforts to educate and win the lawmaker over to your side. No one is going to see everything your way. Just keep the information flowing and keep your cool.

It is a good idea to stay in touch with officials and staff throughout the year, especially on the district office level. This way you can develop

a working relationship and keep your legislator up to date about your issues. If time is a problem, you can spread the responsibility for such contacts among several people in your chapter. For example, one person could serve as the liaison to a particular official for a complete legislative session (one year).

If your chapter has a newsletter, be sure to bring a copy. Include the Congressman, Senator, state representative, or city councilor on your mail list for updates. Be sure you say something kind about his or her support of your position, when that is the case. Include information about your trip to Washington or other visits with federal or local officials in your newsletter, e-mail distribution, or web site.

Let me remind you to be sure you and every member of your household is registered to vote. When it is time to vote, make special arrangements to make it easier for people to get to the polling places. Set up a child-care drop-off for parents who can't take their children to the polling location. Provide transportation for those individuals who are unable to access public transportation. Your group's visibility in getting out the vote will be important on Election Day itself and in subsequent dealings with officials at every level.

Reaching the Media

News Releases

News releases should announce an event or happening that would be of some use to the general community. Such events include regular chapter meetings, guest speakers, and major events like a celebrity fundraiser. In your news release, be sure to provide background information on a particular issue, or make a declaration of support or challenge on an issue (such as a chapter's support on zoning for a group home).

A news release should be written as concisely as possible with the most important information appearing in the first paragraph and the rest of the information included in descending order of importance. The first rule is to remember the five "W's" of journalism: who, what, where, when, and why. It is not a news release without that information.

Be sure to include your contact person's name along with daytime and evening telephone number and an e-mail address (if appropriate) so your local newspaper or news organization can contact you for further information.

If you are trying to interest a news organization in covering a meeting or event, be sure you leave enough time (at least a week) from the time you send or deliver the release and the event itself. About three days before the event, call each news organization and speak to the editor or assignment editor and ask if he or she intends to send a reporter to cover the happening. If the editor does not, ask if you can furnish a report on the event. Some weekly newspapers will accept your own account of the meeting because they cannot cover every event but would like to feature your group.

Local radio stations will sometimes offer you the opportunity to do a "feed." They will record you on tape for 15 to 60 seconds, during which time you describe your event or your opinion on the issue under discussion. They will include this in their regular news coverage.

Do not be afraid to ask editors or assignment editors about the kind of "news" they want to cover. That is the only way you will learn to meet their needs and use them to publicize the important advocacy you are doing. Many times a general assignment editor or reporter will not understand the importance of the issue. You should anticipate that and include some general background about autism as well as the primary issue when you brief the editor or reporter.

Letters to the Editor

Writing letters to the editor can be a most effective and inexpensive way to educate the public about your efforts on behalf of children with autism. Long after reporters or newscasters have lost interest in a story, you can keep the issue in the public's consciousness through letters to the editor. Here are some guidelines to increase your chances of having a letter published in your local newspaper.

- Limit letters to about 150-200 words and strive for tightly composed sentences.
- Use specific examples in order to make specific points.
- Address only one major issue in your letter.

:: LEGISLATIVE ADVOCACY SUMMARY

Grassroots

- Form a cohesive umbrella coalition by contacting members of groups involved with the autism community to come together with the purpose of developing a plan to get legislation passed. Be sure to include a broad cross section of the community and include anyone of particular stature in their field.
- Get the word out using many methods to educate families and interested professionals of the need for services, the current lack thereof, and their necessary involvement for this effort to succeed. Methods to utilize:
- Announcements by related groups at their meetings, workshops, and conferences
- Presentations given to groups on the importance of legislation
- A letter-writing campaign to various group memberships and to those sympathetic to the cause to enlist their involvement or support
- Announcements in statewide newsletters, if available
- Target and educate the general population about the diagnosis and lack of services through various means:
- Use of media—newspapers, TV news stories
- Presentations to community organizations
- Encouraging group members to educate family and professionals within their contact circle
- Fundraising—Individual members of the coalition represent various groups, so a fundraising plan needs to be developed to cover expenses that cannot be circumvented by volunteerism or absorbed by the individual groups involved.

Information in this table courtesy of Lois Rosenwald, President, Greater New Haven PDD/Asperger Support Network and Stacy Hultgren, Editor, PDD Network.

- Use accurate and up-to-date information.
- Always include your signature, address, e-mail, and telephone number. Some newspapers will call you first before they print your letter to verify that you wrote the letter and to inform you that your letter will be printed.

Legislative

- Let the legislature know of the needs, and of the cohesiveness of this group of their constituents by:
  - Developing petitions
  - Instituting an organized letter-writing and e-mail campaign aimed at all legislators, but with a specific focus on influential members (the Appropriations Committee, for example, or members with a personal interest in the disability). This campaign must extend over the long-term.
  - Identifying the four to five members of the legislature in your state that "make things happen;" contact them personally and enlist their support
  - Holding a statewide rally including media coverage to increase public pressure
  - Hosting legislative breakfasts so legislators can get to know the group and understand the needs
  - Speaking at any relevant legislative public hearings
  - Enlisting the aid of a few legislative members (hopefully key people) to work with your group directly in seeing this bill through the entire process
- If not members of your committee, contact a lobbyist (or former member of the legislature) and public relations personnel for advice regarding strategies and timing.
- Contact relevant state agencies and service providers (DMH, DMR, DDD) for their support.
- Target someone within the Governor's office to be "in your corner."
- Make contact with any organizations that might be threatened by your bill in order to develop a relationship and discuss concerns.

If your group wishes to conduct a letters-to-the-editor campaign because of a disagreement with a stand adopted by a paper or a television or radio station, you may wish to stagger your mailings so that only a few letters are sent each week. Keep copies of all letters sent for follow-up possibilities and be sure to maintain a clippings file. This will give you the published copy to send along to your elected officials at appropriate times or use in future public affairs efforts.

In your search for forums in which to air your views, do not overlook general magazines or the more specialized journals for medical, social science, and legal professionals. Many periodicals publish letters to the editor or invite guest editorials on issues of interest to their subscribers. Publishing letters in these periodicals can be the quickest way to reach the people with the most clout. You and your child are direct consumers of these professionals' opinions and actions. Your response to the professionals will be noted.

:: Conclusion

Advocacy can be a powerful tool in the hands of a skilled parent-advocate. You can use it to chisel away at ignorance about autism, to cut through bureaucratic red tape, and to hammer together a better future for children with autism. You can advocate singly or in a group; at home or in a public setting; on local or on national issues.

It is to your advantage—and to your child's advantage—for you to learn how to effectively practice all types of advocacy. Remember, as the expert on your child and her needs, you are in the best, most knowledgeable position to explain these problems to people who can help. If *you* don't speak up on your child's behalf, who will?

:: Parent Statements

Be a loud voice for your child: Advocate!

❦

Nobody is an advocate for your kid but yourself. You see potential when nobody else sees potential and you see problems when nobody else sees problems.

❦

I have a real need to become involved and not just let it happen or turn it over to "professionals."

❦

This year, for the first time in my life, I picked up the phone and called my representatives' and senator's offices to oppose an unjust bill being considered that would affect Lawrence as an adult. It's too early to say whether all the parents who called and wrote will make a difference. But it felt good to take some sort of action, no matter how small. And maybe it will make a difference.

❧

Exposure, time, and practice have taught me how to advocate effectively for my children so that I now have much greater control in educational decision-making.

❧

I believe in power. Money is power. Politics is power. Get yourself in a position to come from power. Don't expect to get anything out of sympathy or moral right. It's a business, like anything else. I mean, they call it a bureaucracy, and it is.

❧

In my opinion, it's not just the squeaky wheel that gets the grease—it's also the most familiar one.

❧

I always make it a point to meet informally with everyone involved in Lawrence's education before any problems or questions arise. This includes teachers, therapists, principals, the people at the area office, and anyone who might be involved in Lawrence's future education. I believe we've avoided an awful lot of conflict this way.

❧

You must be ready to fight for services for your child if that's what it takes. We have taken our concerns to the school superintendent when we had to and all of a sudden doors opened.

❧

If the governor were my cousin, we wouldn't be having this problem. It's that simple.

❧

My best advice: GET INVOLVED. The best thing you can do for yourself is become friends with parents of children who also spit 200 times an hour. They understand you and where you're coming from.

◈

Autistic kids usually can't tell you what they need, and people without everyday contact with autism don't understand your frustration. Step on toes if you must, but don't sit back and assume it will work out.

◈

Something I wish I had done differently from the beginning was to have a professional advocate attend my IEP meetings. I now use an advocate, and she is my voice when I feel uncomfortable expressing an educational concern.

◈

Being a parent of a child with autism is a full-time job and then some. Don't ever give up until you get the answers you need and the results you want.

10

The Years Ahead: Adults with Autism

David L. Holmes, Ed.D.

▪▪ Introduction

Someday your child will grow up. He will become an adult with autism. Right now, while you are concentrating on getting the best possible care for him as a child, this fact may seem irrelevant. But don't forget, the "best possible care" for your child also involves planning toward the best possible future. Understanding what life is presently like for adults with autism, as well as what it *should be* like, is crucial to your child's future. Without this knowledge, you cannot help the "should be" become "is."

Some parents of young children with autism find coping with the present so overwhelming that they just don't feel up to planning for the future. This is understandable. Other parents begin worrying about the future early on, and find that planning helps them cope with their anxieties. Whatever your method of coping, you can use the information in this chapter as a guide when you are ready to plan your child's future.

This chapter reviews the four issues parents worry about most when thinking about the future: 1) nurturing independence in their

child; 2) choosing a place to live for their child; 3) finding employment and training for their child; and 4) coping with the changes the
future may bring. In discussing these concerns, this chapter introduces you to what the future of your child *might* be like: it presents a
combination of what life is like today for adults with autism and what
life *can* and should be like in the future. Remember, as earlier chapters
have emphasized, the future for children with autism is constantly
changing. It is up to you and parents like you to make your child's
future a good one by advocating for better services.[1]

:: Who Are Adults with Autism?

Until recently, children with autism never grew up to be called
adults with autism. Instead, they were called schizophrenic or mentally
retarded, and were usually institutionalized. Why weren't adults with
autism called "autistic?" Until recently, there were no residential, training, or employment services for adults with autism, so the only way they
could receive services was to be labeled something else. And once
labeled, the easiest thing to do was to shut them away in institutions.

Now more services are available for adults with autism, including community-based group homes and apartments and other alternative living arrangements, along with a variety of employment and
training opportunities. This development of services for adults with
autism continues in its infancy, with some states providing a greater
number of adult services, and many other states offering no services
at all. Organizations like the Autism Society of America (ASA) and
other groups and individuals are working hard to enact laws to
improve services for adults with autism, including laws that would
apply the same standards to adults with autism that currently apply to
children under IDEA.

As a result of increased services, we have finally begun to see
adults with autism for who they are. They are people who usually
require intensive, continuing training in order to lead fulfilling lives.
And like children with autism, most of them need structure, supervision, and guidance in much of what they do.

No one can say exactly what your child's life will be like when he
is an adult. We do know that it will depend somewhat on your child's
capacity for learning and achieving—on his cognitive skills, health,

---

[1] *Throughout this chapter, the adult with autism may be referred to as a "child." This is done to reflect
that, no matter what age, a parent always refers to his or her son or daughter as his or her "child."*

work skills, behavior, and level of functioning. But because society's treatment of children with autism has recently improved so much, we just do not know what effect this improved treatment will have on them as adults. Most likely, though, they will have more skills than in the past. For example, adults with autism who receive intensive communication therapy as children are usually far ahead of those raised in institutions. Likewise, stereotyped behavior often diminishes in young adults who continue to receive treatment and therapy.

Children with autism usually carry with them into adulthood the same behavior, preferences, and demands they have had throughout life. This can be both good and bad. The bad news is that undesirable behavior does not end with adulthood. Many adults with autism, for example, retain their need for sameness and continue to have tantrums and outbursts. But the good news is that adults with autism do not usually acquire new behavior problems, nor do they lose the progress they have already made in controlling their behavior and in meeting their own needs if they continue to be challenged and encouraged to learn.

As far as we know, adults with autism should have normal life spans given appropriate services. They do not usually develop new medical problems, such as seizures, that they did not have as children or adolescents. In addition, medication used in childhood to control behavior can often be weaned away in adulthood. Finding quality medical care, however, can be a problem. Some pediatricians are willing to continue treating children with autism when they become adults. More commonly, pediatricians will suggest that an internist or family practitioner become the primary physician. Unfortunately, many physicians have little experience with adults who have developmental problems. But if experienced physicians are available in the community, other parents can be a good source of information about them. Many of the suggestions Chapter 3 gives about choosing a pediatrician can also help you select a new physician for the adult with autism.

▪▪ Do Adults and Children with Autism Have the Same Needs?

In many ways, adults and children have similar needs. To begin with, both need consistency among their many environments—at home, in school, and at the workplace. And like children with autism, adults with autism need individualized programs based upon their unique learning needs. They both require consistent, structured programs that teach them appropriate behavior, as well as training to improve their communication and self-care skills.

The difference between adults and children with autism is in the philosophy used to teach them. With children, the goal is usually to change behavior. With adults, however, the focus should be on trying to channel and direct ingrained problem behavior into more appropriate types of behavior. For example, if years of training have not succeeded in eliminating hand flapping in a young adult with autism, he might be taught instead to pick up a magazine and flip through its pages whenever he feels compelled to flap his hands. A similar strategy might be used for an adult who cannot control a compulsion to arrange the objects in his bathroom. To refocus his energy, teachers might make him responsible for organizing the bathrooms where he lives.

Just as a child's program does, an adult's program should include training in communication, self-care, social skills, controlling impulses, and following directions. But for most adults with autism, training in academic skills such as pure math and science should be phased out and replaced by training in the functional life skills needed for survival in the adult world. "Survival Academic Skills" should include reading signs, following simple written directions, understanding time concepts, handling money, and writing one's name. As you will hear often, the work to build these important skills should begin in childhood. And later on, both residential and employment programs for adults with autism should continue to build on these skills in order to foster as much independence as possible.

■■ Nurturing Independence

Most adults with autism have the potential to become contributing members of society. But they can only reach that potential through active training, beginning in childhood. We now know that, given the right environment—at work, in employment training, or at home—adults with autism can continue to learn and grow all their lives.

The Goal—A Fish Story

You have probably heard the proverb:

"If you give a person a fish, he will eat for a day.
If you teach a person to fish, he will eat for a lifetime."

So it is with people with autism. The more they are capable of satisfying their own needs and wants, the happier they will be. Parents and professionals should therefore not just *give* care to adults with autism, they should *teach* them to care for themselves. As hard as it may be to insist that your child do things for himself, it is the only way he will become independent.

Being helpless is often an attractive condition for people with autism. It allows them to retreat into their own world, and relieves them of the anxiety, frustration, and stress that come with learning new skills. But being helpless robs them of their most basic human dignity. It excuses them for any unacceptable behavior, and it fails to teach the person to be responsible for his behavior. It says, "you are incapable as a human being; you are basically an incompetent."

Commit yourself now to finding and working with programs that will make a good "fisherman" out of your child when he becomes an adult. No one would claim that the road to independence is easy, but in the long run, it offers the best hope for a bright future for your child, your family, and yourself.

"As If"

In nurturing independence, the concept of "as if" is crucial to ensuring that young people are challenged to their full potential. The concept of "as if" is simple: If you treat an adult with autism *as if* he were capable of leading a productive adult life, the chances of him meeting that expectation are greatly improved. On the other hand, if you treat him *as if* he needs constant care, his skills and independence will decline. Your expectations, and the expectations of those who work with your child, will play a critical role in determining the degree of independence he achieves. First at home and at school, and then later in employment and residential programs, everyone must be treated *as if* they have the potential for living and working independently. That is the best way to ensure that greater opportunities open up for all adults with autism.

Learned Helplessness

Just as attitudes like "as if" can help pave the way to independence for an adult with autism, so too can other attitudes pose major stumbling blocks. One of the most harmful of these attitudes is the belief that adults should either be able to be productive or should receive services. In other words, people who can't care for themselves should get help. Yet care giving is the worst possible way to help adults with autism. When you give only care to an adult with autism, you are in fact teaching that adult to be helpless. This condition of "learned helplessness" reduces a person's skills, dignity, sense of responsibility for his future, and self-esteem. Care giving without expectations almost always results in the rapid deterioration of skills, such as shoe tying and self feeding, attained by the adult during his educational years.

:: A Supportive Environment

In order to gain the independence and skills necessary to function in the adult world, adults with autism need a special kind of supportive environment. They need an environment that strikes a balance between the need to encourage—even force—them to be productive at home and at work and the need to provide them with enough care and structure to help them feel secure and less anxious. This type of supportive environment is equally important in both residential placement and in employment training. So whether you are evaluating a potential residential or job opportunity for your child, remember that the *learning* environment is critical, and that for people with autism, every environment—good or bad—is a learning environment. If all an agency provides is care, your child with autism will not be motivated to try to learn the skills needed for greater independence. Remember, merely providing care is not enough for people with autism; if the environment does not also nurture independence, it is not supportive.

Six key elements make up a supportive environment for people with autism:

1. **Individualized Planning.** All services provided to an adult with autism—from personal hygiene to job skills training—must be tailored to his specific needs and abilities. For example, if an adult with autism continues to have communication problems, specific, detailed training should be planned. The staff of the residential or employment program should

be made up of professionals trained in working with people with autism and in providing a supportive environment.

2. **Commitment to Less Restrictive and More Normal Life Experiences.** The goal of a supportive environment is to nurture independence in people with autism and to help them to become integrated into their community as much as possible. If the goal of an agency, school, or organization providing services to your child is different, you should question whether it offers a truly supportive environment or whether its methods actually encourage learned helplessness. Programs that provide too much care giving and not enough training cannot succeed in enabling adults with autism to achieve more normal lives.

A supportive environment will also strive to foster independence in *all* adults with autism, no matter what their abilities. Its programs should be available to all people with autism, from higher-functioning, cooperative people to lower-functioning, less sociable people. No one should be denied services or be removed from the program because he is considered difficult. The commitment should be to individual success for each person served. Independence is not an "all-or-nothing" proposition; everyone should be given as much independence, responsibility, and opportunity as he can handle. In a supportive environment, trained professionals know when to help and when to watch. They know how to establish realistic, yet challenging goals.

3. **A Compatible Physical Environment.** At home and in the workplace, the physical environment—the building, rooms, and outside areas—should be compatible with your child's preferences. For example, if noisy places disturb your child, then he should live and work in a quiet environment. A compatible environment is important because how your child reacts to the layout, color, shape, noise level, and even smell may affect his behavior or ability to learn. You are probably already sensitive to your child's likes and dislikes in these areas; you should make sure that your child's residential or employment training agency is sensitive too.

4. Remedial Programming. If your child is to achieve independence, there are several skills he must have. These skills are "functional;" they allow a person with autism to function as normally as possible in the real world. They include: 1) communication skills; 2) independent self-care skills; and 3) the ability to function without constant supervision. A residential or employment training agency should provide *educational services* to help your child

learn new functional skills or to fill in gaps in his prior education. For example, because most adults with autism continue to need language and communication therapy, the agency should have language therapists on its staff. And if an adult with autism needs help in learning self-care skills, a personal-needs counselor should be available.

Remember, you need not—in fact you *must* not—wait until your child is an adult to start work on these essential skills. The sooner you begin to build these skills, the less remedial programming he will need as an adult. Teach your child domestic and self-care skills at home, and insist that he do as much as possible for himself—for example, take dishes to the sink and make his bed. In addition, make sure that your child's program at school focuses on the functional skills he will need later.

5. Commitment to Encouraging Appropriate Behavior. Success in achieving independence depends greatly on the person with autism, and, in particular, on his behavior. If his behavior is not socially acceptable, he cannot achieve much real independence. An adult who has violent temper tantrums, for example, stands little chance of keeping a job or getting along with the other people in his group home. A supportive environment, therefore, should work to improve the behavior of people with autism and to reduce inappropriate behavior.

6. **Commitment to a Lifetime of Service.** Because people with autism need a supportive environment throughout their lives, agencies should be committed to providing services for a lifetime. This may sound like a lot to ask, but consistency is a critical element in successfully nurturing independence in adults with autism. Because people with autism have difficulty coping with changes in their world, agencies should focus on long-term consistency and stability. Doing less can jeopardize years of progress.

As discussed earlier, all of your child's environments should be supportive. They should provide the care he needs in order to feel secure, but they should also continually challenge your child to become as independent as possible. A good rule of thumb is that for every time care is given to an adult with autism, three opportunities for training or learning should be offered. This holds true whether your child is at home, at work, or receiving education or employment training.

In evaluating adult programs and agencies in the future, you should make sure that each of the elements of a **supportive** environment outlined above is present. Do not, however, confuse the emphasis on nurturing independence with a free-form, unstructured environment. A supportive environment for adults with autism is still far more regimented and controlled than most people's environments. It is how the elements of control, growth, and care are balanced that distinguishes a supportive environment for adults with autism.

∷ Employment Options: A Safety Net Approach

In the real world, grown-ups work. Besides paying the bills, work gives people a sense of accomplishment and pride as well as enhances self-esteem. Your child, too, should be able to reap these benefits of working.

Because your child has autism, there will probably be limitations on the types of jobs he will be able to hold, and there will definitely be differences in the way he is trained for and placed in a job. In most areas, local vocational training agencies or state human services departments train people with disabilities and then search for suitable work for them. In many states, adults with autism receive the same services that adults with other disabilities receive. Sometimes the services provided everyone happen to be effective for people with autism, but too often they are not.

Unfortunately in many areas employment programs provide only a combination of what amounts to adult day care with limited job skills training. Usually this kind of program does not help adults with autism; they need more intensive training in a supportive environment. As a result, inadequate job skills or behavior problems may make it impossible for them to keep jobs, and they may suffer gaps in employment. In addition, they may continually have to wait to get back into training and to receive new placement help.

In the best employment programs, these problems can be avoided by using an approach known as the "safety net approach." The safety net approach is simply a continuing commitment to work with an adult with autism throughout his life. When a person has a gap in employment or needs retraining, the agency automatically serves him in its program. With a safety net approach, the adult with autism is able to return to an employment setting without first having to go to the back of the line for training or services. This approach to the continuing employment training needs of people with autism is gradually being understood around the country, but there is a long way to go.

A "safety net" is not meant to be a "hammock." Employment options must continually challenge people with autism to meet expectations and learn new skills; otherwise they may find themselves "safe" but stagnating. They may find themselves merely resting comfortably in a "hammock," with nothing to do. In contrast, a "safety net" approach is designed to catch someone when they lose their job or experience problems, and then return them to the work force immediately. Good job training programs provide support with a "safety net," not a hammock.

Types of Employment

A wide variety of employment options are identified today for adults with disabilities. These options are usually grouped into four types, according to the kinds of job skills and levels of independence they require. The types are: sheltered, secure, supported, and competitive employment.

Sheltered Employment. Sheltered employment offers the adult with autism a degree of job security. He works at a job site operated by the employment training agency, performing relatively simple tasks such as mail processing, collating and labeling, packaging, woodworking, or product assembly. He is paid for his work. In most programs, his co-workers may also have autism or some other developmental disability. The program may offer training, but the amount of training can vary tremendously. Although sheltered workshops are quite common, they have one major drawback: the adult with autism may stay in the sheltered workshop indefinitely, and may never be prepared for more independent work.

Secure Employment. Although secure employment involves basically the same kinds of work that sheltered employment does, it is fundamentally different in philosophy. Like sheltered employment, it offers structured work and a guaranteed job, but it also trains the adult with autism so he may eventually be able to work in a more independent and competitive workplace. The training focuses not only on improving job skills, but also on improving behavior. For example, staying with a task until finished, moving from one task to another, controlling impulses, working with less supervision, and improving communication and self-care are all important skills that secure employment should teach. Secure employment usually works best with adults more severely affected by autism and those who have had little or no employment training. It is always the better choice for adults who might otherwise work in a sheltered workshop.

Supported Employment. Supported employment is ideal for the adult with autism who has acceptable behavior and has learned the skills necessary to work in the competitive work force, yet still needs supervision to complete the job requirements. In this type of employment, one to four adults with autism work alongside nondisabled adults at a real job site, doing work such as stocking store shelves, pricing merchandise, assembling products, and cleaning offices. The adults with autism are supported by a job coach—a professional or volunteer employed by the employment training agency, not the employer. The job coach teaches the adults with autism the skills needed for the job, reinforces appropriate behavior while working to eliminate inappropriate behavior, supervises each person at work, provides for transportation to and from the job site, and helps maintain a good relationship between the employer and employees. The goal of supported employment is to help the adult with autism become increasingly independent so that he can work without a job coach.

Competitive Employment. Once an adult with autism has mastered both the job skills and the behavior necessary for completely independent work, he is ready for competitive employment. In competitive employment, a person works independently, comes and goes to work on his own, and does not need a job coach. Typical competitive work for an adult with autism includes word processing and data entry, mail sorting and delivery, office assistance, library help, janitorial services, and work in grocery stores, delicatessens, and bakeries. Currently, competitive employment for adults with autism is fairly uncommon. Only about 10 percent of adults with autism achieve this level of employment.

Competitive employment represents almost a graduation from a supportive environment, because the adult with autism no longer needs continuing supervision or training, and is able to function in the world independently. In a truly supportive environment, however, the agency always stands ready to help out if necessary. For example, if behavior problems cause trouble at work in a competitive setting, a job coach can be brought in to help. If problems persist, the person can return to work in a secure employment program, while continuing to receive training to improve both behavior and job skills. The agency never stops caring about the individual.

Secure, supported, and competitive employment programs are all usually designed to keep adults with autism and other disabilities continuously working at the highest level of independence they can handle. Consequently, they provide the adult with autism with the all-important supportive environment described earlier in this chapter. Sheltered workshops, on the other hand, do not foster independence or provide many opportunities for personal growth.

The preceding section provided an overview of the types of employment options usually available for adults with autism. But you need more than a general idea of what is out there. When it comes to employment programs, there is great variety from state to state in eligibility requirements, training methods, and placement success. And once your child turns 21, you cannot expect someone to seek you out to offer services or even to explain what services are available. Long before your child finishes school, you should begin to search for employment services and, if necessary, to demand more appropriate services for your child. It is almost never too early to start this process of investigating options and of advocating for improved employment training services (advocacy is explained in Chapter 9). Start by asking parents of adults with autism about the services available in your community. And as discussed in Chapter 7, make sure that your child with autism receives training to build vocational skills as part of his educational program.

■■ Residential Options: The Dark Ages

Since the early 1970s, federal, state, and local governments have been releasing people with disabilities of all kinds from institutions. The expectation behind this process of *deinstitutionalization* is that people with disabilities will lead happier, more productive lives once they are back in the community. While deinstitutionalization has proven to be moderately successful with people with mental retardation or mental illness, it has been less successful for adults with autism—mainly because there just are not enough community residential placement options for people with autism. As a result, adults with autism still make up a large percentage of people living in institutions. Others wind  up with ineffective placements, expensive placements, or even no placements. Because you will want to avoid these less-than-ideal placements for your child, the drawbacks of each are described below.

No Placement. In the United States today, many adults with autism simply have no residential placement. Most live at home with parents who either do not know about appropriate services for adults with autism or who are unwilling to have their son or daughter placed inappropriately. This situation can be explosive for both the adult with autism and his family, due to the daily stress of living with the behavior and learning problems associated with autism.

Inappropriate Placement. As mentioned earlier, many adults with autism are placed inappropriately in state institutions. Institutions are usually staffed by a variety of professionals, but compared with other residential settings, there is a high resident-to-staff ratio. In most states, institutions house up to one thousand people. Additionally, because these institutions usually house people with many different disabilities, they seldom focus on the unique learning styles of adults with autism. These settings provide little opportunity for helping adults with autism develop greater independence. In fact, they tend to exacerbate the symptoms of autism and to contribute to the general deterioration of the skills and health of an adult with autism because they focus on generic care rather than individualized training.

Ineffective Placement. Many adults with autism live in residential programs that are staffed by workers who are not skilled in providing a supportive environment. In addition, the staff members may use ineffective methods—methods that encourage learned helplessness—to try to teach skills. Such programs primarily provide care rather than training, and do not help the adult with autism. Ineffective placements, like inappropriate placements, generally worsen the condition of the adult with autism.

Expensive Placement. There are a few high quality community-based residential placement options that provide the supportive environment adults with autism need to grow and learn. Unfortunately, because they are unique, they can be quite expensive, with costs ranging from $125,000 to $900,000 per year. And because these placements are not available in all states, there may not be any near the home of the parents of the adult with autism.

Types of Residential Settings

Recently, federal, state, and local agencies have begun to do something about the chronic lack of community-based residential options that has led to the conditions described above. These agencies have finally realized that *public* residential programs should offer adults with disabilities the same high quality services that private programs do. As a result, residential options for adults with autism have gradually begun to expand. Today, although there are no national mandates and too many adults with autism continue to remain in institutions for lack of an appropriate placement in the community, there is ongoing movement toward community living for all adults with autism. But remember, it will take constant advocacy from you and parents like you if this goal is to be met. Here is a summary of the common community-based living arrangements:

Community Group Homes. Over the past decade, there has been a dramatic increase in the number and type of community group homes for adults with all types of disabilities. These homes, which are usually located in residential neighborhoods, house from two to eight adults. During the day, residents typically leave the home to go to work or training. At home, a staff of qualified and trained professionals teaches the residents to take care of the house themselves, and often helps with the housekeeping as well. In many programs, the professional staff may also offer training in other areas, including communication, self-help, and behavior control, but each program is different. Generally, the resident-to-staff ratio ranges from one to one to two to three, so there is much supervision. Group homes are usually operated by city and county governments, local disability organizations such as ASA chapters, local offices of The Arc, and other nonprofit and proprietary organizations. Some group homes have only residents with autism, but more often group homes house people with a variety of disabilities. For adults with autism, a group home that is just for people with autism works better because the programming can be tailored specifically to their needs.

Supported Apartments. A supported apartment is basically just a small group home. Typically, there is only one supported apartment per apartment building. The apartment is usually shared by two adults who require less daily supervision than residents of group homes. Typically there is a full-time supervisor for the apartment. This staff member resides in the apartment. For more independent adults, the supervisor would not reside in the apartment, but might visit one to two days each week, to check on the residents and help train them to care for themselves and the apartment. During the day, the residents go to work or training. Like group homes, supported apartments for adults with autism work best if the other residents also have autism and if the program is tailored to their needs.

Skill Development Homes and Host Family Homes. A skill development home, also known as a host family home, is a fairly recent variation on the group home or supported apartment. In this arrangement, an adult with autism lives with a family that has been trained by an agency or organization in working with people with disabilities. In most cases, the host family is paid by the state. The host family treats the adult with autism like a member of the family, and teaches self-care, housekeeping, recreation, and leisure-time skills. Again, a skill development home works best if the training and approach are tailored to adults with autism.

Other Arrangements. In addition to the arrangements described above, there are other ways of providing supportive and challenging living environments for adults with autism. For example, there are many residential schools, farmsteads, and self-contained communities for adults with disabilities. The key elements—supervision, the number of residents, location, and programming—can vary tremendously from program to program. Thus, a program that is inappropriate or ineffective for one person may work quite well for another. No single approach works best for all people with autism.

What to Look for in Residential Programs

When you investigate residential options for your child, there are several things to look for and to look out for. The most important element, of course, is a commitment to the "supportive environment"

that works best to encourage appropriate behavior, independent life skills, and employment skills in adults with autism. It is also important, however, to look for signs that the program is well managed.

To determine whether a program is supportive, look first at the staff. Are they trained in working with adults with autism? Do they focus on training people toward independence, treating the adults "as if" they have the potential to lead more normal lives in the community? Is there at least one staff member for every three adults with autism? Secondly, look at the program itself. Is it challenging enough for your child? Does it focus on providing opportunities for being out in the community, including food shopping, bowling, field trips, and even community service? Or does the program appear to be isolated and ineffective?

Ineffective programs are actually fairly easy to spot. One of the surest signs is what is known as "couch potato behavior." Couch potato behavior—sitting and "vegging" in front of the T.V.—is all too common in some residential programs. It represents a program's lack of commitment to do what it takes to promote skills and independence, and can only result in deterioration of the residents' skills.

Besides looking for signs that a program is supportive, you should also look for signs that it is well managed. For example, you should examine the physical condition of furniture and of the house, apartment, or building; ask the program administrators about staff turnover rates; and form your own impressions about the overall atmosphere of the residence. Is it clean? Is the food tasty and nutritious? Is there any privacy? All of these elements are important indicators of how seriously a program takes the happiness and well-being of its residents.

Unfortunately, there is no cookbook recipe for finding the right residential program. Just as every adult with autism is unique, so too is every program. It can help you to talk to parents of other residents to find out whether they think the home is an effective environment for their child. Remember, though, what works well for one person may not work as well for another. You should look for a program with the approach to teaching, training, behavior control, and activity that works best for your child. You can refer to the list of characteristics of an appropriate educational program at the end of Chapter 7 for a summary of what to look for in any program for adults with autism.

▪▪ Easing the Transition to Employment and Independent Living

Letting go of a child is never easy. No parent is ever quite prepared for the day his child moves out to live on his own or to begin work. For parents of adults with autism, letting go can be especially hard—not only because of the years they have spent providing intense care, but also because of the added stress of searching for adequate residential and employment programs for their child.

Perhaps most disturbing to parents of children with autism are the feelings of abandonment and guilt that move in when their child moves out. Often parents feel as if they have "given up" on their child by putting someone else in charge of his daily care. They may also feel useless now that they are no longer solely responsible for their child's welfare.

The best antidote for these feelings is to acknowledge ahead of time that your child will have to leave home someday and that he likely will require some type of secure living arrangement all his adult life. If you acknowledge this need early on, you can not only anticipate how you will feel, but you can also plan ahead for residential and employment placements. And if you plan ahead, you will be able to choose the most appropriate programs for your child. This will help you to feel better *and* to be a better advocate for quality services in your child's program.

If you do not consider residential placement until there is a family crisis, you may find the options painfully limited. The best programs frequently have long waiting lists. So it is important to plan early for your child's eventual residential placement in order to secure the best possible program for him when he becomes an adult.

Planning for the future of your child is a daunting task. It requires that you "crystal ball" what you think your child will need and flesh out how you would like to see these needs met. In order to determine what is available, begin to familiarize yourself with the range of options available to adults with autism in your area. You might be pleased with the range of options or, more typically, distressed by their scarcity. Additionally, it is critical to determine the process your state employs for determining who is eligible for adult services. First, talk to other parents of adults who have navigated the process. Speak with school personnel where your child attends. Connect with state representatives at the earliest appropriate time; do not let them put you off. Observe and get to know the programs and personnel in the agencies you believe could serve your child. And be visible and tenacious. It is true that "the squeaky wheel gets the grease."

Once your child has moved out, you, like all parents, will have to adjust to the "empty nest." Finding new family roles and going back to old jobs, hobbies, or activities helps. But what helps most is the passage of time and the discovery that your child can, and will, continue to grow now that he's out in the real world. Again, if you are prepared for the feelings you will have when your adult with autism leaves home, it will be easier to cope with them.

You must also be prepared to help your child cope with his feelings. For the adult with autism, entry into community living and employment training can be traumatic. New surroundings, activities, people, and expectations can all create great stress and make the adjustment lengthy and difficult. With the right help, however, most adults with autism can make the adjustment.

The best way for you to help with the transition is to "desensitize" your child *before* the change occurs. For at least a month before he moves into a residential program or begins job training, take him on daily visits to the place where he will be living or working. Go inside to show him what he will be doing and introduce him to the staff and other participants in the program. Talk with him reassuringly about what is going to happen. This will help your child get used to the idea ahead of time.

∎∎ What the Future Holds

At the start of this chapter, I said I intended to write not only about today, but also about the tomorrow parents and professionals who care about people with autism can create. Briefly, here is what I see for the future:

1. **Full Life Expectancy.** As people with autism receive appropriate services, their life expectancy will rise. In the past, people with autism typically did not live beyond their late 30s or early 40s. Now and in the future this outcome looks much brighter.

2. **Greater Independence for Adults with Autism.** As more and more parents and professionals realize that people with autism can continue to learn throughout their lives, there will be greater and better efforts to teach adults with autism the skills they need to live independently.

3. **Increasingly More Sociable People with Autism.** As we learn more about how to teach children with autism, programs will become more successful in teaching appropriate social behavior. In turn, this improved social behavior will help increase residential and employment opportunities for all people with autism.

4. **Expanded Residential Placements.** More group homes and supported apartments—the residential placements best suited to adults with autism—will be established, and their services will be more tailored to the needs of adults with autism.

5. **Improved Employment Training.** More employment training programs will provide the continual training adults with autism need, and will be there to help between jobs with retraining and new job placements.

6. Greater Employment Opportunities. Improved education and programming plus more social behavior will result in a generation of people with autism who have better skills, and, as a result, increased employment options.

7. More Societal Acceptance. No matter how more capable adults with autism become, they will still require greater societal acceptance. With greater exposure of autism to society through the media and through community placements, acceptance will increase.

8. More Research. There will be increased funding for research into the causes and effective treatment of autism, as more and more advocacy and societal awareness occurs.

9. Greater Recognition of the Importance of Planning. Parents and guardians will begin to plan for the financial security of their children with autism as they would for their own retirement. They will also put into writing their wishes and intentions for the care of their child in the future.

These goals *are* within our grasp. Over the last 25 years, significant progress has been made in the care, education, and training of people with autism, and we are still making headway today. As I said at the beginning of the chapter, it is simply impossible to predict what life will be like for any child with autism when he is an adult.

Remember, the progress that can do so much to improve life for people with autism depends in large part on the commitment and hard work of parents and professionals. Only constant advocacy can achieve our goals. For many other conditions—from Down syndrome to mental illness—advocacy has yielded excellent results. Clearly, doing nothing is the surest way to ensure no progress is made; advocacy by parents, professionals, and organizations is the only guarantee of a better future for people with autism.

▪▪ Conclusion

Currently, appropriate services for adults with autism—services provided in a supportive environment—although increasing in number, remain scarce. There are, however, some excellent examples of what an appropriate program can be. The Center for Outreach and Services for the Autism Community (COSAC), based in Ewing, New Jersey, has identified these programs in its *Directory of Programs Serving Children and Adults with Autism,* which is listed in the references at the end of this chapter. In addition, COSAC has taken a leading role in influencing federal legislation and in advocating for children and adults with autism in this country and abroad.

Armed with the knowledge that an effective national advocacy organization for children and adults with autism exists, parents and professionals should gain strength. There is hope for a brighter tomorrow for adults with autism, but only if everyone works together. Advocates, parents, and professionals must put aside their many differences and rise above the controversies that seem perpetually to plague the field of autism. They must focus instead on pragmatic issues—the development of employment services, community-based residential services, and effective educational programs. With one voice, they must advocate for more programs like the few model programs presently available, and for appropriate, lifetime services for all adults with autism.

Parents will not obtain the best services just because they want them. Professionals will not be able to offer the best services just because there is a need for them. Parents, professionals, and organizations must all work together, guiding and buoying each other when necessary, to ensure that these services come to be.

One final message—a message that is too often forgotten by parents in the day-to-day struggle and frustration of raising a child with autism. There is hope.

■■ References

Ball, J., Gerhardt, P.F., Holmes, D.L., & Allesandri, M. *A Parent's Guide to the Social Security Administration and Social Security Work Incentive Programs.* Princeton, NJ: The Eden Press, 1994.

Center for Outreach and Services for the Autism Community. *Directory of Programs Serving Children and Adults with Autism.* Ewing, NJ: COSAC, 1998.

Eden Family of Services. *Letter of Intent.* Princeton, NJ: The Eden Press, 1998.

Gerhardt, P.F. & Holmes, D.L. "Employment: Options and Issues for Adsolents and Adults with Autism." In *Handbook of Autism and Pervasive Developmental Disabilities, 2nd Ed.* Edited by F. Volkmar & D. Cohen. New York: John Wiley & Sons, 1997.

Gerhardt, P.F. & Holmes, D.L. "The Eden Decision Model: A Model with Practical Applications for the Development of Behavior Decelerative Strategies." In

Behavioral Issues in Autism. Edited by E. Schopler& G.B. Mesibov. New York: Plenum Press, 1994.

Holmes, David L. *Autism through the Lifespan: The Eden Model.* Bethesda, MD: Woodbine House, 1998.

:: Parent Statements

Not too long ago my son took a four-day vacation in the mountains. What's more, he paid for it out of his own earnings. Big deal you say? For a young man with severe disabilities, you bet it was. And for my wife and me, it was a major triumph. You see, my son is autistic, epileptic, and deaf. He cannot talk, but he can stuff shoe pad inserts into plastic packages and box them neatly—and get paid for his efforts. Yet four years ago, he was self-destructive, totally withdrawn, and unable to communicate. Today he knows a dozen signs; he can tell others what he wants and needs.

❧❀❧

It's scary when I think about Janet becoming a teenager. It's scary because there's not enough time.

❧❀❧

Looking at a picture of my son at work, I realize how far he has come. My son's early years were quite difficult for all of us and we never really knew what the future held. Now we can see what all that faith and hard work have accomplished.

❧❀❧

I see other kids and I say, "Hmm, do you think it's going to be like this?" We're fearful of social interaction. That's why we're working on it now, because it's not being dealt with at all in school—that whole social thing is irrelevant to the educators. To them, math and reading are education.

❧❀❧

I don't have time to think too much about the long term except to wonder whether he'll be happy and self-sufficient. I know that he will possibly have social interaction problems later on, but I can't dwell on that now.

❧❀❧

The main thing I hope is that she's independent at doing whatever she's doing and she's happy doing it. If she doesn't go to college, fine.

❧❧❧

I just hope she learns right from wrong.

❧❧❧

It would be nice if she knew how to manage her own life, how to do something. It's so scary. I just hate to think that for the rest of her life she will look at television and just vegetate. That would just be a crime to me.

❧❧❧

I have thoughts—maybe they're way off base—but having a girl, I have thoughts that she might be sexually abused. And the fact that she's so trusting about things makes me worry, too. I think about drugs and I think about things that other regular people have to deal with.

❧❧❧

I remember when I was a kid, I used to think vocational education was for "dummies." Having a child with autism has really changed my perceptions. I'm not expecting a miracle or anything, but I really hope vocational education will be Carl's ticket to self-sufficiency.

❧❧❧

You've got to remember that a lot of the things that seem cute when your child is an adorable little kid aren't going to seem nearly so cute when he's a full-grown man.

❧❧❧

Even though our son is 18, he has just recently learned to respond positively to affection. It's so gratifying to have him initiate or return a hug and kiss that sometimes we forget that his age may make such public displays seem inappropriate. As an example, we were in a museum when my husband and son shared a spontaneous bear hug. A female guard approached and sternly informed my husband that "such behavior was not allowed in this hall." My husband, who was able to gather his wits a lot faster than I could have, innocently asked her to point out the hall where "such behavior" would be tolerated.

❧❧❧

*There just doesn't seem to be any growth in residential services.
Meanwhile, I'm getting older and I'm not sure I can keep up the energy
level I could when I was younger. We need to get these services in
place now.*

✤

*Although my son is only five, I worry constantly about his future. I
know that we will not always be around to watch over him. My husband says that he will be an unhappy man if he knows he is leaving a
child who lacks the skills to be independent. I worry about whether he
will become educated, have a good job, get married, have friends.
Parents of typical kids say they worry about these things too, but it's
not the same.*

✤

*I worry about what it will be like when Peter is an adult. Will he be
able to live independently or in a group home? Will we have enough
money to care for him? Will his siblings feel burdened by him? Will we
be able to enjoy our golden years without him living with us? I try not
to think about it too much since he is only six, but sometimes I wish I
had a crystal ball.*

✤

*What can and should I be doing now so we'll be heading in the right
direction, whatever that may be? What types of educational, vocational, transitional, economic, and living needs should I be anticipating and
preparing for?*

✤

*In a world of computer technology, my son will do well. He under-
stands computers. He won't have to worry about eye contact, body
language, or trying to understand other's people emotions.*

✤

I hope he doesn't get taken advantage of.

✤

I would like for him to have lots of autistic friends.

APPENDIX A

Diagnostic and Statistical Manual of Mental Disorders (DSM-IV)
Diagnostic Criteria for Pervasive Developmental Disorders

:: DIAGNOSTIC CRITERIA FOR 299.00 AUTISTIC DISORDER

A.   A total of six (or more) items from (1), (2), and (3), with at least two from (1), and one each from (2) and (3):

(1) qualitative impairment in social interaction, as manifested by at least two of the following:

    (a) marked impairment in the use of multiple nonverbal behaviors such as eye-to-eye gaze, facial expression, body postures, and gestures to regulate social interaction

    (b) failure to develop peer relationships appropriate to developmental level

    (c) a lack of spontaneous seeking to share enjoyment, interests, or achievements with other people (e.g., by a lack of showing, bringing, or pointing out objects of interest)

    (d) lack of social or emotional reciprocity

(2) qualitative impairments in communication as manifested by at least one of the following:

    (a) delay in, or total lack of, the development of spoken language (not accompanied by an attempt to compensate through alternative modes of communication such as gesture or mime)

    (b) in individuals with adequate speech, marked impairment in the ability to initiate or sustain a conversation with others

> (c) stereotyped and repetitive use of language or idiosyncratic language
> (d) lack of varied, spontaneous make-believe play or social imitative play appropriate to developmental level
> (3) restricted repetitive and stereotyped patterns of behavior, interests, and activities, as manifested by at least one of the following:
> (a) encompassing preoccupation with one or more stereotyped and restricted patterns of interest that is abnormal either in intensity or focus
> (b) apparently inflexible adherence to specific, nonfunctional routines or rituals
> (c) stereotyped and repetitive motor mannerisms (e.g., hand or finger flapping or twisting, or complex whole-body movements)
> (d) persistent preoccupation with parts of objects
> B. Delays or abnormal functioning in at least one of the following areas, with onset prior to age 3 years: (1) social interaction, (2) language as used in social communication, or (3) symbolic or imaginative play.
> C. The disturbance is not better accounted for by Rett's Disorder or Childhood Disintegrative Disorder.

■■ Diagnostic criteria for 299.80 Rett's Disorder

A. All of the following:
   (1) apparently normal prenatal and perinatal development
   (2) apparently normal psychomotor development through the first 5 months after birth
   (3) normal head circumference at birth
B. Onset of all of the following after the period of normal development:
   (1) deceleration of head growth between ages 5 and 48 months
   (2) loss of previously acquired purposeful hand skills between ages 5 and 30 months with the subsequent development of stereotyped hand movements (e.g., hand-wringing or hand washing)
   (3) loss of social engagement early in the course (although often social interaction develops later)
   (4) appearance of poorly coordinated gait or trunk movements
   (5) severely impaired expressive and receptive language development with severe psychomotor retardation

❚❚ DIAGNOSTIC CRITERIA FOR 299.10 CHILDHOOD DISINTEGRATIVE DISORDER

A. Apparently normal development for at least the first 2 years after birth as manifested by the presence of age-appropriate verbal and nonverbal communication, social relationships, play, and adaptive behavior.

B. Clinically significant loss of previously acquired skills (before age 10 years) in at least two of the following areas:
   (1) expressive or receptive language
   (2) social skills or adaptive behavior
   (3) bowel or bladder control
   (4) play
   (5) motor skills

C. Abnormalities of functioning in at least two of the following areas:
   (1) qualitative impairment in social interaction (e.g., impairment in nonverbal behaviors, failure to develop peer relationships, lack of social or emotional reciprocity)
   (2) qualitative impairments in communication (e.g., delay or lack of spoken language, inability to initiate or sustain a conversation, stereotyped and repetitive use of language, lack of varied make-believe play)
   (3) restricted, repetitive, and stereotyped patterns of behavior, interests, and activities, including motor stereotypies and mannerisms

D. The disturbance is not better accounted for by another specific Pervasive Developmental Disorder or by Schizophrenia.

❚❚ DIAGNOSTIC CRITERIA FOR 299.80 ASPERGER'S DISORDER

A. Qualitative impairment in social interaction, as manifested by at least two of the following:
   (1) marked impairment in the use of multiple nonverbal behaviors such as eye-to-eye gaze, facial expression, body postures, and gestures to regulate social interaction
   (2) failure to develop peer relationships appropriate to developmental level
   (3) a lack of spontaneous seeking to share enjoyment, interests, or achievements with other people (e.g., by a lack of showing, bringing, or pointing out objects of interest to other people)

(4) lack of social or emotional reciprocity
B. Restricted repetitive and stereotyped patterns of behavior, interests, and activities, as manifested by at least one of the following:
  (1) encompassing preoccupation with one or more stereotyped and restricted patterns of interest that is abnormal either in intensity or focus
  (2) apparently inflexible adherence to specific, nonfunctional routines or rituals
  (3) stereotyped and repetitive motor mannerisms (e.g., hand or finger flapping or twisting, or complex whole-body movements)
  (4) persistent preoccupation with parts of objects
C. The disturbance causes clinically significant impairment in social, occupational, or other important areas of functioning.
D. There is no clinically significant general delay in language (e.g., single words used by age 2 years, communicative phrases used by age 3 years).
E. There is no clinically significant delay in cognitive development or in the development of age-appropriate self-help skills, adaptive behavior (other than in social interaction), and curiosity about the environment in childhood.
F. Criteria are not met for another specific Pervasive Developmental Disorder or Schizophrenia.

■■ 299.80 PERVASIVE DEVELOPMENTAL DISORDER

Not Otherwise Specified (Including Atypical Autism)
This category should be used when there is a severe and pervasive impairment in the development of reciprocal social interaction or verbal and nonverbal communication skills, or when stereotyped behavior, interests, and activities are present, but the criteria are not met for a specific Pervasive Developmental Disorder, Schizophrenia, Schizotypal Personality Disorder, or Avoidant Personality Disorder. For example, this category includes "atypical autism"—presentations that do not meet the criteria for Autistic Disorder because of late age at onset, atypical symptomatology, or subthreshold symptomatology, or all of these.

(Reprinted with permission from the Diagnostic and Statistical Manual of Mental Disorders, Fourth Edition. *Washington, DC, American Psychiatric Association, 1994.)*

GLOSSARY

ABA: See Applied Behavior Analysis.

ABC's of Behavior Management: A technique for evaluating undesireable behavior that analyzes: *A*-Antecedent or what happens prior to the behavior; *B*-Behavior or what happens as a result of *A*; and *C*-Consequence or what happens as a result of *B*. *See also* Applied Behavior Analysis.

Absence Seizure: Once called a petit mal seizure, this type of *seizure* is characterized by blank staring and eye blinking.

Accommodation: An adaptation of the environment, format, or situation made to suit the needs of those participating.

ADA: *See* Americans with Disabilities Act.

Adaptive Behavior: The ability to adjust to new environments, tasks, objects, and people, and to apply new skills to those situations.

ADD: *See* Attention Deficit Disorder.

ADHD: *See* Attention Deficit Hyperactive Disorder.

Admission, Review, and Dismissal Commitee (ARD Commitee): A committee made up of teachers and other professionals responsible for the admission of children to *special education,* review of the progress of children in special education programs, and dismissal of children from special education.

Advocacy: Supporting or promoting a cause. Speaking out.

Advocacy Groups: Organizations that work to protect the rights and opportunities of people with *disabilities* and their parents.

Americans with Disabilities Act (ADA): The federal law that prohibits *discrimination* against people with *disabilities* in employment, public accommodations, and access to public facilities.

Anafranil™: The trade name for *fluvoxamine.*

Annual Goal: Educational and *developmental* goals set for a child with *disabilities* and outlined in their *IEP.* Progress toward these goals is discussed during the *annual review* meeting.

Annual Review: Yearly meeting to review a student's *IEP.*

Anticipated Regression: The process of assessing the likelihood that a person with *disabilities* will lose skills and knowledge through lack of use or practice.

Anticonvulsant: Medication used to control *seizures.* Although all *seizures* are not convulsions, this term is commonly used.

Applied Behavior Analysis (ABA): A behavioral science that uses researched-based, highly structured teaching procedures to develop skills in individuals. An emphasis is placed on modifying behavior in a precisely measurable manner using repeated trials. Also called *behavior modification. See also* Discrete Trial Teaching; ABC's of Behavior Management; Behavior Management Plan.

ARD Committee: *See* Admission, Review, and Dismissal Committee.

ASA: *See* Autism Society of America.

Asperger's Disorder: A *pervasive developmental disorder* characterized by better-developed early language and cognitive skills, but also an inability to interact appropriately in social situations.

Assessment: The process used to determine a child's strengths and weaknesses. Includes testing and observations performed by an *interdisciplinary team* of professionals and parents. Usually used to determine *special education* needs. Also called *evaluation.*

Asset: Anything owned that has marketable value.

"At Risk of Experiencing Developmental Delay": The term applied to children under the age of three who have not been formally diagnosed with a specific condition. This heading may render them eligible for *special education* services.

Attention: The ability to concentrate on a task. *See also* Attention Span.

Attention Deficit Disorder (ADD): *See* Attention Deficit Hyperactive Disorder. The symptoms for this condition do not include the *hyperactivity* found in *ADHD.*

Attention Deficit Hyperactive Disorder (ADHD): A condition characterized by distractibility, restlessness, short *attention span,* impulsivity, and *hyperactivity.*

Attention Span: The amount of time one is able to concentrate on a task. Also called attending.

Auditory: Relating to the ability to hear.

Auditory Stimulus: Any sound that stimulates the nervous system.

Autism: A form of *pervasive developmental disorder* characterized by *disabilities* in social interaction, *language* acquisition and use, odd or unusual mannerisms, behaviors, and habits, and thinking skills.

Autism Society of America (ASA): A parent organization that *advocates* for the rights of individuals with *autism* and their families, monitors legislation pertaining to individuals with *developmental disabilities,* provides information to interested parties regarding *autism* and issues surrounding *autism,* and functions as a gateway to the media.

Autistic Disorder: The technical term for *autism.*

Autistic-Like Behaviors: Behaviors that include verbal and physical *perseveration* and rituals, poor eye contact, and limited *social awareness;* sometimes seen in individuals with *developmental disorders.*

Autistic Spectrum Disorder: Another term sometimes used for *Pervasive Developmental Disorders.*

Aversive: An unpleasant *stimulus* that follows an undesireable targeted behavior, the application of which is intended to reduce that behavior. *See also* Punishment; ABC's of Behavior Management; Applied Behavior Analysis.

Babbling: The sound a baby makes when he or she combines a vowel and consonant and repeats them over and over again (e.g., "ba-ba-ba," "ga-ga-ga").

Behavior Management Plan: A plan designed to modify or re-shape the behavior of an individual with *disabilities* that addresses existing behavior, *interventions,* support, and goals.

Behavior Modification: *See* Applied Behavior Analysis.

Beneficiary: The person indicated in a *trust* or insurance policy to receive any payments that become due.

Case Manager: A person who coordinates services for individuals with *disabilities. See also* Service Coordinator.

Cause-and-Effect: The concept that actions create reactions.

CDD: *See* Childhood Disintegrative Disorder.

Cerebral Palsy: Brain damage caused at birth or shortly thereafter that affects the *motor* areas of the brain.

Childhood Disintegrative Disorder (CDD): A rare form of *pervasive developmental disorder* in which a child, who has developed typically in early childhood, begins to display *autistic-like* characteristics. His or her abilities are said to "deteriorate" from earlier, more capable behavior.

Childhood Schizophrenia: A psychiatric disorder, probably with multiple causes. Symptoms include disturbances in form and content of thought, perception, emotions, sense of self, volition, relationship to the external world, and *psychomotor* behavior. Childhood schizophrenia is very rare.

Chlordiazepoxide: A medication sometimes prescribed to control anxiety. Also known as *Librium*™.

Chlorpromazine: A medication sometimes prescribed to treat symptoms of *autism*. Also known as *Thorazine*™.

Clomipramine: A medication sometimes prescribed to treat symptoms of *autism* and related disorders. Also known as *Luvox*™.

Cognition: The ability to know and understand the environment and to solve problems.

Competitive Employment: Jobs that pay workers at least minimum wage to produce valued goods or services, and that are performed in settings that include workers without disabilities.

Convulsion: Involuntary contractions of the muscles. A *seizure*.

Cost-of-Care Liability: The right of a state providing care to a person with *disabilities* to charge for the care and to collect from that person's *assets*.

Cue: *Input* that prompts a person to perform a behavior or activity.

Department of Vocational Rehabilitation (DVR): A state agency responsible for administering *vocational training* programs.

Development: The process of growth and learning during which a child acquires skills and abilities.

Developmental Disability: A condition originating before the age of 18 that may be expected to continue indefinitely and that impairs or delays *development*. Such conditions include *autism, pervasive developmental disorders, cerebral palsy,* and *mental retardation*.

Developmental Evaluation: See Assessment.

Developmental Milestone: A *developmental* goal that functions as a measurement of *developmental* progress over time.

Developmentally Delayed: Describes a person whose *development* is slower than average.

Developmentally Disabled Assistance and Bill of Rights Act: The federal law that establishes basic rights for individuals with *disabilities* and ensures the protection of those rights through a national system of law and *advocacy* offices.

Dexedrine™: The trade name for *dextroamphetamine*.

Dextroamphetamine: A *stimulant* medication sometimes prescribed to treat *ADHD.* Also known as *Dexedrine*^{TM}.

Diagnostic and Statistical Manual of Mental Disorders (DSM-IV): A manual published by the American Psychiatric Association that defines and describes the diagnostic criteria for mental disorders, and provides systematic descriptions of them.

Diazepine: A medication sometimes prescribed to control anxiety. Also known as *Valium*^{TM}.

Dilantin^{TM}**:** The trade name for *phenytoin.*

Disability: A term used to describe a delay in physical or cognitive *development.* The older term *"handicap"* is also sometimes used.

Discrete Trial Teaching: An instructional technique that is part of *Applied Behavior Analysis.* This technique involves four steps: 1) presenting a *cue* or *stimulus* to the learner; 2) obtaining the learner's response; 3) providing a positive consequence (reinforcer) or correction; and 4) a brief three-to-five second break until the next teaching trial is provided. Sometimes used in one-to-one or group sessions in which a variety of skills are taught, including *language, social skills, cognitive,* and *academic skills. See* Applied Behavior Analysis.

Discretionary Trust: A *trust,* or account, in which the *trustee* (the person responsible for governing the trust) has the authority to use the *trust* funds for any purpose, providing the funds are expended only for the *beneficiary.*

Discrimination: Showing favor toward one person, race, or group and prejudice toward another.

Disinherit: To deprive someone of an inheritance or legacy. Parents of children with *disabilities* may do this to prevent the state from imposing *cost-of-care liability* on their child's *assets.*

Dispute Resolution Procedures: The procedures established by law and regulation under *IDEA* for the fair resolution of disputes regarding a child's *special education.*

Dopamine: One of the *neurotransmitters* in the brain.

DSM-IV: *See* Diagnostic and Statistical Manual of Mental Disorders (DSM-IV).

DVR: *See* Department of Vocational Rehabilitation.

Early Development: *Development* during the first three years of life.

Early Intervention: The specialized way of interacting with infants to minimize the effects of conditions that can delay *early development.*

Echolalia: A parrot-like repetition of phrases or words just heard (immediate echolalia), or heard hours, days, weeks, or even months before (delayed echolalia).

EEG: *See* Electroencephalogram.

EEOC: *See* Equal Opportunity Employment Commission.

Electroencephalogram (EEG): The machine and test used to determine levels of electrical discharge from nerve cells.

Engagement: The ability to remain focused and interactive with (or responsive to) a person or object.

Epilepsy: A recurrent condition in which abnormal electrical discharges in the brain cause *seizures.*

Equal Employment Opportunity Commission (EEOC): The federal agency responsible for resolving employment *discrimination* complaints and enforcing antidiscrimination laws such as *The Americans with Disabilities Act (ADA).*

Estate Planning: Formal written arrangements for handling the possessions and assets of people after they have died.

ESY: *See* Extended School Year.

Etiology: The study of the cause of disease.

Evaluation: *See* Assessment.

Expressive Language: The use of gestures, words, and written symbols to communicate.

Extended School Year (ESY): Schooling that is provided year-round.

Extinction: A procedure in which *reinforcement* of a previously unintentionally reinforced behavior is withheld in an effort to encourage the behavior's eventual disappearance.

FAPE: *See* "Free Appropriate Public Education."

Fenflouramine: A medication sometimes prescribed to treat symptoms of *autism* in the past, but now used much less frequently because of potential side effects. Also known as *Pondimim*^{TM}.

Fine motor: The use of the small muscles of the body, such as those in the hands, feet, fingers, and toes.

Fluoxetine: A medication sometimes prescribed to treat *autism* and related disorders. Also known as *Prozac*^{TM}.

Fluvoxamine: A medication sometimes prescribed to treat *autism* and related disorders. Also known as *Anafranil*^{TM}.

Formal Complaint: Under *IDEA*, the means by which a parent or legal *guardian* can object to any aspect of his or her child's *special education* or *related services*.

Fragile X Syndrome: A condition caused by a *mutation* in the *genetic* information on the X chromosome. Often causes delays in *development*.

"Free Appropriate Public Education" (FAPE): The right, under *IDEA*, of every child with *disabilities* to an education provided at public expense that is appropriate to his or her *developmental* strengths and needs.

Functional Behavior Analysis: Observing a child's behavior and evaluating its purpose.

Functional Life Skills: The accumulation of knowledge and ability required to live independently. Also called *self-help* skills, functional life skills include hygiene, cooking, and dressing.

Generalization: Transferring a skill taught in one place or with one person to other places and people.

Genetic: Inherited.

Graduated Guidance: Systematically and gradually reducing the amount of physical guidance provided.

Gross Motor: The use of the large muscles of the body, such as those of the back, legs, and arms.

Guardian: A person appointed by law to manage the legal and financial affairs of someone else.

Haldol™: The trade name for *haloperidol*.

Haloperidol: A medication sometimes prescribed to treat symptoms of *autism*. Also known as *Haldol™*.

Hand Flapping/Hand Biting: *Perseverative* behaviors often seen in people with *developmental disorders*. These behaviors may be motivated by a *sensory* need, a desire to focus and calm oneself, to escape from a demand, or to gain access to preferred items or attention from others.

Handicapped: An outdated term referring to people with some form of *disability*, including physical *disability*, *mental retardation*, *sensory* impairment, behavioral disorder, learning *disability*, or combination of the above.

Hepatitis: An inflammation of the liver.

Hyperactivity: A nervous-system-based difficulty that makes it hard for a person to control *motor* (muscle) behavior. It is characterized by frequent movement, flitting from one activity to another, or having difficulty remaining seated.

IDEA: *See* Individuals with Disabilities Education Act.

Identification: The determination that a child should be *evaluated* as a possible candidate for *special education* services.

IEP: *See* Individualized Education Program.

IFSP: *See* Individualized Family Service Plan.

Imitation: The ability to observe the actions of others and to copy them in one's own actions. Also known as *modeling.*

Impartial Due Process Hearing: Part of the procedures established to protect the rights of parents and their children with *disabilities* during disputes under IDEA. These hearings occur before an impartial person to review the *identification, evaluation, placement,* and services provided by the educational agency working on behalf of a child with *disabilities.*

Inclusion: Placing children with *disabilities* in the same schools and classrooms with children who are developing typically. The environment includes the special supports and services necessary for educational success. *See also* Integration; Mainstreaming.

Individualized Education Program (IEP): The written plan that specifies the services the *local education agency* has agreed to provide a child with *disabilities* who is eligible under *IDEA;* for children ages 3 to 21.

Individualized Family Service Plan (IFSP): The written plan that specifies the education and *related services* to be provided to children eligible under *IDEA* and their families; for children birth to age three.

Individualized Plan for Employment (IPE): The written plan that specifies the *vocational training* services that are necessary and will be made available in order for adults with *disabilities* to work productively.

Individuals with Disabilities Education Act (IDEA): A federal law originally passed in 1975 and subsequently amended that requires states to provide a *"free appropriate public education in the least restrictive environment"* to children with *disabilities.*

Input: Information that a person receives through any of the senses (sight, hearing, touch, feeling, smell) that helps that person develop new skills.

Insistence on Sameness: A tendency in many people with autism to become upset when familiar routines or environments are changed.

Integration: When children with *disabilities* and children who are *developing* typically are taught in the same classroom. *See also* Inclusion; Mainstreaming.

Intelligence Quotient (IQ Score): A numerical measurement of intellectual capacity that compares a person's chronological age to his or her "mental age," as shown on *standardized tests.*

Interdisciplinary Team: A team of professionals who observe and *evaluate* children and then develop a comprehensive summary report of strengths and needs. Also known as a *multidisciplinary team.*

Interpretive: The sessions during which parents and teachers review and discuss the results of a child's *evaluation.*

Intervention: Action taken to improve a person's potential for success in compensating for a delay or deficit in their physical, emotional, or mental functioning.

IPE: *See* Individualized Plan for Employment.

IQ Score: *See* Intelligence Quotient.

Job Coach: One who provides employment support and training in order to enable a person with a *disability* to be employed.

Label: The name given to the specific causes of *developmental delays* in children with *disabilities.*

Language: The expression and understanding of human communication.

LEA: *See* Local Education Agency.

Learned Helplessness: A pervasive lack of self-sufficiency and self-respect that results from care-giving without attention to teaching *functional life skills.*

Least Restrictive Environment: The requirement under *IDEA* that children receiving *special education* must be educated to the fullest extent possible with children who do not have *disabilities. See also* Inclusion; Integration.

Liability: Legal accountability for loss or damage.

Librium™: The trade name for *chlordiazepoxide.*

Lithium: A medication sometimes prescribed to treat symptoms of *autism.*

Local Education Agency (LEA): The agency responsible for providing educational services on the local (city, county, and school district) level.

Luvox™: The trade name for *clomipramine.*

Luxury Trust: A *trust* that restricts allowable expenses in a way that excludes the cost of care in state-funded programs in order to avoid cost-of-care *liability.*

Mainstreaming: The practice of involving children with *disabilities* in regular school and preschool environments. *See also* Inclusion; Integration.

Malnutrition: Nutritional intake that is insufficient to promote or maintain growth and *development.*

Mediation: Under *IDEA*, when parents and school officials meet with a neutral third party to discuss a mutually acceptable resolution to a *formal complaint.*

Medicaid: A joint state and federal program that offers medical assistance to people who are financially needy and are therefore entitled to receive *SSI.*

Medicare: A federal program, not based on financial need, that provides payments for medical care to people who are receiving Social Security payments.

Mellaril™: The trade name for *thioridazine.*

Mental Retardation (MR): The term used by some doctors and teachers to describe people who score in the lowest three percentiles on cognitive assessment tests.

Methylphenidate: A drug that stimulates the central nervous system. It is sometimes prescribed to treat *ADHD.* Also known as *Ritalin™.*

Milestone: *See* Developmental Milestone.

Modeling: *See* Imitation.

Motor: Relating to the ability to use muscles to move oneself.

Motor Planning: The ability to think through and carry out a physical task.

MR: *See* Mental Retardation.

Multidisciplinary Team: *See* Interdisciplinary Team.

Multihandicapped: Having more than one *handicap,* or *disability.*

Mutation: A change or alteration in *genetic* information.

Naltrexone: A medication sometimes prescribed to treat symptoms of *autism.* Also known as *Trexan™.*

Negative Reinforcement: Any situation (stimulus event) whose removal increases a specific response. A stimulus is a negative reinforcer if its removal or termination increases the frequency of the response that led to its removal.

Neurologist: A physician specializing in medical problems associated with the brain and spinal cord.

Neurotransmitter: The chemical substance between nerve cells in the brain that allows the transmission of an impulse from one nerve to another.

Objective: In an *IEP,* the specific steps toward meeting an *annual goal.*

Occupational Therapist (OT): A therapist who specializes in improving the *development* of *fine motor* and adaptive skills.

Oral Motor: The use of muscles in and around the mouth.

OT: *See* Occupational Therapist.

P&A: *See* Protection and Advocacy System.

Para-educator: *See* Paraprofessional.

Paraprofessional: Also known as a *para-educator,* this person assists a classroom teacher in providing supports for a child with *disabilities* in educational settings. *See also* Inclusion; Mainstreaming; Integration; Least Restrictive Environment.

Parent Training and Information Center (PTIC): Mandated under *IDEA,* these state organizations provide families with information relating to *special education* rights, laws, and issues. *See* Resource Guide for more information.

Parent-Professional Partnership: The teaming of parents and teachers, doctors, nurses, or other professionals to work together to facilitate the *development* of children with *disabilities.*

PDD: *See* Pervasive Developmental Disorder.

PDD:NOS: *See* Pervasive Developmental Disorder:Not Otherwise Specified.

Perseveration: Seemingly purposeless repetitive movement or speech that is thought to be motivated by a person's inner preoccupations.

Pervasive Developmental Disorder (PDD): A range of conditions, including *autistic disorder, Asperger's Disorder, Rett's Disorder,* and *Childhood Disintegrative Disorder,* that can include symptoms such as verbal and physical perseveration, poor eye contact, limited *social awareness,* and *insistence on sameness. See also* Autistic Spectrum Disorder.

Pervasive Developmental Disorder:Not Otherwise Specified (PDD:NOS): A *pervasive developmental disorder* that includes most characteristics of *Autistic Disorder* but not enough to meet the specific diagnostic criteria for *Autistic Disorder.*

Pervasive Lack of Relatedness: A condition characterized by an individual's extreme difficulty relating to objects or people in a typical or appropriate fashion.

Phenytoin: A medication sometimes prescribed to control *seizures.* Also known as *Dilantin*^{TM}.

Phonetics: The specific sounds that comprise any spoken *language.*

Physical Therapist (PT): A therapist who specializes in improving the *development of motor* skills, particularly the coordination of *gross motor* activities.

Pincer Grasp: The use of the thumb and forefinger to grasp small objects.

Placement: The selection of the educational program for a child who needs *special education* services.

Pondimim™: The trade name for *fenflouramine*.

Positive Reinforcement: Providing a pleasant consequence after a behavior in order to maintain or increase the frequency of that behavior.

Pragmatics: The use of language for social communication. Includes requesting, protesting, commenting, sharing information, and the knowledge of the "rules" governing conversation.

Preschool: Schooling or daycare offered prior to kindergarten for children between the ages of three and five.

Present Level of Development/Functioning: A child's present position on *developmental* scales; a requirement of an *IEP.*

Prompt: *Input* that encourages an individual to perform a movement or activity. *See* Cue.

Prompt Dependence: When an individual requires a *prompt* or *cue* in order to perform a taught task or behavior. An individual's inability to self-motivate impedes his or her potential success in *generalizing* a skill.

Proprioception: The body's innate sense of its position in space.

Protection and Advocacy System (P&A): A nationwide program of state and national offices that *advocates* for the civil and legal rights of people with *developmental disabilities.*

Prozac™: The trade name for *fluoxetine*.

Psychiatrist: A medical doctor who diagnoses and treats mental illness; he or she may utilize prescription medications in treatment.

Psychologist: A professional who specializes in the study of human behavior and treatment of behavioral disorders.

Psychomotor: Voluntary *motor* activity.

Psychotropic: Medications that alter brain function. Pyschotropic drugs are often used in the treatment of mental illness and sometimes for certain *autistic* behaviors.

PT: *See* Physical Therapist.

PTIC: *See* Parent Training and Information Center.

Public Law 94-142: A name for an early version of *IDEA. See* Individuals with Disabilities Education Act.

Punishment: A consequence that is applied following a behavior to reduce the probability of that behavior occurring again. Punishment can be very mild (a frown or scolding), more moderate (a brief timeout), or very severe (electric shock).

Reasonable Accommodation: A requirement of the *ADA* that employers adapt the working environment to remove obstacles that may impede an otherwise qualified inividual's ability to work, despite his or her *disabilities*.

Receptive Language: The ability to understand spoken and written communication as well as gestures.

Redirection: Intentionally changing the focus of attention from one *stimulus* to another in an effort to avoid or curtail an unwanted burgeoning behavior; a nonpunitive approach to shaping behavior.

Regression: The loss of skill or ability due to lack of practice and demonstration. The amount of regression estimated to occur during school breaks determines whether a child qualifies for *Extended School Year (ESY)*.

Rehabilitation Act of 1973: *Section 504* of this federal law prohibits *discrimination* against individuals with *disabilities* in federally funded programs.

Reinforcement: Any consequence that increases the likelihood of the future occurrence of a behavior. A consequence is either presented or withheld in an effort to prompt the desired response. *See* Positive Reinforcement; Negative Reinforcement.

Related Services: Services that enable a child to benefit from *special education*. Related services include *speech, occupational,* and *physical therapies,* as well as transportation.

Repetitive Speech: Also called *echolalia. See also* Perseveration.

Replacement Behaviors: The technique of developing alternative behavior options to replace unwanted behaviors.

Residential Services: Services provided to people with *disabilities* to enable them to live independently in their communities. Examples include community group homes, supervised apartments, and skill development homes.

Respite Care: Skilled adult- or child-care that can be provided in your home, the home of a care-provider, or elsewhere. Respite care may be available for several hours per week or for overnight stays.

Rett's Disorder: A rare *pervasive developmental disorder* that affects females, is characterized by typical *early development,* and later, a pervasive loss of social, cognitive, and physical skills. Some improvement in these areas may take place in late childhood. Many children with Rett's Disorder develop *seizure* disorders.

Risperidal[TM]**:** The trade name for *risperidone.*

Risperdol[TM]**:** The trade name for *risperidol.*

Risperidol: A medication sometimes prescribed to treat symptoms of *autism*. Also known as *Risperdol*^{TM}.

Risperidone: A medication sometimes prescribed to treat symptoms of *autism*. Also known as *Risperidal*^{TM}.

Ritalin^{TM}: The trade name for *methylphenidate*.

Safety Net Approach: The continuing commitment to provide ongoing *vocational training* to individuals with *disabilities* as needed.

Screening Test: A test given to groups of children intended to determine which children need further *evaluation*.

SEA: *See* State Education Agency.

Section 504: *See* Rehabilitation Act of 1973.

Secure Employment: *Vocational training* that prepares adults with *disabilities* to enter the work force. The training is designed specifically to teach the skills needed to survive and succeed in *supported* or *competitive employment* situations. *See also* Department of Vocational Rehabilitation; Individualized Plan for Employment.

Seizure: Abnormal electrical discharges in nerve cells in the brain.

Self-Help: The ability to take care of oneself, employing such skills as eating, dressing, bathing, and cleaning. The process should begin early with awareness, responsiveness, and participation in self-help activities. *See also* Functional Life Skills.

Self Stimulation: The act of providing physical, visual, or *auditory* stimulation for oneself; rocking back and forth and *hand flapping* are examples.

Sensorimotor: Pertaining to *input* from the environment that stimulates the senses and initiates purposeful *motor* response.

Sensory: Relating to the senses.

Sensory Ability: The ability to process sensations, such as touch, sound, light, smell, and movement.

Sensory Integration: The ability to receive *input* from the senses, to organize it into a meaningful message, and to act on it.

Service Coordinator: The individual designated to oversee the education and *related services* for a child with *disabilities* and the services provided to his or her family. *See also* Case Manager.

Sheltered Employment: Employment in work settings where all workers have *disabilities,* are continually supervised, and are paid less than minimum wage.

Side Effect: An effect which results unintentionally from the administration of medication; manifestations of side effects from medication vary from person to person.

SLP: *See* Speech-Language Pathologist.

Social Ability: The ability to function in groups and to interact with people appropriately.

Social Awareness: Being aware of, understanding, and reacting to the behavior of others; requires reading *cues* and reacting to *prompts*.

Social Security Administration (SSA): The federal agency that administers both *SSI* and *SSDI*.

Social Security Disability Insurance (SSDI): Money that has been funneled into the Social Security system through payroll deductions on earnings. Workers who are disabled are entitled to these benefits. People who are born or become disabled before the age of 22 may collect SSDI under a parent's account if the parent is retired, disabled, or deceased.

Social Skills: Learned abilities such as sharing, turn-taking, asserting one's independence, and forming attachments that allow one to effectively interact with others.

Social Worker: A professional who aids and counsels others regarding *social skills.*

Special Education: Specialized instruction to address a student's educational *disabilities* determined by an *interdisciplinary team evaluation.* Instruction must be precisely matched to the child's educational needs and adapted to his or her learning style.

Special Needs: Needs generated by a person's *disabilities.*

Speech/Language Pathologist: A therapist who works to improve speech and *language* skills, as well as to improve *oral motor* abilities.

SSA: *See* Social Security Administration.

SSDI: *See* Social Security Disability Insurance.

SSI: *See* Supplemental Security Income.

Staffing: An *IEP* meeting.

Standardized Test: A test that assesses the *development* of an individual, the results of which are used for comparison with the performance of other individuals.

State Education Agency (SEA): The state agency responsible for implementing the provisions of *IDEA.*

Stereotypic Behavior: *See* Stereotypy.

Stereotypy: Also known as *stereotypic behavior. See* Perseveration.

Stimulant: A *psychotropic* drug, such as *Ritalin*™ or *Dexedrine*™, often used to control *hyperactivity* in children.

Stimulus: A physical object or environmental event that may trigger a response or have an effect upon the behavior of a person. Some stimuli are internal (earache pain), while others are external (a smile from a loved one).

Substantial Gainful Activity: The term used in testing to determine whether or not a person qualifies as "disabled" and is therefore eligible for certain federally funded programs. If a person cannot perform any job that is thought to be suitable for him or her, it is determined that he or she cannot engage in substantial gainful activity.

Supplemental Security Income (SSI): A program of payments available for eligible people who are disabled, blind, or elderly. SSI is based on financial need, not on past earnings.

Supported Employment: Paid employment for people with *developmental disabilities* for whom *competitive employment* at or above minimum wage is unlikely. Individuals receive support, often in the form of a *job coach,* that helps them to maintain employment.

Support Trust: A *trust* that ensures funds be used for the *beneficiary's* living expenses, including housing, food, and transportation.

Symptomatic: Having a cause that is identified.

Syntax: In *language,* the arrangement of words to form proper sentence structure.

Tactile: Relating to touch.

Tactile Defensiveness: Oversensitivity or aversion to touch.

Tardive Dyskinesia: A condition characterized by involuntary jerky movements of the mouth, tongue, lips, and trunk. Some medications prescribed for behavior control contribute to the development of this condition.

Therapist: A professional who works with people with *disabilities* to help them overcome the effects of *developmental* delays.

Thioridazine: A medication sometimes prescribed to treat symptoms of *autism.* Also known as *Mellaril*™.

Thorazine™: The trade name for *chlorpromazine.*

Transition: The period between the end of one activity and the start of another.

Transition Plan: Required under *IDEA*, a plan that details services and *accommodations* provided to children with *disabilities* when moving from *early intervention* services to *preschool*, and school to the work environment at age 21.

Trexan™: The trade name for *naltrexone*.

Triennial Evaluation and Triennial Review: Under *IDEA*, a review of the *IEP* that takes place every three years that includes re-evaluation for continued eligibility.

Trust: A legal arrangement in which a person or institution *(trustee)* maintains responsibility for money or property for another's benefit *(beneficiary)*.

Trustee: Person or institution responsible for governing a *trust*.

Uniform Transfers to Minors Act (UTMA): A law that governs gifts to minors. Under the UTMA, gifts become the property of the recipient at age 18 or 21, depending on the state.

UTMA: *See* Uniform Transfers to Minors Act.

Valium™: The trade name for *diazepine*.

Vestibular: Pertaining to the *sensory* system located in the inner ear that allows the body to maintain balance and enjoyably participate in movement such as swinging and roughhousing.

Visual Motor: The use of the eyes to discriminate and track objects and to perceive environmental *cues*. Visual *motor* skills are required to carry out tasks such as putting a puzzle piece into a puzzle or a key into a keyhole.

Visual Stimulus: That which stimulates the eye. In excess, it can cause confusion or agitation in individuals and can result in *hyperactivity*, perseverative behavior, or withdrawl.

Vocational Training: Training for a job. Learning skills to perform in the workplace.

READING LIST

▪▪ Chapter 1

American Psychiatric Association. **Diagnostic and Statistical Manual of Mental Disorders (DSM-IV), 4th ed.** Washington, DC: American Psychiatric Association, 1994.
   The definitive manual used for the diagnosis of all pervasive developmental disorders, including autism.

Attwood, Tony. **Asperger's Syndrome: A Guide for Parents and Professionals.** London: Jessica Kingsley Publishers, 1997.
   This book details the characteristics of Asperger's Disorder and outlines approaches to reducing undesireable behaviors. Includes a useful question and answer section, diagnostic criteria, and an extensive research guide.

Brill, Marlene Targ. **Keys to Parenting the Child With Autism (Barron's Parenting Keys).** New York: Barron's, 1994.
   Part of a series of guides, this book provides a brief introduction to autism for parents.

Cohen, D.J., and Fred R. Volkmar, M.D., eds. **Handbook of Autism and Pervasive Developmental Disorders, 2nd ed.** John Wiley & Sons, 1997.
   The most comprehensive and up-to-date professional textbook on autism and related conditions. Technical but thorough.

Grandin, Temple. **Thinking in Pictures: And Other Reports from My Life with Autism.** New York: Vintage, 1996.
   A compelling and fascinating look into living with autism, written by a woman who has autism.

Greenspan, Stanley, M.D., and Serena Weidner, Ph.D., Robin Simon, contributor. **The Child with Special Needs: Encouraging Intellectual and Emotional Growth.** New York: Perseus Books, 1998.

Covering many disabilities, this book offers advice on how to help children reach their intellectual potential.

Hart, Charles. **A Parent's Guide to Autism: Answers to the Most Common Questions.** New York: Pocket Books, 1993.

In a question-answer format, this book provides a basic introduction to autism, written by a parent of an individual with autism.

Howlin, Patricia. **Children with Autism and Asperger Syndrome: A Guide for Practitioners and Carers.** New York: John Wiley & Sons, 1998.

Written for professionals, but of use to parents, this book presents a comprehensive look at autism and Asperger's Disorder, covering all the major issues of treatment, education, and behavior.

Schopler, Eric and Gary B. Mesibov. **High Functioning Individuals with Autism.** New York: Plenum, 1992.

Written for professionals, this book provides information specific to the group of people with autism labelled "high functioning."

Siegel, Bryna. **The World of the Autistic Child: Understanding and Treating Autism Spectrum Disorders.** New York: Oxford University Press, 1998.

A comprehensive autism reference, covering a wide range of topics and issues in autism. Technical in tone.

Sweeney, Wilma. **The Special Needs Reading List: An Annotated Guide to the Best Publications for Parents and Professionals.** Bethesda, MD: Woodbine House, 1998.

A comprehensive listing of books for parents and teachers of children with disabilities. The annotations help identify which book is best suited to a specific need.

Weber, Jayne Dixon. **Children with Fragile X Syndrome: A Parents' Guide.** Bethesda, MD: Woodbine House, 2000.

A thorough and compassionate introduction to fragile X syndrome, written for parents and families.

Willey, Liane. **Pretending to be Normal: Living with Asperger's Syndrome.** London: Jessica Kingsley Publishers, 1999.

Written by the mother of a child with Asperger's Disorder who also has the condition herself, this book offers practical advice.

Williams, Donna. **Nobody Nowhere: The Extraordinary Autobiography of an Autistic.** New York: Avon Books, 1994.
Williams, Donna. **Somebody Somewhere: Breaking Free from the World of Autism.** New York: Times Books, 1995.

These two autobiographies trace the life of a woman with autism, but who was not diagnosed until later in life. Well written.

:: Chapter 2

Dillon, Kathleen. **Living With Autism: The Parents' Stories.** Boone, NC: Parkway Publishing, 1995.

After an introduction to autism, this book presents the family and parenting stories of several families with a child with autism.

Gerlach, Elizabeth, **Just This Side of Normal: Glimpses into Life with Autism.** Eugene, OR: Four Leaf Press, 1999.

The personal story of a mother's work to help her child with autism, and the impact of autism on her life.

Kephart, Beth. **A Slant of Sun: One Child's Courage.** New York: Quill, 1999.

A beautifully written account of a mother and her young son with autism. National Book Award Finalist.

Kushner, H.S. **When Bad Things Happen to Good People.** New York: Avon, 1981.

A biographical account of a rabbi and his family following the death of their son from a rare disease. A moving and compassionate work with advice and wisdom about facing adversity.

Maurice, Catherine. **Let Me Hear Your Voice: A Family's Triumph over Autism.** New York: Fawcett Books, 1994.

The personal story of a family's struggle to overcome autism through the use of Applied Behavior Analysis. A compelling story, written very well.

Park, Clara Claiborne. **The Siege: The First Eight Years of an Autistic Child**

with an Epilogue, Fifteen Years Later. New York: Little, Brown, 1990.
A classic account of a family's experiences raising a daughter with autism. Highly recommended.

Schulze, Craig. **When Snow Turns to Rain: One Family's Struggle to Solve the Riddle of Autism.** Bethesda, MD: Woodbine House, 1996.
Although not known to the parents at the time, their son was diagnosed with Childhood Disintegrative Disorder. This book follows the onset and progress of the condition.

■■ Chapter 3

Batshaw, Mark, M.D. **Children with Disabilities, 4th ed.** Baltimore: Paul H. Brookes, 1997.
A layman's medical book about birth defects, developmental disabilities, and other medical conditions of children. Expensive but useful.

Cohen, D.J., and Fred R. Volkmar, M.D., eds. **Handbook of Autism and Pervasive Developmental Disorders, 2nd ed.** John Wiley & Sons, 1997.
The most comprehensive and up-to-date professional textbook on autism and related conditions. Covers medical issues in autism in great detail.

Freeman, John, M.D. **Seizures and Epilepsy in Childhood: A Guide for Parents.** Baltimore: Johns Hopkins University Press, 1997.
An introduction to childhood seizure disorders, written for parents.

■■ Chapter 4

Baker Bruce L., and Alan J. Brightman. **Steps to Independence: Teaching Everyday Skills to Children with Special Needs, 3rd ed.** Baltimore: Paul H. Brookes, 1997.
An excellent, how-to guide for parents on teaching basic skills and managing behavior problems.

Durand, V. Mark. **Sleep Better! A Guide to Improving Sleep for Children with Special Needs.** Baltimore: Paul H. Brookes, 1998.
This book provides practical strategies for encouraging children with special needs to sleep predicably.

Fouse, Beth, and Maria Wheeler. **A Treasure Chest of Behavioral Strategies for Individuals with Autism.** Arlington, TX: Future Horizons, 1997.

A useful book for parents new to Applied Behavior Analysis and its terminology. Provides practical suggestions for dealing with common behavior issues.

Harris, Sandra L., and Mary Jane Weiss. **Right From the Start: Behavioral Intervention for Young Children with Autism (Topics in Autism).** Bethesda, MD: Woodbine House, 1998.

An introductory guide, written for parents, to Applied Behavior Analysis and early intervention programs for young children. Clear explanations in easy-to-understand language.

Kranowitz, Carol Stock. **The Out-of-Sync Child: Recognizing and Coping with Sensory Integration Dysfunction.** New York: Berkley Publishing Group, 1998.

Though not written specifically about children with autism, this easy-to-read book contains lots of basic information about the sensory system and sensory integration problems.

Lovett, Herbert. **Learning to Listen: Positive Approaches and People with Difficult Behavior.** Baltimore: Paul H. Brookes, 1996.

Explaining that all behavior is communication, this book emphasizes understanding difficult behavior as the first step in creating positive behavioral supports.

Maurice, Catherine, Gina Green, and Stephen Luce. **Behavioral Intervention for Young Children with Autism: A Manual for Parents and Professionals.** Austin, TX: Pro-Ed, 1996.

A very detailed program for implementing Applied Behavior Analysis at home. Clear and thorough, if a little complicated. Best used with a professional.

McClannahan, Lynn E., and Patricia J. Krantz. **Activity Schedules for Children With Autism: Teaching Independent Behavior (Topics in Autism).** Bethesda, MD: Woodbine House, 1999.

This short book explains how to use day-planner-like schedules to teach children with autism to complete tasks independently and to manage their own time.

Schopler, Eric, ed. **Parent Survival Manual: A Guide to Crisis Resolution in Autism and Related Developmental Disorders.** New York: Plenum Press, 1995.
A practical book of solutions and advice, covering problems like perseveration, aggression, and communication.

Wheeler, Maria. **Toilet Training for Individuals with Autism and Related Disorders: A Comprehensive Guide for Parents and Teachers.** Arlington, TX: Future Horizons, 1998.
Offers many suggestions in toilet training children with autism. Lots of advice and examples.

** Chapter 5

Buck, Pearl S. **The Child Who Never Grew.** Bethesda, MD: Woodbine House, 1992.
Breaking a national taboo when first published in 1950 by Nobel and Pulitzer prize winner Pearl S. Buck, this brief personal account (supplemented with an extensive Foreword by James Michener) eloquently portrays the life of parenting a child with a disability. Useful for historical perspective.

Featherstone, Helen. **A Difference in the Family: Living with a Disabled Child.** New York: Penguin, 1981.
A highly compassionate account of one family's journey on the road to acceptance of their child's severe disabilities. A classic. Highly recommended.

Gerlach, Elizabeth. **Autism Treatment Guide, rev. ed.** Eugene, OR: Four Leaf Press, 1998.
A review of many of the treatments—traditional and alternative— for children with autism.

Grandin, Temple, and Margaret Scariano. **Emergence: Labeled Autistic.** New York: Warner Books, 1996.
A personal account of growing up with autism, written by a young woman with high-functioning autism. An exceptional book.

Harris, Sandra L. **Siblings of Children With Autism: A Guide for Families (Topics in Autism).** Bethesda, MD: Woodbine House, 1994.
A useful guide to understanding sibling relationships, how autism

affects them, and how parents can support their children in living and growing with a sibling with autism.

Lears, Laurie. **Ian's Walk: A Story about Autism.** Morton Grove, IL: Albert Whitman & Co., 1998.
A beautifully illustrated children's book that shows the joys and challenges of having a sibling with autism.

Marsh, Jayne D.B. **From the Heart: On Being the Mother of a Child with Special Needs.** Bethesda, MD: Woodbine House, 1995.
An engrossing collection of narratives drawn from a parent support group. Mothers of children with disabilities open their hearts in sharing how their child with disabilities shapes their lives.

Meyer, Donald, ed. **Uncommon Fathers: Reflections on Raising a Child with a Disability.** Bethesda, MD: Woodbine House, 1995.
A collection of thoughtful and soul-searching essays written by fathers of children with a variety of disabilities, including autism, that explore their unique experiences and outlook.

Meyer, Donald, ed. **Views from Our Shoes: Growing Up with a Brother or Sister with Special Needs.** Bethesda, MD: Woodbine House, 1997.
An endearing collection of 45 essays and stories written by siblings of children with disabilities about what it's like to be the brother or sister of a child with a disability.

Meyer, Donald, Patricia Vadasy, and Rebecca Fewell. **Living with a Brother or Sister with Special Needs: A Book for Sibs, 2nd ed.** Seattle, WA: University of Washington Press, 1996.
An excellent introduction to the subject of disabilities for siblings. Reviews specific disabilities and discusses what it is like to be a sibling of a child with a disability.

Miller, Nancy and Catherine Sammons. **Everybody's Different: Understanding and Changing Our Reactions to Disabilities.** Baltimore: Paul H. Brookes, 1999.
This book explores the reactions of people to those who have disabilities, and provides advice on how to change attitudes.

Miller, Nancy, **Nobody's Perfect: Living and Growing with Children Who Have Special Needs.** Baltimore: Paul H. Brookes, 1994.

Based on her work with a support group for mothers of children with disabilities, this book provides understanding and advice to parents on coping with a child with a disability.

Siegel, Bryna, and Stuart Silverstein. **What About Me? Growing Up with a Developmentally Disabled Sibling.** New York: Insight Books, 1994.
Written by a sibling of a person with a disability, this book discusses the emotions of siblings of children with disabilities.

Thompson, Mary. **Andy and His Yellow Frisbee.** Bethesda, MD: Woodbine House, 1996.
The illustrated story about the behavior of a child with autism, and a young girl's curiosity. The book explains some "autistic" behaviors in a matter-of-fact way.

❚❚ Chapter 6

Anderson, Johanna. **Sensory Motor Issues in Autism.** San Antonio: The Psychological Corporation, 1998.
A thorough explanation of sensory issues in children with autism, along with many charts, exercises, and suggested activities for teachers and parents. Written by an OT.

Cox, Maureen. **The Child's Point of View, 2nd ed.** New York: Guilford Press, 1991.
A basic overview of what abilities develop in children at what ages, with additional suggestions for educational activities.

Ilg, Frances, Louise Ames, and Sidney Baker. **Child Behavior: The Classic Child Care Manual from the Gesell Institute of Human Development, rev. ed.** New York: HarperCollins, 1981.
Provides a general overview of human development.

Kail, Robert. **Children and Their Develoment.** New York: Prentice-Hall, 1997.
A comprehensive textbook introduction to child development. Written for university-level students studying child development, but contains a wide range of information. Technical.

Miller, Karen. **Ages and Stages: Developmental Descriptions and Activities, Birth through Eight Years.** Beltsville, MD: Telshare Publishing/Gryphon House, 1985.

Although first published in 1985, this book contains good descriptions of typical child development, along with developmental activities for parents and teachers.

Shaffer, David. **Developmental Psychology, 5th ed.** Pacific Grove, CA: Brooks/Cole, 1999.
A well written and comprehensive advanced-level textbook about child development. Focuses on research and developmental theory.

White, Burton L. **The First Three Years of Life, 20th rev. ed.** New York: Fireside, 1995.
One of the classics on child development, covering the first three years of life.

∷ Chapter 7

Berkell Zager, Dianne E. (Editor). **Autism: Identification, Education and Treatment, 2nd ed.** Mahwah, NJ: Lawrence Erlbaum Associates, 1999.
An up-to-date professional text covering a wide range of educational topics. Very useful for teachers and clinicians.

Cohen, Shirley. **Targeting Autism: What We Know, Don't Know, and Can Do to Help Young Children with Autism and Related Disorders.** Berkeley, CA: University of California Press, 1998.
An informative overview of autism and approaches to educating children with autism. Also discusses many current issues in the field of autism.

Coleman, Jeanine. **The Early Intervention Dictionary: A Multi-disciplinary Guide to Terminology, 2nd ed.** Bethesda, MD: Woodbine House, 1999.
A comprehensive guide to the terminology used in early intervention and special education. Useful for parents and teachers in understanding each other.

Freeman, Sabrina. **Teach Me Language: A Language Manual for Children with Autism, Asperger's Syndrome and Related Developmental Disorders.** Langley, BC: SKF Books, 1997.
An excellent, practical resource addressing pragmatic language for students with autism spectrum disorders.

Harris, Sandra L., and Mary Jane Weiss. **Right From the Start: Behavioral Intervention for Young Children with Autism (Topics in Autism).** Bethesda, MD: Woodbine House, 1998.

An introductory guide, written for parents, to Applied Behavior Analysis and early intervention programs for young children. Clear explanations in easy-to-understand language.

Hodgdon, Linda. **Solving Behavior Problems in Autism: Improving Communication with Visual Strategies.** Troy, MI: QuirkRoberts, 1999.

Explains how to use visual strategies to diffuse difficult behavior and self-management challenges in children with autism. Includes information for parents.

Hodgdon, Linda. **Visual Strategies for Improving Communication: Volume 1: Practical Supports for School and Home.** Troy, MI: QuirkRoberts, 1995.

Explains how to use visual methods to structure and organize classroom routines to enable children with autism to succeed. Includes information for parents.

Holmes, David. **Autism through the Lifespan: The Eden Model.** Bethesda, MD: Woodbine House, 1998.

An in-depth look at the educational approach of The Eden Family of Services, a successful behavioral-based educational program. Provides a detailed and useful look into the educational philosophy at Eden and its behavioral intervention processes.

Koegel, Robert, and Lynn Kern Koegel. **Teaching Children With Autism: Strategies for Initiating Positive Interactions and Improving Learning Opportunities.** Baltimore: Paul H. Brookes, 1996.

Though technical, this book explains positive behavioral support strategies that can be applied to classroom and home settings.

Myles, Brenda Smith, and Jack Southwick. **Asperger Syndrome and Difficult Moments: Practical Solutions for Tantrums, Rage, and Meltdowns.** Shawnee Mission, KS: Autism Asperger Publishing Co., 1999.

A brief guide to managing problem behavior in children with Asperger's Disorder and other PDDs, using functional analysis. Written for teachers, but also useful to parents.

Quill, Kathleen Ann. **Teaching Children with Autism: Strategies to Enhance Communication and Socialization.** Albany, NY: Delmar Publishers, 1996.

Although intended for professionals, this book provides helpful classroom strategies for children with autism.

Simons, Jeanne, and Sabine Oishi. **The Hidden Child: The Linwood Method of Reaching the Autistic Child.** Bethesda, MD: Woodbine House, 1987.

A well-written account of one pioneering teacher's approach to treating children with autism.

∷ Chapter 8

Anderson, Winifred, Stephen Chitwood, and Deidre Hayden. **Negotiating the Special Education Maze: A Guide for Parents and Teachers, 3rd ed.** Bethesda, MD: Woodbine House, 1997.

A step-by-step guide to help parents make sure their children receive appropriate education services under the Individuals with Disabilities Education Act.

Baldwin, Ben. **The Complete Book of Insurance: The Consumer's Guide to Insuring Your Life, Health, Property, and Income.** Chicago: Irwin Professional Publishing, 1996.

Written to help parents make informed decisions about buying insurance; covers all of the types of insurance and selecting an agent.

Bateman, Barbara and Mary Anne Linden. **Better IEPs: How to Develop Legally Correct and Educationally Useful Programs, 3rd ed.** Longmont, CO: Sopris West, 1992.

A useful and practical guide to the IEP process, written for parents. Contains information on the 1997 IDEA amendments.

Detlefs, Dale, and Robert J. Myers. **2000 Mercer Guide to Social Security and Medicare (Mercer Guide to Social Security and Medicare, 2000).** William M. Mercer, Inc., 2000.

These two critical and complex subjects are presented in a way that makes them easy to understand. This book describes your rights and benefits under these programs.

Fouse, Beth. **Creating a Win-Win IEP for Students with Autism: A How-To Manual for Parents and Educators.** Arlington, TX: Future Horizons, 1999.

An easy-to-understand basic guide to IDEA and its application to students with autism. Filled with suggestions and examples.

Russell, L. Mark. **Planning for the Future: Providing a Meaningful Life for a Child with a Disability after Your Death.** Evanston, IL: American Publishing Co., 1995.

A guide to estate planning for parents of children with disabilities.

Schlachter, Gail. **Financial Aid for the Disabled and Their Families.** San Carlos, CA: Reference Service Press, 1998.

A guide to a wide range of financial aid programs offered to people with disabilities and their familes.

Siegel, Lawrence. **The Complete IEP Guide: How to Advocate for Your Special Ed Child.** Berkeley, CA: 1999.

A practical, hands-on guide to navigating the special education laws. Filled with forms and resources, along with much useful information.

■■ Chapter 9

Alberti, Robert, and Michael Emmons. **Your Perfect Right: A Guide to Assertive Living.** San Luis Obispo, CA: Impact Publishers, 1995.

A general guide to fostering the attitude of feeling comfortable in advocating for rights.

Charlton, James. **Nothing About Us Without Us: Disability Oppression and Empowerment.** Berkeley, CA: University of California Press, 1998.

Based on interviews with disability activists around the world, this book reveals the oppression of people with disabilities.

Dekieffer, Donald E. **The Citizen's Guide to Lobbying Congress.** Chicago: Chicago Review Press, 1997.

A practical guidebook to how to advocate for legislation before Congress (and state legislators).

Des Jardins, Charlotte. **How to Get Services by Being Assertive, 2nd ed.** Chicago, IL: Family Resource Center on Disabilities, 1993.

This guide describes your child's legal rights to an education and how to get the services he or she needs.

Des Jardins, Charlotte. **How to Organize an Effective Parent/Advocacy Group and Move Bureaucracies, 2nd ed.** Chicago, IL: Family Resource Center on Disabilities, 1993.

Instructions on starting a parent advocacy group along with ideas on how to keep the group active.

Shaw, Randy. **The Activist's Handbook: A Primer for the 1990s and Beyond.** Berkeley, CA: University of California Press, 1996.

A guide to advocating for social change through lobbying, public awareness campaigns, and social action.

∷ Chapter 10

Smith, Marcia Datlow, Ronald G. Belcher, and Patricia D. Juhrs. **A Guide to Successful Employment for Individuals with Autism.** Baltimore: Paul H. Brookes, 1997.

A thorough overview of the issues and challenges facing adults with autism in community employment. Many case examples.

Stengle, Linda. **Laying Community Foundations for Your Child with a Disability: How to Establish Relationships That Will Support Your Child after You're Gone.** Bethesda, MD: Woodbine House, 1996.

A practical guide that shows families how to build a network of relationships to support the independence and dignity of an adult with disabilities in his or her community.

Wehman, Paul, and John Kregel, eds. **More Than a Job: Securing Satisfying Careers for People with Disabilities.** Baltimore: Paul H. Brookes, 1998.

A guide to supported employment for people with disabilities.

∷ Spanish-Language Books

Powers, Michael. **Niños Autistas Guía para padres, terapeutas y educadores.** Mexico: Trillas, 1999.

The Spanish language edition of the first edition of **Children with Autism: A Parents' Guide,** available from Woodbine House.

∷ Magazines and Newsletters

AA News. Asperger's Association of New England, P.O. Box 68, 526 Main Street, Henderson, MN 56044; (507) 248-3294; E-mail: info@aane.org;

Web: http://www.aane.org.

Includes informative and down-to-earth articles for and about people with Asperger's Disorder and their families.

ABTA News. Autism Behavior Therapy Alliance, 1360-F University Avenue West, No. 101-110, St. Paul, MN 55104; (612) 927-0017; E-mail: info@behaviortherapy.org; Web: http://www.autismbehaviortherapy.org.

This newsletter focuses on current legislation regarding the education of children with autism; discusses advances and hurdles in the field of Applied Behavior Analysis.

The Advocate. The Autism Society of America, 7910 Woodmont Avenue, Suite 300, Bethesda, MD 20814-3015; (800) 3AUTISM ext. 150; (301) 657-0869 (fax); E-mail: action_alert@autism-society.org; Web: http://www.autism-society.org.

Especially informative! Free with membership in ASA.

The ARC. The Arc of the United States, 1010 Wayne Avenue, Suite 650, Silver Spring, MD 20910; (301) 565-3842; (301) 565-5342 (fax); E-mail: info@thearc.org; Web: http://www.thearc.org.

News and information on mental retardation and the activities of the national office of the ARC and its affiliates. Website posts weekly reports regarding current legislation, upcoming conferences, and current projects. Available in Spanish.

Autism Asperger's Digest. Future Horizons, Inc., 721 West Abram Street, Arlington, TX 76013; (800) 489-0727.

This monthly magazine offers a broad spectrum of topical information related to autism and features a recommended reading list in each publication.

Autism Research Review International. Autism Research Institute, 4182 Adams Avenue, San Diego, CA 92116; (619) 281-7165; (619) 563-6840 (fax); Web: http://www.autism.com/ari.

A quarterly newsletter of up-to-date information from the bio-medical and educational literature on autism. Articles published are of interest and value to both parents and professionals concerned with the care of children with autism.

Closing the Gap. Enabling Technologies, P.O. Box 68, 526 Main Street, Henderson, MN 56044; (507) 248-3294; (507) 248-3810 (fax); E-mail:

info@closingthegap.com; Web: http://www.closingthegap.com.

A bi-monthly newspaper focusing on how computer technology can and is being used to aid individuals with disabilities.

Connections Newsletter. Gutstein, Sheely & Associates, P.C., 1177 West Loop South, Suite 530, Houston, TX 77027.

A bi-monthly newsletter for individuals with Asperger's Disorder and high-functioning autism.

Disability Solutions. 9220 SW Barbur Blvd., #119-179, Portland, OR 97219-5428; (503) 244-7662; (503) 246-3869 (fax); E-mail: subscription@disabilitysolutions.org; Web: http://www.disabilitysolutions.org/.

A free newsletter written in parent-friendly language covering a wide range of topics concerning children with disabilities and their education. Its recent special issue on children with Down syndrome and autism is of special interest.

Exceptional Parent. Psy-Ed Corp., 555 Kinderkamack Road, Oradell, NJ 07649-1517; (877) 372-7368; E-mail: Webmaster@eparent.com; Web: http://www.eparent.com.

Magazine focusing on timely topics that affect the lives of parents of children with disabilities.

Journal of Autism and Developmental Disorders. Kluwer Academic/Plenum Publishers, 233 Spring Street, New York, NY 10013-1578; (212) 620-8468; (212) 807-1047 (fax); E-mail: services@wkap.nl; Web: http://www.wkap.nl/journalhome.htm/0162-3257.

Professional and academic journal. Inquire about special price for ASA members.

Looking Up: The Monthly International Autism Newsletter, P.O. Box 25727, London, SW19 1WF, England; (181) 542-7702; E-mail: LookingUp@compuserve.com; Web: http://www.feinst.demon.co.uk/looking-up.html.

Aimed at parents and professionals, the articles in this magazine explore the impact of autism on family, school, employment, politics, and society.

MAAP Newsletter. More Able Autistic Persons, Inc., P.O. Box 524, Crown Point, IN 46307; (219) 662-1311; E-mail: chart@netnitco.net; Web: http://ww2.netnitco.net/users/chart/maap.html.

This quarterly newsletter presents information relevant to individuals with high-functioning autism; offers support and advice to parents.

The Morning News. Jenison Public School, editor: Carol Gray, 2140 Bauer Road, Jenison, MI 49428; (616) 457-8955; (616) 457-4070 (fax); E-mail: edfuture@onramp.net; Web: http://www.futurehorizons-autism.com.
Articles in this newsletter relate primarily to helping individuals with autism and developmental disabilities acquire social skills.

Naarrative. National Alliance for Autism Research, 414 Wall Street, Research Park, Princeton, NJ 08540; (609) 430-9160; (888) 777-NAAR; E-mail: vickih@artsci.net; Web: http://babydoc.home.pipeline.com/naar/naar.htm.
A newsletter dedicated to reporting current research and medical interventions pertaining to autism spectrum disorders.

News Digest, Parent Guides, and Basics for Parents. NICHCY, P.O. Box 1492, Washington, DC 20013; (800) 695-0285; E-mail: nichcy@aed.org; Web: http://www.nichcy.org.
These publications are useful and up-to-date. Available in Spanish.

Our Voice. Autism Network International, P.O. Box 448, Syracuse, NY 13210-0448; E-mail: bordner@uiuc.edu; Web: www.staff.uiuc.edu/~bordner/ani.
A newsletter written for and about people with autism.

Pacesetter Newsletter. Parent Advocacy Coalition for Educational Rights, 4826 Chicago Avenue South, Minneapolis, MN 55417-1098; (612) 827-2966; (612) 827-3065 (fax); E-mail: Webmaster@pacer.org; Web: http://www.pacer.org.
A newsletter, mailed three times a year, for parents interested in special education issues.

PDD NETWORK Newsletter. PDD/Asperger's Support Group, contact: Stacy Hultgren, 21 Sharon Court, Shelton, CT 06484; (203) 924-0457; E-mail: BHULT40@aol.com; Web: http://www.PDDAspergerSupportCT.org.
A valuable resource that presents opportunities for parents of individuals with PDD and Asperger's Disorder to exchange information.

Sib to Sib! The Sibling Support Project, contact: Andrew Lanier, c/o Rhoda Berlin, Little Red Schoolhouse, P.O. Box 992, Lynnwood, WA 98046; E-mail: dmeyer@chmc.org; Web:http://www.chmc.org/departmt/sibsupp/default.htm.
This newsletter includes articles written for and about siblings of kids with health and developmental needs.

The Source. Asperger Syndrome Education Network, Inc., P.O. Box 2577, Jacksonville, FL 32203-2577; (904) 745-6741; E-mail: aspen@cyber-max.net; Web: http://www.asperger.org.

Articles in this quarterly newsletter focus on research in the field of social and communication disorders.

RESOURCE GUIDE

∷ National Organizations

American Association of University Affiliated Programs
8630 Fenton Street, Suite 410
Silver Spring, MD 20910
(301) 588-8252
E-mail: gjesien@aauap.org
Web: http://www.aauap.org/
The national organization for UAPs, which provide developmental, clinical, and research services. This organization can locate the UAP that is nearest to you.

American Hyperlexia Association (AHA)
195 W. Spangler, Suite B
Elmhurst, IL 60126
(630) 415-2212; (630) 530-5909 (Fax)
E-mail: president@hyperlexia.org
Web: http://www.hyperlexia.org/
This organization is made up of parents and relatives of children with hyperlexia, speech and language professionals, education professionals, and other concerned individuals. The organization's goal is to increase awareness of hyperlexia, and promote effective teaching techniques.

The Arc of the United States
1010 Wayne Avenue, Suite 650
Silver Spring, MD 20910
(301) 565-3842; (301) 565-3843 (Fax)
E-mail: Info@thearc.org
Web: http://www.thearc.org/

A national grassroots organization of persons with mental retardation and their advocates. Publishes information about all types of mental retardation, advocates on behalf of people with intellectual disabilities, and supports an extensive national network of local affiliates.

ASPEN of America (Asperger Syndrome Education Network of America)
P.O. Box 2577
Jacksonville, FL 32203-2577
(904) 745-6741
E-mail: aspen@cybermax.net
Web: http://www.asperger.org/
A national organization that provides information about Asperger's Disorder to parents and professionals.

Autism Research Institute
4182 Adams Avenue
San Diego, CA 92116
(619) 281-7165; (619) 563-6840 (Fax)
Web: http://http://www.autism.com/ari/
Conducts research into autism, methods of preventing, diagnosing and treating autism, and other severe behavioral disorders of childhood. Provides information based on research to parents and professionals throughout the world.

Autism Society of America
7910 Woodmont Avenue, Suite 300
Bethesda, MD 20814
(800) 3-AUTISM; (301) 657-0881; (301) 657-0869 (Fax)
Web: www.autism-society.org
A national organization of parents and professionals that promotes a better understanding of autism, encourages the development of services, supports research related to autism, and advocates on behalf of people with autism and their families. Acts as information clearinghouse about autism and services for people with autism. Publishes the Advocate, a bi-monthly newsletter. Coordinates a national network of affiliated state and local chapters. For the location of the state or local chapter nearest you, call the 800 number listed above.

Beach Center on Families and Disability

3111 Haworth
University of Kansas
Lawrence, KS 66045.
(785) 864-7600; (785) 864-7605 (Fax)
E-mail: beach@dole.lsi.ukans.edu
Web: http://www.lsi.ukans.edu/beach/
A national center of support for families of children with disabilities. Provides a wide range of information and resources on families of children with disabilities, including autism. Publishes newsletters and information about many family-centered topics.

Center for the Study of Autism

P.O. Box 4538
Salem, OR 97302
Web: http://www.autism.org/
Conducts research into therapies and provides information to parents through its website. Affiliated with the Autism Research Institute.

Children's Defense Fund

25 E Street, NW
Washington, DC 20001
(800) CDF-1200; (202) 628-8787; (202) 662-3510 (Fax)
E-mail: cdfinfo@childrensdefense.org
Web: http://www.childrensdefense.org
A national organization which advocates for the rights of children.

Closing the Gap

526 Main Street
P.O. Box 68
Henderson, MN 56004
(612) 248-3294; (612) 248-3810 (Fax)
E-mail: info@closingthegap.com
Web: http://www.closingthegap.com
An organization that focuses on computer technology for people with special needs through its bi-monthly newspaper, annual international conference, and extensive web site.

Cure Autism Now

5225 Wilshire Blvd., Suite 226,
Los Angeles, CA 90036

(323) 549-0500
Web: http://www.canfoundation.org/
A non-profit organization of parents, physicians, and researchers dedicated to promoting and funding research with direct clinical implications for the treatment and cure of autism.

Division TEACCH
CB# 7180; 310 Medical School Wing E
The University of North Carolina at Chapel Hill
Chapel Hill, NC 27599-7180
(919) 966-2174; (919) 966-4127 (Fax)
E-mail: teacch@unc.edu
Web: http://www.unc.edu/depts/teacch/
The nationally acclaimed program provides educational and behavioral services to people with autism.

The Doug Flutie, Jr. Foundation for Autism
c/o The Giving Back Fund
54 Canal Street, Suite 320
Boston, MA 02114
(617) 556-2820; (617) 973-9463 (Fax)
E-mail: giveback@ma.ultranet.com
This non-profit foundation provides funding for services for economically disadvantaged families and for research into the causes and treatment of autism. It also serves as a clearinghouse of information about innovative programs and services for children with autism.

Epilepsy Foundation of America
4351 Garden City Drive
Landover, MD 20785
(800) EFA-1000; (301) 459-3700; (301) 577-4941 (Fax)
Email: webmaster@efa.org
Web: http://www.efa.org/
The national organization for families of children with seizure disorders. Promotes awareness, support research, and provides information and referral through its toll-free number.

Families for Early Autism Treatment (FEAT)
P.O.Box 255722
Sacramento, California, 95865-5722
(916) 843-1536

Web: http://www.feat.org/
A network of organizations in many states, sometimes called "Families for Effective Autism Treatment." It has many state and local branches; links to them can be found at their website.

FRAXA Research Foundation
45 Pleasant St.
Newburyport, MA 01950
(978) 462-1866; (978) 463-9985 (Fax)
E-mail: kclapp@fraxa.org
Web: http://www.fraxa.org/
This organization funds research into finding a treatment or cure for fragile X syndrome.

The Indiana Resource Center for Autism
Institute for the Study of Developmental Disabilities
Indiana University
2853 East Tenth Street
Bloomington, IN 47408-2601
(812) 855-6508; (812) 855-9630 (Fax); (812) 855-9396 (TTY)
E-mail: prattc@indiana.edu
Web: http://www.iidc.indiana.edu/~irca/
Conducts outreach training and consultations, engages in research, and develops and disseminates information focused on building the capacity of local communities, organizations, and families to support children and adults across the autism spectrum in typical work, school, home, and community settings.

International Rett Syndrome Association
9121 Piscataway Road
Clinton, MD 20735
(800) 818-RETT; (301) 856-3334
(301) 856-3336 (Fax)
E-mail: irsa@rettsyndrome.org
Web: http://www.rettsyndrome.org/
The national organization for families affected by Rett Syndrome. Provides information, referral, resources, encourages research, and works to increase public awareness of the condition.

Learning Disabilities Association of America (LDA)
4156 Library Road
Pittsburgh, PA 15234-1349
(412) 341-1515; (412) 344-0224 (Fax)
E-mail: ldanatl@usaor.net
Web: http://www.ldanatl.org/

With over 500 local affiliates, this national organization supports people with learning disabilities and their families. It publishes a wide variety of information about the many different learning disabilities, and can provide information on educational programs, laws, and advocacy.

Lovaas Institute for Early Intervention (LIFE)
UCLA Young Autism Project
Department of Psychology
1282A Franz Hall
Box 951563
Los Angeles, CA 90095
(310) 840-5983; (310) 840-5987 (Fax)
E-mail: info@lovaas.com
Web: http://www.lovaas.com

This researched-based psychology clinic specializes in developing and implementing behavior modification treatment programs for children with autism. Backed by 35 years of research; the methodologies utilized by the clinic were developed by Dr. Ivar Lovaas, professor of Psychology at the University of California, Los Angeles.

National Alliance for Autism Research
414 Wall St., Research Park
Princeton, New Jersey 08540
(888)-777-NAAR; (609) 430-9160; (609) 430-9163 (Fax)
E-mail: naar@naar.org
Web: http://www.naar.org

A national organization that works to encourage and support research into effective treatment and, ultimately, cure for autism and related PDDs. It is a nationwide alliance of families, researchers and others concerned with autism united in their efforts to fund and accelerate autism research.

National Fragile X Foundation
P.O. Box 190488
San Francisco, CA 94119
(800) 688-8765; (510) 763-6030
(510) 763-6223 (Fax)
E-mail: natlfx@sprintmail.com
Web: http://www.nfxf.org/
This organization's mission is to promote awareness of fragile X syndrome, encourage research into fragile X syndrome, and provide information and support to families of children with this condition. Supports a network of affiliates.

National Information Center for Children and Youth with Disabilities (NICHCY)
P.O. Box 1492
Washington, DC 20013-1492
(800) 695-0285; (202) 884-8200; (202) 884-8441 (Fax)
E-mail: nichcy@aed.org
Web: http://www.nichcy.org
An invaluable organization that can link parents to practically every government and non-profit agency and organization involved in any way with disabilities. NICHCY's website provides extensive links and resources, organized into "State Resource Sheet."

New Jersey Center for Outreach & Services for the Autism Community (COSAC)
1450 Parkside Avenue, Suite 22
Ewing, NJ 08638
(609) 883-8100; (800) 4-AUTISM (in NJ)
E-mail: njautism@aol.com
Web: http://members.aol.com/njautism
An organization that provides parent support, information and referral, advocacy on behalf of people with autism and related conditions, and provides community support services. Its National Directory of Programs and Services for the Autism Community is extremely useful.

PACER Center, Inc.
8161 Normandale Blvd.
Minneapolis, MN 55437
(952) 838-9000; (952) 838-0190 (TTY)
(800) 53-PACER (in MN)

E-mail: pacer@pacer.org
Web: http://www.pacer.org
PACER's mission is "to improve and expand opportunities that enhance the quality of life for children and young adults with all disabilities—physical, mental, emotional, learning—and their families. PACER now offers 20 major programs, including Parent Training programs, programs for students and schools, and technical assistance to parent centers both regionally and nationally.

Sibling Support Project
Children's Hospital and Medical Center
P.O. Box 5371, CL-09
Seattle, WA 98105
(206) 368-4911; (206) 368-4816 (Fax)
E-mail: dmeyer@chmc.org
Web: http://www.chmc.org/departmt/sibsupp/DEFAULT.HTM
The Sibling Support Project is a national program dedicated to the interests of brothers and sisters of people with special health and developmental needs. Through its award-winning "Sibshops" program, it provides peer support for siblings of children with disabilities.

TASH (formerly The Association for Persons with Severe Handicaps)
29 W. Susquehanna Avenue, Suite 210
Baltimore, MD 21204
(410) 828-8274; (410) 828-6706
E-mail: nweiss@tash.org
Web: http://www.tash.org/
This international organization advocates for and provides information about people with a wide range of disabilities, including autism. Publishes newsletters and journals.

Tourette Syndrome Association
42-40 Bell Boulevard
Bayside, NY 11361-2820
(718) 224-2999; (718) 279-9596 (Fax)
E-mail: tourette@ix.netcom.com
Web: http://tsa.mgh.harvard.edu/
The national organization for families of children with Tourette syndrome. Promotes awareness, support research, and provides information and referral through its toll-free number.

:: Network of Collaborative Programs of Excellence in Autism (CPEAs)

The National Institutes of Health has recognized the following autism research centers and investigators for excellence in clinical service and research in autism

University of California, Los Angeles
Neuropsychiatric Institute
Marian Sigman, Ph.D.
760 Westwood Plaza
Los Angeles, CA 90024-1759
(310) 825-0180;
(310) 825-2682 (Fax)
E-mail: msigman@ucla.edu

Department of Pediatrics, 4482
University of California Irvine
Medical Center
M. Anne Spence, Ph.D.
101 City Drive
Orange, CA 92868
(714) 456-8848;
(714) 456-8384 (Fax)
E-mail: maspence@uci.edu

University of Colorado Health Sciences Center
Campus Box C-234
Sally J. Rogers, Ph.D.
4200 East 9th
Denver, CO 80262
(303) 315-6509;
(303) 315-6844 (Fax)
E-mail: Sally.Rogers@UCHSC.edu

Yale Child Study Center
Fred R. Volkmar, M.D.
230 South Frontage Road
P.O. Box 207900

New Haven, CT 06520-7900
(203) 785-2510;
(203) 737-4197 (Fax)
E-mail: fred.volkmar@yale.edu

Psychological Sciences Division
Eunice Kennedy Shriver Center
Helen Tager-Flushbery, Ph.D.
Waltham, MA 02452
(781) 642-0181;
(781) 642-0185 (Fax)
E-mail: htagerf@shriver.org

Rose F. Kennedy Center
Michelle Dunn, Ph.D.
Room 808
Albert Einstein College of Medicine
1300 Morris Park Avenue
Bronx, NY 10461
(718) 430-2130;
(718) 430-8786 (Fax)
E-mail: dunn@aecom.yu.edu

University of Rochester Medical Center
Department of OB/GYN, Box 668
Patricia M. Rodier, Ph.D.
601 Elmwood Avenue
Rochester, NY 19642
(716) 275-2582;
(716) 244-2209 (Fax)
E-mail: rodierp@
ehsct7.envmen.rochester.edu

Western Psychiatric
Institute & Clinic
Nancy J. Minshew, M.D.
3811 O'Hara Street
430 Bellefield Towers
Pittsburgh, PA 15213
(412) 624-0818;
(412) 624-0930 (Fax)
E-mail:
minshewnj@msx.upmc.edu

University of Washington
Department of Psychology
Geraldine Dawson, Ph.D.
Box 351525

Seattle, WA 98195
(206) 543-1051;
(206) 685-3157 (Fax)
E-mail:
dawson@u.washington.edu

University of Utah
Red Butte Clinic
William M. McMahon, M.D.
546 Chipeta Way, Box 896
Salt Lake City, UT 84108-1241
(801) 585-7781;
(801) 585-9096 (Fax)
E-mail:
William.McMahon@hsc.utah.edu

▪▪ International Organizations

Africa

Ghana
Rights of the Child Foundation
C 415/7
Senya Breku Street
P.O. Box 2502
Accra, Ghana

Kenya
Special Education Professionals
c/o Acorn Special Tutorials
General Mathenge Close
Off General Mathenge Drive
P.O. Box 40301
Nairobi, Kenya 732911

Nigeria
Nigerian Autistic Society
P.O. Box 7173
Wuse, Abuja, Nigeria

Republic of Niger
Association Espoir C.C. Pc n°

31665 X Niamey R.P.
Boîte postale 11.509
Niamey, Republic Of Niger

South Africa
Association for Autism (AFA)
P.O. Box 35833 Menlo Park
Pretoria 0102
South Africa
012-47-27820

Society for Children & Adults with
Autism
P.O. Box 87190 Houghton
Johannesburg 2041
South Africa

South African Society for Autistic
Children
Private Bag X4
Clareinch 7740
Cape Town 8001
South Africa

Tanzania
National Association for Care of
Autistics (NACA)
Department of Psychiatry
Muhimbili Medical Centre
P.O. Box 65001
Dar es Salaam

North America
Canada
Association for Community Living
Kinsmen Building, York University
4700 Keele Street
North York, Ontario M3J 1P3
(416) 661-9611;
(416) 661-5701 (Fax)
E-mail: info@cacl.ca
Web: http://www.cacl.ca

Autism Society of British Columbia
Suite 200 - 3550 Kingsway
Vancouver, B.C. V5R 5L7
(604) 434-0880; (888) 437-0880
(in Canada);
(604) 434-0801 (Fax)
E-mail: autismbc@istar.ca
Home page:
http://www.enet.ca/autism/

Autism Society of Manitoba
825 Sherbrook Street
Winnipeg, Manitoba R3A 1M5
(204) 783-9563
E-mail: asm@escape.ca

Autism Society of Newfoundland
and Labrador
P.O.Box 14078
St. John's, Newfoundland A1B 4G8
(709) 722-2803

Autism/PDevelopmental
Disabilities Society of Mainland
Nova Scotia
(902) 429-5529

Society for Treatment of Autism
(N.S.)
P.O. Box 392
Sydney, Nova Scotia B1P 6H2
(902) 567-6441

Autism Society Ontario
1 Greensboro Drive, Suite 306
Etobicoke, Ontario M9W 1C8
(416) 246-9592;
(416) 246-9417 (Fax)
E:mail: mail@autismsociety.on.ca

Quebec Society for Autism
Société québécoise de l'autisme
65 de Castelnau O.
Montréal, Québec H2R 2W3
(514) 270-7386;
(514) 270-9261 (Fax)
E-mail: sqa@sympatico.ca
Web: http://people.sca.uqam.ca/
~sqa/sqa_home.html

Saskatoon Society for Autism
2229 Avenue C North
Saskatoon, Saskatchewan S7L 5Z2
(306)665-7013
E-mail: aa093@
sfn.saskatoon.sk.ca
Web: http://www.sfn.saskatoon.
sk.ca/health/autism/

McMaster University
Department of Psychology
1200 Maine Street
West Hamilton, Ontario L8N 3Z5

(905) 521-7367
Contact: Peter Szatmari, M.D.

Mexico
ASA (Asociacion Sinaloense de
Autismo)
Callejon Zaragoza #48 Ote.
Centic. CP 80000
Culiacan, Sinaba, Mexico
E-mail: ernesto@informacion.acs-
conacyt-mx

Australia
University of Melbourne
Department of Psychology
Royal Children's Hospital
Flemington Road
Parkville, Victoria
(61)3-345-5881; (61) 3-345-6002
(Fax)
Contact: Professor Margot Prior

Asperger's Syndrome Support
Network
C/O VACCA
PO Box 235
Ashburton Victoria 3147
(03)-9543-2935;
(03)-9459-8163

Europe
World Autism Organisation
Avenue Van Becelaere 26B
bte21, B - 1170
Belgique
(32)-2-675-72-70 (Fax)
E-mail: autisme.europe@
arcadis.be
Web: http://worldautism.org/

Autism-Europe
Avenue E. Van Becelaere 26B, bte
21
B-1170 Brussels, Belgium
32(0)2-675-75-05;
32(0)2-675-72-70 (Fax)
E-mail:
autisme.europe@arcadis.be
Web: http://www.autismeurope.
arc.be/

Hungary
Autism Foundation and Autism
Research Group
Budapest
Delej U. 24-26
1089 Hungary
Contact: Dr. Anna Balazs

Ireland
The Irish Society for Autism
Unity Building
16/17 Lower O'Connell Street
Dublin 1
(071) 744684; (071) 744224 (Fax)
E-mail: aru@
sunderland.ac.uk
Web: http://osiris.sunderland.ac.uk/
autism/irish.html

ASPIRE: The Asperger's Syndrome
Association of Ireland
85 Woodley Park
Kilmacud, Dublin 14
(01) 2951389
E-mail: tonerj@indigo.ie

PAPA: Parents and Professionals in
Autism: Northern Ireland
Knockbracken Healthcare Park
Saintfield Road

Belfast, BT8 8BH
Northern Ireland
(01232) 401729;
(01232) 403467 (Fax)

The Netherlands
Divisie Psychiatrie
Kinder en Jeugdpsychiatrie
Academeisch Ziekenhuis Utrecht
Postbus 85500, 3508 GA
Utrecht, The Netherlands
(31) 30-254-2286 (Fax)
Contact: Jan Buitelaar, M.D.

University Centre for Child and
Adolescent Psychiatry
P.O. Box 30,001
9700 RB Groningen
The Netherlands
(31) 50-681158;
(31) 50-681120 (Fax)
Contact: Dr. Ellen F. Luteijn

Serbia
Autism Society of Serbia
Djure Djakovica 13, Beograd
11000
Yugoslavia
(381) 11-763-941

Turkey
Marmara University Hospital
Tophanelioglu Cad.
Altunizade, 81190, Istanbul

United Kingdom
The National Autistic Society
393 City Road
London EC1V 1NG
(44)-(0)-20-7833-2299;
(44)-(0)-20-7833-9666 (Fax)
E-mail: nas@nas.org.uk

Autism Initiatives
Pat Minshull House
7 Chesterfield Road
Liverpool L23 9XL
(0151) 330-9500
E-mail: membership@
autism-initiatives.co.uk

Institute of Psychiatry
Department of Psychology
DeCrespigny Park
Denmark Hill
London SE5 8AF, England
(44) 71-703-5411
Contact: Simon Baron-Cohen, M.D.

The Scottish Society for Autism
Hilton House,
Alloa Business Park
Whins Road
Alloa FK10 3SA Scotland
(01259) 720044;
(01259)720051 (Fax)

Asia
India
Action for Autism
T370 Chiragh Gaon
3rd Floor
New Delhi 110 017
(91) 11-641-6469;
(91) 11-641-6470;
(91) 11-641-6470 (Fax)
E-mail: autism@vsnl.com

Japan
Fukushima Medical College
Department of Neuropsychiatry
Hikarigaoka
Fukushima-shi, Japan, 960
(81) 24-548-1281;

(81) 24-548-6735
Contact: Yoshihiko Hoshino, M.D.

Jordan
Specialty Institute for Special
Education
Amman, Jordan
(962) 6-5817-083;
(962) 6-5354-697 (Fax)
E-mail: scse@firstnet.com.jo
Contact: Khalid Rasheed, M.A.

Singapore
Autistic Association (Singapore)
Blk 381, Clementi Avenue 5,
#01-398
Singapore 120381
Tel: (65)7746649
Fax: (65)7746957
E-mail: autism@singnet.com.sg

■■ State and Local Resources

The following list contains names, addresses, phone numbers, and e-mail and website addresses (where avaiable) for public and private agencies and organizations in each state that provide a wide variety of services and assistance to people with autism and their families. We wish to thank the National Information Center for Children and Youth with Disabilities (NICHCY) and the Autism Society of America (ASA) for contributing much of this information.

Here are brief descriptions of the types of agencies and organizations listed:

The State Departments of Education, Offices of Special Education, Early Intervention Systems are the state agencies responsible for ensuring that the requirements of the Individuals with Disabilities Education Act (IDEA)are followed. These agencies oversee how local school districts implement IDEA. In almost all states, these agencies also administer programs for very young children with disabilities: early intervention programs for children birth through age two and preschool programs for children ages three through five.

The State Vocational Rehabilitation Agency provides education, training, and counseling, as well as medical, therapeutic, and other services, to prepare people with disabilities to work. The state agency will refer you to the local office nearest you.

The Developmental Disabilities Council provides funding for direct services for people with developmental disabilities. Most provide services such as diagnosis, evaluation, information and referral, social services, group homes, advocacy, and legal protection.

The Protection & Advocacy Agency is a legal organization established to protect the rights of people with disabilities. It can supply information about the educational, health care, residential, social, and legal services available for children with autism in your state. In some cases, attorneys from these offices can provide representation on behalf of your child.

University Affiliated Programs (UAP) are federally funded centers that offer services to parents of children with developmental disabilities. They are a good source for interdisciplinary diagnostic teams described in Chapter 1.

Parent Programs include privately and publicly funded groups that offer support, information, and referral services to parents of children with disabilities.

Autism Society of America (ASA) Chapters are local and state affiliates of the national organization that provide support and information to parents of children with autism, and can help direct them to resources in their area who can help them. Call ASA's national office (800- 3-AUTISM) for referral to the ASA chapter nearest you.

The Arc (formerly The Association for Retarded Citizens) provides a wide variety of services to people with developmental disabilities and their families, including education, social, vocational training and support, and residential services. Each state has its own office, and there are many local offices of The Arc. Contact your state office of The Arc or visit The Arc's website (http://www.thearc.org).

Alabama
AL Dept of Educ, Div of Special
Education Services
P.O. Box 302101
Montgomery, AL 36130-2101
(334) 242-8114;
(800) 392-8020 (in AL)
E-mail: mabreyw@sdenet.alsde.edu
Web: http://www.alsde.edu/
speced/speced.html

Alabama's Early
Intervention System
Department of Rehabilitation
Services/Division of

Early Intervention
2129 East South Blvd.,
P.O. Box 11586
Montgomery, AL 36111-0586
(334) 281-8780
E-mail: oholder@rehab.state.al.us
Web: http://www.rehab.state.al.us

Department of
Rehabilitation Services
2129 East South Blvd.,
P.O. Box 11586
Montgomery, AL 36111-0586
(334) 281-8780
E-mail: webinfo@rehab.state.al.us

Web: http://www.rehab.state.al.us/
vr.html

Special Needs Programs, Department
of Education
Gordon Persons Building
P.O. Box 302101
Montgomery, AL 36130-2101
(334) 242-9108

Alabama Developmental Disabilities
Planning Council
RSA Union Bldg.
100 N. Union Street
P.O. Box 301410
Montgomery, AL 36130-1410
(800) 232-2158; (334) 242-3973

Alabama Disabilities Advocacy
Program (ADAP)
526 Martha Parham West
The University of Alabama
P.O. Box 870395
Tuscaloosa, AL 35487-0395
(800) 826-1675; (205) 348-4928;
(205)348-9484 (TTY)
E-mail: ADAP@law.ua.edu
Web: http://www.adap.net

Children's Rehabilitation Service
Alabama Department of Rehabilitation
Services
2129 East South Blvd.,
P.O. Box 11586
Montgomery, AL 36111-0586
(800) 846-3697; (334) 281-8780
E-mail: ckendall@rehab.state.al.us
Web: http://www.rehab.state.al.us

Autism Society of Alabama
P.O. Box 248
Alabaster, AL 35207-0248
(877) 428-8476 (toll-free)
E-mail: julieASA@ucmail.com
Web: http://www.autism-
alabama.org

Civitan International
Research Center
University of Alabama at Birmingham
1719 Sixth Avenue South

Birmingham, AL 35294-0021
(205) 934-8900
Web: http://www.circ.uab.edu

Special Education Action Committee
Inc. (SEAC)
600 Bel Air Blvd., Suite 210
P.O. Box 161274
Mobile, AL 36616-2274
(334) 478-1208;
(800) 222-7322 (in AL)
E-mail: seacofmobile@zebra.net
Web: http://www.hsv.tis.net/
~seachsv/

The Arc of Alabama
444 South Decatur
Montgomery, AL 36104
205-262-7688

Alaska
Office of Special Education
Alaska Department of Education
801 West 10th St, Suite 200
Juneau, AK 99801-1894
(907) 465-8702
Web: http://www.educ.state.ak.us/
tls/sped/

Office of Special Services and
Supplemental Programs
Department of Education
801 West 10th Street, Suite 200
Juneau, AK 99801-1894
(907) 465-2972
E-mail: Wendy_Tada@
educ.state.ak.us
Web: http://www.educ.state.ak.us/
tls/sped/

State of Alaska Department of Health
& Social Services
Special Needs Services Unit
1231 Gambell Street
Anchorage, AK 99501-4627
(907) 269-3460

Health Care Program for Children with
Special Needs
Section of Maternal, Child, and Family
Health

1231 Gambell Street
Anchorage, AK 99501-4627
(907) 269-3460

Division of Vocational Rehabilitation
801 West 10th Street, M.S. 0581
Juneau, AK 99801
(907) 269-3573;
(907) 269-3570 (TTY)
E-mail: Duane_French@
educ.state.ak.us

Governor's Council on Disabilities &
Special Education
PO Box 240249
Anchorage, AK 99524-0249
(907) 269-8990
E-mail: dmaltman@
health.state.ak.us
Web: http://www.hss.state.ak.us/
htmlstuf/BOARDS/gcdse/
ak_cdse.html

Disability Law Center of Alaska
615 East 82nd, Suite 101
Anchorage, AK 99518
(907) 344-1002
E-mail: disablaw@anc.ak.net

University of Alaska Anchorage
Center for Human Development
2330 Nichols Street
Anchorage, AK 99508
(907) 272-8270

P.A.R.E.N.T.S., Inc.
4743 E. Northern Lights Boulevard
Anchorage, AK 99508
(907) 337-7678;
(800) 478-7678 (in AK)
E-mail: parents@alaska.net
Web: http://www.alaska.net/
~parents

Arc/Alaska
2211-A Arca Drive
Anchorage, AK 99508
907-277-6677

American Samoa
Special Education Division
Department of Education

Pago Pago, AS 96799
(684) 633-1323

LBJ Tropical Medical Center
AS. Samoa Hospital Authority
Pago Pago, AS 96799
(684) 633-4929 or -2697

Department of Human & Social
Services
Division of Vocational Rehabilitation
Pago Pago, AS 96799
(684) 699-1371/1372/1373

AS Developmental Disabilities Council
P.O. Box 194
Pago Pago, AS 96799
(684) 633-5908

Office of Protection and Advocacy for
the Disabled
P.O. Box 3937
Pago Pago, AS 96799
(684) 633-2441

Protection and Advocacy for
Developmental Disabilities (PA
Developmental Disabilities)
Office of Protection and Advocacy for
the Disabled
P.O. Box 3937
Pago Pago, AS 96799
(684) 633-2441

Protection and Advocacy for Individual
Rights (PAIR)
Office of Protection and Advocacy for
the Disabled
P.O. Box 3937
Pago Pago, AS 96799
(684) 633-2441

American Samoa PAVE
P.O. Box 3432
Pago Pago, AS 96799
011 (684) 699-6946
E-mail: SAMPAVE@
samoatelco.com
Web: http://www.taalliance.org/
ptis/amsamoa/

Arizona
Exceptional Student Services,
Department of Education
1535 West Jefferson
Phoenix, AZ 85007
(602) 542-4013
E-mail: lbusenb@
mail1.ade.state.az.us
E-mail: smishlo@
mail1.ade.state.az.us
Web: http://ade.state.az.us

(Ages 3 through 5)
Exceptional Student Services,
Department of Education
1535 West Jefferson
Phoenix, AZ 85007
(602) 364-4011
E-mail: lshield@mail1.ade.state.az.us
Web: http://ade.state.az.us

(Birth through 2)
Interagency Coordinating Council for
Infants & Toddlers
Department of Economic Security
1717 West Jefferson
P.O. Box 6123 (801-A-6)
Phoenix, AZ 85005
(602) 542-5577
E-mail: azeip@aztec.asu.edu

Rehabilitation Services Bureau 930A
Department of Economic Security
1789 West Jefferson 2NW
Phoenix, AZ 85007
(602) 542-3332
Web: http://www.azrsa.org

Governor's Council on Developmental
Disabilities
1717 West Jefferson Street
Site Code (074Z)
Phoenix, AZ 85007
(602) 542-4049

Arizona Center for Disability Law
3839 N 3rd Street #209
Phoenix, AZ 85012
(602) 274-6287
E-mail: lorraineazl@juno.com
Web: http://www.nau.edu/~ihd/acdl
Office for Children with Special Health

Care Needs
Department of Health
1740 W. Adams
Phoenix, AZ 85007
(602) 542-1860

Institute for Human Development
Northern Arizona University
P.O. Box 5630
Flagstaff, AZ 86011
(520) 523-4791
Web: http://www.nau.edu/~ihd

RAISING Special Kids
4750 N. Black Canyon Highway, Suite
101
Phoenix, AZ 85017-3621
(602) 242-4366;
(800) 237-3007 (in AZ)

Pilot Parents of Southern Arizona
2600 North Wyatt Drive
Tucson, AZ 85712
(520) 324-3150
E-mail: ppsa@azstarnet.com
Web: http://www.azstarnet.com/
~ppsa

Families Reaching Harmony
(PTI serving Native Americans)
P.O. Box 5423
Window Rock, AZ 86515
(520) 729-2468
E-mail: TMGenigma@aol.com

The Arc of Arizona
5610 S Central
Phoenix, AZ 85040
(602) 243-1787
E-mail: Arcofariz@aol.com

Arkansas
Special Education Unit, Department of
Education
State Education Building C,
Room 105
#4 Capitol Mall
Little Rock, AR 72201-1071
(501) 682-4225
E-mail: dsydoriak@
arkedu.k12.ar.us

(Ages 3 through 5)
Preschool Programs, Special Education
Department of Education
#4 Capitol Mall, Room 105-C
Little Rock, AR 72201-1071
(501) 682-4225

(Birth through 2)
Division of Developmental Disabilities
Services
Department of Human Services
P.O. Box 1437, Donaghey Plaza
North-5th Floor, Slot 2520
Little Rock, AR 72203-1437
(501) 682-8676

Department of Workforce Education
Arkansas Rehabilitation Services
1616 Brookwood Drive
P.O. Box 3781
Little Rock, AR 72203-3781
(501) 296-1616
E-mail: BCSimpson@
ARS.state.ar.us

Governor's Developmental
Disabilities Council
Freeway Medical Tower
5800 West 10th, Suite 805
Little Rock, AR 72204
(501) 661-2589

Disability Rights Center
1100 N. University, Suite 201
Little Rock, AR 72207
(800) 482-1174; (501) 296-1775
E-mail: panda@
advocacyservices.org
Web: http://www.
advocacyservices.org

Children's Medical Services
Department of Human Services
P.O. Box 1437, Slot #256
Little Rock, AR 72203-1437
(501) 682-2277
E-mail: gail.buchanan@
medicaid.state.ar.us

University Affiliated
Program of Arkansas
501 Woodlane, Suite 210

Little Rock, AR 72201
(501) 682-9900;
(800) 831-4827
E-mail: swansonmarke@
exchange.uams.edu

Arkansas Disability Coalition
1123 S. University Avenue
Suite 225
Little Rock, AR 72204
(800) 223-1330; (501) 614-7020
E-mail: adc@alltel.net

Arkansas Support Network, Inc.
614 East Emma Ave., Suite 235
Springdale, AR 72764
(800) 759-8788
E-mail: ldonald49@hotmail.com

Arkansas Fathers' Network
P.O. Box 1437, Slot 526
Little Rock, AR 72203-1437
(800) 482-5850, ext. 22277

The Arc of Arkansas
2000 Main St.
Little Rock, AR 72206-1597
(501)375-7770

California
Special Education, Department of
Education
515 L Street, Suite 270
Sacramento, CA 95814
(916) 445-4729
Web: http://www.cde.ca.gov/
spbranch/sed/index.htm

(Ages 3 through 5)
Special Education Div./California
Dept. of Educ.
515 L Street, Suite 270
Sacramento, CA 95814
(916) 445-4623
Web: http://www.cde.ca.gov/
spbranch/sed/index.htm

(Birth through 2)
Prevention & Children Services Branch
Department of Developmental
Services
1600 9th Street, Room #310

Sacramento, CA 95814
(916) 654-2773

State Council on Developmental
Disabilities
2000 "O" Street, Room 100
Sacramento, CA 95814
(916) 322-8481

Protection & Advocacy, Inc.
100 Howe Avenue, Suite 185N
Sacramento, CA 95825
(916) 488-9950;
(800) 776-5746 (in CA)
E-mail: legalmail@pai-ca.org
Web: http://www.pai-ca.org

State Children's Medical
Services Branch
Department of Health Services
714 P Street, Room 350
Sacramento, CA 95814
(916) 654-0832

University of California at Los Angeles,
UAP
760 Westwood Plaza
Los Angeles, CA 90024
(310) 825-0470
E-mail: jmccracken@
mednet.ucla.edu

Center for Child Development &
Developmental Disabilities
Children's Hospital LA
USC — University Affiliated Program
P. O. Box 54700, MS #53
Los Angeles, CA 90054-0700
(323) 669-2300

Team of Advocates for Special Kids
(TASK)
100 West Cerritos Avenue
Anaheim, CA 92805-6546
(714) 533-TASK
E-mail: taskca@aol.com

Team of Advocates for Special Kids
(TASK), San Diego
3750 Convoy Street, Suite 303
San Diego, CA 92111
(619) 874-2386

E-mail: tasksdl@aol.com
Northern California Coalition for
Parent Training & Information (NCC)
Parents Helping Parents
3041 Olcott Street
Santa Clara, CA 95054-3222
(408) 727-5775;
 (408) 727-0182 (Fax)
E-mail: info@php.com
Web: http://www.php.com

Parents Helping Parents—
San Francisco
594 Monterey Boulevard
San Francisco, CA 94127
(415) 841-8820

Disability Rights Education and
Defense Fund, Inc. (DREDF)
2212 6th Street
Berkeley, CA 94710
(510) 644-2555
E-mail: dredf@dredf.org
Web:http://www.dredf.org

MATRIX, A Parent Network &
Resource Center
94 Galli Drive, Suite C
Novato, CA 94949
(415) 884-3535;
(415) 884-3554 (TTY)
E-mail: matrix@matrixparents.org
Web: http://matrixparents.org

Support for Families of Children with
Disabilities
2601 Mission Street, Suite 804
San Francisco, CA 94110
(415) 282-7494
E-mail: sfcdmiss@aol.com

Parents Helping Parents
594 Monterey Blvd.
San Francisco, CA 94127
(415) 841-8820

Center for Autism and Related
Disorders
23300 Ventura Boulevard
Woodland Hills, CA 91364
(818) 223-0123
(818) 223-0133 (Fax)

Email: CARDLA@aol.com
Web: http://www.cardhq.com/

Center for Early Education
4735 Clairemont Drive #293
San Diego, CA 92117
(619) 272-1708;
(619) 272-2124 (Fax)
E-mail: info@earlyed.com

Claremont Autism Center
Claremont McKenna College
850 Columbia Avenue
Claremont, CA 91711
(909)621-8598;
(909) 621-8419 (Fax)
E-mail: mhcharlop@aol.com

Institute for Applied Behavior Analysis
5777 West Century Blvd. #675
Los Angeles, CA 90045
(310) 649-0499;
(310) 649-3109 (Fax)
E-mail: iabala@attmail.com
Web: http://www.iaba.net

University of California
Santa Barbara Autism Center
c/c/s Psychology Clinic
Graduate School of Education
Santa Barbara, CA 93106-9490
(805) 893-2176;
 (805) 893-2049 (Fax)
E-mail: doniel@
education.ucsb.edu
Web: http://education.ucsb.edu/
autism/

Autism Society of California
P.O. Box 1295
Escondido, CA 92033
(800) 700-0037
E-mail: ASAASC@aol.com
Web: http://hometown.aol.com/
asaasc/myhomepage/index.html

Autism Partnership
200 Marina Drive, Suite C
Seal Beach, CA 90740-6057
(562) 431-9293;
(562) 431-8386 (Fax)

Arc California
120 I Street, 2nd Floor
Sacramento, CA 95814
(916)552-6619
E-mail: arcgary@quiknet.com

Colorado
Spec. Educ. Svcs. Unit/
CO Dept. of Educ.
201 East Colfax Avenue
Denver, CO 80203
(303) 866-6694
E-mail: Harkess_L@cde.state.co.us

(Ages 3 through 5)
Department of Education/Prevention
Initiatives
201 East Colfax Avenue, Room 305
Denver, CO 80203
(303) 866-6712
E-mail: Amundson_j@cde.state.co.us

(Birth through 2)
Early Childhood Initiatives
State Department of Education
201 East Colfax, Room 305
Denver, CO 80203
(303) 866-6709

Division of Vocational Rehabilitation
Department of Human Services
110 16th Street, 2nd Floor
Denver, CO 80202
(303) 620-4153

Colorado Developmental Disabilities
Planning Council
777 Grant Street, Suite 304
Denver, CO 80203
(303) 894-2345
E-mail: cddpc@aol.com

The Legal Center for People with
Disabilities and Older People
455 Sherman Street, Suite 130
Denver, CO 80203-4403
(303) 722-0300; (800) 288-1376 (in
CO); (303) 722-0720 (Fax)
Web: http://www.thelegalcenter.org

JFK Partners
University of CO
Health Sciences Center
4200 E. 9th Avenue, Suite C-234
Denver, CO 80262
(303) 864-5266;
(303) 315-6844 (Fax)
E-mail: jfk.partners@
tchdem.org
Web: http://www.uchse.edu/sm/jfk

PEAK Parent Center, Inc.
6055 Lehman Drive, Suite 101
Colorado Springs, CO 80918
(719) 531-9400; (800) 284-0251 (in
CO)
E-mail: info@peakparent.org
Web: http://www.peakparent.org

The Arc of Colorado
4155 E. Jewell Ave.
Suite 916
Denver, CO 80222
(303) 756-7234

Connecticut
Bur. of Special Educ. & Pupil Svcs.
CT Dept. of Education
25 Industrial Park Road
Middletown, CT 06457-1520
(860) 807-2025
E-mail: george.dowaliby@
po.state.ct.us

(Ages 3 through 5)
Bureau of Early Childhood Education
& Social Svcs.
CT Department of Education
25 Industrial Park Road
Middletown, CT 06457
(860) 807-2054
E-mail: maria.synodi@
po.state.ct.us
Web: http://www.state.ct.us/sde

(Birth through 2)
State Birth to Three System
Department of Mental Retardation
460 Capitol Avenue
Hartford, CT 06106
(860) 418-6147;

(800) 505-7000 (in CT)
(860) 571-7556
Web: http://www.birth23.org

Council on Developmental Disabilities
460 Capitol Avenue
Hartford, CT 06106-1308
(860) 418-6160;
(860) 418-6172 (TTY)

Office of P & A for Persons with
Disabilities
60 B Weston Street
Hartford, CT 06120-1551
(860) 297-4300;
(800) 842-7303 (in CT)
(860) 566-2102 (TTY)
E-mail: hn2571@earthlink.net

Maternal & Child Health Unit
410 Capital Avenue, MF #911MAT
P. O. Box 340308
Hartford, CT 06134-0308
(860) 509-8074

Connecticut Childrens Medical Center
Child Development Center
Ann Milanese, M.D., Medical Director
282 Washington Street
Hartford, CT 06106
(860) 545-8589

Connecticut Center for Child
Development
Susanne Letso, Executive Director
925 Bridgeport Avenue
Milford, CT 06460
(203) 882-8810

The Center for Children with Special
Needs
Michael D. Powers, Psy.D., Director
384 Z Merrow Road
Tolland, CT 06084
(860) 870-5313;
(860) 870-5316 (Fax)

A. J. Pappanikou Ctr. on
Disability Studies
A University Affiliated Program
249 Glenbrook Road, 2064

Storrs, CT 06269-2064
(860) 486-5035;
(860) 486-5069 (TTY)
E-mail: mclean@
unconnvm.uconn.edu
Web: http://www.ucc.uconn.edu/
~http://wwwpcse

Yale Child Study Center
230 South Frontage Road
P.O. Box 207900
New Haven, CT 06520-7900
(203) 785-2510;
(203) 737-4197 (Fax)
E-mail: lori.casalini@yale.edu
Web: http://info.med.yale.edu/
chldstdy/autism/index.html

Connecticut Parent Advocacy Center
(CPAC)
338 Main Street
Niantic, CT 06357
(860) 739-3089;
(800) 445-2722 (in CT)
E-mail: cpacinc@aol.com
Web: http://members.aol.com/
cpacinc/cpac.htm

Parent-to-Parent Network of CT
Connecticut Children's Medical Center
282 Washington Street
Hartford, CT 06106
(860) 545-9021
E-mail: mameade@ccmckids.org

Autism Society of Connecticut
125 Harrington Street
Meriden, CT 06451
(203) 235-7629
E-mail: asconn@geocities.com
Web: http://www.geocities.com/
HotSprings/Spa/7896

River Street School
601 River Street
Windsor, CT 06095
(860) 298-9079;
(860) 298-8413 (Fax)
E-mail: rstreet@crec.org
Web: http://www.crec.org/

The Arc of Connecticut
1030 New Britain Ave
Suite 102-B
West Hartford, CT 06110
(203) 953-8335

Delaware
Exceptional Children and Early
Childhood Group
Department of Education
P.O. Box 1402
Dover, DE 19903
(302) 739-5471
E-mail: mbrooks@state.de.us
Web: http://www.doe.state.de.us/
Exceptional_Child/ececehome.htm

(Ages 3 through 5)
Exceptional Children and Early
Childhood Group
Department of Education
P.O. Box 1402
Dover, DE 19903
(302) 739-4667
E-mail: mtoomey@state.de.us
Web: http://www.doe.state.de.us/
Exceptional_Child/ececehome.htm

(Birth through 2)
Management Svcs. Division
Health and Social Services, 2nd Floor,
Room 204
1901 North DuPont Highway
New Castle, DE 19720
(302) 577-4647
E-mail: rcabelli@state.de.us

Delaware Division of Vocational
Rehabilitation
4425 North Market Street
P. O. Box 9969
Wilmington, DE 19809-0969
(302) 761-8275;
(302) 761-8336 (TTY)

Delaware Developmental Disabilities
Council
821 Silver Lake Boulevard,
Suite 108
Townsend Building
Dover, DE 19904

(302) 739-3333
E-mail: jlinehan@state.de.us
Web: http://www.state.de.us/ddc

Disabilities Law Program
913 Washington Street
Wilmington, DE 19801
(302) 575-0660;
(302) 575-0696 (TTY)

Division of Public Health
P.O. Box 637, Jesse Cooper Building
Dover, DE 19903
(302) 739-4785
E-mail: 1weeks@state.de.us

University of Delaware
Center for Disabilities Studies
A University Affiliated Program
101 Alison Hall
Newark, DE 19716
(302) 831-6974

Parent Information
Center of DE (PIC)
700 Barksdale Road, Suite 16
Newark, DE 19711
(302) 366-0152; (302) 366-0178
(TTY)
E-mail: picofdel@picofdel.org
Web: http://www.picofdel.org

Autism Society of Delaware
P.O. Box 7336
Wilmington, DE 19803-0336
(302) 366-0152
E-mail: DelAutism@aol.com
Web: http://www.wserv.com/
delautism/

The Arc of Delaware
1016 Centre Road
Suite 1
Wilmington, DE 19805-1234
(302)996-9400

District of Columbia
(Birth through 3)
DC Early Intervention Program
609 H Street, NE, 5th Floor
Washington, DC 20002
(202) 727-5930

Rehabilitation Services Administration
Department of Human Services
810 First Street, NE, 10th Floor
Washington, DC 20002
(202) 442-8663

DC Developmental Disabilities State
Planning Council
2700 Martin L. King, Jr. Avenue, SE
Department of Human Services/801
East Building
Washington, DC 20032
(202) 279-6086

University Legal Services: Protection
and Advocacy
300 I Street, NE, Suite 202
Washington, DC 20002
(202) 547-0198;
(202) 547-2657 (TTY)

Health Services for Children with
Special Needs Clinic
D.C. General Hospital, Bldg. 10
19th & Massachusetts Avenue, S.E.
Washington, DC 20003
(202) 675-5214

Georgetown University Child
Development Center
3307 M Street, NW, Suite 401
Washington, DC 20007
(202) 687-8635

Advocates for Justice and Education
2041 Martin Luther King Jr. Ave., SE,
Suite 301
Washington, DC 20020
(888) 327-8060; (202) 678-8060
E-mail: justicel@bellatlantic.net
Web: http://aje.qpg.com

DC Parent Training & Information
Center
817 Varnum St., NE, Room 145
Washington, DC 20017
(202) 832-6860

District of Columbia Arc
900 Varnum Street NE
Washington, DC 20017
202-636-2950

Florida
Bureau of Instructional
Support & Community Services
Division of Public Schools &
Community Education
Department of Education
325 West Gaines Street, Suite 614
Tallahassee, FL 32399-0400
(850) 488-1570

(Ages 3 through 5)
Office of Early Intervention & School
Readiness
Division of Public Schools &
Community Education
Department of Education
325 West Gaines Street, Suite 325
Tallahassee, FL 32399-0400
(850) 488-6830
E-mail: Ballthp@mail.doe.state.fl.us

(Birth through 2)
Children's Medical Services
Department of Health
2020 Capital Circle, S.E.
Mail Bin A-06
Tallahassee, FL 32399-0700
(850) 487-2690
E-mail: Fran_Wilber@
doh.state.fl.us

Division of Vocational Rehabilitation
Department of Labor & Employment
Security
2002 Old St. Augustine Road,
Building A
Tallahassee, FL 32399-0696
(850) 488-6210
Web: http://www.state.fl.us/
vocrehab

Florida Developmental
Disabilities Council
124 Marriott Drive, Suite 203
Tallahassee, FL 32301-2981
(850) 488-4180
E-mail: joek.fddc@nettally.com

Advocacy Center for
Persons with Disabilities
2671 Executive Center Circle West,

Suite 100
Tallahassee, FL 32301-5029
(800) 342-0823; (850) 488-9071;
(800) 346-4127 (TTY); (800) 350-
4566 (Spanish & Creole Speaking
Clients)
E-mail: advocacyn@aol.com
Web: http://www.AdvocacyCenter.org

Children's Medical Services Programs
Department of Health & Rehabilitative
Services
1309 Winewood Blvd., Bldg. 6, Room
130
Tallahassee, FL 32399-0700
(850) 487-2690

Autism Society of Florida, Inc.
2858 Remington Green Circle
Tallahassee, FL 32308
(850) 997-7233

Mailman Center for Child
Development, UAP
University of Miami School of
Medicine
1601 NW 12th Avenue
P.O. Box 016820 - D-820
Miami, FL 33136
(305) 243-6810
Web: http://pediatrics.med.
miami.edu/../../mailman.htm

Family Network on Disabilities of
Florida
2735 Whitney Road
Clearwater, FL 33760
(800) 541-6682; (727) 523-1130;
(800) 825-5736
E-mail: fnd@fndfl.org
Web: http://fndfl.org/

Parent to Parent of Florida
Family Network on Disabilities of
Florida, Inc.
2735 Whitney Road
Clearwater, FL 33760
(800) 825-5736; (727) 523-1130
E-mail: fnd@fndfl.org
Web: http://fndfl.org/

Center for Autism and
Related Disorders
University of Miami
Department of Psychology
1500 Monza Avenue
Coral Gables, FL 33146-3004
(800) 9-AUTISM; (305) 284-6563
(305) 284-6555 (Fax)
Web: http://www.psy.miami.edu/
card

Center for Autism and Related
Disorders
Nova Southeastern University
3301 College Avenue
Ft. Lauderdale, FL 33314
(954) 262-7111;
(954) 262-1725 (Fax)

Center for Autism and
Related Disorders
The Richard & Pat Johnson Children's
Hospital
Dept. of Child Development
St. Mary's Medical Center
5313 Greenwood Avenue
West Palm Beach, FL 33407
(561) 840-6739;
(561) 881-0934 (Fax)

Center for Autism and Related
Disorders
Department of Exceptional Student
Education
Florida Atlantic University
777 Glades Road
Boca Raton, FL 33431
(561) 297-3239;
(561) 297-2507 (Fax)

Center for Autism and Related
Disorders
University of South Florida
Florida Mental Health Institute
13301 N. Bruce B. Downs Blvd.
Tampa, FL 33612-3899
(800) 333-4530; (813) 974-2532
(813) 974-6115 (Fax)
E-mail: usf@fmhi.usf.edu
Web: http://card-usf.fmhi.usf.edu/

Center for Autism and Related
Disorders
University of Florida
Department of Psychiatry
P.O. Box 100234
Gainesville, FL 32610
(352) 846-2761;
(352) 846-0941 (Fax)

Center for Autism and Related
Disorders
Florida State University
RRC107
Tallahassee, FL 32306-2007
(800) 769-7926; (850) 644-4367;
(850) 644-3644 (Fax)

Center for Autism and
Related Disorders
University of Florida at Jacksonville
820 Prudential Drive
Howard Bldg., Suite 412
Jacksonville, FL 32207
(904) 306-0002;
(904) 396-4718 (Fax)

Center for Autism and Related
Disorders
University of Central Florida
P.O. Box 162202
Orlando, FL 32816-1908
(888) 558-1908; (407) 823-2176;
(407) 823-6180 (Fax)

ARC/Florida
411 E. College Avenue
Tallahassee, FL 32301
(904)921-0460
Email: arcfl@supernet.net

Georgia
Division for Exceptional Students
GA Department of Education
1870 Twin Towers East
Atlanta, GA 30334
(404) 656-3963
E-mail: pbragg@doe.k12.ga.us
Web: http://www.doe.k12.ga.us/
sla/exceptional/exceptional.html

(Ages 3 through 5)
Preschool Special Education
GA Department of Education
1870 Twin Towers East
Atlanta, GA 30334-5060
(404) 657-9955
E-mail: pbragg@doe.k12.ga.us
Web: http://www.doe.k12.ga.us/
sla/exceptional/exceptional.html

(Birth through 2)
Babies Can't Wait Program
Division of Public Health
Department of Human Resources
2 Peachtree Street, Room 7-315
Atlanta, GA 30303-3166
(404) 657-2726
Web: http://www2.state.ga.us/
departments/DHR/

Department of Human Resources
Division of Rehabilitation Services
2 Peachtree Street, NW,
Room 35-403
Atlanta, GA 30303-3166
(404) 657-3053
E-mail: vathomas@dhr.state.ga.us
Web: http://www2.state.ga.us/
departments/dhr/rehab.html

Governor's Council on Developmental
Disabilities
2 Peachtree Street, NW, 3rd Floor,
Suite 210
Atlanta, GA 30303-3142
(404) 657-2126; (888) 275-4233
E-mail: eej@dhr.state.ga.us
Web: http://www.ga-ddcouncil.org

Georgia Advocacy Office, Inc.
999 Peachtree Street, NE, Suite 870
Atlanta, GA 30309
(404) 885-1234;
(800) 537-2329 (in GA)

Adolescent Health & Youth Develop.
DHR/DPH/FHB
2 Peachtree Street, NW,
Suite 8-206
Atlanta, GA 30303
(404) 657-2850
E-mail: rkb@dhr.state.ga.us

Institute on Human Development and
Disability
University Affiliated Program
The University of Georgia
850 College Station Road
Athens, GA 30602-4806
(706) 542-3457

Emory Autism Resource Center
Emory University
718 Gatewood Road
Atlanta, GA 30322
(404) 727-8350;
(404) 727-3969 (Fax)

Parents Educating Parents &
Professionals for All Children (PEP-
PAC)
6613 Church Street, Suite 100
Douglasville, GA 30134
(770) 577-7771
E-mail: peppac@bellsouth.net
Web: http://www.peppac.org

Parent to Parent of Georgia, Inc.
2872 Woodcock Boulevard, Suite 230
Atlanta, GA 30341
(770) 451-5484
E-mail: info@parenttoparentofga.org
Web: http://www.
parenttoparentofga.org

Greater Georgia Chapter
Autism Society of America
2971 Flowers Road, South,
Suite 140
Atlanta, GA 30341
(770) 451-0954
(770) 451-8066 (Fax)
E-mail: asa-ga@mindspring.com
Web: http://www.asaga.com/

The Arc of Georgia
PO Box 4363
Atlanta, GA 30336
(770)732-1122
E-mail: Tomquery@
worldnet.att.net

Guam
Special Education Division
GU Department of Education
P.O. Box DE
Hagatna, GU 96932
671) 475-0552;
(671) 475-0550 (TTY)

(Ages 3 through 5)
Pre-School & Elementary
School Program
Dept. of Education/Division of Special
Education
P.O. Box DE
Hagatna, GU 96932
(671) 475-0575;
(671) 475-0550 (TTY)

(Birth through 2)
303 Dean Circle
University Drive
UOG Station
Mangilao, GU 96923
(671) 735-2414;
(671) 734-6531 (TTY0
E-mail: eeclavea@ite.net

Dept. of Integrated Services for
Individuals with Disabilities
1313 Central Avenue
Tiyan, GU 96913
(671) 475-4646;
(671) 475-2892 (TTY)
E-mail: dvrcam@ite.net

GU Developmental Disabilities Council
104 E. Street
Tiyan, GU 96913
(671) 475-9127;
(671) 475-9128(TTY)

GLSC Disability Law Center Services
113 Bradley Place
Hagatna, GU 96910
(671) 477-9811;
(671) 477-3416 (TTY)
E-mail: glsc@netpci.com

Department of Public Health & Social
Services
Government of Guam
P.O. Box 2816

Hagatna, GU 96932
(671) 735-7102;
(671) 734-7822 (TTY)
E-mail: dennisr@ns.gov.gu

University of Guam, College of
Education
UOG Station
Mangilao, GU 96923
(671) 735-2481;
(671) 734-6531 (TTY)
E-mail: heidisan@ite.net

Hawaii
Special Education Section
Hawaii Department of Education
637 18th Avenue, Room 102
Honolulu, HI 96816
(808) 733-4990
Web: http://www2.k12.hi.us/
special-programs

(Ages 3 through 5)
Special Education Section
Department of Education
637 18th Avenue Avenue, Bldg. C
Honolulu, HI 96816
(808) 733-4840
E-mail: Michael_Fahey@
notes.k12.hi.us

(Birth through 2)
Zero-to-Three Services Section
Department of Health
1600 Kapiolani Blvd., Suite 1401
Honolulu, HI 96814
(808) 957-0066

Division of Vocational Rehabilitation
Department of Human Services
601 Kamokila Blvd., Room 515
Kapolei, HI 96707
(808) 586-5355
E-mail: hivrsbd@kestrok.com

State Planning Council on
Developmental Disabilities
919 Ala Moana Blvd., #113
Honolulu, HI 96814
(808) 586-8100
E-mail: hiddc@pixi.com

Protection and Advocacy Agency
1580 Makaloa Street, Suite 1060
Honolulu, HI 96814
(808) 949-2922;
(800) 882-1057 (in HI)
E-mail: pahi@pixi.com
Web: http://www.pixi.com/~pahi

Children with Special Health Needs
Branch
Department of Health
741 Sunset Avenue
Honolulu, HI 96816
(808) 733-9070
E-mail: plheu@
mail.fhsd.health.state.hi.us

Hawaii University Affiliated Program
for Developmental Disabilities
University of Hawaii at Manoa
1776 University Avenue, UA 4-6
Honolulu, HI 96822
(808) 956-5011

Hawaii Center for Autism Sprectrum
Disorders
1600 Kapiolani Blvd., Suite 620
Honolulu, HI 96814
(808) 947-4693;
(808) 942-5232 (Fax)
E-mail: wmbolman@msn.com

Assisting With Appropriate Rights in
Education (AWARE)
200 North Vineyard Blvd., #310
Honolulu, HI 96817
(800) 533-9684;
(808) 536-9684 (V/TTY)
E-mail: lda@gte.net

Special Parent Information Network
(SPIN)
919 Ala Moana Blvd. #101
Honolulu, Hawaii 96814
(808) 586-8126 (V/TTY)
E-mail: cpdppp@aloha.net

Autism Society of Hawaii
P.O. Box 2995
Honolulu, HI 96802
(808) 256-7540

(808) 735-3771 (Fax)
The Arc in Hawaii
3989 Diamond Head Road
Honolulu, HI 96816
808-737-7995
E-mail: arc-hi@aloha.com

Idaho
Bureau of Special Education Section
Idaho Department of Education
P.O. Box 83720
Boise, ID 83720-0027
(208) 332-6910
E-mail: nbweaver@sde.state.id.us

(Birth through 2)
Infant Toddler Program
Bureau of
Developmental Disabilities
Department of Health and Welfare
P.O. Box 83720
450 West State Street, 5th Floor
Boise, ID 83720-0036
(208) 334-5514
E-mail: jonesm@dhw.state.id.us

Division of Vocational Rehabilitation
P.O. Box 83720
Boise, ID 83720-0096
(208) 334-3390 (V/TTY)

Idaho State Council on Developmental
Disabilities
280 North 8th Street, Suite 208
P.O. Box 83720
Boise, ID 83720-0280
(208) 334-2178
E-mail: msword@icdd.state.id.us
Web: http://www.state.id.us/icdd/

Comprehensive Advocacy, Inc.
4477 Emerald Street, Suite B-100
Boise, ID 83706
(208) 336-5353; (800) 632-5125
E-mail: coadinc@cyberhighway.net
Web: http://users.moscow.com/co-ad

Children's Special Health Program
Bureau of Clinical and Preventive
Services
Idaho Department of Health & Welfare
P.O. Box 83720

Boise, ID 83720-0036
(208) 334-5962
E-mail: harrellb@idhw.state.id.us

Center on Disabilities and Human
Development
University Affiliated
Program/University of Idaho
129 W. Third Street
Moscow, ID 83843
(208) 885-3559
E-mail: lparks@uidaho.edu
Web: http://www.ets.uidaho.edu/
cdhd/

Idaho Parents Unlimited (IPUL)
4696 Overland Road, #568
Boise, ID 83705
(208) 342-5884 (V/TTY); (800) 242-
4785 (in ID)
E-mail: ipul@rmci.net
Web: http://home.rmci.net/IPUL

Autism Society of America—Treasure
Valley Chapter
2811 East Migratory Drive
Boise, ID 83706
E-mail: asatvc@micronnet
Web: http://netnow.micron.net/
~asatvc/

Illinois
Center for Educational Innovation &
Reform
Program Compliance
100 North First Street, E-228
Springfield, IL 62777-0001
(217) 782-5589

(Birth through 2)
Bureau of Part C/Early Intervention
Dept. of Human Services
P.O. Box 19429
Springfield, IL 62794-9429
(217) 782-1981;
(800) 323-4769 (in IL)

(Ages 3 through 5)
Division of Early
Childhood Education
100 North First Street, E-230
Springfield, IL 62777-0001

(217) 524-4835
E-mail: hhenders@
smtp.isbe.state.il.us

Office of Rehabilitation Services
Department of Human Services
P.O. Box 19429
Springfield, IL 62794-9429
(217) 524-3824 (V);
(217) 782-5734 (TTY)
E-mail: ilvr@rehabnetwork.org

Illinois Planning Council on
Developmental Disabilities
830 S. Spring St.
Springfield, IL 62704
(217) 782-9696 (V/TTY)

Equip for Equality
11 East Adams, Suite 1200
Chicago, IL 60603
(800) 537-2632; (312) 341-0022;
(800) 610-2779 (TTY)
E-mail: hn6177@handsnet.org

Division of Specialized Care for
Children
University of Illinois at Chicago
P.O. Box 19481
2815 West Washington, Suite 300
Springfield, IL 62794-9481
(217) 793-2340
E-mail: cnonufer@uic.edu
Web: http://www.uic.edu/hsc/dscc/

Institute on Disability & Human
Development
University of Illinois at Chicago
1640 West Roosevelt Road
Chicago, IL 60608
(312) 413-1647;
(312) 413-0453 (TTY)
E-mail: braddock@
uic.edu

Family Resource Center
on Disabilities
20 East Jackson Blvd., Suite 300
Chicago, IL 60604
(312) 939-3513;
(800) 952-4199 (in IL)
E-mail: frcdptiil@ameritech.net

Council for Disability Rights
205 W. Randolph, Suite 1650
Chicago, IL 60606
(312) 444-9484;
(312) 444-1967 (TTY)
E-mail: cdrights@interaccess.com
Web: http://www.disabilityrights.org

Autism Society of Illinois
2200 South Main Street, Suite 317
Lombard, IL 60148
(708) 691-1270

University of Chicago
Department of Psychology
5841 South Maryland MC 3077
Chicago, IL 60637
Contact: Edwin Cook, M.D.; Catherine
Lord, Ph.D.

The Arc of Illinois
925 W. 175th St.
Homewood, IL 60430
(708)206-1930

Indiana
Division of Special Education, Dept. of
Education
State House, Room 229
Indianapolis, IN 46204-2798
(317) 232-0570
E-mail: MARRAB@
speced.doe.state.in.us
Web: http://web.indstate.edu/
soe/iseas/dse.html

(Ages 3 through 5)
Division of Special Education,
Department of Education
State House, Room 229
Indianapolis, IN 46204-2798
(317) 232-0570
E-mail: COCHRA@
speced.doe.state.in.us

(Birth through 2)
Indiana Family & Social Services
Administration
Div. of Families & Children/Bur. of
Child Development
402 West Washington Street,

Room W-386
Indianapolis, IN 46207-7083
(317) 232-2429;
(317) 232-7948 (Fax)
E-mail: mgreer@fssa.state.in.us

Indiana Family & Social Services
Administration
Vocational Rehabilitation Services
Division of Disability, Aging &
Rehabilitative Services
402 W. Washington St., Rm. W453,
P.O. Box 7083
Indianapolis, IN 46207-7083
(800) 545-7763, ext. 1319;
(317) 232-1319;

Governor's Planning Council on
Disabilities
143 West Market Street, Suite 404
Indianapolis, IN 46204
(317) 722-5555;
(317) 722-5563 (TTY)
E-mail: suellen@In.net

Indiana Protection
and Advocacy Services
4701 N. Keystone Avenue,
Suite 222
Indianapolis, IN 46205
(800) 622-4845; (317) 722-5555;
(800) 838-1131 (TTY)

Children's Special
Health Care Services
Indiana State Department
of Health
2 N. Meridian Street, Section 7-B
Indianapolis, IN 46204
(317) 233-5578

Indiana Resource
Center for Autism
2853 East Tenth Street
Bloomington, IN 47408-2601
(812) 855-6508;
(812) 855-9630 (Fax)
E-mail: prattc@
isdd.ibdd.indiana.edu
Web: http://www.isdd.indiana.edu/
~irca

IN*SOURCE
809 North Michigan Street
South Bend, IN 46601-1036
(219) 234-7101; (219) 234-7101
(TTY); (800) 332-4433 (in IN)
E-mail: insourc1@aol.com
Web: http://home1.gte.net/
insource

Indiana Parent
Information Network
4755 Kingsway Drive, Suite 105
Indianapolis, IN 46205-1545
(317) 257-8683
E-mail: ipin@indy.net
Web: http://www.ipininc.com

Riley Child Development Center
Indiana University
School of Medicine
James Whitcomb Riley Hospital for
Children
702 Barnhill Drive, Room 5837
Indianapolis, IN 46202-5225
(317) 274-8167
E-mail: jdrau@indyuap.iupui.edu

The Arc of Indiana
22 E. Washington, Suite 210
Indianapolis, IN 46204
(317)977-2375
E-mail: arcin@in.net

Iowa
Bureau of Family and
Community Services
Department of Education
Grimes State Office Building
Des Moines, IA 50319-0146
(515) 281-5735
E-mail: Brenda.Oas@ed.state.ia.us
Web: http://www.state.ia.us/
educate/index.html

(Ages 3 through 5)
Bureau of Family and
Community Services
Grimes State Office Building
Des Moines, IA 50319-0146
(515) 281-5433
E-mail: Mary.Schertz@
ed.state.ia.us

(Birth through 2)
Early Access
Grimes State Office Building
Des Moines, IA 50319-0146
(515) 281-7145
E-mail: lpletch@ed.state.ia.us

Governor's Developmental Disabilities
Council
617 E. Second Street
Des Moines, IA 50309
(515) 281-9083
E-mail: bharker@dhs.state.ia.us

Iowa Protection and Advocacy
Services, Inc.
3015 Merle Hay Road, Suite 6
Des Moines, IA 50310
(800) 779-2502; (515) 278-2502;
(515) 278-0571 (TTY)
E-mail: info@ipna.org

Iowa Child Health Specialty Clinics
University Hospital School
100 Hawkins Drive, Room 247
Iowa City, IA 52242-1011
(319) 356-1118
E-mail: jeffrey-lobas@uiowa.edu

Iowa University Affiliated Program
University Hospital School
The University of Iowa
Iowa City, IA 52242
(319) 353-6390
E-mail: disability-resources@
uiowa.edu
Web: http://www.uiowa.edu/uhs

Parent Training and Information
Center of Iowa
321 E. 6th Street
Des Moines, IA 50309
(800) 450-8667; (515) 243-1713
E-mail: PTIIowa@aol.com
Web: http://www.taalliance.org/
ptis/ia

Autism Society of Iowa
3135 Spring Valley Road
Dubuque, IA 52001
(319) 557-1169
E-mail: asiowa@mhte.net

The Arc of Iowa
715 East Locust
Des Moines, IA 50309
515-283-2358

Kansas
Student Support Services
Kansas State Department of Education
120 East 10th Avenue
Topeka, KS 66612
(785) 291-3097
E-mail: mremus@ksbe.state.ks.us

(Ages 3 through 5)
Student Support Services
Kansas State Department of Education
120 East Tenth Avenue
Topeka, KS 66612-1182
(785) 296-7454
E-mail: cdermyer@
ksbe.state.ks.us

(Birth through 2)
State Department of
Health & Environment
Landon State Office Bldg.
900 S.W. Jackson, 10th Floor
Topeka, KS 66612-1290
(785) 296-6135
E-mail: jgarcia@kdhe.state.ks.us

Developmental Disabilities Services
SRS/ MH & Developmental Disabilities
Docking State Office Bldg., 5th Floor
North
Topeka, KS 66612-1570
(785) 296-3561
E-mail: DFH@srskansas.org

Kansas Advocacy & Protective Services
3218 Kimball Ave.
Manhattan, KS 66503
(800) 432-8276; (785) 776-1541
E-mail: Michelle@ksadv.org

Services for Children with Special
Health Care Needs
Department of Health & Environment
Landon State Office Bldg., 10th Floor
900 S.W. Jackson

Topeka, KS 66612-1220
(785) 296-1316;
(800) 332-6262 (in KS)
Web: http://www.kdhe.state.ks.us/
shs/services.html

Life Span Institute
University of Kansas
1052 Robert Dole Human
Development Center
Lawrence, KS 66045
(785) 864-4295
E-mail: schroede@
dole.lsi.ukans.edu

Families Together, Inc.
3340 W. Douglas, Suite 102
Witchita, KS 67203
(316) 945-7747; (888) 815-6364
(Witchita); (800) 264-6343 (Topeka)
(888) 820-6364 (Garden City); (800)
499-9443 (Espanol)
E-mail: fmin@feist.com
Web: http://www.kansas.net/
~family

Kansas Autism Foundation (KAF)
1605 Vermont Avenue
Lawrence, KS 66044
(785) 865-0915
E-mail: autism@midusa.net
Web: http://www.kansasautism.com

The Arc of Kansas
3601 SW 29th, S-105
Topeka, KS 66614
(913)271-8783

Kentucky
Division of Exceptional
Children's Services
Kentucky Department of Education
Capitol Plaza Tower, 8th Floor
500 Mero Street
Frankfort, KY 40601
(502) 564-4970
E-mail: marmstro@kde.state.ky.us
Web: http://www.kde.state.ky.us

(Ages 3 through 5)
Office of Learning Program
Development
500 Mero Street, Capitol Plaza Tower,
17th Floor
Frankfort, KY 40601
(502) 564-7056
E-mail: dschumac@kde.state.ky.us
Web: http://www.kde.state.ky.us

(Birth through 2)
Infant and Toddler Program
Department of Mental Health &
Mental Retardation Services
100 Fair Oaks Lane, 4E-E
Frankfort, KY 40621-0001
(502) 564-7700
E-mail: jhenson@mail.state.ky.us

Department of Vocational
Rehabilitation
Cabinet for Workforce Development
209 St. Clair
Frankfort, KY 40601
(502) 564-4440
E-mail: sam.serraglio@mail.state.ky.us

Kentucky Developmental Disabilities
Planning Council
Dept. For Mental Health/Mental
Retardation Services
100 Fair Oaks Lane, 4E-F
Frankfort, KY 40621-0001
(502) 564-7842
E-mail: pfseybold@mail.state.ky.us

Department for Public Advocacy, P&A
Division
100 Fair Oaks Lane, Third Floor
Frankfort, KY 40601
(502) 564-2967;
 (800) 372-2988 (in KY)

Commission for Children with Special
Health Care Needs
982 Eastern Parkway
Louisville, KY 40217-1566
(800) 232-1160; (502) 595-4459
E-mail: Beverly.Hampton@
mail.state.ky.us

Human Development Institute
University Affiliated Facility
University of Kentucky
126 Mineral Industries Building
Lexington, KY 40506-0051
(606) 257-1714
E-mail: ronh@ihdi.uky.edu

Kentucky Special Parent Involvement
Network (KY-SPIN)
2210 Goldsmith Lane, Suite 118
Louisville, KY 40218
(800) 525-7746; (502) 456-0923
E-mail: familytrng@aol.com

Parent Outreach: Parents Supporting
Parents
1146 South Third Street
Louisville, KY 40203
(502) 584-1239
E-mail: CRC@iglou.com

The Arc of Kentucky
833 East Main
Frankfort, KY 40601
(502)875-5225

Louisiana
Division of Special Populations
Louisiana State Department of
Education
P.O. Box 94064
Baton Rouge, LA 70804-9064
(225) 342-3633

(Ages 3 through 5)
Preschool Programs, Division of
Special Populations
Louisiana State Department of
Education
P.O. Box 94064
Baton Rouge, LA 70804-9064
(225) 342-1190

(Birth through 2)
Infant/Toddler Program
Division of Special Populations
Louisiana State Department of
Education
P.O. Box 94064
Baton Rouge, LA 70804-9064

(225) 342-3730
E-mail: edjohnson@
mail.doe.state.la.us

Dept. of Social Services/LA
Rehabilitation Svcs.
8225 Florida Boulevard
Baton Rouge, LA 70806-4834
(225) 925-4131
E-mail: mnelson@
lrs.dss.state.la.us

LA State Planning Council on
Developmental Disabilities
P.O. Box 3455
Baton Rouge, LA 70821-3455
(225) 342-6804;
(800) 922-3425 (in LA)
E-mail: swinchel@
dhhmail.dhh.state.la.us
Web: http://www.laddc.org

The Advocacy Center
225 Baronne Street, Suite 2112
New Orleans, LA 70112-2112
(504) 522-2337;
(800) 960-7705 (in LA)
E-mail: simplo@advocacyla.org

Children's Special Health Services
Office of Public Health
Department of Health & Hospitals
P.O. Box 60630, Room 607
New Orleans, LA 70160
(225) 568-5055
E-mail: lrose@
dhhmail.dhh.state.la.us

Human Development Center
LA State University Medical Center
1100 Florida Avenue, Building 138
New Orleans, LA 70119
(225) 942-8202

Project PROMPT
4323 Division Street, Suite 110
Metairie, LA 70002-3179
(225) 888-9111; (800) 766-7736 (in
LA)
E-mail: fhfgno@ix.netcom.com
Web: http://www.projectprompt.com

The Arc of Louisiana
PO Box 65129
Columbia Med Center
17050 Medical Center Dr. #304
Baton Rouge, LA 70896-5129
(504) 383-0742

Maine
Department of Education, Office of
Special Services
State House, Station #23
Augusta, ME 04333-0023
(207) 287-5950; (207) 287-2550
E-mail: DStockford@
doe.k12.ed.us
Web: http://www.state.me.us/
education/specserv.htm

Part C and Section 619 Coordinator
Child Development Services
State House, Station #146
Augusta, ME 04333
(207) 287-3272
E-mail: jaci.holmes@state.me.us
Web: http://www.state.me.us/
education

Bureau of Rehabilitation Services
Department of Labor
150 State House Station
Augusta, ME 04333-0150
(207) 287-5100
E-mail: John.G.Shattuck@
state.me.us

ME Developmental
Disabilities Council
139 State House Station,
Nash Building
Capitol and Sewall Streets
Augusta, ME 04333-0139
(207) 287-4213;
(800) 244-3990 (in ME)

Disability Rights Center of Maine
P.O. Box 2007
Augusta, ME 04338-2007
(207) 626-2774;
(800) 452-1948 (V/TTY in ME)
E-mail:
advocate@disabilityrightsctr.org

Coordinated Care Svcs for Children
with Special
Health Needs,
Department of Human Services
151 Capitol Street, #11 State House
Station
Augusta, ME 04333
(207) 287-5139
E-mail: toni.g.wall@state.me.us

Autism Society of America
693 Western Avenue, Suite 2
Manchester, ME 04351
(207) 626-2708;
(800) 273-5200 (in ME)
E-mail: asm@mint.net
Web: http://www.mainetoday.
koz.com/maine/asm

Center for Community Inclusion, UAP
5717 Corbett Hall, Room 100
University of Maine
Orono, ME 04469-5717
(207) 581-1084
Web: http://www.ume.maine.edu/
~cci

Maine Parent Federation/SPIN
P.O. Box 2067
Augusta, ME 04338-2067
(207) 582-2504;
(800) 870-7746 (in ME)
E-mail: jlachance@mpf.org
Web: http://www.mpf.org

Maryland
Department of Education, Division of
Special Education
Early Intervention Services
200 West Baltimore Street
Baltimore, MD 21201-2595
(410) 767-0238
E-mail: cbaglin@msde.state.md.us
Web: http://www.msde.state.md.us

(Birth through 3)
Program Development and Assistance
Branch
Division of Special Education
Early Intervention Services
200 West Baltimore Street

Baltimore, MD 21201
(410) 767-0237;
(800) 535-0182 (in MD)

Department of Education
Division of Special Education
Early Intervention Services
200 West Baltimore Street
Baltimore, MD 21201
(410) 767-0249
E-mail: jwhite@msde.state.md.us

Division of Rehabilitation Services
Department of Education, Maryland
Rehabilitation Center
2301 Argonne Drive
Baltimore, MD 21218-1696
(410) 554-9385
E-mail: dors@state.md.us
Web: http://www.dors.state.md.us/

MD Developmental
Disabilities Council
300 West Lexington Street, Box 10
Baltimore, MD 21201-2323
(410) 333-3688
E-mail: MDDC@erols.com

Maryland Disability Law Center
1800 N. Charles, Suite 204
Baltimore, MD 21201
(410) 727-6352; (800) 233-7201
E-mail: philf@MDLCBALTO.org

Department of Health &
Mental Hygiene
Children's Medical Services Program—
Unit 50
20l West Preston Street
Baltimore, MD 21201
(800) 638-8864; (410) 225-5580
E-mail: Malones@DHMH.state.md.us

The Kennedy Krieger Institute
707 North Broadway
Baltimore, MD 21205-1890
(410) 502-9483
E-mail: goldstein@
kennedykrieger.org
Web: http://www.kennedykrieger.org

Parents Place of Maryland
7484 Candlewood Road, Suite S
Hanover, MD 21076
(410) 859-5300
E-mail: parplace@aol.com
Web: http://www.somerset.net/
ParentsPlace

The Arc of Maryland
49 Old Solomon's Island Road
Suite 205
Annapolis, MD 21401
(410) 571-9320

Massachusetts
Educational Improvement Group
Department of Education
350 Main Street
Malden, MA 02148-5023
(781) 338-3000; (781) 338-3388
(Fax)
E-mail: mmittnacht@
doe.mass.edu
Web: http://www.doe.mass.edu

(Ages 3 through 5)
Early Learning Services
Department of Education
350 Main Street
Malden, MA 02148-5023
(781) 338-3000
E-mail: eschaefer@doe.mass.edu
Web: http://www.doe.mass.edu

(Birth through 2)
Early Intervention Services
Dept. of Public Health
250 Washington Street, 4th Floor
Boston, MA 02108
(617) 624-5070
E-mail: ronbenham@state.ma.us

MA Rehabilitation Commission
Fort Point Place
27-43 Wormwood Street
Boston, MA 02210-1616
(617) 204-3600

MA Developmental Disabilities Council
174 Portland Street, 5th Floor
Boston, MA 02114
(617) 727-6374;

(617) 727-1885 (TTY)
E-mail: Daniel.Shannon@
state.ma.us

Disability Law Center, Inc.
11 Beacon Street, Suite 925
Boston, MA 02108
(800) 872-9992; (617) 723-8455; (617)
227-9464(TTY);
(800) 381-0577 (TTY)
Web: http://www.dlc-ma.org/

Division for Children with Special
Health Care Needs
Department of Public Health
250 Washington Street, 4th Floor
Boston, MA 02108-4619
(617) 624-5070
E-mail: deborah.allen@
state.ma.us
Web: http://www.magnet.state.
ma.us/dph

Institute for Community Inclusion,
UAP
Children's Hospital
300 Longwood Avenue
Boston, MA 02115
(617) 355-6506;
(617) 355-6956 (TTY)
Web: http://web1.tch.harvard.
edu/ici/

Eunice Shriver Center UAP
200 Trapelo Road
Waltham, MA 02254
(781) 642-0001;
(800) 764-0200 (TTY)
Web: http://www.shriver.org

Federation for Children with Special
Needs
1135 Tremont Street
Boston, MA 02120
(617) 236-7210 (V/TTY);
(800) 331-0688
E-mail: fcsninfo@fcsn.org
Web: http://www.fcsn.org/

Families Ties
c/o MA Dept. of Public Health

250 Washington Street
Boston, MA 02108
(617) 624-5070

Massachusetts Families
Organizing for Change
P.O. Box 61
Raynham, MA 02768
(800) 406-3632
E-mail: mfofc@tmlp.com
Web: http://personal.tmlp.
com/mfofc

Community Resources for People with
Autism
116 Pleasant Street
Easthampton, MA 01027
(413) 529-2428;
(413) 529-2567 (Fax)
E-mail: crautism@crocker.com
Web: http://www.crocker.com/
~crautism

The New England Center for Children
33 Turnpike Road
Southborough, MA 01772
(508) 481-1015;
(508) 485-3421 (Fax)
E-mail: cwelch@NECC.org
Web: http://www.NECC.org

TAP—The Autism Partnership
P.O. Box 605
Milford, MA 01757
(508) 478-7TAP

The Asperger's Association of New
England
P.O. Box 242
Newton, MA 02166
(617) 964-6860
E-mail: info@aane.org
Web: http://www.aane.org

The Arc Massachusetts
217 South Street
Waltham, MA 02154
(617)891-6270
arcmass@gis.net

Michigan
Office of Special Education and Early

Intervention Services
Department of Education
P.O. Box 30008
Lansing, MI 48909-7508
(517) 373-9433
E-mail: ThompsonJJ@state.mi.us
Web: http://www.mde.state.mi.us/
off/sped/index.html

(Ages 3 through 5)
Office of Special Education and Early
Intervention Services
Department of Education
P.O. Box 30008
Lansing, MI 48909
(517) 373-2949
E-mail: Regniec@state.mi.us

(Birth through 2)
Michigan Department of Education
Office of Special Education and Early
Intervention Services
P.O. Box 30008
Lansing, MI 48909
(517) 373-6335
E-mail: WinborneV@state.mi.us

Michigan Dept. of Career Development
Michigan Rehabilitation Services
P.O. Box 30010
Lansing, MI 48909
(517) 373-3391
E-mail: davisr1@state.mi.us

MI Developmental Disabilities Council
Lewis Cass Building
Lansing, MI 48913
(517) 334-6123
E-mail: collinsve@state.mi.us

Michigan Protection and Advocacy
Service
106 West Allegan, Suite 300
Lansing, MI 48933-1706
(517) 487-1755 (V/TTY);
(800) 288-5923 (V/TTY)
E-mail: molson@mpas.org
Web: http://www.mpas.org

Children's Special Health Care
Services Plan Division
Medical Services Administration

Department of Community Health
400 S. Pine, P.O. Box 30479
Lansing, MI 48909-7979
(517) 335-8207

Developmental Disabilities Institute
Wayne State University
326 Justice Building
6001 Cass Avenue
Detroit, MI 48202
(313) 577-2654
E-mail: B_Le_Roy@wayne.edu

Citizens Alliance to Uphold Special
Education (CAUSE)
3303 West Saginaw Street,
Suite F1
Lansing, MI 48917-2303
(517) 886-9167;
(800) 221-9105 (in MI)
E-mail: info-cause@voyager.net
Web: http://www.pathwaynet.com/
cause

Parents Training Parents
Project/Parents are Experts
23077 Greenfield Road, Suite 205
Southfield, MI 48075-3745
(800) 827-4843; (248) 557-5070
E-mail: ucp@ameritech.net

Parent Participation Program
Family Support Network of Michigan
Children's Special
Health Care Services
MI Dept. of Community Health
1200 6th St, Suite 316
Detroit, MI 48226-2418
(800) 359-3722; (313) 256-2186

The Arc Michigan
333 S. Washington Square
Suite 200
Lansing, MI 48933
(517) 487-5426

Minnesota
Minnesota Department of Children,
Families and Learning
Division of Special Education
1500 Highway 36 West

Roseville, MN 55113-4266
(651) 582-8289;
(651) 582-8201 (TTY)
E-mail: norena.hale@state.mn.us
Web: http://children.state.mn.us/
speced/speced.htm

(Ages 3 through 5)
Early Childhood & Family Initiatives
Team
Minnesota Department of Children,
Families and Learning
1500 Highway 36 West
Roseville, MN 55112
(651) 582-8473
E-mail: robyn.widley@state.mn.us

(Birth through 2)
Part C-Infants & Toddlers with
Disabilities Interagency
Minnesota Department of Children,
Families and Learning
1500 Highway 36 West
Roseville, MN 55113-4266
(651) 582-8436;
(651) 582-8201 (TTY)
E-mail: jan.rubenstein@
state.mn.us

Rehabilitation Services Branch
Department of Economic Security
390 North Robert Street, 5th Floor
St. Paul, MN 55101
(651) 296-1822
E-mail: mick.coleman@
state.mn.us
Web: http://www.des.state.mn.us

Governor's Council on Developmental
Disabilities
300 Centennial Office Bldg.
658 Cedar Street
St. Paul, MN 55155
(612) 296-4018
E-mail: admin.dd@state.mn.us
Web: http://www.mncdd.org

Minnesota Disability Law Center
430 First Avenue, N., Suite 300
Minneapolis, MN 55401-1780
(612) 332-1441

MN Children with Special Health
Needs
MN Department of Health
85 East 7th Place, Suite 400
P.O. Box 64882
St. Paul, MN 55164-0882
(651) 215-8956;
(800) 728-5420
Web: http://www.health.
state.mn.us

Institute on Community Integration,
UAP
University of Minnesota
102 Pattee Hall
150 Pillsbury Drive SE
Minneapolis, MN 55455
(612) 624-6300
E-mail: ici@mail.ici.coled.umn.edu
Web: http://www.ici.coled.
umn.edu/ici/

PACER Center, Inc.
4826 Chicago Avenue South
Minneapolis, MN 55417-1098
(612) 827-2966; (612) 827-7770
(TTY); (800) 53-PACER (in MN)
E-mail: alliance@taalliance.org
Web: http://www.taalliance.org

Arc Minnesota
3225 Lyndale Avenue South
Minneapolis, MN 55408
612-827-5641
arcminn@mtn.org

Mississippi
Office of Special Education,
Department of Education
P.O. Box 771—Central High School
Building
Jackson, MS 39205-0771
(601) 359-3498
Web: http://mdek12.state.ms.us

(Ages 3 through 5)
Office of Special Education,
Department of Education
P.O. Box 771
Jackson, MS 39205-0771
(601) 359-3498

E-mail: dbowman@
mdek.12.state.ms.us
Web: http://mdek12.state.ms.us

(Birth through 2)
First Steps Early
Intervention System
MS State Department of
Health (MSDH)
P.O. Box 1700
2423 North State Street,
Room 107
Jackson, MS 39215-1700
(601) 576-7427;
(800) 451-3903 (in MS)
E-mail: rhart@msdh.state.ms.us

MS Office of Vocational Rehabilitation
Department of Rehabilitation Services
P.O. Box 1698
Jackson, MS 39215-1698
(601) 853-5230

Developmental Disabilities Planning
Council
1101 Robert E. Lee Bldg.
239 N. Lamar Street
Jackson, MS 39201
(601) 359-1288
E-mail: mspna@bellsouth.net
Web: http://www.dmh.state.ms.us

Mississippi P&A System
5330 Executive Place, Suite A
Jackson, MS 39206
(800) 772-4057; (601) 981-8207
E-mail: mspna@bellsouth.net

Children's Medical Program
Department of Health
P.O. Box 1700
Jackson, MS 39215
(800) 844-0898; (601) 987-3965

MS University Affiliated Program
University of Southern Mississippi
P.O. Box 5163
Hattiesburg, MS 39406-5163
(601) 266-5163;
(800) 467-4488 (in MS)
E-mail: jzsiders@ocean.st.usm.edu

Parent Partners
1900 N. West Street, Suite C-100
Jackson, MS 39202
(601) 714-5707;
(800) 366-5707 (in MS)
E-mail: ptiofms@misnet.com
Web: http://www.taalliance.org/
ptis/ms

Project EMPOWER
136 South Poplar Avenue
Greenville, MS 38701
(800) 337-4852; (601) 332-4852
E-mail: empower@techinfo.com

Living Independence for
Everyone (L.I.F.E)
301 Humble Avenue, Suite 197
Hattiesburg, MS 39401
(601) 583-2108; (800) 898-8977

Living Independence for
Everyone (L.I.F.E)
754 N. President Street
Jackson, MS 39202
(800) 748-9398; (601) 969-4009

Living Independence for
Everyone (L.I.F.E)
1914 East University Avenue
Oxford, MS 38655
(800) 748-7471; (601) 234-7010;

Coalition for Citizens
with Disabilities
754 N. President Street
Jackson, MS 39202
(800) 748-9420; (601) 969-0601
E-mail: MsLife@tsbbso2.tnet.com
Web: http://www.ccd-life.org

The Arc of Mississippi
3111 North State Street
Jackson, MS 39216
(601) 362-4830

Missouri
Division of Special Education
Department of Elementary and
Secondary Education
P.O. Box 480
Jefferson City, MO 65102

(573) 751-2965
E-mail: mfriedeb@
mail.dese.state.mo.us
Web: http://www.dese.state.mo.us/
divspeced/

(Ages 3 through 5)
Department of Elementary and
Secondary Education
P.O. Box 480
Jefferson City, MO 65102
(573) 751-0185
E-mail: pgoff@
mail.dese.state.mo.us
Web: http://www.dese.state.mo.us/
divspeced/ecse.html

(Birth through 2)
Section of Early Childhood Special
Education
Department of Elementary and
Secondary Education
P.O. Box 480
Jefferson City, MO 65102
(573) 751-0187
E-mail: pgoff@
maildese.state.mo.us
Web: http://www.dese.state.mo.us/
divspeced/firststeps.html

Division of Vocational Rehabilitation
Department of Education
3024 W. Trauma Boulevard
Jefferson City, MO 65109-0525
(573) 751-3251
E-mail: kkendle@
vr.dese.state.mo.us
Web: http://www.dese.state.mo.us/
divvocrehab/

MO Planning Council for
Developmental Disabilities
Division of MR/Developmental
Disabilities, Department of Mental
Health
1706 East Elm, P.O. Box 687
Jefferson City, MO 65102
(573) 751-8611;
(800) 500-7878 (in MO)
Web: http://www.modmh.state.
mo.us/mrdd/moplan/moplan.html

MO Protection &
Advocacy Services
925 South Country Club Dr., Unit B-1
Jefferson City, MO 65109
(573) 893-3333; (800) 392-8667
E-mail: mopasjc@socket.net

Bureau of Special
Heath Care Needs
Department of Health
P.O. Box 570, 930 Wildwood
Jefferson City, MO 65109
(573) 751-6246

Institute for Human Development
University of MO at Kansas City
2220 Holmes Street, 3rd Floor
Kansas City, MO 64108
(816) 235-1770
Web: http://www.ihd.umkc.edu

Judevine Center for Autism
9455 Rott Road
St. Louis, MO 63127-1915
(314) 849-4440;
(314) 849-2721 (Fax)
E-mail: judevine@judevine.org
Web: http://www.judevine.org

Missouri Parents Act (MPACT)
1901 Windriver Drive
Jefferson City, MO 65101
(573) 635-1189

Missouri Parents Act (MPACT)
2100 South Brentwood, Suite G
Springfield, MO 65804
(417) 882-7434;
(800) 743-7634 (in MO)
E-mail: mpac01@MCIONE.com
Web: http://www.crn.org/mpact

Missouri Parents Act (MPACT)
4144 Lindell Boulevard, Suite 405
St. Louis, MO 63108
(314) 531-5922;
(800) 995-3160 (in MO)

Missouri Parents Act (MPACT)
One West Armour Boulevard,
Suite 301

Kansas City, MO 64111
(816) 531-7070
E-mail: mpactcs@.crn.org

Montana
Special Education Division
Office of Public Instruction
P.O. Box 202501
Helena, MT 59620-2501
(406) 444-4429
E-mail: brunkel@opi.state.mt.us

(Ages 3 through 5)
Office of Public Instruction
P. O. Box 202501
Helena, MT 59620-2501
(406) 444-4425

(Birth through 2)
Developmental Disabilities Program
Department of Public Health
and Human Services
P.O. Box 4210
Helena, MT 59604-4210
(406) 444-4181
E-mail: jspiegle@state.mt.us

Vocational Rehabilitation Programs
Department of Public Health & Human
Services
111 N. Sanders Street, Room 305
P. O. Box 4210
Helena, MT 59604-4210
(406) 444-2590

Developmental Disabilities Planning &
Advisory Council
P. O. Box 526
Helena, MT 59624
(406) 444-1334;
(800) 337-9942 (in MT)

Montana Advocacy Program
P.O. Box 1680, 316 North Park,
Room 211
Helena, MT 59624
(406) 444-3889;
(800) 245-4743 (V/TTY, in MT)
E-mail: bernie@mtadv.org
Web: http://www.mt.net/
~advocate

Parents, Let's Unite For Kids (PLUK)
516 N. 32nd Street
Billings, MT 59101-6003
(406) 255-0540;
(800) 222-7585 (in MT)
E-mail: plukmt@wtp.net
Web: http://www.pluk.org

ARC/Montana
400 Echo Rd
Big Fork, MT 59911
(406)837-4652

Nebraska
Special Populations
Department of Education
P.O. Box 94987
Lincoln, NE 68509-4987
(402) 471-2471
E-mail: gsherman@edneb.org
Web: http://www.edneb.org/
SPED/sped.html

(Ages 3 through 5)
Special Populations Office
Department of Education
P.O. Box 94987
Lincoln, NE 68509
(402) 471-4319
E-mail: jthelen@edneb.org

(Birth through 2)
Special Populations Office
State Department of Education
P.O. Box 94987
Lincoln, NE 68509
(402) 471-2463
E-mail: luebbers@edneb.org

Developmental Disabilities Planning
Council/HHS
P.O. Box 95044
301 Centennial Mall South
Lincoln, NE 68509
(402) 471-2330
E-mail: DOH7111@
vmhost.cdp.state.ne.us
Web: http://www.hhs.state.ne.us

Nebraska Advocacy Services
522 Lincoln Center Bldg.

215 Centennial Mall South
Lincoln, NE 68508
(402) 474-3183; (800) 422-6691
E-mail: nas@navix.net

NE Health & Human Services
Special Services for Children & Adults
P.O. Box 95044
Lincoln, NE 68509-5044
(402) 471-9345
E-mail: dss0065@
vmhost.cdp.state.ne.us

Autism Society of Nebraska
1026 Twin Ridge Rd.
Lincoln, NE 68510
(402) 423-3796

Munroe-Meyer Institute
98540 Nebraska Medical Center
Omaha, NE 68198-5450
(402) 559-6400
Web: http://www.unmc.edu/mmi

Nebraska Parent's Center
1941 South 42nd St., Suite 122
Omaha, NE 68105-2942
(402) 346-0525;
(800) 284-8520 (in NE)
E-mail: gdavis@
neparentcenter.org
Web: http://www.neparentcenter.org

Pilot Parents
1941 South 42nd Street, Suite 121
Omaha, NE 68105
(402) 346-5220
E-mail: aadamson@olliewebb.org
Web: http://www.olliewebb.org

The Arc of Nebraska
645 M St., S-105
Lincoln, NE 68508
402-475-4407

Nevada
Educational Equity
Department of Education
700 E. Fifth Street, Suite 113
Carson City, NV 89701-5096
(775) 687-9171

(Ages 3 through 5)
Educational Equity
Department of Education
1820 E. Sahara #208
Las Vegas, NV 89104
(702) 486-6454
E-mail: kallred@nsn.k12.nv.us

(Birth through 2)
Department of Human Resources
3987 S. McCarran Boulevard
Reno, NV 89502
(775) 688-2284
E-mail: jamulven@
govmail.state.nv.us

Rehabilitation Division
Dept. of Employment, Training &
Rehabilitation
505 East King St., Room 502
Carson City, NV 89710
(775) 684-4040

Office of Community Based Services
711 South Stewart Street
Carson City, NV 89701
(775) 687-4452

Nevada Disability Advocacy
and Law Center
6039 Eldora Avenue,
Suite C - Box 3
Las Vegas, NV 89146
(702) 257-8150; (888) 349-3843 (toll-free)
(702) 257-8160 (TTY)
E-mail: ndalc@earthlink.net
Web: http://www.ndalc.org

Nevada Disability Advocacy
and Law Center
1201 Terminal Way, Suite 219
Reno, NV 89502
(775) 333-7878;
(800) 992-5715 (toll-free)
(775) 788-7824 (TTY)
E-mail: reno@ndalc.org

Bureau of Family Health Services,
Division of Health
Dept. of Human Resources
505 East King Street, Room 200

Carson City, NV 89701-4792
(775) 687-4885
E-mail: jwright@
govmail.state.nv.us

Research and Education Planning
Center, UAP
College of Education/MS285
University of Nevada, Reno
Reno, NV 89557
(775) 784-4921 (V/TTY); (800) 216-7988

Nevada PEP
2810 W. Charleston, Suite G68
Las Vegas, NV 89102
(702) 388-8899;
(800) 216-5188 (in NV)
E-mail: nvpep@vegas.infi.net
Web: http://www.nvpep.org

New Hampshire
New Hampshire Department of
Education
101 Pleasant Street
Concord, NH 03301-3860
(603) 271-1536
E-mail: rwells@ed.state.nh.us

(Ages 3 through 5)
Bureau of Special Education, Dept. of
Education
101 Pleasant Street
Concord, NH 03301-3860
(603) 271-2178
E-mail: rlittlefield@ed.state.nh.us

(Birth through 2)
NH Family-Centered Early Support &
Services
Division of Developmental Services
State Office Park South
105 Pleasant Street
Concord, NH 03301-3860
(603) 271-5122
E-mail: cohara@dhhs.state.nh.us
Div. of Adult Learning & Rehabilitation

New Hampshire Department of
Education
78 Regional Drive, Bldg. 2
Concord, NH 03301

(603) 271-3471
E-mail: pleather@ed.state.nh.us

NH Developmental Disabilities
Council, The Concord Center
10 Ferry Street, Unit 315
Concord, NH 03301-5004
(603) 271-3236
E-mail: nhddcncl@aol.com

Disabilities Rights Center, Inc.
P.O. Box 3660
Concord, NH 03302-3660
(800) 834-1721; (603) 228-0432

Autism Society of New Hampshire
P.O. Box 68
Concord, NH 03302
(603) 898-0916

Institute on Disability, UAP
University of New Hampshire
7 Leavitt Lane, Suite 101
Durham, NH 03824-3522
(603) 862-4320 (V/TTY)
E-mail: institute.disability@
unh.edu
Web: http://iod.unh.edu

Parent Information Center (PIC)
P.O. Box 2405
Concord, NH 03302-2405
(603) 224-7005;
(800) 232-0986 (in NH)
E-mail: picnh@aol.com
Web: http://taalliance.org/
ptis/nhpic

Parent to Parent
P.O. Box 622
Hanover, NH 03755
(603) 448-6393;
(800) 698-5465 (in NH & VT)
E-mail: parent.to.parent@
dartmouth.edu

The Arc of New Hampshire
10 Ferry Street - Box 4
The Concord Center
Concord, NH 03301
(603) 228-9092

New Jersey
Office of Special Education Programs,
Dept. of Education
100 Riverview Plaza, P. O. Box 500
Trenton, NJ 08625-0500
(609) 633-6833

(Ages 3 through 5)
Office of Special Education Programs
Department of Education
P. O. Box 500
Trenton, NJ 08625-0500
(609) 292-2912

(Birth through 2)
Division of Family Health Services
Early Intervention System
P. O. Box 364
Trenton, NJ 08625
(609) 777-7734
E-mail: tlh@doh.state.nj.us
Web: http://www.state.nj.us/
health/fhs/eiphome.htm

Division of Vocational Rehabilitation
Svcs.
NJ Department of Labor
P. O. Box 398
Trenton, NJ 08625-0398
(609) 292-5987;
(609) 292-2919 (TTY)
Web: http://www.wnjpin.state.nj.us/

New Jersey Developmental Disabilities
Council
20 West State Street, 7th floor
P. O. Box 700
Trenton, NJ 08625
(609) 292-3745

NJ Protection and Advocacy
210 South Broad Street, 3rd Floor
Trenton, NJ 08608
(609) 292-9742; (609) 633-7106
(TTY); (800) 922-7233 (in NJ)
E-mail: advoca@njpanda.org
Web: http://www.njpanda.org

NJ Department of Health &
Senior Services
Special Child & Adult Health Services
50 E. State Street, P. O. Box 364

Trenton, NJ 08625
(609) 984-0755
E-mail: mg5@doh.state.nj.us

NJ Center for Outreach &
Services for the Autism Community
(COSAC)
1450 Parkside Avenue, Suite 22
Ewing, NJ 08638
(609) 883-8100;
(800) 4-AUTISM (in NJ)
E-mail: njautism@aol.com
Web: http://members.aol.com/
njautism

Douglass Developmental Disabilities
Center
Rutgers-The State University
25 Gibbons Circle
New Brunswick, NJ 08901-8528
(732) 932-9137; (732) 932-8011
(Fax); (732) 932-3902 (Outreach)

The Elizabeth M. Boggs Center on
Developmental Disabilities
The University Affiliated Program of
New Jersey
University of Medicine and Dentistry
of New Jersey
Robert Wood Johnson Medical School
335 George Street, 3rd Floor
P.O. Box 2688
New Brunswick, NJ 08903-2688
(732) 235-9300;
(732) 235-9328 (TTY)
E-mail: spitalde@umdnj.edu

UMDNJ-Robert Wood Johnson
Medical School
Department of Pediatrics
Division of Neurodevelopmental
Pediatrics
97 Paterson Street
New Brunswick, NJ 08903
(732) 235-7895;
(732) 235-7346 (Fax)

ASPEN
9 Aspen Circle
Edison, NJ 08820
(732) 906-8043;

(732) 744-1622 (Fax)
E-mail: LoriSue59@aol.com
Web: http://www.aspennj.org

Bancroft NeuroHealth
Hopkins Lane
P.O. Box 20
Haddonfield, NJ 08033-0018
(856) 429-0010;
(856) 429-1613 (Fax)
E-mail: inquiry@
bancroftneurohealth.org
Web: http://www.
bancroftneurohealth.org

Statewide Parent Advocacy Network
(SPAN)
35 Halsey Street
Newark, NJ 07102
(973) 642-8100; (973) 642-8080
E-mail: SPAN@bellatlantic.net
Web: http://www.taalliance.org/
ptis/nj

NJ Statewide Parent-to-Parent
35 Halsey Street
Newark, NJ 07102
(973) 642-8100;
(800) 372-6510
E-mail: njptp@ptd.net
Web: http://community.nj.com/
cc/njparenttoparent

Princeton Child Development Institute
300 Cold Soil Road
Princeton, NJ 08540
(609) 924-6280;
(609) 924-4110 (Fax)
E-mail: njpcdi@earthlink.net

Eden Institute
One Logan Drive
Princeton, NJ 08540
(609) 987-0099; (609) 987-0243
(Fax)
E-mail: EdenSvcs@aol.com
Web: http://members.aol.com/
EdenSvcs/index.html

Pyramid Educational Consultants
1930 State Highway 70,

Suite D-20
Cherry Hill, NJ 08003
(888) 732-7462; (856) 489-1644
E-mail: pyramid@pecs.com
Web: http://www.pecs.com

Rutgers Autism Program
41 Gordon Road, Suite A
Piscataway, NJ 08854
(732) 445-1141;
(732) 445-7970 (Fax)

The Arc of New Jersey
985 Livingston Ave.
N. Brunswick, NJ 08902
(201) 246-2525
E-mail: Arcblues@aol.com

New Mexico
Special Education
Department of Education
300 Don Gaspar Avenue
Santa Fe, NM 87501-2786
(505) 827-6541
E-mail: bpasternack@
sde.state.nm.us
Web: http://www.sde.state.nm.us

(Ages 3 through 5)
Early Childhood Consultant
Special Education Unit, Department of
Education
300 Don Gasper Avenue
Santa Fe, NM 87501-2786
(505) 827-6788
E-mail: mlandazvri@
sde.state.nm.us

(Birth through 2)
New Mexico Department of Health
1190 St. Francis Drive
P.O. Box 26110
Santa Fe, NM 87502-6110
(505) 827-2578

Div. of Vocational Rehabilitation, Dept.
of Education
435 St. Michaels Drive, Building D
Santa Fe, NM 87505
(505) 954-8511
Web: http://www.state.nm.us

New Mexico Developmental
Disabilities Planning Council
435 Saint Michael's Drive, Bldg D
Santa Fe, NM 87505
(505) 827-7590;
(505) 827-7589 (Fax)

Protection and Advocacy System
1720 Louisiana Blvd., NE,
Suite 204
Albuquerque, NM 87110
(505) 256-3100;
(800) 432-4682 (in NM)

Family Health Bureau
Department of Health
1190 Saint Francis Drive
Santa Fe, NM 87502
(505) 476-8589

University of New Mexico
Health Sciences Center
Center for Development and Disability
2300 Menaul Boulevard, NE
Albuquerque, NM 87106
(505) 272-3000
E-mail: cmcclain@unm.edu

New Mexico Autism Project
2300 Menaul NE
Albuquerque, NM 87107
(505) 272-1852;
(505) 272-5280 (Fax)
E-mail: jliddell@unm.edu

Parents Reaching Out (P.R.O.)
1000 A Main Street, NW
Los Lunas, NM 87031
(505) 865-3700;
(800) 524-5176 (in NM)
E-mail: nmproth@aol.com
Web: http://www.
parentsreachingout.org

The Arc of New Mexico
3500-G Comanche NE
Albuquerque, NM 87107
(505).883-4630

New York
Office of Vocational & Educational

Services for Individuals with
Disabilities
1 Commerce Plaza,
Room 1606
Albany, NY 12234
(518) 474-2714
Web: http://www.nysed.gov

(Ages 3 through 5)
State Education Department
Office of Vocational and Education
Services
for Individuals with Disabilities
1 Commerce Plaza, Room 1607
Albany, NY 12234
(518) 473-6108
E-mail: mplotzke@mail.nysed.gov

(Birth through 2)
Early Intervention Program
Bureau of Child and Adolescent Health
Corning Tower, Room 208
Albany, NY 12237
(518) 473-7016
E-mail: dmn02@health.state.ny.us

NYS Developmental Disabilities
Planning Council
155 Washington Avenue,
2nd Floor
Albany, NY 12210
(518) 486-7505; (800) 395-3372
Web: http://www.ddpc.state.ny.us

NY Committee on Quality of Care
401 State Street
Schenectady, NY 12305-2397
(518) 381-7098
Web: http://www.cqc.state.ny.us

Bureau of Child and Adolescent Health
Department of Health
Tower Building, Room 208
Albany, NY 12237-0618
(518) 474-2084
E-mail: dpmo4@health.state.ny.us

Developmental Disabilities Center
St. Lukes - Roosevelt Hospital Center
1000 10th Avenue
New York, NY 10019
(212) 523-6230

WIHD/University Affiliated Program
Westchester Medical Center
Valhalla, NY 10595
(914) 493-8204
E-mail: Ansley_Bacon@NYMC.edu
Web: http://www.nymc.edu/wihd

Univ. Affiliated Program/Rose F.
Kennedy Center
Albert Einstein Coll. of
Medicine/Yeshiva University
1410 Pelham Parkway South
Bronx, NY 10461
(718) 430-8522
E-mail: hcohen@aecom.yu.edu

Strong Center for Developmental
Disabilities
University of Rochester Medical Center
601 Elmwood Avenue, Box 671
Rochester, NY 14642
(716) 275-2986
E-mail: scdd@
cc.urmc.rochester.edu
Web: http://www.urmc.rochester.
edu/strong/scdd

Institute for Child Development
State University at Binghamton
Department of Psychology
P.O. Box 6000
Binghamton, NY 13902-6000
(607) 777-2829;
(607) 777-6981 (Fax)
E-mail: icdadmin@
binghamton.edu
Web: http://www.binghamton.
edu/icd

Seaver Autism Research Center
Mt. Sinai Medical Center
100th 8 Madison
Annenberg Bldg, Suite 22-66
New York, NY 10029
(212) 241-8164;
(212) 987-4031 (Fax)

The Advocacy Center
277 Alexander Street, Suite 500
Rochester, NY 14607
(716) 546-1700;
(800) 650-4967 (in NY)

E-mail: advocacy@frontiernet.net
Web: http://www.
advocacycenter.com

Advocates for Children of New York
(NY City)
105 Court Street, 4th Floor
Brooklyn, NY 11201
(718) 624-8450
E-mail: advocat1@idt.net
Web: http://www.
advocatesforchildren.org

Autism Advocacy and
Outreach Group
86 Boyce Avenue
Staten Island, NY 10306
(718) 980-1983

Resources for Children with Special
Needs
200 Park Avenue South, Suite 816
New York, NY 10003
(212) 667-4650
E-mail: resourcesnyc@prodigy.net
Web: http://www.resourcesnyc.org

Singergia/Metropolitan Parent Center
15 West 65th Street, 6th Floor
New York, NY 10023
(212) 496-1300
E-mail: Sinergia@panix.com
Web: http://www.panix.com/
~sinergia

Parent to Parent of New York State
500 Balltown Road
Schenectady, NY 12304
(800) 305-8817; (518) 381-4350
E-mail: Parent2Par@aol.com
Web: http://www.
parenttoparentnys.org

Family Support Project for the
Developmental Disabilities
North Central Bronx Hospital
3424 Kossuth Avenue, Room 15A10
Bronx, NY 10467
(718) 519-4797

The New York Autism Network
Department of Psychology
University at Albany, SUNY
Albany, New York 12222
(518) 442-5132;
(518) 442-4867 (Fax)
Web: http://www.albany.edu/psy/
autism/autism.html

Autistic Services, Inc.
169 Sheridan Parkside Drive
Tonawanda, NY 14150
(888)-AUTISM4; (716) 873-6997;
(716) 873-7428 (Fax)

NYSArc
393 Delaware Ave.
Delmar, NY 12054
518-439-8311

North Carolina
Exceptional Children Division
Department of Public Instruction
301 N. Wilmington St., Education
Bldg., #670
Raleigh, NC 27601-2825
(919) 715-1565
E-mail: lharris@dpi.state.nc.us

Child & Adolescent Services
Developmental Disabilities Services
Section
Division of MH, Developmental
Disabilities & Substance Abuse
Services
Department of Health and Human
Services
3006 Mail Service Center
Raleigh, NC 27699-3006
(919) 733-3654
E-mail: Duncan.Munn@ncmail.net
Web: http://www.dhhs.state.nc.us

NC Council on Developmental
Disabilities
1001 Navahoe Drive, Suite GL-103
Raleigh, NC 27609
(800) 357-6916; (919) 850-2833
E-mail: Holly.Riddle@ncmail.net
Web: http://www.nc-ddc.org

Governor's Advocacy Council for
Persons with Disabilities
Bryan Building
2113 Cameron Street, Suite 218
Raleigh, NC 27605
(919) 733-9250;
(800) 821-6922 (in NC)
E-mail: allen_perry@
mail.doa.state.nc.us
Web: http://www.doa.state.nc.us/
doa/gacpd/gacpd.htm

Children and Youth Branch
Women's and Children's Health
Section Center
Department of Health and Human
Services
1916 Mail Service Center
1330 St. Mary's Street
Raleigh, NC 27699-1916
(919) 733-7437
E-mail: tom.vitaglione@
ncmail.net

Autism Society of North Carolina
505 Oberlin Road, Suite 230
Raleigh, NC 27605-1345
(800) 442-2762; (919) 743-0204

Asheville TEACCH Center
168-B South Liberty Street
Asheville, NC 28801
(828) 251-6319;
(828) 251-6358 (Fax)
E-mail: SLove5@juno.com
Web: http://www.unc.edu/
depts/teacch/

Chapel Hill TEACCH Center
400 Roberson Street
(919) 966-5156;
(919) 966-4003 (Fax)
E-mail: Lee_Marcus@unc.edu
Web: http://www.unc.edu/
depts/teacch/

Charlotte TEACCH Center
James K. Polk Building
500 West Trade Street, Suite 361
Charlotte, NC 28202-1334
(704) 342-6346;
(704) 342-6417 (Fax)

E-mail: AJack5941@aol.com
Web: http://www.unc.edu/
depts/teacch/

Fayetteville TEACCH Center
806 Stamper Road, Suite 101
Fayetteville, NC 28303
(910) 437-2517;
(910) 437-2520 (Fax)
E-mail: SKROUPA@aol.com
Web: http://www.unc.edu/
depts/teacch/

Greensboro TEACCH Center
Self Help Public Interest Center
122 North Elm Street, Suite 920
Greensboro, NC 27401
(336) 334-5773;
(336) 334-5811 (Fax)
E-mail: JPopeNC@AOL.com
Web: http://www.unc.edu/
depts/teacch/grns_c.htm

Greenville TEACCH Center
South Hall Professional Center
108-D West Fire Tower Road
Winterville, NC 28590
(252) 830-3300;
(252) 830-3322 (Fax)
E-mail: pimayfie@
eastnet.educ.ecu.edu
Web: http://www.unc.edu/
depts/teacch/

Wilmington TEACCH Center
1320 South 16th Street
Wilmington, NC 28401
(910) 251-5700;
(910) 251-5809 (Fax)
E-mail: teacch@wilmington.net
Web: http://www.unc.edu/
depts/teacch/

Clinical Center for the Study of
Development and Learning
CB# 7255
University of North Carolina
Chapel Hill, NC 27599-7255
(919) 966-5171
E-mail: cdlweb@css.unc.edu
Web: http://www.cdl.unch.unc.edu

Exceptional Children's Assistance
Center (ECAC)
P.O. Box 16
Davidson, NC 28036
(704) 892-1321;
(800) 962-6817 (in NC)
E-mail: ECAC1@aol.com
Web: http://www.
ECAC-parentcenter.org

Family Support Network of North
Carolina/Central Directory of
Resources
CB #7340
University of NC at Chapel Hill
Chapel Hill, NC 27599-7340
(800) 852-0042; (919) 966-2841
E-mail: cdr@med.unc.edu
Web: http://www.med.unc.edu/
commedu/familysu

The Arc of North Carolina
16 Rowan Street
P. O. Box 20545
Raleigh, NC 27619
(919) 782-4632
E-mail: Rsewell108@aol.com

North Dakota
Special Education, Department of
Public Instruction
600 East Boulevard Avenue,
 Dept. 201
Bismarck, ND 58505-0440
(701) 328-2277;
(701) 328-4920 (TTY)
E-mail: brutten@
mail.dpi.state.nd.us
Web: http://www.dpi.state.nd.us/
dpi/speced/index.htm

(Ages 3 through 5)
Special Education Div., Dept. of Public
Instruction
600 E. Boulevard Avenue
Bismarck, ND 58505-0440
(701) 328-2277
E-mail: jkolberg@
mail.dpi.state.nd.us

(Birth through 2)
Developmental Disabilities Unit
North Dakota Department of Human
Services
600 S. 2nd Street, Suite 1A
Bismarck, ND 58504-5729
(701) 328-8936;
(800) 755-8529 (in ND)
E-mail: sobald@state.nd.us

Disabilities Services Division
ND Department of Human Services
600 S. 2nd Street, Suite 1B
Bismarck, ND 58504-5729
(701) 328-8950; (701) 328-8968
(TTY); (800) 755-2745 (in ND)

North Dakota Developmental
Disabilities Council
Department of Human Services
600 S. 2nd Street, Suite 1B
Bismarck, ND 58504-5729
(701) 328-8953
E-mail: sowalt@state.nd.us

Protection & Advocacy Project
400 East Broadway, Suite 616
Bismarck, ND 58501-4073
(701) 328-2950; (800) 472-2670 (in
ND); (800) 366-6888 (ND Relay)
E-mail: panda@state.nd.us
Web: http://www.ndcd.org/
ndcpd/uapdis/pa.html

Children's Special Health Services
Department of Human Services
State Capitol, 600 East Blvd. Avenue,
Dept. 325
Bismarck, ND 58505-0269
(701) 328-2436;
(800) 755-2714 (in ND)
E-mail: SONELR@state.nd.us

North Dakota Center for Persons with
Disabilities
Minot State University
500 University Avenue West
Minot, ND 58707
(800) 233-1737;
(701) 858-3580

E-mail: ndcpd@
farside.cc.misu.nodak.edu
Web: http://www.ndcpd.org

Pathfinder Family Center
1600 2nd Avenue, S.W., Suite 19
Minot, ND 58701-3459
(701) 837-7500; (701) 837-7501
(TTY); (800) 245-5840 (in ND)
E-mail: ndpath01@
minot.ndak.net
Web: http://www.ndcd.org/
pathfinder

North Dakota Parent Assistance and
Supportive Schools (NDPASS)
1600 2nd Avenue, S.W., Suite 19
Minot, ND 58701-3459
(701) 837-7510;
(888) 763-7277 (in ND)
E-mail: ndpass1@minot.com
Web: http://www.ndpass.minot.com

Family to Family Support Network
University of North Dakota School of
Medicine
P.O. Box 9037
Grand Forks, ND 58202-9037
(701) 777-2359;
(888) 434-7436
E-mail: F2F@
medicine.nodak.edu/f2f

The Arc of North Dakota
418 E. Rosser Ave., Suite 110
P.O. Box 2776
Bismarck, ND 58502-2776
(701)223-5349

Northern Marina Island
Northern Mariana Island
Special Education, Public School
System
P.O. Box 1370 CK
Saipan, MP 96950
(670) 664-3730;
(670) 664-3796 (Fax)

Early Childhood Education
Public School System

P.O. Box 1370 CK
Saipan, MP 96950
(670) 664-3751/3754;
(670) 664-3796 (Fax)

Governor's Developmental Disabilities
Council
P.O. Box 2565
Saipan, MP 96950
(670) 322-3014;
(670) 322-4168 (Fax)
E-mail: dd.council@saipan.com

Northern Mariana's Protection and
Advocacy System
P.O. Box 3529 CK
Saipan, MP 96950
(670) 235-7273;
(670) 235-7275 (Fax)

Department of Public Health Services
P.O. Box 409 CK
Saipan, MP 96950
(670) 234-8950;
(670) 8930 (Fax)

Ohio
Division of Special Education
Ohio Department of Education
933 High Street
Worthington, OH 43085-4017
(614) 466-2650
E-mail: se_herner@ode.ohio.gov
Web: http://www.ode.ohio.gov/
http://www/se/se.html

(Ages 3 through 5)
Division of Early Childhood Education
Ohio Department of Education
65 South Front Street, Room 309
Columbus, OH 43215-4183
(614) 466-0224
E-mail: ece_wiechel@ode.ohio.gov

(Birth through 2)
Bureau of Early Intervention Services
Ohio Department of Health
P.O. Box 118, 246 North High Street,
5th Floor
Columbus, OH 43266-0118

(614) 644-8389
E-mail: dwright@
gw.odh.state.oh.us

Rehabilitation Services Commission
400 East Campus View Blvd.
Columbus, OH 43235-4604
(614) 438-1210 (V/TTY)
E-mail: RSC_RLR@ohio.gov
Web: http://www.state.oh.us/RSC

Ohio Developmental Disabilities
Planning Council
8 East Long Street, Atlas Bldg., 12th
Floor
Columbus, OH 43266-0415
(614) 466-5205
E-mail: david.zwyer@
dmr.state.oh.us
Web: http://www.state.oh.us/ddc

Ohio Legal Rights Services
8 East Long Street, 5th Floor
Columbus, OH 43215
(614) 466-7264; (614) 728-2553
(TTY); (800) 282-9181 (in OH)

Bureau for Children with Medical
Handicaps
Ohio Department of Health
P.O. Box 1603
Columbus, OH 43216-1603
(800) 755-4769; (614) 466-1549
E-mail: JBryant@gw.odh.state.us
Web: http://www.odh.state.oh.us

Cincinnati Center for Developmental
Disorders, UAP
Pavilion Building
3333 Burnet Avenue
Cincinnati, OH 45229-3039
(513) 636-8383

The Nisonger Center
Ohio State University
1581 Dodd Drive
Columbus, OH 43210-1296
(614) 292-8365

OH Coalition for the Education of
Children with Disabilities
Bank One Building

165 West Center Street, Suite 302
Marion, OH 43302-3741
(740) 382-5452;
(800) 374-2806 (V/TTY)
E-mail: ocecdmb@gte.net
Web: http://taalliance.org/
ptis/regohio

Child Advocacy Center
1821 Summit Rd., #110
Cincinnati, OH 45237
(513) 821-2400 (V/TTY)
E-mail: CADCenter@aol.com

OH Coalition for the Education of
Children with Disabilities
165 W. Center Street, Suite 302
Bank One Building
Marion, OH 43302-3741
(800) 374-2806
E-mail: ocecd@gte.net
Web: http://taalliance.org/
ptis/regohio

Ohio Society of Northwest Ohio
One Stranahan Square
Suite 540
Toledo, OH 43604-1900
(419) 242-9587;
(419) 242-0631 (Fax)

The Arc of Ohio
1335 Dublin Road, Suite 205-C
Columbus, OH 43215
(614) 487-4720
E-mail: arcoh@coil.com

Oklahoma
Special Education Services
Department of Education
2500 N. Lincoln Boulevard
Oklahoma City, OK 73105-4599
(405) 521-3351
E-mail: darla_griffin@
mail.sde.state.ok.us

(Ages 3 through 5)
Special Education Section
Department of Education
2500 North Lincoln Blvd.,
Room 411

Oklahoma City, OK 73105-4599
(405) 521-3351
E-mail: Amber_Villines-Hackney@
mail.sde.state.ok.us

(Birth through 2)
Sooner Start
Special Education Section
Department of Education
2500 North Lincoln Blvd.,
Room 411
Oklahoma City, OK 73105-4599
(405) 521-4880
E-mail: mark_sharp@
mail.sde.state.ok.us
Web: http://www.sde.state.ok.us/
pro/ei.html

Department of Rehabilitation Services
3535 NW 58th, Suite 500
Oklahoma City, OK 73112
(405) 951-3400
E-mail: LSParker@drs.state.ok.us

OK Developmental Disabilities Council
3033 N. Walnut, Suite 105E
P.O. Box 25352
Oklahoma City, OK 73125
(800) 836-4470; (405) 528-4984
E-mail: OPCDevelopmental
Disabilities@aol.com

Oklahoma Disability Law Center, Inc.
2915 Classen Blvd.
300 Cameron Building
Oklahoma City, OK 73106
(405) 525-7755; (800) 880-7755 (in
OK)
E-mail: kbower1@flash.net
Web: http://www.flash.net/
~odlcokc

Family Support Services
Department of Human Services
P.O. Box 25352
Oklahoma City, OK 73125
(405) 521-3076

UAP of Oklahoma
University of Oklahoma Health
Sciences Center
P.O. Box 26901, ROB 316

Oklahoma City, OK 73190-3042
(405) 271-2688; (405) 271-4500;
(405) 271-1464 (TTY)
E-mail: valerie-williams@
ouhsc.edu

Parents Reaching Out in OK (PRO-
Oklahoma)
1917 South Harvard Avenue
Oklahoma City, OK 73128
(405) 681-9710; (800) PL94-142
E-mail: prook1@aol.com
Web: http://www.ucp.org/
probase.htm

Oregon
Office of Special Education
Department of Education
255 Capitol Street NE
Salem, OR 97310-0203
(503) 378-3598;
(503) 378-2892 (TTY)
E-mail: steve.johnson@state.or.us
Web: http://www.ode.state.or.us/
sped/index.htm

(Ages 3 through 5)
Office of Special Education,
Department of Education
255 Capitol Street N.E.
Salem, OR 97310-0203
(503) 378-3598
Web: http://www.ode.state.or.us

(Birth through 2)
Office of Special Education
Department of Education
255 Capitol Street N.E.
Salem, OR 97310-0203
(503) 378-3598
Web: http://www.ode.state.or.us

Vocational Rehabilitation Division
Department of Human Services
500 Summer Street, NE
Salem, OR 97310-1018
(503) 945-5880
E-mail: sally.s.zuelke@state.or.us

Oregon Developmental Disabilities
Council
540 24th Place, NE

Salem, OR 97301-4517
(503) 945-9941;
(800) 292-4154 (in OR)
E-mail: oddc@oddc.org
Web: http://www.oddc.org

Oregon Advocacy Center
620 SW 5th Avenue, Fifth Floor
Portland, OR 97204-1428
(503) 243-2081;
(503) 323-9161 (TTY)
E-mail: oradvocacy@aol.com

Child Development & Rehab. Center
Oregon Health Sciences University
P.O. Box 574
Portland, OR 97207-0574
(503) 494-8362
E-mail: sellsc@OHSU.edu

State Services for Autism
255 Capitol Street, NE
Salem, OR 97310-0203
(503) 585-0855
E-mail: marilyn.gense@state.or.us
Web: http://www.ode.state.or.us

Center on Human Development—
Clinical Services
1265 University of Oregon
Eugene, OR 97403-1265
(503) 346-3591
Web: http://darkwing.uoregon.
edu/~uap/

Child Development & Rehabilitation
Center
OR Health Sciences University
P.O. Box 574
Portland, OR 97207-0574
(503) 494-8364
E-mail: oidd@ohsu.edu
Web: http://www.ohsu.edu/cdrc/uap/

Oregon COPE Project (Coalition in OR
for Parent Education)
999 Locust Street, N.E.
Salem, OR 97303
(503) 581-8156;
(888) 505-COPE (in OR)
E-mail: orcope@open.org
Web: http://www.open.org/orcope

Autism Society of Oregon
P.O. Box 13884
Salem, OR 97309
E-mail: aso@teleport.com
The Arc of Oregon
1745 State Street
Salem, OR 97301
(503) 581-2726
E-mail: arcoforg@open.org

Pennsylvania
Bureau of Special Education
Department of Education
333 Market Street, 7th Floor
Harrisburg, PA 17126-0333
(717) 783-6913
Special Education Consultline: (800)
879-2301 (V/TTY)
Web: http://www.cas.psu.edu/
pde.html

(Ages 3 through 5)
Division of Early Intervention
Bureau of Special Education
Department of Education
333 Market Street, 7th Floor
Harrisburg, PA 17126-0333
(717) 772-2647
E-mail: rprice@ed.state.pa.us

(Birth through 2)
Children's Services Division, Office of
Mental Retardation
Department of Public Welfare
P.O. Box 2675
Harrisburg, PA 17105-2675
(717) 783-7213

Office of Vocational Rehabilitation
Department of Labor & Industry
1300 Labor & Industry Bldg.
Seventh and Forster Streets
Harrisburg, PA 17120
(717) 787-5244
E-mail: saldrete@dli.state.pa.us

Developmental Disabilities Planning
Council
561 Forum Bldg., Commonwealth
Avenue
Harrisburg, PA 17120
(717) 787-6057

E-mail: gmulholland@
dpw.state.pa.us

PA Protection & Advocacy Inc.
116 Pine Street
Harrisburg, PA 17101
(717) 236-8110;
(800) 692-7443 (in PA)
E-mail: ppa@ppainc.org

Division of Special Health Care
Programs
Department of Health, Room 724
P.O. Box 90
Harrisburg, PA 17108
(717) 783-5436; (800) 852-4453
E-mail: gstock@health.state.pa.us

Institute on Disabilities, UAP
Temple University, Ritter Annex, Room
423
1301 Cecil B. Moore Avenue
Philadelphia, PA 19122
(215) 204-1356 (V/TTY)
E-mail: dianeb@
astro.ocis.temple.edu
Web: http://www.temple.edu/
inst_disabilities

John Merck Program
Western Psychiatric Institute and
Clinic
University of Pittsburgh Health System
3811 O'Hara Street
Pittsburgh, PA 15213
(412) 624-2331;
(412) 624-2282 (Fax)
E-mail: lubetskymj@
msx.upmc.edu

Children's Seashore House of the
Children's Hospital of Philadelphia
3405 Civic Center Boulevard
Philadelphia, PA 19104-4388
(215) 590-7466
E-mail: coplan@email.CHOP.edu

Parents Union for Public Schools
The Philadelphia Building
1315 Walnut Street, Suite 1124
Philadelphia, PA 19107

(215) 546-1166
E-mail: ParentsU@aol.com

Parent Education Network
2107 Industrial Highway
York, PA 17402
(717) 600-0100; (800) 522-5827 (in
PA); (800) 441-5028 (Spanish)
E-mail: pen@parentednet.org
Web: http://www.parentednet.org

Parent to Parent of Pennsylvania
150 South Progress Avenue
Harrisburg, PA 17109
(800) 986-4550; (717) 540-4722;
(717)-540-7603 (Fax)
E-mail: bril1134@cdc.gov
Web: http://www.enter.net/
~kidstogether/p2p.html

Autism Society of Pittsburgh
500-G Garden City Drive
Monroeville, PA 15146-1128
(412) 856-7223;
(412) 856-7428 (Fax)
E-mail: http://www.asapgh@
aol.com
Web: http://www.trfn.clpgh.org/
autism

The Arc—Pennsylvania
Building #2, Suite 221
2001 N. Front St
Harrisburg, PA 17102
(717) 234-2621

Puerto Rico
Assistant Secretary of Special
Education
Department of Education
P.O. Box 190759
San Juan, PR 00919-0759
(787) 759-7228;
(787) 753-0015 (Fax)

(Ages 3 through 5)
Preschool Programs
Department of Education
P.O. Box 190759
San Juan, PR 00919
(787) 753-6594

(Birth through 2)
Infants & Toddlers Program
Department of Health
P.O. Box 190759
San Juan, PR 00936
(787) 274-5659
E-mail: nperez@salud.gov.pr

Vocational Rehabilitation
Administration
Department of the Family
P.O. Box 191118
San Juan, PR 00919-1118
(787) 729-0160
E-mail: vra@vrapr.gov
Web: http://www.vrapr.gov

Puerto Rico Developmental Disabilities
Council
P.O. Box 9543
San Juan, PR 00908
(787) 722-0595; (787) 722-0590
E-mail: cedd@jp.gov.pr

Office of the Ombudsman for Persons
with Disabilities
P.O. Box 4234
San Juan, PR 00940-1309
(787) 725-2333
E-mail: vcruz@oppe.prstar.net

Maternal & Child Health & Crippled
Children's Programs
Department of Health
Call Box 70184
San Juan, PR 00936
(809) 274-5660 or 5659

Parents Society for Children & Adults
with Autism in PR
Autism Society of America Chapter
P.O. Box 190594
San Juan, PR 00919-0594
(787) 723-4566

Asociación de Padres Pro Bienestar de
Niños con Impedidos de PR (APNI)
P.O. Box 21301
San Juan, PR 00928-1301
(800) 981-8492; (787) 763-4665;

(787) 753-7185 (TTY);
(800) 981-8393 (TTY)
E-mail: apnipr@prtc.net

Rhode Island
Office of Special Needs
Department of Education, Shepard
Building
255 Westminster Street, Room 400
Providence, RI 02903-3400
(401) 222-4600
E-mail: ride0032@ride.ri.net

(Ages 3 through 5)
Offices of Integrated Social Services
Shepard Building
255 Westminster Street
Providence, RI 02903-3414
(401) 222-4600

(Birth through 2)
Division of Family Health
State Department of Health
3 Capital Hill, Rm. 302
Providence, RI 02908-5097
(401) 222-4612
E-mail: ronc@doh.state.ri.us

Office of Rehabilitation Services
Department of Human Services
40 Fountain Street
Providence, RI 02903
(401) 421-7005
E-mail: rcarroll@ors.state.ri.us
Web: http://www.ors.state.ri.us

R.I. Developmental
Disabilities Council
14 Harrington Road
Cranston, RI 02920
(401) 464-3191;
(401) 462-3191 (Fax)
E-mail: riddc@riddc.org
Web: http://www.riddc.org

Rhode Island Disability
Law Center
349 Eddy Street
Providence, RI 02903
(401) 831-3150; (401) 831-5335
TTY); (800) 733-5332 (in RI)

Office for Children with Special Health Care Needs
Department of Health
3 Capitol Hill
Providence, RI 02908
(401) 222-4612; (401) 222-2312
E-mail: ronc@doh.state.ri.us
Web: http://www.health.state.ri.us

UAP of Rhode Island
600 Mount Pleasant Avenue
Providence, RI 02908
(401) 456-8072;
(401) 456-8773 (TTY)
E-mail: aantosh@ric.edu

Bradley Hospital
1011 Veterans Memorial Parkway
East Providence, RI 02915
(401) 432-1189;
(401) 438-5149 (Fax)
E-mail: rbarrett@lifespan.org

The Groden Center
86 Mt. Hope Avenue
Providence, RI 02906
(401) 274-6310;
(401) 421-3280 (Fax)
E-mail: grodencenter@
grodencenter.org
Web: http://www.grodencenter.org

RI Parent Info Network (RIPIN)
175 Main Street
Pawtucket, RI 02860
(401) 727-4144;
(800) 464-3399 (in RI)
E-mail: ripin@ripin.org
Web: http://www.ripin.org

Rhode Island Arc
99 Bald Hill Road
Cranston, RI 02920
(401) 463-9191

South Carolina
State Department of Education
Office of Exceptional Children
1429 Senate Street, Room 808
Columbia, SC 29201
(803) 734-8806
E-mail: ospann@sde.state.sc.us

(Ages 3 through 5)
State Department of Education
Office of Exceptional Children
1429 Senate Street, 8th Floor
Columbia, SC 29201
(803) 734-8811
E-mail: njenkins@sde.state.sc.us

(Birth through 2)
Dept. of Health & Environmental Control/Baby Net
Robert Mills Complex, Box 101106
Columbia, SC 29211
(803) 898-0591
E-mail: hartkf@
colum61.dhec.state.sc.us
Web: http://www.scbabynet.org

Vocational Rehabilitation Department
1410 Boston Avenue, P.O. Box 15
West Columbia, SC 29171-0015
(803) 896-6504

SC Developmental Disabilities Council
1205 Pendleton Street, Room 372
Columbia, SC 29201
(803) 734-0465
E-mail: clang@govoepp.state.sc.us

P&A for People with Disabilities
3710 Landmark Drive, Suite 208
Columbia, SC 29204
(803) 782-0639; (800) 922-5225 (in SC); (800) 531-9781 (Spanish)
E-mail: scpa@sc-online.net

Children's Rehabilitative Services Branch
Department of Health & Environmental Control
1751 Calhoun Street, Box 101106
Columbia, SC 29211
(803) 737-4072

South Carolina Autism Society
229 Parson Street, Suite A-1
W. Columbia, SC 29169
(803) 794-2300; (800) 438-4790
E-mail: scas@scautism.org

University of South Carolina
School of Medicine

Center for Disability Resources
8301 Sarrow Road
Columbia, SC 29208
(803) 935-5231
E-mail: richardf@cdd.sc.edu

PRO-PARENTS of South Carolina
2712 Middleburg Drive, Suite 203
Columbia, SC 29204
(803) 779-3859;
(800) 759-4776 (in SC)
E-mail: PROparents@aol.com

South Carolina Services Information
System
Center for Disability Resources
University of South Carolina School of
Medicine
8301 Sarrow Road
Columbia, SC 29208
(800) 922-1107; (803) 935-5231;
(803) 935-5300 (Columbia Area)
E-mail: deniser@cdd.sc.edu

South Dakota
Office of Special Education
700 Governors Drive
Pierre, SD 57501-2291
(605) 773-3678;
(605) 773-6302 (TTY)
E-mail: debb@deca.state.sd.us
Web: http://www.state.sd.us/
deca/special/special.htm

(Ages 3 through 5)
Office of Special Education
700 Governors Drive
Pierre, SD 57501-2291
(605) 773-3678

(Birth through 2)
Education Program
Assistant Manager
Office of Special Education
700 Governor's Drive
Pierre, SD 57501-2291
(605) 773-3678

Division of Rehabilitation Services
Hillsview Plaza, E. Hwy 34
500 East Capitol

Pierre, SD 57501-5070
(605) 773-3195
Web: http://www.state.sd.us/
state/executive/dhs/drs/drs.htm

SD Governor's Planning Council on
Developmental Disabilities
Hillsview Plaza, E. Hwy 34
c/o 500 East Capitol
Pierre, SD 57501-5070
(605) 773-6369
E-mail: arlene.poncelet@
state.sd.us
Web: http://www.state.sd.us/state/
executive/dhs/ddc/council.htm

South Dakota Advocacy Services
221 S. Central Avenue
Pierre, SD 57501
(605) 224-8294;
(800) 658-4782 (in SD)
E-mail: sdas@sdadvocacy.com
Web: http://www.sdadvocacy.com

Children's Special Health Services
Health & Medical Services
Department of Health
615 E. Fourth Street
Pierre, SD 57501
(605) 773-3737
E-mail: nancyh@doh.state.sd.us

South Dakota University Affiliated
Program
Health Science Center
1400 West 22nd Street
Sioux Falls, SD 57105
(800) 658-3080; (605) 357-1439

SD Parent Connection
3701 W. 49th Street, Suite 200B
Sioux Falls, SD 57106
(605) 361-3171;
(800) 640-4553 (in SD)
E-mail: bschreck@dakota.net
Web: http://www.taalliance.org/
ptis/sd/

Parent to Parent, Inc.
3701 West 49th Street, Suite 200-B
Sioux Falls, SD 57106

(605) 361-9838;
(800) 658-5411 (in SD)

The Arc of South Dakota
208 W Capitol
P. O. Box 220
Pierre, SD 57501-0220
(605) 224-8211

Tennessee
Division of Special Education
Department of Education
Andrew Johnson Tower, 5th Floor
710 James Robertson Pkwy.
Nashville, TN 37243-0380
(615) 741-2851
E-mail: jfisher@mail.state.tn.us
Web: http://www.state.tn.us/
education/msped.htm

Division of Rehabilitation Services
Department of Human Svcs.
400 Deaderick Street, 15th Floor
Nashville, TN 37248-0060
(615) 313-4714
E-mail: carlbrown@mail.state.tn.us

Tennessee Developmental Disabilities
Council
Cordell Hull Building, 5th Floor
425 5th Avenue North
Nashville, TN 37243-0675
(615) 532-6615
E-mail: tnddc@mail.state.tn.us

Tennessee Protection and Advocacy
P.O. Box 121257
Nashville, TN 37212
(615) 298-1080; (800) 342-1660 (in
TN); (615) 298-2471 (TTY)

Children's Special Services
Department of Health, Title 5 CSHCN
Cordell Hull Building, 5th Floor
425 5th Avenue North
Nashville, TN 37247-4750
(615) 741-0310
E-mail: jcundall@mail.state.tn.us
Web: http://www.state.tn.us/health

Boling Center for
Developmental Disabilities
The University of Tennessee, Memphis
711 Jefferson Avenue
Memphis, TN 38105
(901) 448-6512; (888) 572-2249
(901) 448-4677 (TTY)
E-mail: fpalmer@utmem.edu
Web: http://www.utmem.edu/
bcdd/boling.html

Support and Training for Exceptional
Parents (STEP)
424 East Bernard Avenue, Suite 3
Greeneville, TN 37745
(423) 639-0125; (800) 280-7837
(Toll-free in TN)
(423) 636-8217 (TTY)
E-mail: tnstep@aol.com
Web: http://www.tnstep.org

Parents Encouraging Parents (PEP)
Program
Cordell Hull Building, 5th Floor
426 5th Avenue North
Nashville, TN 37247-4750
(615) 741-0353
E-mail: srothacker@
mail.state.tn.us

The Arc of Tennessee
1805 Hayes, Suite 100
Nashville, TN 37203
615-327-0294
arctn@worldnet.att.net

Texas
Texas Education Agency
Division of Special Education
1701 North Congress Avenue
Austin, TX 78701-1494
(512) 463-9414
E-mail: sped@tea.tetn.net
Web: http://www.tea.state.tx.us/
special.ed

(Ages 3 through 5)
Special Education Programs
Texas Education Agency
1701 North Congress Avenue
Austin, TX 78701-1494

(512) 463-9414
E-mail: kclayton@
tmail.tea.state.tx.us

(Birth through 2)
Early Childhood Intervention
4900 N. Lamar Boulevard
Austin, TX 78751-2399
(800) 250-2246; (512) 424-6754
E-mail: mary.elder@eci.state.tx.us
Web: http://www.eci.state.tx.us

Texas Rehabilitation Commission
4900 North Lamar, Room 7102
Austin, TX 78751-2399
(512) 424-4001
E-mail: max.arrell.rehab@
rehab.state.tx.us

Texas Council for Developmental
Disabilities
4900 North Lamar Blvd.
Austin, TX 78751-2399
(800) 262-0334; (512) 424-4080;
(512) 424-4099 (TTY)
E-mail: TXDDC@rehab.state.tx.us
Web: http://www.rehab.state.tx.us/
tpcdd/index.htm

Advocacy, Inc.
7800 Shoal Creek Blvd., Suite 171-E
Austin, TX 78757
(512) 454-4816;
(800) 252-9108 (in TX)

CSHCN Planning & Policy
Development
Bureau of Children's Health
TX Department of Health
1100 West 49th Street
Austin, TX 78756-3179
(512) 458-7355
E-mail: susan.penfield@
tdh.state.tx.us

Texas UAP for Developmental
Disabilities
University of Texas at Austin
SZB 252/D5100

Austin, TX 78712-1290
(800) 828-7839; (512) 471-7621;
(512) 471-1844 (TTY)
E-mail: pseay@mail.utexas.edu
Web: http://uap.edb.utexas.edu

Partners Resource Network
1090 Longfellow Drive, Suite B
Beaumont, TX 77706-4819
(409) 898-4684;
(800) 866-4726 (in TX)
E-mail: txprn@juno.com
Web: http://partnerstx.org

Grassroots Consortium
6202 Belmark
P.O. Box 61628
Houston, TX 77208-1628
(713) 643-9576
E-mail: SpecKids@aol.com

Project PODER
1017 N. Main Avenue, Suite 207
San Antonio, TX 78212
(210) 222-2637;
(800) 682-9747 (in TX)
E-mail: poder@tfepoder.org
Web: http://www.tfepoder.org

Parents Supporting Parents Network
601 N. Texas Blvd., Suite C
Weslaco, TX 78596
(888) 857-8668; (956) 447-8408
E-mail: weslaco@gte.net

The Arc of Texas
P.O. Box 5368
Jefferson Bldg, 2nd Fl
Austin, TX 78763
(512)454-6694

Utah
At Risk and Special Education Services
State Office of Education
250 East 500 South
Salt Lake City, UT 84111-3204
(801) 538-7706
E-mail: mtaylor@usoe.k12.ut.us
Web: http://www.usoe.k12.ut.us/sars

(Ages 3 through 5)
Special Education Services Unit, State
Office of Education
250 East Fifth South
Salt Lake City, UT 84111
(801) 538-7708
E-mail: bbroadbe@usoe.k12.ut.us
Web: http://www.usoe.k12.ut.us

(Birth through 2)
Utah Dept. of Health
Community & Family Health Services
Children with Special Health Care
Needs - BWEIP
Box 144720
Salt Lake City, UT 84114-4720
(801) 584-8226; (801) 584-8496
E-mail: sord@doh.state.ut.us
Web: http://hlunix.hl.state.ut.us/
cfhs/cshcn/babywatch/default.htm

Utah State Office of Rehabilitation
250 East 500 South
Salt Lake City, UT 84111
(801) 538-7530 (V/TTY)
E-mail: bpeterse@usor.state.ut.us
Web: http://www.usor.state.ut.us

UT Governor's Council for People with
Disabilities
555 East 300 South, Suite 201
Salt Lake City, UT 84102
(801) 533-4128
E-mail: gcpd@state.ut.us
Web: http://www.gcpd.state.ut.us

Disability Law Center
455 East 400 South, Suite 410
Salt Lake City, UT 84111
(801) 363-1347;
(800) 662-9080 (in UT) (V/TTY)
E-mail: info@
disabilitylawcenter.org
Web: http://www.
disabilitylawcenter.org

Utah Department of Health
Community & Family Health Services
Children with Special
Health Care Needs
44 North Medical Drive
P.O. Box 144610

Salt Lake City, UT 84114-4610
(801) 584-8240
E-mail: ftait@doh.state.ut.us

Center for Persons with Disabilities,
UAP
Utah State University
Logan, UT 84322-6800
(801) 797-1981
E-mail: marv@cpd2.usu.edu
Web: http://www.cpd.usu.edu

University of Utah Autism Clinic
546 Chipeta Way, Suite 2264
Salt Lake City, UT 84108
(801) 585-1212;
(801) 585-9096 (Fax)

Autism Society of Utah
668 South 1300 East
Salt Lake City, UT 84102
(801) 583-7049

Utah Parent Center
2290 East 4500 South, Suite 110
Salt Lake City, UT 84117
(801) 272-1051 (V/TTY); (800) 468-
1160 (in UT)
E-mail: upc@inconnect.com
Web: http://www.utahparentcenter.org

Hope—A Parent to Parent Network
2290 East 4500 South, Suite 110
Salt Lake City, UT 84117
(801) 856-9795;
(800) 468-1160 (in UT)

Access Utah Network
(Statewide Information and Referral
for Disability Issues)
555 East 300 South #201
Salt Lake City, UT 84102
(800) 333-8824 (outside SLC); (801)
533-4636 (SLC area)
E-mail: accessut@state.ut.us
Web: http://www.accessut.org

The Arc of Utah
455 East 400 South, Suite 300
Salt Lake City, UT 84111
(801) 364-5060
E-mail: Arcutah@burgoyne.co

Vermont
Family & Educational
Support Team
120 State Street, State Office Building
Montpelier, VT 05620-2501
(802) 828-2755
Web: http://www.state.vt.us/
educ/sped.htm

(Ages 3 through 5)
Special Education Unit, Department of
Education
120 State Street
Montpelier, VT 05620-2501
(802) 828-5115
E-mail: kandrews@doe.state.vt.us
Web: http://www.state.vt.us/educ

(Birth through 2)
Family, Infant and Toddlers Project
P.O. Box 70
Burlington, VT 05402
(802) 651-1786
E-mail: bmaccar@vdh.state.vt.us

Vocational Rehabilitation Division
Dept. of Aging & Disabilities, Agency
of Human Services
103 South Main Street
Waterbury, VT 05671-2303
(802) 241-2186
E-mail: carmen@dad.state.vt.us
Web: http://www.dad.state.vt.us/

Vermont Developmental Disabilities
Council
103 South Main Street
Waterbury, VT 05671-0206
(802) 241-2612 (TTY)
E-mail: tomp@
wpgate1.ahs.state.vt.us
Web: http://www.ahs.state.vt.us/
vtddc

Disability Law Project
57 N. Main Street
Rutland, VT 05701
(800) 769-7459; (802) 775-0021
E-mail: nbreiden@vtlegalaid.org

Vermont Protection and Advocacy
15 E. State Street, #101
Montpelier, VT 05602
(802) 229-1355;
(800) 834-7890 (in VT)
E-mail: info@vtpa.org

Division for Children with Special
Health Needs
Department of Health
108 Cherry St, P.O. Box 70
Burlington, VT 05402
(802) 863-7338
E-mail: chassle@vdh.state.vt.us

Center on Disability and Community
Inclusion
The University Affiliated Program of
Vermont
University of Vermont
499C Waterman Building
Burlington, VT 05405-0160
(802) 656-4031
E-mail: wfox@zoo.uvm.edu
Web: http://www.uvm.edu/
~uapvt/index.html

VT Parent Information Center
Chace Mill
1 Mill St., Suite A7
Burlington, VT 05401
(802) 658-5315;
(800) 639-7170 (in VT)
E-mail: vpic@together.net
Web: http://www.together.net/
~vpic

Virgin Islands
Special Education/Department of
Education
44-46 Kongens Gade
Charlotte Amalie
St. Thomas, VI 00802
(340) 774-4399

(Ages 3 through 5)
Special Education/Department of
Education
#44-46 Kongens Gade
St. Thomas, VI 00802
(340) 776-5802

(Birth through 2)
Division of Maternal and Child Health
Birth to Three Program
Department of Health
Charles Harwood Hospital
3500 Estate Richmond
St. Croix, VI 00820
(340) 773-1311, ext. 3006
E-mail: kimmie@virginislands.com

Division Disabilities and Rehabilitation
Services
Knud Hansen Complex, Building A
1303 Hospital Ground
Charlotte Amalie
St. Thomas, VI 00802
(340) 774-0930, ext. 4191

Developmental Disabilities Council
P.O. Box 2671, Kings Hill
St. Croix, VI 00851
(340) 778-9681

Virgin Island Advocacy Agency
7A Whim, Suite #2
Fredericksted, St. Croix, VI 00840
(340) 772-1200
E-mail: viadvocacy@
worldnet.att.net

Department of Health
Maternal Child Health &
Children with Special Health
Care Needs Program
3012 Vitraco Mall
Estate Golden Rock
Christiansted, St. Croix 00820-4370
(340) 713-9924
E-mail: vimchstx@viaccess.net

University of the Virgin Islands
2 John Brewers Bay
St. Thomas, VI 00802-9990
(340) 693-1323

V.I. FIND
2 Nye Gade
St. Thomas, VI 00802
(340) 775-3962
E-mail: vifind@islands.vi
Web: http://www.taalliance.org/
ptis/vifind/

VI Coalition of Citizens with
Disabilities
St. Thomas
P.O. Box 9500
St. Thomas, VI 00801
(340) 776-1277
E-mail: DAR@viaccess.net

VI Coalition of Citizens with
Disabilities
St. Croix Chapter
P.O. Box 5156 Sunny Isles
St. Croix, VI 00820
(340) 778-7370

Virginia
Office of Special Education and
Student Services
Department of Education
P.O. Box 2120
Richmond, VA 23218-2120
(804) 225-2402
E-mail: dougcox@pen.k12.va.us
Web: http://www.pen.k12.va.us/

(Ages 3 through 5)
Office of Special Education Services
Department of Education
P.O. Box 2120
Richmond, VA 23218-2120
(804) 225-2675
E-mail: lbradfor@pen.k12.va.us
Web: http://www.pen.k12.va.us/
VDOE/newvdoe/div.html

(Birth through 2)
Children/Family Services
Office of Mental Retardation Services
Department of Mental Health, Mental
Retardation & Substance Abuse
Services
P.O. Box 1797
Richmond, VA 23218
(804) 786-0992
E-mail: sricks@
dmhmrsas.state.va.us

Department of Rehabilitative Services
P. O. Box K300
8004 Franklin Farm Drive

Richmond, VA 23288-0300
(804) 662-7081
E-mail: walshms@DRS.state.va.us

Virginia Board for People with
Disabilities
Ninth Street Office Building
202 North Ninth Street, 9th Floor
Richmond, VA 23219
(804) 786-0016 (V/TTY); (800) 846-
4464 (in VA)
Web: http://www.cns.state.va.us/
vbpd

Department for Rights of Virginians
with Disabilities
Ninth St. Office Building,
9th Floor
202 North 9th Street
Richmond, VA 23219
(804) 225-2042 (Voice/TTY); (800)
552-3962 (in VA)
Web: http://www.cns.state.va.us/
drvd

Children with Special Health Care
Needs Program
Division of Child & Adolescent Health,
Room 137
Virginia Department of Health
P.O. Box 2448
Richmond, VA 23218
(804) 786-7367
E-mail: nbullock@vdh.state.va.us
Web: http://www.vdh.state.va.us

Virginia Institute for Developmental
Disabilities
Virginia Commonwealth University
700 East Franklin Street,
Box 843020
Richmond, VA 23284-3020
(804) 828-3876
E-mail: forelove@saturn.vcu.edu
Web: http://www.vcu.edu/vidd

Parent Educational Advocacy Training
Center (PEATC)
6320 Augusta Drive, Suite 1200
Springfield, VA 22150
(703) 923-0010;

(800) 869-6782 (in VA)
E-mail: partners@peatc.org
Web: http://www.peatc.org/

Office of Special Education and
Student Services
Virginia Department of Education
P.O. Box 2120
Richmond, VA 23218-2120
(800) 422-2083; (804) 371-7420
E-mail: aswan@pen.k12.va.us

The Autism Program of Virginia (TAP-
VA)
P.O. Box 1417
Richmond, VA 23218
(800) 649-8481
E-mail: autismVA@aol.com
Web: http://www.autismva.org

Parent to Parent of Virginia
c/o The Arc of Virginia
6 North 6th Street, Suite 403-A
Richmond, VA 23219
(804) 649-8481

Autism Society of America-Peninsula
Chapter
3421 West Lewis Road
Hampton, VA 23666-3830
(757) 827-8226;
(757) 827-8226 (Fax)
Web: http://www.orion1.gateway.com

The Arc of Virginia
6 North 6th St
Suite 403-A
Richmond, VA 23219
(804) 649-8481
E-mail: arcva@richmond.infi.net

Washington
Special Education Section
Superintendent of Public Instruction
P.O. Box 47200
Olympia, WA 98504-7200
(360) 753-6733;
(360) 586-0126 (TTY)
E-mail: speced@ospi.wednet.edu
Web: http://www.k12.wa.us

(Ages 3 through 5)
Early Childhood Services
Office of Superintendent of Public
Instruction
P.O. Box 47200
Olympia, WA 98504-7200
(360) 753-0317;
(360) 586-0126 (TTY)
E-mail: ashureen@
ospi.wednet.edu
Web: http://www.k12.wa.us

(Birth through 2)
Infant Toddler Early Intervention
Program
Division of Developmental Disabilities
Department of Social & Health
Services
P.O. Box 45201
Olympia, WA 98504-5201
(360) 902-8490;
(360) 902-7864 (TTY)
Web: http://www.wa.gov/
dshs/iteip/iteip.html

Division of Vocational Rehabilitation
Department of Social and Health
Services
P.O. Box 45340
Olympia, WA 98504-5340
(360) 438-8008
E-mail: munroj@dshs.wa.gov

Developmental Disabilities Council
P.O. Box 48314
Olympia, WA 98504-8314
(360) 753-3908;
(800) 634-4473 (V/TTY)
E-mail: EdH@cted.wa.gov
Web: http://www.wa.gov/ddc

Washington Protection & Advocacy
System
1401 East Jefferson, Suite 506
Seattle, WA 98122
(206) 324-1521
E-mail: wpas@halcyon.com
Web: http://www.halcyon.com/
wpas

Community & Family Health
Department of Health
P.O. Box 47830
Olympia, WA 98504-7830
(360) 236-3703
E-mail: maxine.hayes@
doh.wa.gov

Center on Human Development and
Disability
Box 357920, University of Washington
Seattle, WA 98195-7920
(206) 543-2832
E-mail: chdd@u.washington.edu
Web: http://depts.washington.edu/
chdd/

Parents Are Vital in Education (PAVE)
6316 South 12th Street
Tacoma, WA 98465
(800) 572-7368; (253) 565-2266
E-mail:
wapave9@washingtonpave.com
Web: http://www.washingtonpave.org

Washington State P2P Programs
State Coordinating Office
10550 Lake City Way, N.E., Suite A
Seattle, WA 98125
(800) 821-5927; (206) 364-4645
E-mail: statep2p@earthlink.net

Autism Society of Washington
203 East 4th, Suite 507
Olympia, WA 98501
(360) 943-2205
(360) 943-5015 (Fax)
E-mail: autism@olywa.net
Web: http://www.olywa.net/
autism

The Arc of Washington State
1703 East State Street
Olympia, WA 98506
(206) 357-5596
E-mail: thearc@nwrain.com

West Virginia
Office of Special Education
Department of Education

1900 Kanawha Boulevard East
Bldg. 6, Room B-304
Charleston, WV 25305-0330
(304) 558-2696
E-mail: dbodkins@
access.k12.wv.us

(Ages 3 through 5)
Preschool Disabilities
Office of Special Education
1900 Kanawha Boulevard East
Bldg. 6, Room 304
Charleston, WV 25305-0330
(304) 558-2696
E-mail: vhuffman@
access.k12.wv.us

(Birth through 2)
WV Birth to Three
Office of Maternal and Child Health
Bureau of Public Health
1116 Quarrier Street
Charleston, WV 25301
(304) 558-3071
E-mail: pamroush@wvdhhr.org

Division of Rehabilitation Services
State Capitol Complex
P.O. Box 50890
Charleston, WV 25305-0890
(304) 766-4601
E-mail: jeffers@
mail.drs.state.wv.us
Web: http://www.wvdrs.org

Developmental Disabilities Council
110 Stockton Street
Charleston, WV 25312
(304) 558-0416;
(304) 558-2376 (TTY)
E-mail: wisems@
wvnvm.wvnet.edu

Autism Services Center
605 Ninth Street
P.O. Box 507
Huntington, WV 25710-0507
(304) 525-8014;
(304) 525-8026 (Fax)

West Virginia Advocates
Litton Bldg., 4th Floor
1207 Quarrier Street
Charleston, WV 25301
(304) 346-0847;
(800) 950-5250 (in WV)
E-mail: wvadvocates@
newwave.net
Web: http://www.newwave.net/
~wvadvocates

Children's Specialty Care
1116 Quarrier Street East
Charleston, WV 25301
(304) 558-3071
E-mail: janetlucas@wvdhhr.org

The West Virginia Autism/
Training Center
Marshall University
College of Education and Human
Services
400 Hal Greer Blvd., Suite 316
Huntington, WV 25755
(304) 696-2332;
(800) 344-5115 (in WV)
Web: http://www.marshall.edu/
coe/atc/

West Virginia University
University Affiliated Center for
Developmental Disabilities (UAC
Developmental Disabilities)
Research & Office Park
955 Hartman Run Road
Morgantown, WV 26505
(304) 293-4692

WV Parent Training & Information
Project (WVPTI)
371 Broaddus Avenue
Clarksburg, WV 26301
(304) 624-1436;
(800) 281-1436 (in WV)
E-mail: wvpti@aol.com
Web: http://www.iolinc.net/
wvpti/default.asp

Parent-Educator Resource Center
116 East King Street
Martinsburg, WV 25401

(304) 263-5717
E-mail: carolt7@intrepid.net

Wisconsin
Division for Learning Support: Equity
and Advocacy
125 South Webster Street, P.O. Box
7841
Madison, WI 53707-7841
(608) 266-1649;
(800) 441-4563
E-mail: juanita.pawlisch@
dpi.state.wi.us
Web: http://www.dpi.state.wi.us/
dpi/dlsea/een

(Ages 3 through 5)
Early Childhood: Exceptional
Educational Needs Programs
Division for Learning Support: Equity
and Advocacy
Department of Public Instruction
P.O. Box 7841
Madison, WI 53707
(800) 441-4563; (608) 267-9625;
(608) 267-9172 (Fax)

(Birth to 3)
Division of Supportive Living
Department of Health & Family
Services
P.O. Box 7851
Madison, WI 53707-7851
(608) 267-3270
E-mail: kremema@
dhfs.state.wi.us

Vocational Rehabilitation
Department of Workforce
Development
2917 International Lane, Suite 300
P.O. Box 7852
Madison, WI 53707-7852
(608) 243-5603
E-mail: dixonth@dwd.state.wi.us
Web: http://www.dwd.state.
wi.us/dvr

Wisconsin Council on Developmental
Disabilities
600 Williamson Street

P.O. Box 7851
Madison, WI 53707-7851
(608) 266-7826
E-mail: wiswcdd@dhfs.state.wi.us

Wisconsin Coalition for Advocacy
16 North Carroll Street, Suite 400
Madison, WI 53703
(608) 267-0214;
(800) 928-8778 (in WI)
E-mail: wcamsn@globaldialog.com

Waisman Center UAP
University of Wisconsin - Madison
1500 Highland Avenue
Madison, WI 53705-2280
(608) 263-5940
E-mail: dolan@
waisman.wisc.edu
Web: http://www.waisman.
wisc.edu

Early Intervention Program
229 Waisman Center
1500 Highland Avenue
Madison, WI 53705
(608) 263-5022
E-mail: Tuchman@
waisman.wisc.edu
Web: http://www.waisman.
wisc.edu/earlyint/

Parent Education Project of Wisconsin
2192 South 60th Street
West Allis, WI 53219
(414) 328-5520; (414) 328-5525
(TTY); (800) 231-8382 (in WI)
E-mail: pmcolletti@aol.com
Web: http://members.aol.com/
pepofwi

Native American Family
Empowerment
Great Lakes-Inter-Tribal Council, Inc.
2932 Highway 47 North
P.O. Box 9
Lac du Falmbeau, WI 54538
(800) 472-7207; (715) 588-3324
E-mail: drosin@glitc.org

MUMS—National Parent to Parent
Network
150 Custer Court
Green Bay, WI 54301-1243
(920) 336-5333
E-mail: mums@netnet.net
Web: http://www.netnet.net/mums/

Autism Society of Wisconsin
103 W. College Avenue, Suite 601
Appleton, WI 54911-5744
(920) 993-0279
(888) 4-AUTISM (WI)
E-mail: griffinl@athenet.net
Web: http://www.asw4autism.org/

The Arc—Wisconsin
121 South Hancock
Madison, WI 53703
(608) 251-9272

Wyoming
Department of Education, Special
Programs Unit
Hathaway Building, 2nd Floor
2300 Capitol Avenue
Cheyenne, WY 82002
(307) 777-7417
E-mail: pmuhle@educ.state.wy.us
Web: http://www.k12.wy.us

(Ages 3 through 5)
Department of Health, Division of
Developmental Disabilities
Herschler Bldg, 1st Floor West
122 West 25th St.
Cheyenne, WY 82002
(307) 777-5246

(Birth through 2)
Division of Developmental Disabilities
Department of Health
Herschler Building, 1st Floor West
122 West 25th St.
Cheyenne, WY 82002
(307) 777-6972

Division of Vocational Rehabilitation
Department of Employment
1100 Herschler Bldg.
Cheyenne, WY 82002
(307) 777-7389

E-mail: GCHILD@missc.state.wy.us
Web: http://wydoe.state.wy.us/
vocrehab

Governor's Planning Council on
Developmental Disabilities
122 West 25th St.
Herschler Bldg., 1st W
Cheyenne, WY 82002
(307) 777-7230 (TTY);
(800) 442-4333 (in WY)
Web: http://ddd.state.wy.us

Wyoming P&A System
2424 Pioneer Avenue, Suite #101
Cheyenne, WY 82001
(307) 632-3496;
(800) 624-7648 (in WY)
E-mail: wypanda@vcn.com

Division of Public Health
Department of Health
4th Floor, Hathaway Bldg.
Cheyenne, WY 82002
(307) 777-7941

Wyoming Institute for Disabilities
112 Education Building
Box 4298, University Station
University of Wyoming
Laramie, WY 82071-4298
(307) 766-2761
E-mail: WIND.UW@uwyo.edu
Web: http://wind.uwyo.edu/

Parent Information Center
5 N. Lobban
Buffalo, WY 82834
(307) 684-2277;
(800) 660-9742 (in WY)
E-mail: tdawsonpic@vcn.com
Web: http://www.wpic.org

Wyoming Family Support Network
1110 E. 5th Avenue
Cheyenne, WY 82001
(800) 567-9376; (307) 632-0839

The Arc of Wyoming
P. O. Box 2161
Casper, WY 82602
(307) 237-9110

■■ Internet Resources

Americans with Disabilities Act Document Center
Web: http://janweb.icdi.wvu.edu/kinder/index.htm

Provides online copies of ADA Statute, Regulations, ADAAG (Americans with Disabilities Act Accessibility Guidelines), Federally Reviewed Tech Sheets, and Other Assistance Documents.

Asperger's Disorder Homepage
Web:www.ummed.edu/pub/o/ozbayrak/asperger.html

Provides information about Asperger's Disorder, along with resource listings.

The #Autism Channel
Web: http://www.autism.clarityconnect.com/

This website enables parents and teachers of children with autism (and other PDDs) to chat about therapies, treatment options, and parenting.

Autism Network International
Web: http://www.ani.ac

Autism Network International, an autistic-run self-help and advocacy organization.

Autism Resources
Web: http://autism-info.com/

A massive collection of autism-related resources, information, and links.

Autism-Resources
Web: http://www.autism-resources.com

The most comprehensive collection of useful links on autism and related topics available anywhere online. Maintained by John Wobus.

BehaveNet(r) :Behavioral health care information & publishing on the World Wide Web since 1995
Web: http://www.behavenet.com/

Provides information and links to resources on a wide range of behavioral conditions, treatment approaches, and issues.

Disability Resources Monthly
Web: http://www.disabilityresources.org

Provides extensive list and database of online information sources on many disabilities.

Family Village: A Global Community of Disability-Related Resources
Web: http://www.familyvillage.wisc.edu/index.htmlx

Excellent resource for families of children with disabilities. Contains lots of useful information and links.

National Institutes of Mental Health (NIMH)
Web: http://www.nimh.nih.gov/publicat/autism.cfm
    Information about autism from the National Institutes of Mental Health.

Online Asperger Syndrome Information & Support (OASIS)
Web: http://www.udel.edu/bkirby/asperger/
    An important and useful website containing a wide variety of information and resources on Asperger's Disorder.

Special Child
Web: http://www.specialchild.com
    An online magazine for parents of children with disabilities.

CONTRIBUTORS

Carolyn Thorwarth Bruey, Psy.D., is a psychologist in private practice in Lancaster, Pennsylvania and Managing Partner of Developmental Disabilities Resources. She received her doctorate in psychology from Rutgers University. Dr. Bruey is the author or co-author of chapters in several books including *Handbook of Behavioral Family Therapy* (Guilford, 1988) and *Expanding Systems of Service Delivery for Persons with Developmental Disabilities* (Paul H. Brookes, 1988).

Andrew L. Egel, Ph.D., is a Professor in the Department of Special Education at the University of Maryland, College Park. He received his M.A. and Ph.D. from the University of California at Santa Barbara. Dr. Egel has received numerous federal grants designed to develop model educational programs for children with autism. He is co-editor of *Educating and Understanding Autistic Children* (College-Hill, 1982) and author of numerous research articles, book chapters, and presentations on the education of children with autism.

Bernice Friedlander was the public information and legislative affairs consultant in the national office of the Autism Society of America. Ms. Friedlander holds a master's degree in public administration from Harvard University. Presently, she is the senior Public Affairs Specialist with the Women's Bureau, Office of the Secretary, U.S. Department of Labor, Washington, D.C.

Temple Grandin is one of the foremost experts in the design and construction of livestock handling facilities in the world. She received her Ph.D. from the University of Illinois, and currently is a faculty member at Colorado State University. Perhaps the most well-known individual with autism in the world, Dr. Grandin's presentations throughout the world have helped thousands of parents and professionals understand how to help individuals with autism. She is the author of two books: *Emergence: Labeled Autistic* (Warner Books, 1996) and *Thinking in Pictures: And Other Reports from My Life with Autism* (Vintage, 1996).

Beverly Sills Greenough is an internationally renowned coloratura soprano and the retired General Director of the New York City Opera.

Sandra L. Harris, Ph.D., is Professor and Dean, Graduate School of Applied and Professional Psychology, Rutgers University. She is also the Executive Director of the Douglass Developmental Disabilities Center for children with autism. Dr. Harris received her Ph.D. from SUNY-Buffalo, and is the author of *Siblings of Children with Autism: A Guide for Families* (Woodbine House, 1994), co-author of *Right from the Start: Intensive Behavioral Intervention for Young Children with Autism* (Woodbine House, 1998), and co-editor with Jan S. Handleman of *Preschool Education Programs for Children with Autism* (Pro-Ed, 1994).

David L. Holmes, Ed. D., holds a master's and doctorate degrees in educational psychology from Rutgers University. He is the President and Executive Director of the Eden Family of Services, which serves children and adults with autism with facilities in Princeton, New Jersey, Fort Myers/Naples, Florida, and Chaplin, Connecticut. Dr. Holmes is Chairman of the Autism Society of America's Panel of Professional Advisors, a founding trustee of the Autism Society of America Foundation, and past Chairman of the Board of The National Commission for the Accreditation of Special Education Services (NCASES). He is the author of numerous research articles, book chapters, and books, including *Autism Through the Lifespan: The Eden Model* (Woodbine House, 1997) for which he received the 1998 Outstanding Literary Work of the Year Award from the Autism Society of America. Dr. Holmes is an Adjunct Professor in the Department of Psychology, Princeton University.

Ralph J. Moore, Jr., and **James E. Kaplan** are both active in the area of the legal rights of children with disabilities. They are the co-authors of the "Legal Rights and Hurdles" chapters in Woodbine House's parents' guides to children with mental retardation, epilepsy, cerebral palsy, spina bifida, autism, and Down syndrome. Mr. Moore, a partner in the law firm of Shea & Gardner in Washington, D.C., is the author of *Handbook on Estate Planning for Families of Developmentally Disabled Persons in Maryland, the District of Columbia, and Virginia* (MD. DD Council, 3rd ed, 1989). Mr. Kaplan is Of Counsel in the law firm of Jensen, Baird, Gardner & Henry in Portland, Maine.

Bernard Rimland, Ph.D., a research psychologist, founded the Autism Research Institute in 1967. He is also the founder of the Autism Society of America, and is the editor of the *Autism Research Review International*. His prize-winning book, *Infantile Autism: The Syndrome and Its Implications for a Neural Theory of Behavior*, changed the field of psychiatry from claiming that autism is an emotional illness caused by destructive mothers to its current recognition that autism is a biological disorder. He has lectured on autism and related problems throughout the world, and is the author of numerous publications. Dr. Rimland has received many awards for his work on autism. He served as primary advisor on autism for the film *Rain Man*.

Joe and Lillian Tommasone are the parents of Michael, an adult with autism, and Jon, an adult with multiple handicaps. Joe works for a major airline as a jet mechanic and Lillian is a teacher of children with multiple disabilities in Carteret, New Jersey. Lillian holds a master's degree in special education from Kean University (NJ) and writes frequently on the subjects of respite care and advocacy.

Fred Volkmar, M.D., is Professor of Child Psychiatry, Pediatrics, and Psychology at Yale University School of Medicine. He received his M.D. from Stanford University School of Medicine. Dr. Volkmar is an editor of the *Handbook of Autism and Pervasive Developmental Disorders, 2nd edition* (John Wiley & Sons, 1997), as well as an associate editor of the *Journal of Autism and Developmental Disorders and the Journal of Child Psychology and Psychiatry*.

INDEX

■■
■■

ABOUT THE EDITOR

Michael D. Powers, Psy.D., is a pediatric psychologist and the Director of the Center for Children with Special Needs in Tolland, Connecticut. He specializes in the diagnosis, evaluation, and treatment of individuals with autism and related developmental disabilities. He recieved his master's in special education from Columbia University and his doctorate in psychology from the Graduate School of Applied and Professional Psychology at Rutgers University. Dr. Powers holds an appointment as an Assistant Clinical Professor of Psychology at the Yale Child Study Center, Yale University. In 1990 he was awarded the Literary Achievement Award by the Autism Society of America for the first edition of *Children With Autism: A Parents' Guide* (Woodbine House, 1989). He is the author of numerous articles and book chapters on autism as well as *Behavioral Assessment of Severe Developmental Disabilities* (with J. Handleman, Aspen Press, 1984) and *Expanding Systems of Service Delivery for Persons with Developmental Disabilities* (Paul H. Brookes, 1988). Dr. Powers is a former member of the Board of Directors of the Autism Society of America.